EXPLORING MICROSOFT® ACCESS 97

Robert T. Grauer / Maryann Barber

University of Miami

Prentice Hall, Upper Saddle River, New Jersey 07458

Acquisitions Editor: Carolyn Henderson
Assistant Editor: Audrey Regan
Editorial Assistant: Lori Cardillo
Executive Marketing Manager: Nancy Evans
Editorial/Production Supervisor: Greg Hubit
Project Manager: Lynne Breitfeller
Senior Manufacturing Supervisor: Paul Smolenski
Manufacturing Coordinator: Lisa DiMaulo
Manufacturing Manager: Vincent Scelta
Senior Designer/Interior and Cover Design: Suzanne Behnke
Composition: GTS Graphics

ISBN 0-13-754227-5

PRENTICE-HALL INTERNATIONAL (UK) LIMITED, *LONDON*
PRENTICE-HALL OF AUSTRALIA PTY. LIMITED, *SYDNEY*
PRENTICE-HALL CANADA INC., *TORONTO*
PRENTICE-HALL HISPANOAMERICANA, S.A., *MEXICO*
PRENTICE-HALL OF INDIA PRIVATE LIMITED, *NEW DELHI*
PRENTICE-HALL OF JAPAN, INC., *TOKYO*
PEARSON EDUCATION ASIA PTE. LTD., *SINGAPORE*
EDITORA PRENTICE-HALL DO BRASIL, LTDA., *RIO DE JANEIRO*

Printed in the United States of America

10 9 8 7

CONTENTS

2

Tables and Forms: Design, Properties, Views, and Wizards   37

3

Information from the Database: Reports and Queries   87

4

One-to-Many Relationships: Subforms and Multiple Table Queries   137

5

Many-to-Many Relationships: A More Complex System   189

6

Building Applications: Introduction to Macros and Prototyping   251

To Marion, Benjy, Jessica, and Ellie

—Robert Grauer

To Frank, Jessica, and My Parents

—Maryann Barber

PREFACE

We are proud to announce the third edition of the *Exploring Windows* series in conjunction with the release of Microsoft Office 97. There is a separate book for each major application—*Word 97, Excel 97, Access 97,* and *PowerPoint 97*—as well as a book on Windows 95, and, eventually, Windows 97. There are also two combined texts, *Exploring Microsoft Office Professional 97, Volumes I and II. Volume I* contains the introductory chapters from each application, supplementary modules on Internet Explorer and Windows 95, and a PC Buying Guide. It is designed for the instructor who seeks to cover the basics of all Office applications in a single course, but who does not need the extensive coverage that is provided in the individual books. *Volume II* consists of the advanced chapters from each application and was developed for the rapidly emerging second course in PC applications. The complete set of titles appears on the back cover.

Exploring Microsoft Access 97 is a revision of our existing book on *Microsoft Access for Windows 95.* In addition to modifying the text to accommodate the new release, we have revised the end-of-chapter material to include a greater number of practice exercises and case studies. We also added Appendix D, which describes a semester project that is the essence of a course on Access. The many exercises provide substantial opportunity for students to master the material while simultaneously giving instructors considerable flexibility in student assignments.

Our most significant change, however, is the incorporation of the Internet and World Wide Web throughout the text. Students learn Office applications as before, and in addition are sent to the Web as appropriate for supplementary exercises. Students can download the practice files (or "data disk") from the *Exploring Windows* home page (**www.prenhall.com/grauer**). This site also contains additional practice exercises and case studies, which can be downloaded to supplement the text. The icon at the left of this paragraph appears throughout the text whenever there is a Web reference.

Each book in the *Exploring Windows* series is accompanied by an Instructor's Resource Manual with solutions to all exercises, PowerPoint lectures, and the printed version of our test bank. (The Instructor's Resource Manual is available on a CD-ROM, which contains a Windows-based testing program.) Instructors can also use the Prentice Hall Computerized Online Testing System to prepare customized tests for their courses and may obtain Interactive Multimedia courseware as a further supplement.

The *Exploring Windows* series is part of the Prentice Hall custom binding program, enabling you to create your own text by selecting any module(s) in *Office Volume I* to suit the needs of a specific course. You could, for example, create a custom text consisting of the introductory (essential) chapters in Word, Excel, and Internet Explorer. You get exactly the material you need, and students realize a cost saving. You can also take advantage of our ValuePack program to shrink-wrap multiple books together. If, for example, you are teaching a course that covers Excel and Access, and you want substantial coverage of both applications, a ValuePack results in significant savings for the student.

We look forward to continuing to provide quality textbooks for all of your Microsoft Office requirements.

FEATURES AND BENEFITS

Exploring Microsoft Office 97 is written for the computer novice and assumes no previous knowledge of Windows 95. A detailed supplement introduces the reader to the operating system and emphasizes the file operations he or she will need.

An introductory section on Microsoft Office emphasizes the benefits of the common user interface. Although the text assumes no previous knowledge, some users may already be acquainted with another Office application, in which case they can take advantage of what they already know.

PREREQUISITES: ESSENTIALS OF WINDOWS 95

OBJECTIVES

After reading this appendix you will be able to:

1. Describe the objects on the Windows desktop; describe the programs available through the Start button.
2. Explain the function of the minimize, maximize, restore, and close buttons; move and size a window.
3. Discuss the function of a dialog box; describe the elements in a dialog box and the various ways in which information is supplied.
4. Use the Help menu to learn about features in Windows 95; format a floppy disk and implement a screen saver by following instructions from the Help menu.
5. Use the Internet Explorer to access the Internet and download the practice files for the *Exploring Windows* series.
6. Use Windows Explorer to locate a specific file or folder; describe the views available for Windows Explorer.
7. Describe how folders are used to organize a disk; create a new folder; copy and/or move a file from one folder to another.
8. Delete a file, then recover the deleted file from the Recycle Bin.

OVERVIEW

Windows 95 is a computer program (actually many programs) that controls the operation of your computer and its peripherals. *Windows 97* improves on Windows 95 to bring elements of the Internet to the desktop. Windows 97 was not available when we went to press, but we expect it to follow the same conventions as Windows 95. Thus, our introduction applies to both, as it emphasizes the common features of file management in support of Microsoft Office 97. (Microsoft Office runs equally well under Windows 95, Windows 97, or Windows NT.)

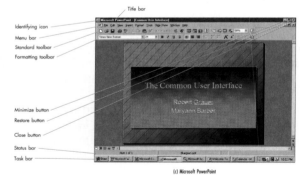

(c) Microsoft PowerPoint

(d) Microsoft Access

FIGURE 1   The Common User Interface (continued)

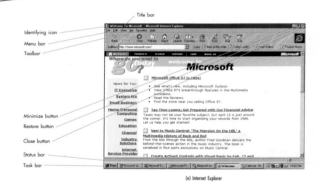

(e) Internet Explorer

(f) Microsoft Outlook

FIGURE 1   The Common User Interface (continued)

Subforms and Multiple Table Queries

Objective: To use multiple table queries as the basis for a main form and its associated subform; to create the link between a main form and subform manually. Use Figure 5.6 as a guide in the exercise.

STEP 1: Create the Subform Query

➤ Open the **Computer Store database** from the previous exercise. Click the **Queries tab** in the Database window, click **New** to display the New Query dialog box, select **Design View** as the means of creating the query, then click **OK.**

➤ The Show Table dialog box appears in Figure 5.6a with the Tables tab already selected.

➤ Double click the **Products table** to add this table to the query. Double click the **Order Details table** to add this table to the query. A join line showing the one-to-many relationship between the Products and Order Details table appears automatically.

➤ Click **Close** to close the Show Table dialog box. If necessary, click the **Maximize button.**

Double click Order Details table to add it to the query

(a) Add the Tables (step 1)

FIGURE 5.6   Hands-on Exercise 2

CUSTOMIZE THE QUERY WINDOW

The Query window displays the field list and design grid in its upper and lower halves, respectively. To increase (decrease) the size of either portion of the window, drag the line dividing the upper and lower sections. Drag the title bar to move a field list. You can also size a field list by dragging a border just as you can size any other window.

STEP 2: Create the Subform Query (continued)

➤ Add the fields to the query as follows:
- Double click the **ProductID** and **OrderID fields** in that order from the Order Details table.
- Double click the **ProductName** and **UnitPrice fields** in that order from the Products table.
- Double click the **Quantity field** from the Order Details table.

➤ Click the **Sort row** under the **OrderID field.** Click the **drop-down arrow,** then specify an **ascending** sequence.

➤ Click the first available cell in the Field row. Type **=[Quantity]*[UnitPrice].** Do not be concerned if you cannot see the entire expression, but be sure you put square brackets around each field name.

➤ Press **enter.** Access has substituted Expr1: for the equal sign you typed. Drag the column boundary so that the entire expression is visible as in Figure 5.6b. (You may need to make the other columns narrower in order to see all of the fields in the design grid.)

➤ Click and drag to select **Expr1.** (Do not select the colon.) Type **Amount** to substitute a more meaningful field name.

➤ Point to the expression and click the **right mouse button** to display a shortcut menu. Click **Properties** to display the Field Properties dialog box in Figure 5.6b.

➤ Click the box for the **Format property.** Click the **drop-down arrow,** then scroll until you can click **Currency.** Close the Properties dialog box.

➤ Save the query as **Order Details with Product Information.** Click the **Run button** to test the query so that you know the query works prior to using it as the basis of a form.

THE ZOOM BOX

Creating a long expression can be confusing in that you cannot see the entire expression as it is entered. Access anticipates the situation and provides a Zoom box to increase the space in which you can work. Press Shift+F2 as you enter the expression (or select Zoom from the shortcut menu) to display the Zoom box. Click OK to close the Zoom box and continue working in the design grid.

A total of 20 in-depth tutorials (hands-on exercises) guide the reader at the computer. Each tutorial is illustrated with large, full-color screen captures that are clear and easy to read. Each tutorial is accompanied by numerous tips that present different ways to accomplish a given task, but in a logical and relaxed fashion.

Database design is stressed throughout the text, beginning in Chapter 1, where the reader is shown the power of a relational database. Full-color illustrations help to clarify the relationships between the various tables. Appendix B provides additional information.

FIGURE 1.7   The Bookstore Database

University of Miami Book Store

Publisher	ISBN Number	Author	Title	List Price
IDG Books Worldwide				
	1-56884-453-0	Livingston/Straub	Windows 95 Secrets	$39.95
			Number of Books:	1
			Average List Price:	$39.95
Macmillan Publishing				
	1-56686-127-6	Rosch	The Hardware Bible	$35.00
			Number of Books:	1
			Average List Price:	$35.00
MIS Press				
	1-55828-353-6	Banks	Welcome to CompuServe	$24.95
			Number of Books:	1
			Average List Price:	$24.95
New Riders Publishing				
	1-56205-306-X	Maxwell/Grycz	New Riders Internet Yellow Pages	$29.95
			Number of Books:	1
			Average List Price:	$29.95
Osborne-McGraw Hill				
	0-07-882023-5	Hahn/Stout	The Internet Yellow Pages	$27.95
	0-07-881980-6	Hahn/Stout	The Internet Complete Reference	$29.95
			Number of Books:	2
			Average List Price:	$28.95
Prentice Hall				
	0-13-754235-6	Grauer/Barber	Exploring PowerPoint 97	$30.95
	0-13-065541-4	Grauer/Barber	Exploring Windows 3.1	$24.95

Saturday, January 11, 1997   Page 1 of 2

FIGURE 3.12   Screen for Practice Exercise 4

Super Bowl

http://www.nfl.com

Year	AFC Team	AFC Score	NFC Team	NFC Score
1997	New England	21	Green Bay	35
1996	Pittsburgh	17	Dallas	27
1995	San Diego	26	San Francisco	49
1994	Buffalo	13	Dallas	30
1993	Buffalo	17	Dallas	52
1992	Buffalo	24	Washington	37
1991	Buffalo	19	Giants	20
1990	Denver	10	San Francisco	55
1989	Cincinnati	16	San Francisco	20
1988	Denver	10	Washington	42
1987	Denver	20	Giants	39
1986	New England	10	Chicago	46
1985	Miami	16	San Francisco	38
1984	Los Angeles	38	Washington	9
1983	Miami	17	Washington	27
1982	Cincinnati	21	San Francisco	26
1981	Oakland	27	Philadelphia	10
1980	Pittsburgh	31	Los Angeles	19
1979	Pittsburgh	35	Dallas	31
1978	Denver	10	Dallas	27
1977	Oakland	32	Minnesota	14
1976	Pittsburgh	21	Dallas	17
1975	Pittsburgh	16	Minnesota	6
1974	Miami	24	Minnesota	7
1973	Miami	14	Washington	7
1972	Miami	3	Dallas	24
1971	Baltimore	16	Dallas	13

Saturday, January 11, 1997   Page 1 of 2

FIGURE 3.13   Screen for Practice Exercise 5

Every chapter contains a large number of practice exercises, in sufficient quantity to avoid repetition from one semester to the next. There are objective multiple-choice questions and guided computer exercises, as well as less structured case studies.

Object Linking and Embedding (OLE) is stressed throughout the series. All references to OLE are identified by a special icon to highlight this important technology.

PRACTICE WITH MICROSOFT ACCESS 97

1. Use the Our Students database as the basis for the following queries and reports:
   a. Create a select query for students on the Dean's List (GPA >= 3.50). Include the student's name, major, quality points, credits, and GPA. List the students alphabetically.
   b. Use the Report Wizard to prepare a tabular report based on the query in part a. Include your name in the report header as the academic advisor.
   c. Create a select query for students on academic probation (GPA < 2.00). Include the same fields as the query in part a. List the students in alphabetical order.
   d. Use the Report Wizard to prepare a tabular report similar to the report in part b.
   e. Print both reports and submit them to your instructor as proof that you did this exercise.

2. Use the Employee database in the Exploring Access folder to create the reports listed below. (This is the same database that was used earlier in Chapters 1 and 2.)
   a. A report containing all employees in sequence by location and alphabetically within location. Show the employee's last name, first name, location, title, and salary. Include summary statistics to display the total salaries in each location as well as for the company as a whole.
   b. A report containing all employees in sequence by title and alphabetically within title. Show the employee's last name, first name, location, title, and salary. Include summary statistics to show the average salary for each title as well as the average salary in the company.
   c. Add your name to the report header in the report so that your instructor will know the reports came from you. Print both reports and submit them to your instructor.

3. Use the United States database in the Exploring Access folder to create the report shown in Figure 3.11. (This is the same database that was used in Chapters 1 and 2.) The report lists states by geographic region, and alphabetically within region. It includes a calculated field, Population Density, which is computed by dividing a state's population by its area. Summary statistics are also required as shown in the report.
   Note that the report header contains a map of the United States that was taken from the Microsoft Clip Gallery. The instructions for inserting an object can be found on page 81 in conjunction with an earlier problem. Be sure to include your name in the report footer so that your instructor will know that the report comes from you.

4. Use the Bookstore database in the Exploring Access folder to create the report shown in Figure 3.12. (This is the same database that was used in the hands-on exercises in Chapter 1.)
   The report header in Figure 3.12 contains a graphic object that was taken from the Microsoft Clip Gallery. You are not required to use this specific image, but you are required to insert a graphic. The instructions for inserting an object can be found on page 81 in conjunction with an earlier problem. Be sure to include your name in the report header so that your instructor will know that the report comes from you.

Chapter 6 shows the student how to develop a complete application through macros and prototyping. This "capstone" chapter is the ideal basis for a semester-long project and enables students to develop realistic applications.

Students learn concepts as well as keystrokes and mouse clicks, which in turn increases their proficiency in Access. All discussions are accompanied by multiple illustrations to further explain and reinforce the material.

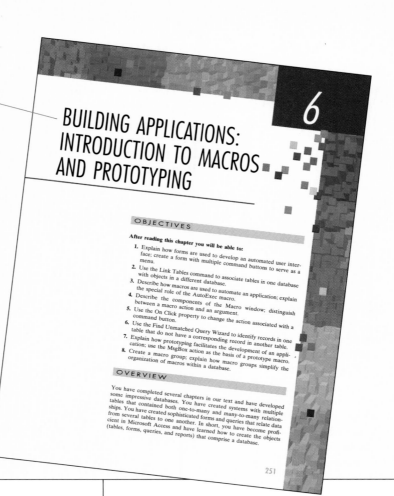

6

BUILDING APPLICATIONS: INTRODUCTION TO MACROS AND PROTOTYPING

OBJECTIVES

After reading this chapter you will be able to:

1. Explain how forms are used to develop an automated user interface; create a form with multiple command buttons to serve as a menu.
2. Use the Link Tables command to associate tables in one database with objects in a different database.
3. Describe how macros are used to automate an application; explain the special role of the AutoExec macro.
4. Describe the components of the Macro window; distinguish between a macro action and an argument.
5. Use the On Click property to change the action associated with a command button.
6. Use the Find Unmatched Query Wizard to identify records in one table that do not have a corresponding record in another table.
7. Explain how prototyping facilitates the development of an application; use the MsgBox action as the basis of a prototype macro.
8. Create a macro group; explain how macro groups simplify the organization of macros within a database.

OVERVIEW

You have completed several chapters in our text and have developed some impressive databases. You have created systems with multiple tables that contained both one-to-many and many-to-many relationships. You have created sophisticated forms and queries that relate data from several tables to one another. In short, you have become proficient in Microsoft Access and have learned how to create the objects (tables, forms, queries, and reports) that comprise a database.

251

Selection Criteria

To specify selection criteria in the design grid, enter a value or expression in the Criteria row of the appropriate column. Figure 3.7 contains several examples of simple criteria and provides a basic introduction to select queries.

The criterion in Figure 3.7a selects the students majoring in Business. The criteria for text fields are case-insensitive. Thus, *"Business"* is the same as *"business"* or *"BUSINESS"*.

Values entered in multiple columns of the same Criteria row implement an **AND condition** in which the selected records must meet *all* of the specified criteria. The criteria in Figure 3.7b select students who are majoring in Business and who are from the state of Florida. The criteria in Figure 3.7c select Communications majors who are receiving financial aid.

Values entered in different Criteria rows are connected by an **OR condition** in which the selected records may satisfy *any* of the indicated criteria. The criteria in Figure 3.7d select students who are majoring in Business *or* who are from Florida or both.

(a) Business Majors

(b) Business Majors from Florida

(c) Communications Majors Receiving Financial Aid

(d) Business Majors or Students from Florida

FIGURE 3.7 Criteria

Relational operators (>, <, >=, <=, =, and <>) are used with date or number fields to return records within a designated range. The criteria in Figure 3.7e select Engineering majors with fewer than 60 credits. The criteria in Figure 3.7f select Communications majors who were born on or after April 1, 1974.

(e) Engineering Majors with Fewer than 60 Credits

(f) Communications Majors Born on or after April 1, 1974

(g) Engineering Majors with Fewer than 60 Credits or Communications Majors Born on or after April 1, 1974

(h) Students with between 60 and 90 Credits

(i) Students with Majors Other Than Liberal Arts

FIGURE 3.7 Criteria (continued)

Acknowledgments

We want to thank the many individuals who helped bring this project to fruition. We are especially grateful to our editor at Prentice Hall, Carolyn Henderson, without whom the series would not have been possible. Cecil Yarbrough and Susan Hoffman did an outstanding job in checking the manuscript and proofs for technical accuracy. Suzanne Behnke developed the innovative and attractive design. John DeLara and David Nusspickel were responsible for our Web site. Carlotta Eaton of Radford University and Karen Vignare of Alfred University wrote the instructor manuals, and Dave Moles produced the CD. Paul Smolenski was manufacturing supervisor. Lynne Breitfeller was project manager. Greg Hubit was in charge of production and kept the project on target from beginning to end. Nancy Evans, our marketing manager at Prentice Hall, developed the innovative campaigns, which made the series a success. Lori Cardillo, editorial assistant at Prentice Hall, helped in ways too numerous to mention. We also want to acknowledge our reviewers who, through their comments and constructive criticism, greatly improved the *Exploring Windows* series.

Lynne Band, Middlesex Community College
Stuart P. Brian, Holy Family College
Carl M. Briggs, Indiana University School of Business
Kimberly Chambers, Scottsdale Community College
Alok Charturvedi, Purdue University
Jerry Chin, Southwest Missouri State University
Dean Combellick, Scottsdale Community College
Cody Copeland, Johnson County Community College
Larry S. Corman, Fort Lewis College
Janis Cox, Tri-County Technical College
Martin Crossland, Southwest Missouri State University
Paul E. Daurelle, Western Piedmont Community College
David Douglas, University of Arkansas
Carlotta Eaton, New River Community College
Raymond Frost, Central Connecticut State University
James Gips, Boston College
Vernon Griffin, Austin Community College
Michael Hassett, Fort Hays State University
Wanda D. Heller, Seminole Community College
Bonnie Homan, San Francisco State University
Ernie Ivey, Polk Community College
Mike Kelly, Community College of Rhode Island
Jane King, Everett Community College
John Lesson, University of Central Florida

David B. Meinert, Southwest Missouri State University
Bill Morse, DeVry Institute of Technology
Alan Moltz, Naugatuck Valley Technical Community College
Kim Montney, Kellogg Community College
Kevin Pauli, University of Nebraska
Mary McKenry Percival, University of Miami
Delores Pusins, Hillsborough Community College
Gale E. Rand, College Misericordia
Judith Rice, Santa Fe Community College
David Rinehard, Lansing Community College
Marilyn Salas, Scottsdale Community College
John Shepherd, Duquesne University
Helen Stoloff, Hudson Valley Community College
Margaret Thomas, Ohio University
Mike Thomas, Indiana University School of Business
Suzanne Tomlinson, Iowa State University
Karen Tracey, Central Connecticut State University
Karen Vignare, Alfred State College
Sally Visci, Lorain County Community College
David Weiner, University of San Francisco
Connie Wells, Georgia State University
Wallace John Whistance-Smith, Ryerson Polytechnic University
Jack Zeller, Kirkwood Community College

A final word of thanks to the unnamed students at the University of Miami, who make it all worthwhile. And most of all, thanks to you, our readers, for choosing this book. Please feel free to contact us with any comments and suggestions.

Robert T. Grauer
rgrauer@umiami.miami.edu
www.bus.miami.edu/~rgrauer
www.prenhall.com/grauer

Maryann Barber
mbarber@homer.bus.miami.edu
www.bus.miami.edu/~mbarber

MICROSOFT OFFICE 97: SIX APPLICATIONS IN ONE

OVERVIEW

Word processing, spreadsheets, and data management have always been significant microcomputer applications. The early days of the PC saw these applications emerge from different vendors with radically different user interfaces. WordPerfect, Lotus, and dBASE, for example, were dominant applications in their respective areas, and each was developed by a different company. The applications were totally dissimilar, and knowledge of one did not help in learning another.

The widespread acceptance of Windows 3.1 promoted the concept of a common user interface, which required all applications to follow a consistent set of conventions. This meant that all applications worked essentially the same way, and it provided a sense of familiarity when you learned a new application, since every application presented the same user interface. The development of a suite of applications from a single vendor extended this concept by imposing additional similarities on all applications within the suite.

This introduction will acquaint you with *Microsoft Office 97* and its four major applications—*Word, Excel, PowerPoint,* and *Access.* The single biggest difference between Office 97 and its predecessor, Office 95, is that the Internet has become an integral part of the Office suite. Thus, we also discuss *Internet Explorer,* the Web browser included in Office 97, and *Microsoft Outlook,* the e-mail and scheduling program that is built into Office 97. The icon at the left of this paragraph appears throughout the text to highlight references to the Internet and enhance your use of Microsoft Office. Our introduction also includes the Clip Gallery, WordArt, and Office Art, three tools built into Microsoft Office that help you to add interest to your documents. And finally, we discuss Object Linking and Embedding, which enables you to combine data from multiple applications into a single document.

Our primary purpose in this introduction is to emphasize the similarities between the applications in Office 97 and to help you transfer your knowledge from one application to the next. You will find the same commands in the same menus. You will also recognize familiar toolbars and will be able to take advantage of similar keyboard shortcuts. You will learn that help can be obtained in a variety of ways, and that it is consistent in every application. Our goal is to show you how much you already know and to get you up and running as quickly as possible.

TRY THE COLLEGE BOOKSTORE

Any machine you buy will come with Windows 95 (or Windows 97), but that is only the beginning since you must also obtain the application software you intend to run. Some hardware vendors will bundle (at no additional cost) Microsoft Office as an inducement to buy from them. If you have already purchased your system and you need software, the best place to buy Microsoft Office is the college bookstore, where it can be obtained at a substantial educational discount.

MICROSOFT OFFICE 97

All Office applications share the ***common Windows interface*** with which you may already be familiar. (If you are new to Windows 95, then read the appendix on the "Essentials of Windows.") Microsoft Office 97 runs equally well under Windows 95, Windows 97, or Windows NT.

Figure 1 displays a screen from each major application in Microsoft Office—Word, Excel, PowerPoint, and Access. Our figure also includes screens from Internet Explorer and Microsoft Outlook, both of which are part of Office 97. Look closely at Figure 1, and realize that each screen contains both an application window and a document window, and that each document window has been maximized within the application window. The title bars of the application and document windows have been merged into a single title bar that appears at the top of the application window. The title bar displays the application (e.g., Microsoft Word in Figure 1a) as well as the name of the document (Web Enabled in Figure 1a) on which you are working.

All six screens in Figure 1 are similar in appearance even though the applications accomplish very different tasks. Each application window has an identifying icon, a menu bar, a title bar, and a minimize, maximize or restore, and a close button. Each document window has its own identifying icon, and its own minimize, maximize or restore, and close button. The Windows taskbar appears at the bottom of each application window and shows the open applications. The status bar appears above the taskbar and displays information relevant to the window or selected object.

Each major application in Microsoft Office uses a consistent command structure in which the same basic menus are found in all applications. The File, Edit, View, Insert, Tools, Window, and Help menus are present in all six applications. The same commands are found in the same menus. The Save, Open, Print, and Exit commands, for example, are contained in the File menu. The Cut, Copy, Paste, and Undo commands are found in the Edit menu.

The means for accessing the pull-down menus are consistent from one application to the next. Click the menu name on the menu bar, or press the Alt key plus the underlined letter of the menu name; for example, press Alt+F to pull down the File menu. If you already know some keyboard shortcuts in one application, there is a good chance that the shortcuts will work in another application. Ctrl+Home and Ctrl+End, for example, move to the beginning and end of a document, respectively. Ctrl+B, Ctrl+I, and Ctrl+U boldface, italicize, and underline text. Ctrl+X (the "X" is supposed to remind you of a pair of scissors), Ctrl+C, and Ctrl+V will cut, copy, and paste, respectively.

Title bar

Identifying icon

Menu bar

Standard toolbar

Formatting toolbar

Minimize button

Restore button

Close button

Status bar

Task bar

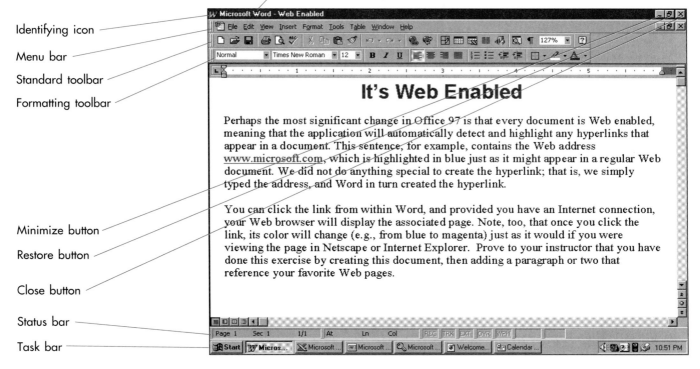

(a) Microsoft Word

Title bar

Identifying icon

Menu bar

Standard toolbar

Formatting toolbar

Minimize button

Restore button

Close button

Status bar

Task bar

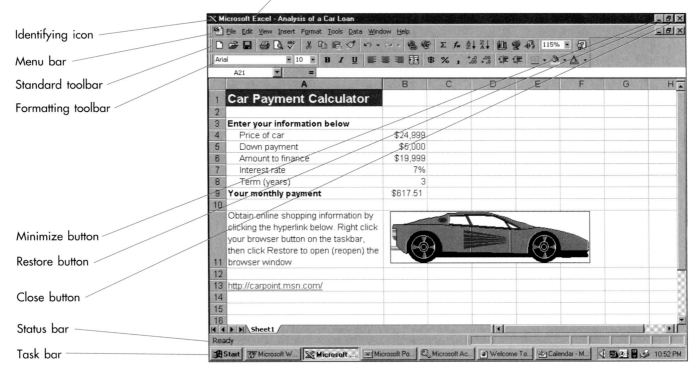

(b) Microsoft Excel

FIGURE 1   The Common User Interface

Title bar

Identifying icon

Menu bar

Standard toolbar

Formatting toolbar

Minimize button

Restore button

Close button

Status bar

Task bar

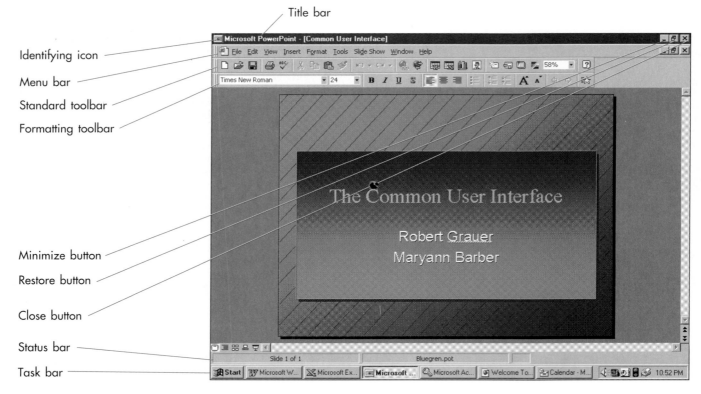

(c) Microsoft PowerPoint

Title bar

Identifying icon

Menu bar

Toolbar

Minimize button

Restore button

Close button

Status bar

Task bar

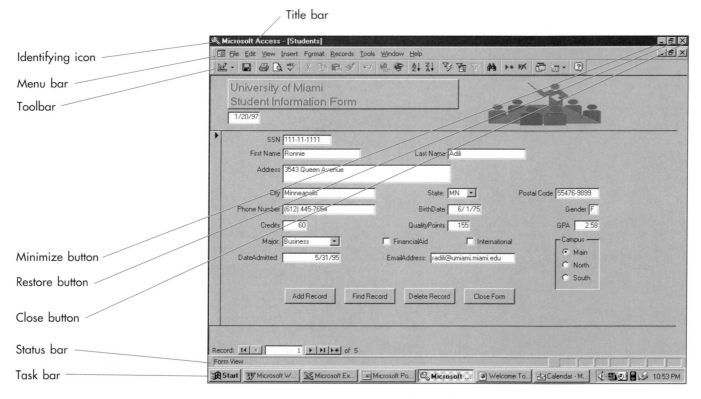

(d) Microsoft Access

FIGURE 1 The Common User Interface (continued)

Title bar

Identifying icon

Menu bar

Toolbar

Minimize button

Restore button

Close button

Status bar

Task bar

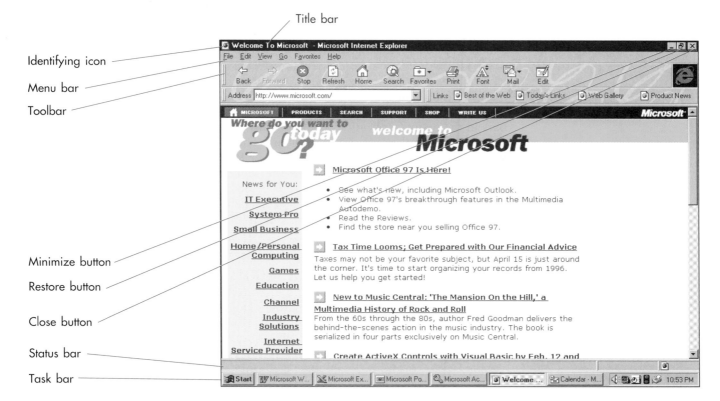

(e) Internet Explorer

Title bar

Identifying icon

Menu bar

Toolbar

Minimize button

Restore button

Close button

Status bar

Task bar

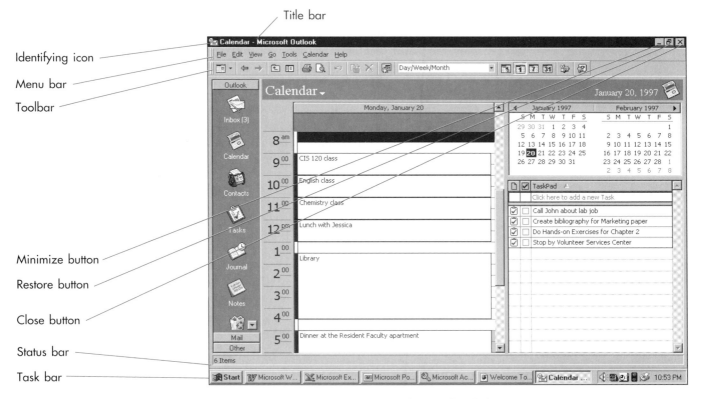

(f) Microsoft Outlook

FIGURE 1   The Common User Interface (continued)

The four major applications use consistent (and often identical) dialog boxes. The dialog boxes to open and close a file, for example, are identical in every application. All four applications also share a common dictionary. The AutoCorrect feature (to correct common spelling mistakes) works identically in all four applications. The help feature also functions identically.

There are, of course, differences between the applications. Each application has unique menus and toolbars. Nevertheless, the Standard and Formatting toolbars in the major applications contain many of the same tools (especially the first several tools on the left of each toolbar). The *Standard toolbar* contains buttons for basic commands such as Open, Save, or Print. It also contains buttons to cut, copy, and paste, and these buttons are identical in all four applications. The *Formatting toolbar* provides access to common operations such as boldface or italics, or changing the font or point size; again, these buttons are identical in all four applications. ScreenTips are present in all applications.

STANDARD OFFICE VERSUS OFFICE PROFESSIONAL

Microsoft distributes both a Standard and a Professional edition of Office 97. Both versions include Word, Excel, PowerPoint, Internet Explorer, and Outlook. Office Professional also has Microsoft Access. The difference is important when you are shopping and you are comparing prices from different sources. Be sure to purchase the version that is appropriate for your needs.

Help for Office 97

Several types of help are available in Office 97. The most basic is accessed by pulling down the Help menu and clicking the Contents and Index command to display the Help Contents window as shown in Figures 2a and 2b. (The Help screens are from Microsoft Word, but similar screens are available for each of the other applications.) The *Contents tab* in Figure 2a is analogous to the table of contents in an ordinary book. It displays the major topics in the application as a series of books that are open or closed. You can click any closed book to open it, which in turn displays additional books and/or help topics. Conversely, you can click any open book to close it and gain additional space on the screen.

The *Index tab* in Figure 2b is similar to the index of an ordinary book. Enter the first several letters of the topic to look up, such as "we" in Figure 2b. Help then returns all of the topics beginning with the letters you entered. Select the topic you want, then display the topic for immediate viewing, or print it for later reference. (The Find tab, not shown in Figure 2, contains a more extensive listing of entries than does the Index tab. It lets you enter a specific word, then it returns every topic that contains that word.)

The *Office Assistant* in Figure 2c is new to Office 97 and is activated by clicking the Office Assistant button on the Standard toolbar or by pressing the F1 function key. The Assistant enables you to ask a question in English, then it returns a series of topics that attempt to answer your question.

Additional help can be obtained from the Microsoft Web site as shown in Figure 2d, provided you have access to the Internet. The easiest way to access the site is to pull down the Help menu from any Office application, click Microsoft on the Web, then click Online Support. This, in turn, will start the Internet Explorer and take you to the appropriate page on the Web, where you will find the most current information available as well as the most detailed support. You can, for example, access the same knowledge base as that used by Microsoft support engineers when you call for technical assistance.

Topic may be viewed or
printed by clicking
appropriate command button

Double click closed book to
open it and display additional
help topics

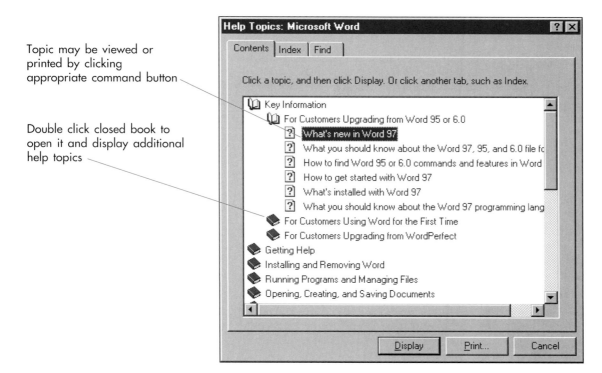

(a) Contents Tab

Type the first few letters in
the topic to look up

Select the desired topic

Click Display button to
view the information

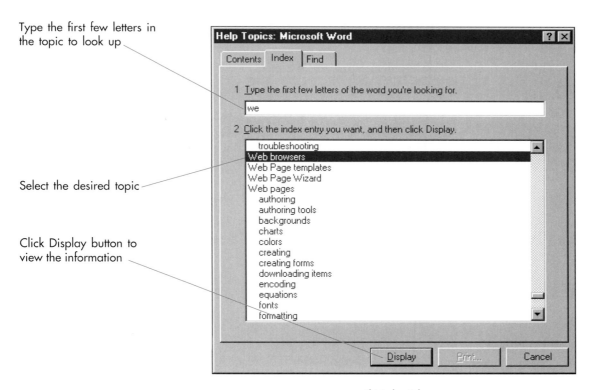

(b) Index Tab

FIGURE 2   Help with Microsoft Office

Help screen contains links
to additional information

Click any topic to display
the help screen

Enter your question, then
click the Search button

Office Assistant (other images
are available)

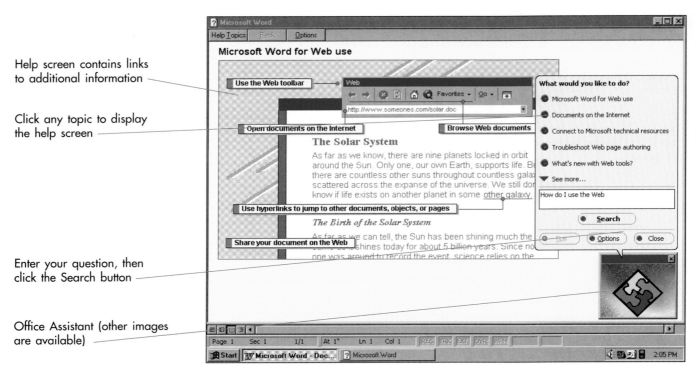

(c) The Office Assistant

Internet Explorer
opens automatically

Web address

Link to Frequently
Asked Questions

Click the link to
desired information

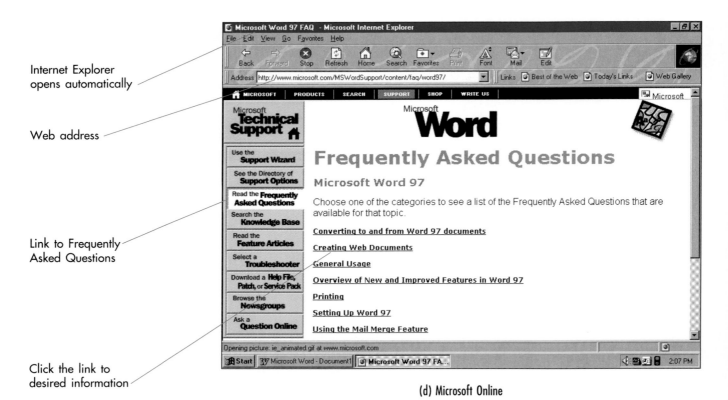

(d) Microsoft Online

FIGURE 2   Help with Microsoft Office (continued)

Office Shortcut Bar

The **Microsoft Office Shortcut Bar** provides immediate access to each application within Microsoft Office. It consists of a row of buttons and can be placed anywhere on the screen. The Shortcut Bar is anchored by default on the right side of the desktop, but you can position it along any edge, or have it "float" in the middle of the desktop. You can even hide it from view when it is not in use.

Figure 3a displays the Shortcut Bar as it appears on our desktop. The buttons that are displayed (and the order in which they appear) are established through the Customize dialog box in Figure 3b. Our Shortcut Bar contains a button for each Office application, a button for the Windows Explorer, and a button for Bookshelf Basics.

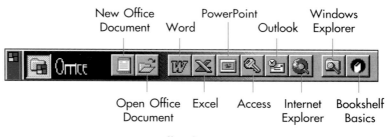

(a) Office Shortcut Bar

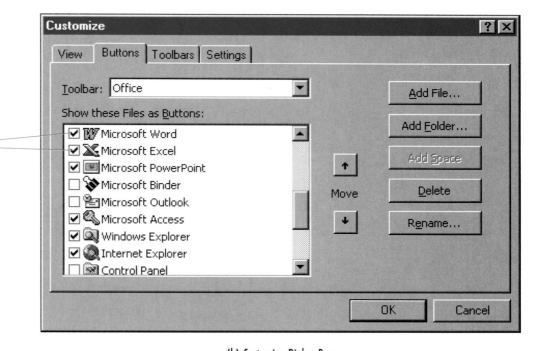

(b) Customize Dialog Box

FIGURE 3   Microsoft Office Shortcut Bar

Docucentric Orientation

Our Shortcut Bar contains two additional buttons: to open an existing document and to start a new document. These buttons are very useful and take advantage of the "docucentric" orientation of Microsoft Office, which lets you think in terms

Selected folder

Double click document name to open it

List of files in the folder

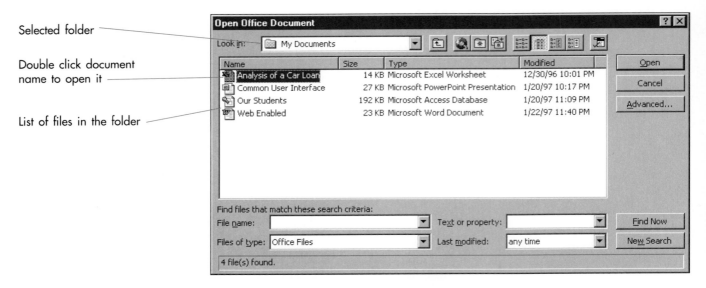

(a) Open an Existing Document

Letters & Faxes tab

Double click template name to open it

Details button

Preview of template

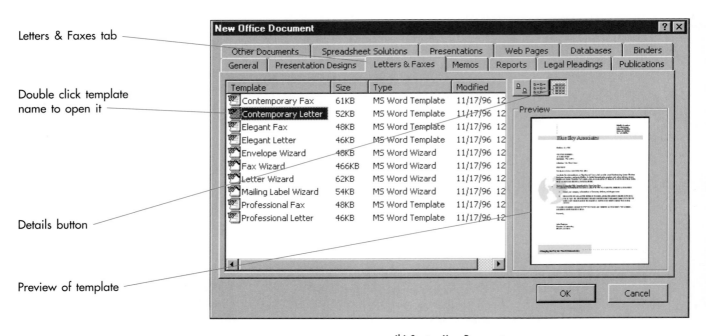

(b) Start a New Document

FIGURE 4   Document Orientation

of a document rather than the associated application. You can still open a document in traditional fashion, by starting the application (e.g., clicking its button on the Shortcut Bar), then using the File Open command to open the document. It's easier, however, to locate the document, then double click its icon, which automatically loads the associated program.

Consider, for example, the Open dialog box in Figure 4a, which is displayed by clicking the Open a Document button on the Shortcut Bar. The Open dialog box is common to the major Office applications, and it works identically in each application. The My Documents folder is selected in Figure 4a, and it contains four documents of various file types. The documents are displayed in the Details view, which shows the document name, size, file type, and date and time the document was last modified. To open any document—for example, "Analysis of a Car Loan"—just double click its name or icon. The associated application (Microsoft Excel in this example) will be started automatically; and it, in turn, will open the selected workbook.

The "docucentric" orientation also applies to new documents. Click the Start a New Document button on the Office Shortcut Bar, and you display the New dialog box in Figure 4b. Click the tab corresponding to the type of document you want to create, such as Letters & Faxes in Figure 4b. Change to the Details view, then click (select) various templates so that you can choose the one most appropriate for your purpose. Double click the desired template to start the application, which opens the template and enables you to create the document.

CHANGE THE VIEW

The toolbar in the Open dialog box contains buttons to display the documents within the selected folder in one of several views. Click the Details button to switch to the Details view and see the date and time the file was last modified, as well as its size and type. Click the List button to display an icon representing the associated application, enabling you to see many more files than in the Details view. The Preview button lets you see a document before you open it. The Properties button displays information about the document, including the number of revisions.

SHARED APPLICATIONS AND UTILITIES

Microsoft Office includes additional applications and shared utilities, several of which are illustrated in Figure 5. The *Microsoft Clip Gallery* in Figure 5a has more than 3,000 clip art images and almost 150 photographs, each in a variety of categories. It also contains a lesser number of sound files and video clips. The Clip Gallery can be accessed from every Office application, most easily through the Insert Picture command, which displays the Clip Gallery dialog box.

The *Microsoft WordArt* utility adds decorative text to a document, and is accessed through the Insert Picture command from Word, Excel, or PowerPoint. WordArt is intuitive and easy to use. In essence, you choose a style for the text from among the selections in the dialog box of Figure 5b, then you enter the specific text in a second dialog box (which is not shown in Figure 5). It's fun, it's easy, and you can create some truly dynamite documents that will add interest to a document.

Office Art consists of a set of drawing tools that is found on the Drawing toolbar in Word, Excel, or PowerPoint. You don't have to be an artist—all it takes is a little imagination and an appreciation for what the individual tools can do. In Figure 5c, for example, we began with a single clip art image, copied it several times within the PowerPoint slide, then rotated and colored the students as shown. We also used the AutoShapes tool to add a callout for our student.

Microsoft Bookshelf Basics contains three of the nine books available in the complete version of Microsoft Bookshelf (which is an additional cost item). The *American Heritage Dictionary,* the *Original Roget's Thesaurus,* and the *Columbia Dictionary of Quotations* are provided at no charge. An excerpt from the *American Heritage Dictionary* is illustrated in Figure 5d. Enter the word you are looking for in the text box on the left, then read the definition on the right. You can click the sound icon and hear the pronunciation of the word.

Choose the type of object

Choose the category

Choose the image

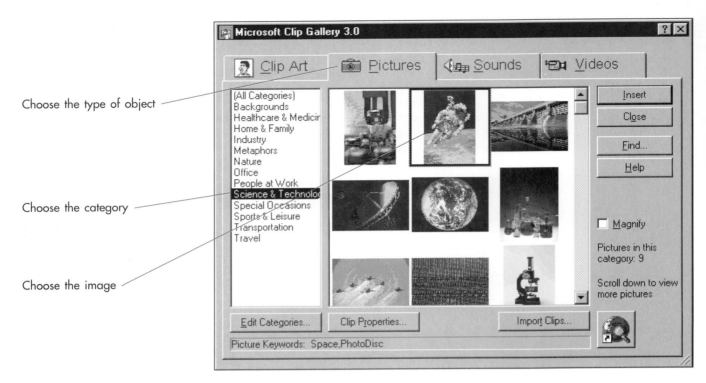

(a) Microsoft Clip Gallery

Select the style to display a
second dialog box in which
you enter your text

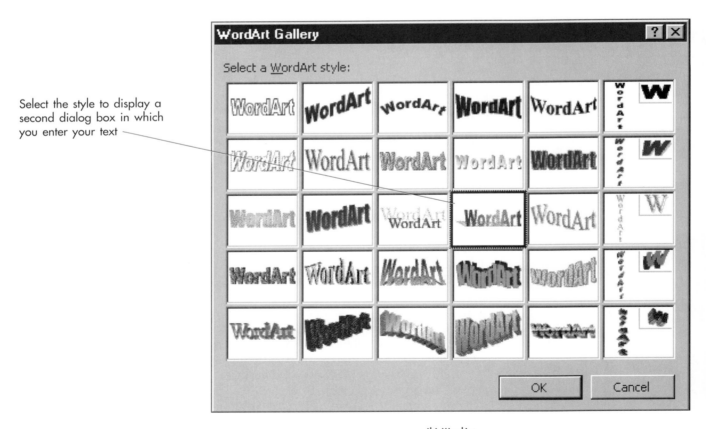

(b) WordArt

FIGURE 5   Shared Applications

Color objects in clip art

Create callout

Callout tool

Drawing toolbar

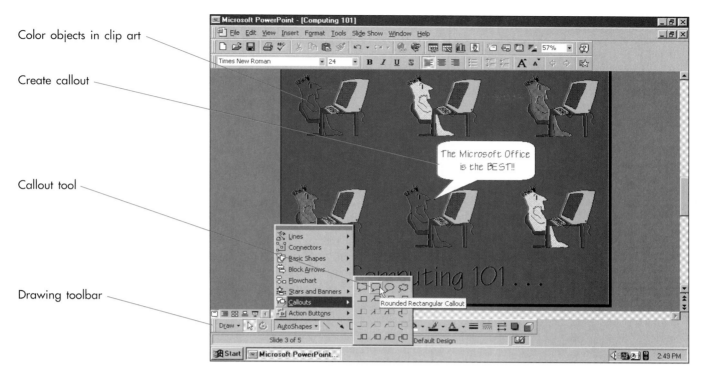

(c) Office Art

Enter word

Click to
hear pronunciation

(d) Bookshelf Basics

FIGURE 5   Shared Applications (continued)

OBJECT LINKING AND EMBEDDING

The applications in Microsoft Office are thoroughly integrated with one another. They look alike and they work in consistent fashion. Equally important, they share information through a technology known as **Object Linking and Embedding (OLE),** which enables you to create a **compound document** containing data (objects) from multiple applications.

The compound document in Figure 6 was created in Word, and it contains objects (a worksheet and a chart) that were created in Excel. The letterhead uses a logo that was taken from the Clip Gallery, while the name and address of the recipient were drawn from an Access database. The various objects were inserted into the compound document through linking or embedding, which are actually two very different techniques. Both operations, however, are much more sophisticated than simply pasting an object, because with either linking or embedding, you can edit the object by using the tools of the original application.

The difference between linking and embedding depends on whether the object is stored within the compound document (*embedding*) or in its own file (*linking*). An *embedded object* is stored in the compound document, which in turn becomes the only user (client) of that object. A *linked object* is stored in its own file, and the compound document is one of many potential clients of that object. The compound document does not contain the linked object per se, but only a representation of the object as well as a pointer (link) to the file containing the object. The advantage of linking is that the document is updated automatically if the object changes.

The choice between linking and embedding depends on how the object will be used. Linking is preferable if the object is likely to change and the compound document requires the latest version. Linking should also be used when the same object is placed in many documents so that any change to the object has to be made in only one place. Embedding should be used if you need to take the object with you (to a different computer) and/or if there is only a single destination document for the object.

Office of Residential Living

| University of Miami | • | P.O. Box 248904 | • | Coral Gables, FL 33124 |

January 10, 1998

Mr. Jeffrey Redmond, President
Dynamic Dining Services
4329 Palmetto Lane
Miami, FL 33157

Dear Jeff,

As per our conversation, occupancy is projected to be back up from last year. I have enclosed a spreadsheet and chart that show the total enrollment for the past four school years. Please realize, however, that the 1997–1998 figures are projections, as the Spring 1998 numbers are still incomplete. The final 1997–1998 numbers should be confirmed within the next two weeks. I hope that this helps with your planning. If you need further information, please contact me at the above address.

Dorm Occupancy				
	94-95	95-96	96-97	97-98
Beatty	330	285	270	250
Broward	620	580	620	565
Graham	450	397	352	420
Rawlings	435	470	295	372
Tolbert	550	554	524	635
Totals	2385	2286	2061	2242

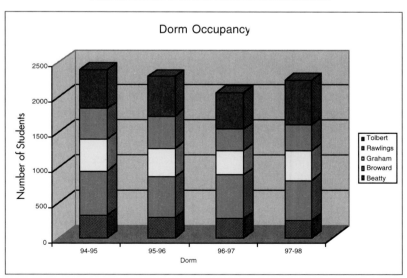

FIGURE 6   A Compound Document

The common user interface requires every Windows application to follow a consistent set of conventions and ensures that all applications work basically the same way. The development of a suite of applications from a single vendor extends this concept by imposing additional similarities on all applications within the suite.

Microsoft distributes both a Standard and a Professional edition of Office 97. Both versions include Word, Excel, PowerPoint, Internet Explorer, and Outlook. Office Professional also has Microsoft Access. The single biggest difference between Office 97 and its predecessor, Office 95, is that the Internet has become an integral part of the Office suite.

Help for all Office applications is available in a variety of formats. The Help Contents window provides access to a Contents and Index tab in which you look up specific topics. The Office Assistant enables you to ask a question in English. Still additional help is available from the Microsoft Web site, provided you have access to the Internet.

Microsoft Office includes several additional applications and shared utilities that can be used to add interest to a document. The Clip Gallery has more than 3,000 clip art images, 150 photographs, and a lesser number of sound files and video clips. WordArt enables you to create decorative text, while Office Art consists of a powerful set of drawing tools.

The Microsoft Office Shortcut Bar provides immediate access to each application in Microsoft Office. The Shortcut Bar is fully customizable with respect to the buttons it displays, its appearance, and its position on the desktop. The Open a Document and Start a New Document buttons enable you to think in terms of a document rather than the associated application.

Object Linking and Embedding (OLE) enables you to create a compound document containing data (objects) from multiple applications. Linking and embedding are different operations. The difference between the two depends on whether the object is stored within the compound document (embedding) or in its own file (linking).

KEY WORDS AND CONCEPTS

Common Windows
    interface
Compound document
Contents tab
Docucentric orientation
Embedding
Formatting toolbar
Index tab
Internet Explorer
Linking
Microsoft Access

Microsoft Bookshelf
    Basics
Microsoft Clip Gallery
Microsoft Excel
Microsoft Office
    Professional
Microsoft Office
    Shortcut Bar
Microsoft Outlook
Microsoft PowerPoint
Microsoft Standard
    Office

Microsoft Word
Microsoft WordArt
Object Linking and
    Embedding (OLE)
Office Art
Office Assistant
Online help
Shared applications
Standard toolbar

INTRODUCTION TO MICROSOFT ACCESS: WHAT IS A DATABASE?

OBJECTIVES

After reading this chapter you will be able to:

1. Define the terms *field, record, table,* and *database.*
2. Start Microsoft Access; describe the Database window and the objects in an Access database.
3. Add, edit, and delete records within a table; use the Find command to locate a specific record.
4. Describe the record selector; explain when changes are saved to a table.
5. Explain the importance of data validation in table maintenance.
6. Describe a relational database; distinguish between a one-to-many and a many-to-many relationship.

OVERVIEW

All businesses and organizations maintain data of one kind or another. Companies store data about their employees. Schools and universities store data about their students and faculties. Magazines and newspapers store data about their subscribers. The list goes on and on, and while each of these examples refers to different types of data, they all operate under the same basic principles of database management.

This chapter provides a broad-based introduction to database management through the example of a college bookstore. We begin by showing how the mechanics of manual record keeping can be extended to a computerized system. We discuss the basic operations in maintaining data and stress the importance of data validation.

The chapter also introduces you to Microsoft Access, the fourth major application in the Microsoft Office Professional suite. We describe the objects within an Access database and show you how to add, edit, and delete records in an Access table. We also explain how the real power of Access is derived from a database with multiple tables that are related to one another.

The hands-on exercises in the chapter enable you to apply all of the material at the computer, and are indispensable to the learn-by-doing philosophy we follow throughout the text. As you do the exercises, you may recognize many commands from other Windows applications, all of which share a common user interface and consistent command structure.

CASE STUDY: THE COLLEGE BOOKSTORE

Imagine, if you will, that you are the manager of a college bookstore and that you maintain data for every book in the store. Accordingly, you have recorded the specifics of each book (the title, author, publisher, price, and so on) in a manila folder, and have stored the folders in one drawer of a file cabinet.

One of your major responsibilities is to order books at the beginning of each semester, which in turn requires you to contact the various publishers. You have found it convenient, therefore, to create a second set of folders with data about each publisher such as the publisher's phone number, address, discount policy, and so on. You also found it necessary to create a third set of folders with data about each order such as when the order was placed, the status of the order, which books were ordered, how many copies, and so on.

Normal business operations will require you to make repeated trips to the filing cabinet to maintain the accuracy of the data and keep it up to date. You will have to create a new folder whenever a new book is received, whenever you contract with a new publisher, or whenever you place a new order. Each of these folders must be placed in the proper drawer in the filing cabinet. In similar fashion, you will have to modify the data in an existing folder to reflect changes that occur, such as an increase in the price of a book, a change in a publisher's address, or an update in the status of an order. And, lastly, you will need to remove the folder of any book that is no longer carried by the bookstore, or of any publisher with whom you no longer have contact, or of any order that was canceled.

The preceding discussion describes the bookstore of 40 years ago—before the advent of computers and computerized databases. The bookstore manager of today needs the same information as his or her predecessor. Today's manager, however, has the information readily available, at the touch of a key or the click of a mouse, through the miracle of modern technology. The concepts are identical in both the manual and computerized systems.

You can think of the file cabinet, which contains the various sets of folders, as a *database.* Each set of folders in the file cabinet corresponds to a *table* within the database. In our example the bookstore database consists of three separate tables—for books, publishers, and orders. Each table, in turn, consists of multiple *records,* corresponding to the folders in the file cabinet. The Books table, for example, contains a record for every book title in the store. The Publishers table has a record for each publisher, just as the Orders table has a record for each order.

Each fact (or data element) that is stored within a record is called a *field.* In our example each book record consists of six fields—ISBN (a unique identifying number for the book), title, author, year of publication, price, and publisher. The table is constructed in such a way that every record has the same fields in the same order. In similar fashion, every record in the Publishers table will have the same fields for each publisher, just as every record in the Orders table has the same fields for each order. This terminology (field, record, table, and database) is extremely important and will be used throughout the text.

Microsoft Access, the fourth major application in the Microsoft Office, is used to create and manage a database such as the one for the college bookstore. Consider now Figure 1.1, which shows how Microsoft Access appears on the desktop. Our discussion assumes a basic familiarity with Windows 95 and the user interface that is common to all Windows applications. You should recognize, therefore, that the desktop in Figure 1.1 has two open windows—an application window for Microsoft Access and a document (database) window for the database that is currently open.

Each window has its own title bar and Minimize, Maximize (or Restore), and Close buttons. The title bar in the application window contains the name of the application (Microsoft Access). The title bar in the document (database) window contains the name of the database that is currently open (Bookstore). The application window for Access has been maximized to take up the entire desktop, and hence the Restore button is visible. The database window has not been maximized.

A menu bar appears immediately below the application title bar. A toolbar (similar to those in other Office applications) appears below the menu bar and offers alternative ways to execute common commands. The Windows 95 taskbar appears at the bottom of the screen and shows the open applications.

The Database Window

The *Database window* displays the various objects in an Access database. There are six types of objects—tables, queries, forms, reports, macros, and modules. Every database must contain at least one table, and it may contain any or all (or

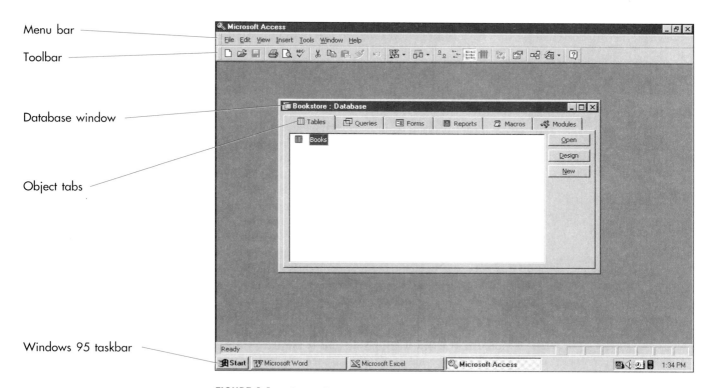

Menu bar

Toolbar

Database window

Object tabs

Windows 95 taskbar

FIGURE 1.1   The Database Window

none) of the other objects. Each object type is accessed through the appropriate tab within the Database window. In this chapter we concentrate on tables, but we briefly describe the other types of objects as a preview of what you will learn as you read our book.

- A *table* stores data about an entity (a person, place, or thing) and is the basic element in any database. A table is made up of records, which in turn are made up of fields. It is columnar in appearance, with each record in a separate row of the table and each field in a separate column.
- A *form* provides a more convenient and attractive way to enter, display, and/or print the data in a table. Forms are discussed in Chapter 2.
- A *query* answers a question about the database. The most common type of query specifies a set of criteria, then searches the database to retrieve the records that satisfy the criteria. Queries are introduced in Chapter 3.
- A *report* presents the data in a table or query in attractive fashion on the printed page. Reports are described in Chapter 3.
- A *macro* is analogous to a computer program and consists of commands that are executed automatically one after the other. Macros are used to automate the performance of any repetitive task.
- A *module* provides a greater degree of automation through programming in Access Basic. Modules are beyond the scope of this text.

ONE FILE HOLDS ALL

All of the objects in an Access database (tables, forms, queries, reports, macros, and modules) are stored in a single file on disk. The database itself is opened through the Open command in the File menu or by clicking the Open button on the Database toolbar. The individual objects within a database are opened through the database window.

Tables

A table (or set of tables) is the heart of any database, as it contains the actual data. In Access a table is displayed in one of two views—the Design view or the Datasheet view. The **Design view** is used to define the table initially and to specify the fields it will contain. It is also used to modify the table definition if changes are subsequently necessary. The Design view is discussed in detail in Chapter 2. The **Datasheet view**—the view you use to add, edit, or delete records—is the view on which we focus in this chapter.

Figure 1.2 shows the Datasheet view for the Books table in our bookstore. The first row in the table contains the *field names.* Each additional row contains a record (the data for a specific book). Each column represents a field (one fact about a book). Every record in the table contains the same fields in the same order: ISBN Number, Title, Author, Year, List Price, and Publisher.

The status bar at the bottom of Figure 1.2a indicates that there are five records in the table and that you are positioned on the first record. This is the record you are working on and is known as the *current record.* (You can work on only one record at a time.) There is a *record selector symbol* (either a triangle or a pencil) next to the current record to indicate its status.

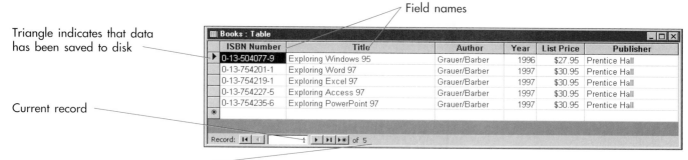

Field names

Triangle indicates that data has been saved to disk

Current record

Total number of records

(a) All Data Has Been Saved

Pencil indicates that data has not yet been saved to disk

Asterisk represents the blank record at end of every table

Insertion point indicates that data is being entered

(b) During Data Entry

FIGURE 1.2 Tables

A *triangle* indicates that the record has been saved to disk. A *pencil* indicates that you are working on the record and that the changes have not yet been saved. As soon as you move to the next record, however, the pencil changes to a triangle to indicate that the record on which you were working has been saved. (Access, unlike other Office applications, automatically saves changes made to a record without your having to execute the Save command.) An *asterisk* appears next to the blank record at the end of every table.

Figure 1.2a shows the table as it would appear immediately after you opened it. The first field in the first record is selected (highlighted), and anything you type at this point will replace the selected data. (This is the same convention as in any other Windows application.) The triangle next to the current record (record 1) indicates that changes have not yet been made. An asterisk appears as the record selector symbol next to the blank record at the end of the table. The blank record is used to add a record to the table and is not counted in determining the number of records in the table.

Figure 1.2b shows the table as you are in the process of entering data for a new record at the end of the table. The current record is now record 6. The *insertion point* (a flashing vertical bar) appears at the point where text is being entered. The record selector for the current record is a pencil, indicating that the record has not yet been saved. The asterisk has moved to the blank record at the end of the table, which now contains one more record than the table in Figure 1.2a.

Note, too, that each table in a database must have a field (or combination of fields) known as the *primary key,* which is unique for every record in the table. The ISBN (International Standard Book Number) is the primary key in our example, and it ensures that each record in the Books table is different from every other record. (Other fields may also have a unique value for every record, but only one field is designated as the primary key.)

Objective: To open an existing database; to add a record to a table within the database. Use Figure 1.3 as a guide in the exercise.

STEP 1: Welcome to Windows

➤ Turn on the computer and all of its peripherals. The floppy drive should be empty prior to starting your machine. This ensures that the system starts by reading from the hard disk, which contains the Windows files, as opposed to a floppy disk, which does not.

➤ Your system will take a minute or so to get started, after which you should see the desktop in Figure 1.3a. Do not be concerned if the appearance of your desktop is different from ours. If necessary, click the **Close button** to close the Welcome window.

TAKE THE WINDOWS 95 TOUR

Windows 95 greets you with a Welcome window that contains a command button to take you on a 10-minute tour. Click the command button and enjoy the show. If you do not see the Welcome window, click the Start button, click Run, type WELCOME in the Open text box, and press enter. Windows 97 was not available when we went to press, but we expect it to have a similar option.

(a) Welcome to Windows (step 1)

FIGURE 1.3   Hands-on Exercise 1

STEP 2: Obtain the Practice Files:

➤ We have created a series of practice files for you to use throughout the text. Your instructor will make these files available to you in a variety of ways:

- You can download the files from our Web site if you have access to the Internet and World Wide Web (see boxed tip).
- The files may be on a network drive, in which case you use the Windows Explorer to copy the files from the network to a floppy disk.
- There may be an actual "data disk" that you are to check out from the lab in order to use the Copy Disk command to duplicate the disk.

➤ Check with your instructor for additional information.

DOWNLOAD THE PRACTICE FILES

Download the practice files for any book in the *Exploring Windows* series from the *Exploring Windows* home page www.prenhall.com/grauer. Use any Web browser to get to this site, click the Office 97 book, then click the link to Student data disks, where you choose the appropriate book and download the file. Be sure to read the associated "read me" file which provides additional information about downloading the file.

STEP 3: Start Microsoft Access

➤ Click the **Start button** to display the Start menu. Click (or point to) the **Programs menu,** then click **Microsoft Access** to start the program. Close the Office Assistant if it appears. (The Office Assistant is described in the next hands-on exercise.)

➤ You should see the Microsoft Access dialog box with the option button to **Open an Existing Database** already selected. Click **More Files,** then click **OK** to display the Open dialog box in Figure 1.3b.

➤ Click the **Details button** to change to the Details view. Click and drag the vertical border between columns to increase (or decrease) the size of a column.

➤ Click the **drop-down arrow** on the Look In list box. Click the appropriate drive (drive C is recommended rather than drive A), depending on the location of your data. Double click the **Exploring Access folder.**

➤ Click the **down scroll arrow** until you can click the **Bookstore database.** Click the **Open command button** to open the database.

WORK ON DRIVE C

Even in a lab setting it is preferable to work on the local hard drive, as opposed to a floppy disk. The hard drive is much faster, which becomes especially important when working with the large file sizes associated with Access. Use the Windows Explorer to copy the database from the network drive to the local hard drive prior to the exercise, then work on drive C throughout the exercise. Once you have completed the exercise, use the Explorer a second time to copy the modified database to a floppy disk that you can take with you.

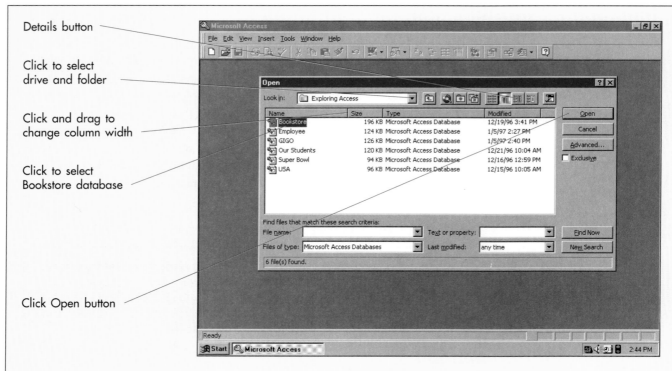

Details button

Click to select drive and folder

Click and drag to change column width

Click to select Bookstore database

Click Open button

(b) Open an Existing Database (step 3)

FIGURE 1.3   Hands-on Exercise 1 (continued)

STEP 4: Open the Books Table

➤ You should see the database window for the Bookstore database with the **Tables tab** already selected. Double click the icon next to **Books** to open the table as shown in Figure 1.3c.

➤ Click the **Maximize button** so that the Books table fills the Access window and reduces the clutter on the screen.

➤ If necessary, click the **Maximize button** in the application window so that Access takes the entire desktop.

A SIMPLER DATABASE

The real power of Access is derived from a database with multiple tables that are related to one another. For the time being, however, we focus on a database with only one table so that you can learn the basics of Access. After you are comfortable working with a single table, we will show you how to work with multiple tables and how to relate them to one another.

STEP 5: Moving within a Table

➤ Click in any field in the first record. The status bar at the bottom of the Books Table indicates record 1 of 22.

➤ The triangle symbol in the record selector indicates that the record has not changed since it was last saved.

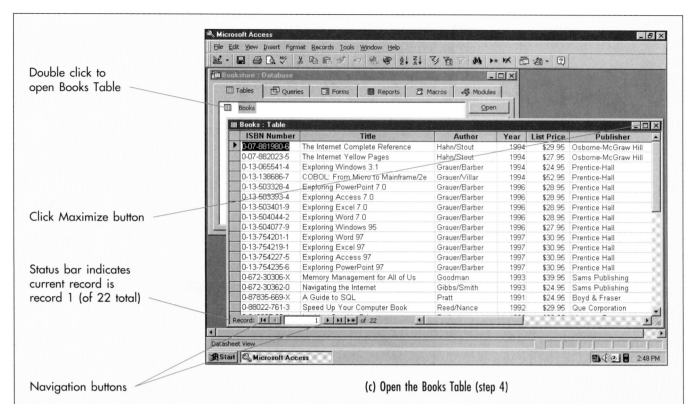

Double click to
open Books Table

Click Maximize button

Status bar indicates
current record is
record 1 (of 22 total)

Navigation buttons

(c) Open the Books Table (step 4)

FIGURE 1.3   Hands-on Exercise 1 (continued)

➤ You can move from record to record (or field to field) using either the mouse
or the arrow keys:

• Click in any field in the second record. The status bar indicates record 2
of 22.

• Press the **down arrow key** to move to the third record. The status bar indicates record 3 of 22.

• Press the **left and right arrow keys** to move from field to field within the
third record.

➤ You can also use the navigation buttons above the status bar to move from
one record to the next:

• Click |◄ to move to the first record in the table.

• Click ► to move forward in the table to the next record.

• Click ◄ to move back in the table to the previous record.

MOVING FROM FIELD TO FIELD

Press the Tab key, the right arrow key, or the enter key to move to the
next field in the current record (or the first field in the next record if you
are already in the last field of the current record). Press Shift+Tab or the
left arrow key to return to the previous field in the current record (or the
last field in the previous record if you are already in the first field of the
current record).

- Click ▶| to move to the last record in the table.
- Click ▶* to move beyond the last record in order to insert a new record.

➤ Click |◀ to return to the first record in the table.

STEP 6: Add a Record

➤ Pull down the **Insert menu** and click **New Record** (or click the **New Record button** on the Table Datasheet toolbar). The record selector moves to the last record (now record 23). The insertion point is positioned in the first field (ISBN Number).

➤ Enter data for the new record as shown in Figure 1.3d. The record selector changes to a pencil as soon as you enter the first character in the new record.

➤ Press the **enter key** when you have entered the last field for the record. The new record is saved, and the record selector changes to a triangle and moves automatically to the next record.

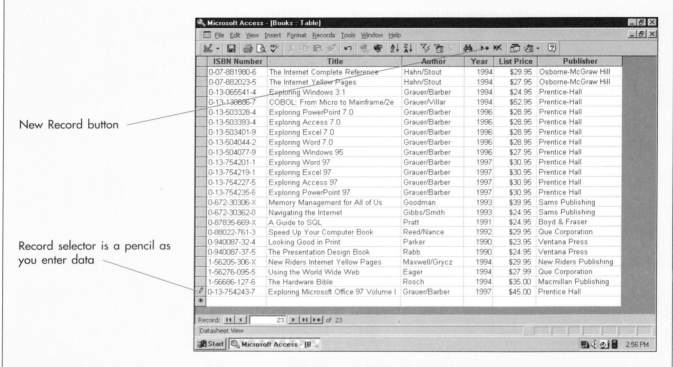

New Record button

Record selector is a pencil as you enter data

(d) Add a New Record (step 6)

FIGURE 1.3   Hands-on Exercise 1 (continued)

WHEN IS DATA SAVED?

There is one critical difference between Access and other Office applications such as Word for Windows or Microsoft Excel. *Access automatically saves any changes in the current record as soon as you move to the next record or when you close the table.* In other words, you do *not* have to execute the Save command explicitly to save the data in the table.

STEP 7: Add a Second Record

➤ The record selector is at the end of the table where you can add another record. Enter **0-13-271693-3** as the ISBN number for this record. Press the **Tab, enter,** or **right arrow key** to move to the Title field.

➤ Enter the title of this book as **Exploring teh Internet/2nd Edition** (deliberately misspelling the word "the"). Try to look at the monitor as you type to see the AutoCorrect feature (common to all Office applications) in action. Access will correct the misspelling and change *teh* to *the.*

➤ If you did not see the correction being made, press the **backspace key** several times to erase the last several characters in the title, then re-enter the title.

➤ Complete the entry for this book. Enter **Grauer/Marx** for the author. Enter **1997** for the year of publication. Enter **28.95** for the list price. Enter **Prentice Hall** for the publisher, then press **enter.**

CREATE YOUR OWN SHORTHAND

Use the AutoCorrect feature that is common to all Office applications to expand abbreviations such as "PH" for Prentice Hall. Pull down the Tools menu, click AutoCorrect, type the abbreviation in the Replace text box and the expanded entry in the With text box. Click the Add command button, then click OK to exit the dialog box and return to the document. The next time you type PH (in upper- or lowercase) as you enter a record, it will automatically be expanded to Prentice Hall.

STEP 8: Print the Table

➤ Pull down the **File menu.** Click **Page Setup** to display the Page Setup dialog box in Figure 1.3e.

➤ Click the **Page tab.** Click the **Landscape option button.** Click **OK** to accept the settings and close the dialog box.

➤ Click the **Print button** on the toolbar to print the table. Alternatively, you can pull down the **File menu,** click **Print** to display the Print dialog box, click the **All options button,** then click **OK.**

ABOUT MICROSOFT ACCESS

Pull down the Help menu and click About Microsoft Access to display the specific release number as well as other licensing information, including the product serial number. This help screen also contains two very useful command buttons, System Info and Tech Support. The first button displays information about the hardware installed on your system, including the amount of memory and available space on the hard drive. The Tech Support button provides telephone numbers for technical assistance.

Print button

Click Page tab

Select Landscape

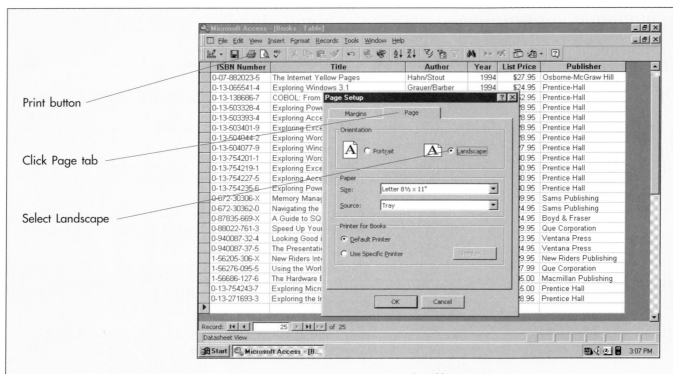

(e) Print the Table (step 8)

FIGURE 1.3   Hands-on Exercise 1 (continued)

STEP 9: Exit Access

➤ You need to close both the Books table and the Bookstore database:

- Pull down the **File menu** and click **Close** (or click the **Close button)** to close the Books table. Answer **Yes** if asked to save changes to the layout of the table.

- Pull down the **File menu** and click **Close** (or click the **Close button)** to close the Bookstore database.

➤ Pull down the **File menu** and click **Exit** to close Access if you do not want to continue with the next exercise at this time.

OUR FAVORITE BOOKSTORE

This exercise has taken you through our hypothetical bookstore database. It's more fun, however, to go to a real bookstore. Amazon Books (www.amazon.com), with a virtual inventory of more than one million titles, is one of our favorite sites on the Web. You can search by author, subject, or title, read reviews written by other Amazon visitors, or contribute your own review. It's not as cozy as your neighborhood bookstore, but you can order any title for mail-order delivery. And you never have to leave home.

The exercise just completed showed you how to open an existing table and add records to that table. You will also need to edit and/or delete existing records in order to maintain the data as changes occur. These operations require you to find the specific record and then make the change. You can search the table manually, or more easily through the Find and Replace commands.

Find and Replace Commands

The Find and Replace commands are similar in function to the corresponding commands in all other Office applications. The ***Find command*** in Microsoft Access enables you to locate a specific record(s) by searching a table for a particular value. You could, for example, search the Books table for the title of a book as in Figure 1.4a, then move to the appropriate field to change its price. The ***Replace command*** incorporates the Find command and allows you to locate and optionally replace (one or more occurrences of) one value with another. The Replace command in Figure 1.4b, for example, searches for *PH* in order to substitute *Prentice Hall.*

Searches can be made more efficient by making use of the various options. A case-sensitive search, for example, matches not only the specific characters, but also the use of upper- and lowercase letters. Thus, *PH* is different from *ph*, and a case-sensitive search on one will not identify the other. A case-insensitive search (where Match Case is *not* selected) will find both *PH* and *ph*. Any search may specify a match on whole fields to identify *Davis*, but not *Davison*. And finally, a

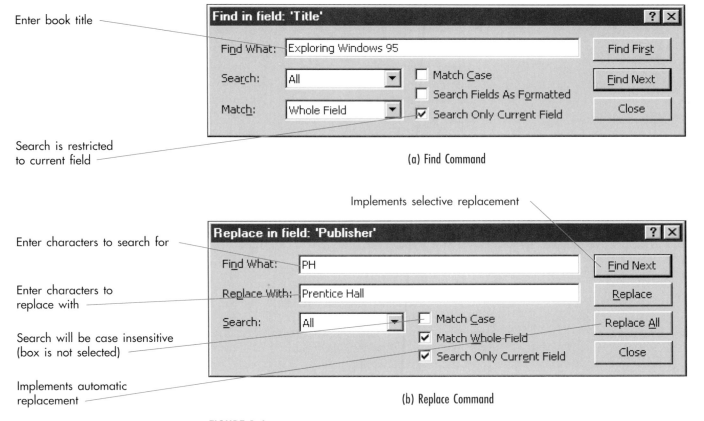

Enter book title

Search is restricted to current field

(a) Find Command

Implements selective replacement

Enter characters to search for

Enter characters to replace with

Search will be case insensitive (box is not selected)

Implements automatic replacement

(b) Replace Command

FIGURE 1.4   Find and Replace Commands

search can also be made more efficient by restricting it to the current field (e.g., Publisher), as opposed to searching every field.

The replacement can be either selective or automatic. Selective replacement lets you examine each successful match in context and decide whether to replace it. Automatic replacement makes the substitution without asking for confirmation (and is generally not recommended). Selective replacement is implemented by clicking the Find Next command button, then clicking (or not clicking) the Replace button to make (or not make) the substitution. Automatic replacement (through the entire table) is implemented by clicking the Replace All button.

Data Validation

It is unwise to simply add (edit or delete) a record without adequate checks on the validity of the data. Ask yourself, for example, whether a search for all books by Prentice Hall (without a hyphen) will also return all books by *Prentice-Hall* (with a hyphen). The answer is *no* because the publisher's name is spelled differently and a search for one will not locate the other. *You* know the publisher is the same in both instances, but the computer does not.

Data validation is a crucial part of any system. Good systems will anticipate errors you might make and reject those errors prior to accepting data. Access automatically implements certain types of data validation. It will not, for example, let you enter letters where a numeric value is expected (such as the Year and List Price fields in our example.) More sophisticated types of validation are implemented by the user when the table is created. You may decide, for example, to reject any record that omits the title or author. Data validation is described more completely in Chapter 2.

GARBAGE IN, GARBAGE OUT (GIGO)

A computer does exactly what you tell it to do, which is not necessarily what you want it to do. It is absolutely critical, therefore, that you validate the data that goes into a system, or else the associated information may not be correct. No system, no matter how sophisticated, can produce valid output from invalid input. In other words: *garbage in, garbage out.*

FORMS, QUERIES, AND REPORTS

As previously indicated, an Access database can contain as many as six different types of objects. Thus far we have concentrated on tables, but now we extend the discussion to include forms, queries, and reports as illustrated in Figure 1.5.

Figure 1.5a contains the Books table as it exists after the first hands-on exercise. There are 24 records in the table and six fields for each record. The status bar indicates that you are currently positioned in the first record. You can enter new records in the table as was done in the previous exercise. You can also edit or delete an existing record, as will be illustrated in the next exercise.

Figure 1.5b displays a form that is based on the table of Figure 1.5a. A form provides a friendlier interface than does a table and is easier to understand and use. Note, for example, the command buttons in the form to add a new record, or to find and/or delete an existing record. The status bar at the bottom of the form indicates that you are on the first of 24 records, and is identical to the status bar for the table in Figure 1.5a.

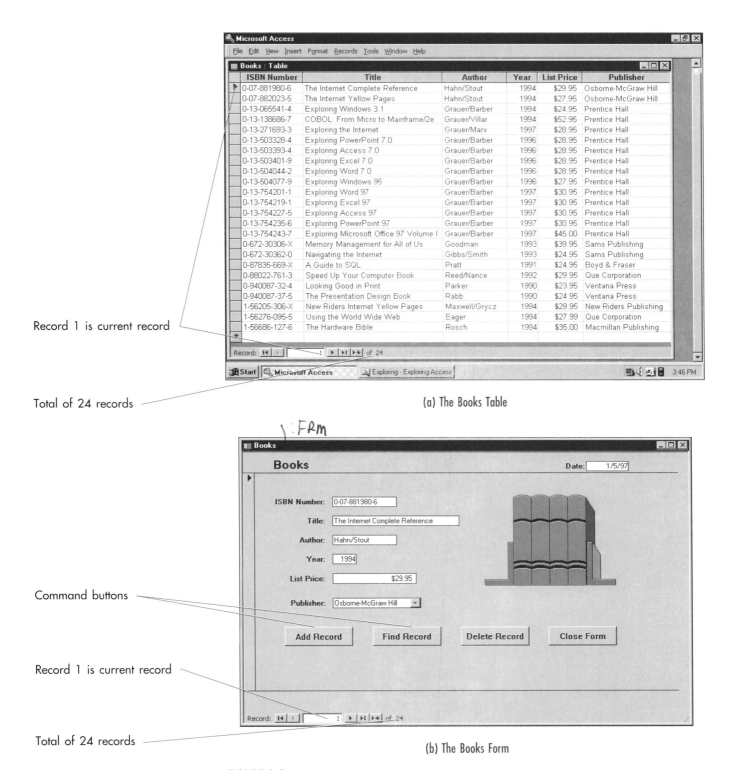

Record 1 is current record

Total of 24 records

(a) The Books Table

Command buttons

Record 1 is current record

Total of 24 records

(b) The Books Form

FIGURE 1.5   The Objects in a Database

Figure 1.5c displays a query to list the books for a particular publisher (Prentice Hall in this example). A query consists of a question (e.g., enter the publisher name) and an answer (the records that satisfy the query). The results of the query are similar in appearance to the underlying table, except that the query contains selected records and/or selected fields for those records. The query may also list the records in a different sequence from that of the table.

Books are in sequence by author, and within the same author, by title

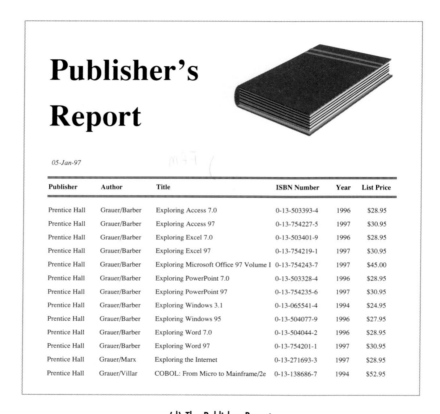

Publisher	Author	Title	ISBN Number	Year	List Price
Prentice Hall	Grauer/Barber	Exploring Access 7.0	0-13-503393-4	1996	$28.95
Prentice Hall	Grauer/Barber	Exploring Access 97	0-13-754227-5	1997	$30.95
Prentice Hall	Grauer/Barber	Exploring Excel 7.0	0-13-503401-9	1996	$28.95
Prentice Hall	Grauer/Barber	Exploring Excel 97	0-13-754219-1	1997	$30.95
Prentice Hall	Grauer/Barber	Exploring Microsoft Office 97 Volume I	0-13-754243-7	1997	$45.00
Prentice Hall	Grauer/Barber	Exploring PowerPoint 7.0	0-13-503328-4	1996	$28.95
Prentice Hall	Grauer/Barber	Exploring PowerPoint 97	0-13-754235-6	1997	$30.95
Prentice Hall	Grauer/Barber	Exploring Windows 3.1	0-13-065541-4	1994	$24.95
Prentice Hall	Grauer/Barber	Exploring Windows 95	0-13-504077-9	1996	$27.95
Prentice Hall	Grauer/Barber	Exploring Word 7.0	0-13-504044-2	1996	$28.95
Prentice Hall	Grauer/Barber	Exploring Word 97	0-13-754201-1	1997	$30.95
Prentice Hall	Grauer/Marx	Exploring the Internet	0-13-271693-3	1997	$28.95
Prentice Hall	Grauer/Villar	COBOL: From Micro to Mainframe/2e	0-13-138686-7	1994	$52.95

Record: 1 of 13

(c) The Publisher Query

Publisher's Report

05-Jan-97

Publisher	Author	Title	ISBN Number	Year	List Price
Prentice Hall	Grauer/Barber	Exploring Access 7.0	0-13-503393-4	1996	$28.95
Prentice Hall	Grauer/Barber	Exploring Access 97	0-13-754227-5	1997	$30.95
Prentice Hall	Grauer/Barber	Exploring Excel 7.0	0-13-503401-9	1996	$28.95
Prentice Hall	Grauer/Barber	Exploring Excel 97	0-13-754219-1	1997	$30.95
Prentice Hall	Grauer/Barber	Exploring Microsoft Office 97 Volume I	0-13-754243-7	1997	$45.00
Prentice Hall	Grauer/Barber	Exploring PowerPoint 7.0	0-13-503328-4	1996	$28.95
Prentice Hall	Grauer/Barber	Exploring PowerPoint 97	0-13-754235-6	1997	$30.95
Prentice Hall	Grauer/Barber	Exploring Windows 3.1	0-13-065541-4	1994	$24.95
Prentice Hall	Grauer/Barber	Exploring Windows 95	0-13-504077-9	1996	$27.95
Prentice Hall	Grauer/Barber	Exploring Word 7.0	0-13-504044-2	1996	$28.95
Prentice Hall	Grauer/Barber	Exploring Word 97	0-13-754201-1	1997	$30.95
Prentice Hall	Grauer/Marx	Exploring the Internet	0-13-271693-3	1997	$28.95
Prentice Hall	Grauer/Villar	COBOL: From Micro to Mainframe/2e	0-13-138686-7	1994	$52.95

(d) The Publisher Report

FIGURE 1.5   The Objects in a Database (continued)

Figure 1.5d illustrates a report that includes only the books from Prentice Hall. A report provides presentation-quality output and is preferable to printing the results of a table or query. Note, too, that a report may be based on either a table or a query. You could, for example, base the report in Figure 1.5d on the Books table, in which case it would list every book in the table. Alternatively, the report could be based on a query, as in Figure 1.5d, and list only the books that satisfy the criteria within the query.

Later chapters discuss forms, queries, and reports in depth. The exercise that follows is intended only as a brief introduction to what can be accomplished in Access.

Maintaining the Database

Objective: To add, edit, and delete a record; to demonstrate data validation; to introduce forms, queries, and reports. Use Figure 1.6 as a guide in doing the exercise.

STEP 1: Open the Bookstore Database

➤ Start Access. The Bookstore database should appear within the list of recently opened databases as shown in Figure 1.6a.

➤ Select the **Bookstore database** (its drive and folder may be different from that in Figure 1.6a). Click **OK** to open the database.

➤ Close the Office Assistant if it appears.

Select the
Bookstore database

Close the
Office Assistant

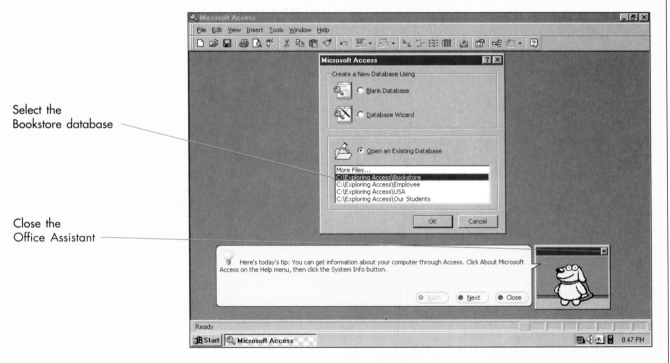

(a) Open the Bookstore Database (step 1)

FIGURE 1.6   Hands-on Exercise 2

CHOOSE YOUR OWN ASSISTANT

You can choose your own personal assistant from one of several available images. Click the Office Assistant button on any visible toolbar to display the Assistant, click the Options button to display the Office Assistant dialog box, click the Gallery tab, then click the Next button repeatedly to cycle through the available images. Click OK to select the character and close the dialog box. (The Office 97 CD is required for certain characters.)

STEP 2: The Find Command

➤ Click the **Tables tab** in the Database window. Double click the icon for the **Books table** to open the table from the previous exercise.

➤ You should see the Books table in Figure 1.6b. (The Find dialog box is not yet displayed).

➤ If necessary, click the **Maximize button** to maximize the Books table within the Access window.

➤ Exploring Office 95 and Exploring the Internet, the books you added in the previous exercise, appear in sequence according to the ISBN number because this field is the primary key for the Books table.

➤ Click in the **Title field** for the first record. Pull down the **Edit menu** and click **Find** (or click the **Find button** on the toolbar) to display the dialog box in Figure 1.6b. (You are still positioned in the first record.)

➤ Enter **Exploring Windows 95** in the Find What text box. Check that the other parameters for the Find command match the dialog box in Figure 1.6b. Be sure that **Search Only Current Field** is selected.

➤ Click the **Find First command button.** Access moves to record 10, the record containing the designated character string, and selects the Title field for that record. Click **Close** to close the Find dialog box.

➤ Press the **tab key** three times to move from the Title field to the List Price field. The current price ($27.95) is already selected. Type **28.95,** then press the **enter key** to change the price to $28.95.

Find button

Click in Title field for first record

The new books are in order according to ISBN (primary key)

Enter title

Select Search Only Current Field

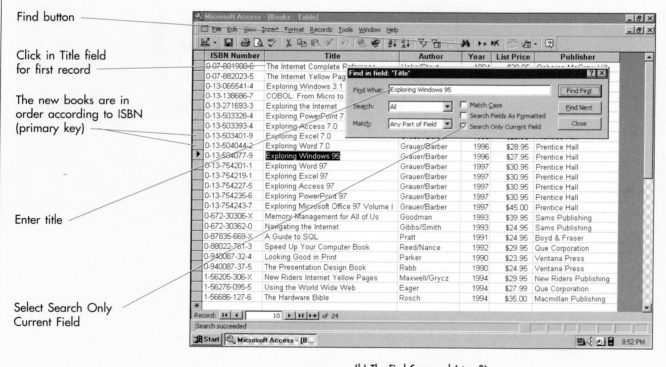

(b) The Find Command (step 2)

FIGURE 1.6   Hands-on Exercise 2 (continued)

EDITING A RECORD

The fastest way to replace the value in an existing field is to select the field, then type the new value. Access automatically selects the field for you when you use the keyboard (Tab, enter, or arrow keys) to move from one field to the next. Click the mouse within the field (to deselect the field) if you are replacing only one or two characters rather than the entire field.

STEP 3: The Undo Command

➤ Pull down the **Edit menu** and click **Undo Current Field/Record** (or click the **Undo button** on the toolbar). The price for Exploring Windows 95 returns to its previous value.

➤ Pull down the **Edit menu** a second time. The Undo command is dim (as is the Undo button on the toolbar), indicating that you can no longer undo any changes. Press **Esc.**

➤ Correct the List Price field a second time and move to the next record to save your change.

THE UNDO COMMAND

The Undo command is common to all Office applications, but is implemented differently from one application to the next. Microsoft Word, for example, enables you to undo the last 100 operations. Access, however, because it saves changes automatically as soon as you move to the next record, enables you to undo only the most recent command.

STEP 4: The Delete Command

➤ Click any field in the record for **A Guide to SQL.** (You can also use the **Find command** to search for the title and move directly to its record.)

➤ Pull down the **Edit menu.** Click **Select Record** to highlight the entire record.

➤ Press the **Del key** to delete the record. You will see a dialog box as shown in Figure 1.6c, indicating that you are about to delete a record and asking you to confirm the deletion. Click **Yes.**

➤ Pull down the **Edit menu.** The Undo command is dim, indicating that you cannot undelete a record. Press **Esc** to continue working.

THE RECORD SELECTOR

Click the record selector (the box immediately to the left of the first field in a record) to select the record without having to use a pull-down menu. Click and drag the mouse over the record selector for multiple rows to select several sequential records at the same time.

Undo button ————

Click Yes to confirm deletion ———

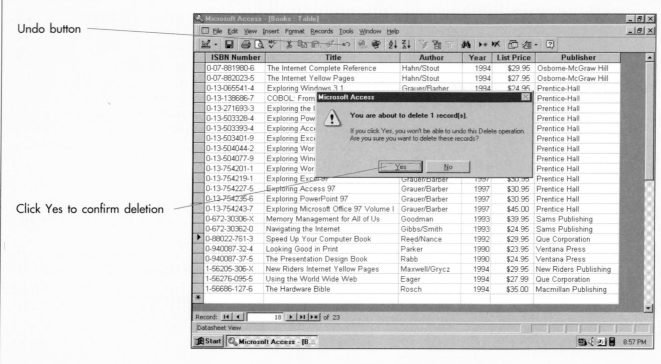

(c) The Delete Command (step 4)

FIGURE 1.6   Hands-on Exercise 2 (continued)

STEP 5: Data Validation

➤ Click the **New Record button** on the toolbar. The record selector moves to the last record (record 24).

➤ Add data as shown in Figure 1.6d, being sure to enter an invalid price **(XXX)** in the List Price field. Press the **Tab key** to move to the next field.

➤ Access displays the dialog box in Figure 1.6d, indicating that the value you entered (XXX) is inappropriate for the List Price field; in other words, you cannot enter letters when Access is expecting a numeric entry.

➤ Click the **OK command button** to close the dialog box and return to the table. Drag the mouse to select XXX, then enter the correct price of **$39.95.**

➤ Press the **Tab key** to move to the Publisher field. Type **IDG Books World-wide.** Press the **Tab key, right arrow key,** or **enter key** to complete the record.

➤ Click the **Close button** to close the Books table.

STEP 6: Open the Books Form

➤ Click the **Forms tab** in the Database window. Double click the **Books form** to open the form as shown in Figure 1.6e, then (if necessary) maximize the form so that it takes the entire window.

➤ Click the **Add Record command button** to move to a new record. The status bar shows record 25 of 25.

➤ Click in the text box for **ISBN number,** then use the **Tab key** to move from field to field as you enter data for the book as shown in Figure 1.6e.

➤ Click the **drop-down arrow** on the Publisher's list box to display the available publishers and to select the appropriate one. The use of a list box ensures that you cannot misspell a publisher's name.

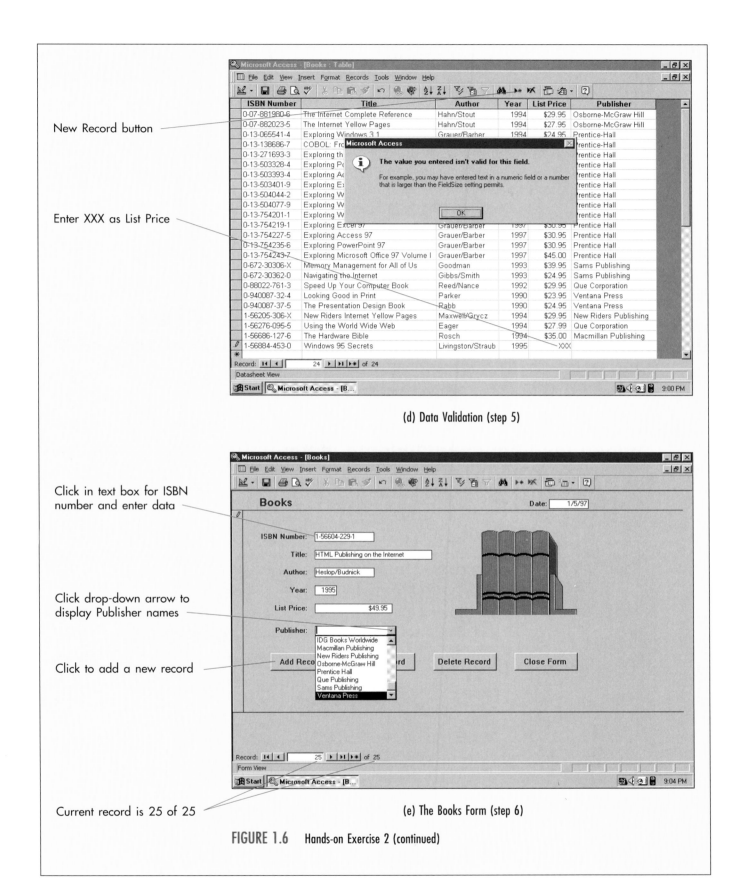

New Record button

Enter XXX as List Price

(d) Data Validation (step 5)

Click in text box for ISBN number and enter data

Click drop-down arrow to display Publisher names

Click to add a new record

Current record is 25 of 25

(e) The Books Form (step 6)

FIGURE 1.6   Hands-on Exercise 2 (continued)

STEP 7: The Replace Command

➤ Pull down the **View menu.** Click **Datasheet** to switch from the Form view to the Datasheet view to display the table on which the form is based.

➤ Press **Ctrl+Home** to move to the first record in the Books table, then click in the **Publisher field** for that record. Pull down the **Edit menu.** Click **Replace** to display the dialog box in Figure 1.6f.

➤ Enter the parameters as they appear in Figure 1.6f, then click the **Find Next button** to move to the first occurrence of Prentice-Hall.

➤ Click **Replace** to make the substitution in this record and move to the next occurrence.

➤ Click **Replace** to make the second (and last) substitution, then close the dialog box when Access no longer finds the search string.

➤ Click the **Close button** to close the table.

Click Publisher field

Enter text to search for

Enter text to replace with

Search only current field

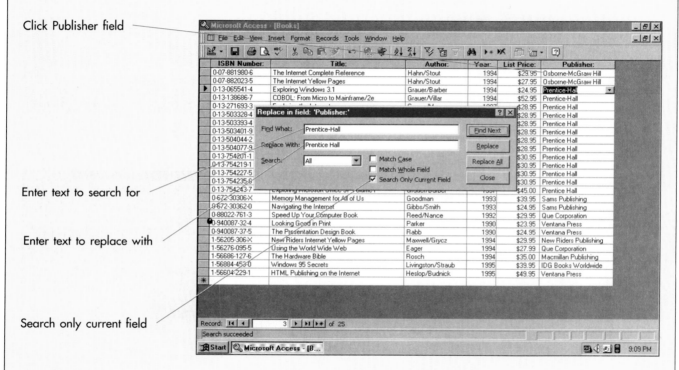

(f) The Replace Command (step 7)

FIGURE 1.6   Hands-on Exercise 2 (continued)

THE COMMON USER INTERFACE

Ctrl+Home and Ctrl+End are keyboard shortcuts that apply universally to virtually every Windows application and move to the beginning and end of a document, respectively. Microsoft Access is no exception. Press Ctrl+Home to move to the first field in the first record of a table. Press Ctrl+End to move to the last field in the last record. Press Home and End to move to the first and last fields in the current record, respectively. Other common shortcuts you may find useful are Ctrl+X, Ctrl+C, and Ctrl+V to cut, copy, and paste, respectively.

STEP 8: Run a Query

➤ Click the **Queries tab** in the Database window. Double click the **Publisher query** to run the query.

➤ You will see the Enter Parameter Value dialog box in Figure 1.6g. Type **Prentice Hall,** then press **enter** to see the results of the query, which should contain 13 books by Prentice Hall. (If you do not see all of the books, it is probably because you failed to replace Prentice-Hall with Prentice Hall in step 7.)

➤ Click the **Close button** to close the query, which returns you to the Database window.

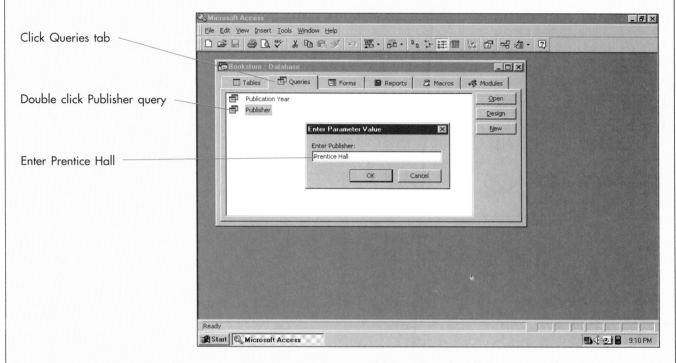

Click Queries tab

Double click Publisher query

Enter Prentice Hall

(g) Run a Query (step 8)

FIGURE 1.6   Hands-on Exercise 2 (continued)

STEP 9: Print a Report

➤ Click the **Reports tab** in the Database window to display the available reports.

➤ Double click the icon for the **Publisher report.** Type **Prentice Hall** (or the name of any other publisher) in the Parameter dialog box. Press **enter** to create the report.

➤ If necessary, click the **Maximize button** in the Report Window so that the report takes the entire screen as shown in Figure 1.6h.

➤ Click the **arrow** on the Zoom box on the Report toolbar, then click **Fit** to display the whole page. Note that all of the books in the report are published by Prentice Hall, which is consistent with the parameter you entered earlier.

➤ Click the **Print button** on the Report toolbar.

➤ Click the **Close Window button** to close the Report window.

Print button

Click down arrow
on Zoom box

Close Window button

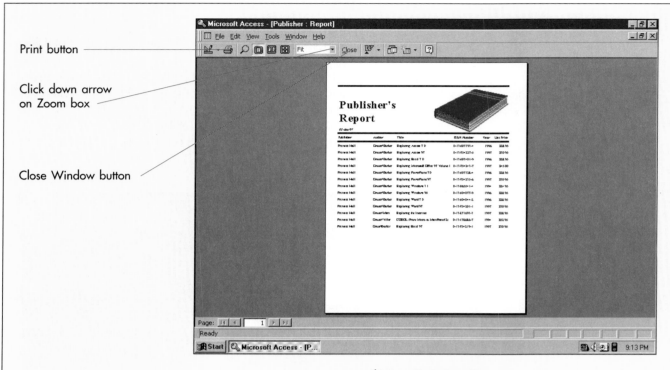

(h) Run a Report (step 9)

FIGURE 1.6   Hands-on Exercise 2 (continued)

TIP OF THE DAY

You can set the Office Assistant to greet you with a "Tip of the Day" whenever you start Access. If the Office Assistant is not visible, click the Office Assistant button on the Standard toolbar to start the Assistant, then click the options button to display the Office Assistant dialog box. Check the Show the Tip of the Day at startup box, then click OK. The next time you start Access, the Assistant will greet you with a tip of the day.

STEP 10: The Office Assistant

➤ Click the **Office Assistant button** on the Standard toolbar to display the Office Assistant. (You may see a different character than the one we have selected.)

➤ Enter your question, for example, **What is a table** as shown in Figure 1.6i, then click the **Search button** to look for the answer.

➤ The size of the dialog box expands as the Assistant suggests several topics that may be appropriate to answer your question.

➤ Click the topic **Tables: What they are and how they work** to display a help screen that reviews (and extends) much of the material in this chapter.

➤ There are three help screens in this topic, each of which contains several graphic elements. You go from one screen to the next by clicking the number (1, 2, or 3) at the upper left of the Help Window.

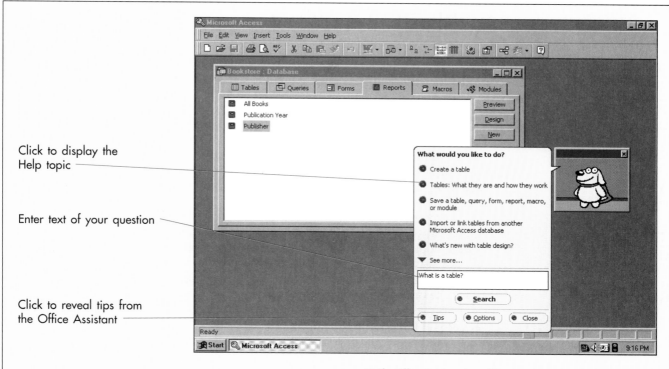

Click to display the
Help topic

Enter text of your question

Click to reveal tips from
the Office Assistant

(i) The Office Assistant (step 10)

FIGURE 1.6   Hands-on Exercise 2 (continued)

➤ These help screens also contain a series of screen tips (indicated by a red border). Point to any tip (the mouse pointer changes to a hand), then click to
display additional information.

➤ Continue to read the help screen(s), then close the Help Window.

ADVICE FROM THE OFFICE ASSISTANT

The Office Assistant indicates it has a suggestion by displaying a lightbulb.
Click the lightbulb to display the tip, then click the Back or Next buttons
as appropriate to view additional tips. The Assistant will not, however,
repeat a tip from an earlier session unless you reset it at the start of a new
session. To reset the tips, click the Assistant to display a balloon asking
what you want to do, click the Options button in the balloon, click the
Options tab, then click the button to Reset My Tips.

STEP 11: Exit Access
➤ Pull down the **File menu.** Click **Exit** to close the Bookstore database and also
exit from Access.

➤ Remember to use the Windows Explorer to copy the Bookstore database
from drive C to a floppy disk that you will keep as backup.

The database we have been using is a simple database in that it contains only one table. The real power of Access, however, is derived from multiple tables and the relationships between those tables. This type of database is known as a ***relational database.***

This section extends the Bookstore example by including the additional tables for Publishers and Orders. We will ask you to look at the data in those tables in order to answer questions about the database. You will need to consider several tables at the same time, but that is precisely what Access does. Once you see how the tables are related to one another, you will be well on your way to designing your own applications.

Pretend again that you are the manager of the bookstore and think about how you would actually use the database. You want information about the individual books, but you also need information about the publishers of those books. At the very least you need the publishers' addresses and phone numbers so that you can order the books. And once you order the books, you need to be able to track the orders, to know when each order was placed, which books were ordered, and how many of each. These requirements give rise to a database with several additional tables as shown in Figure 1.7.

The Books table in Figure 1.7a is similar to the table in the hands-on exercise, with one modification. This is the substitution of a (shorter) PublisherID field instead of the publisher's name. The Books table contains only fields that pertain to a specific book, such as the book's ISBN, Title, Author, Year (of publication), List Price, and PublisherID. The Publishers table has fields that pertain to the publisher: PublisherID, Publisher Name, Address, City, State, Zipcode, and Phone. The PublisherID appears in both tables, enabling us to obtain the publisher's address and phone number for a particular book. Consider:

Query: What are the address and telephone number for the publisher of the book *Exploring Windows 95?*

Answer: *Exploring Windows 95* is published by Prentice Hall, which is located at 1 Lake Street, Upper Saddle River, NJ 07458. The telephone number is (800) 526-0485.

To determine the answer, Access would search the Books table for *Exploring Windows 95* to obtain the PublisherID (P4 in this example). It would then search the Publishers table for the publisher with this PublisherID and obtain the address and phone number from that record. The relationship between the publishers and books is an example of a ***one-to-many relationship.*** One publisher can have many books, but a book can have only one publisher.

Query: Which books are published by Ventana Press?

Answer: Three books—*Looking Good in Print, The Presentation Design Book,* and *HTML Publishing on the Internet*—are published by Ventana Press.

To answer this query, Access would begin in the Publishers table and search for Ventana Press to determine the PublisherID. It would then select all records in the Books table with a PublisherID of P6. It's easy once you recognize the relationship between the tables.

The Bookstore database in Figure 1.7 has a second one-to-many relationship between publishers and orders. One publisher can receive many orders, but a given order goes to only one publisher. Use this relationship to answer the following queries:

ISBN	Title	Author	Year	List Price	PublisherID
0-07-881980-6	The Internet Complete Reference	Hahn/Stout	1994	$29.95	P3
0-07-882023-5	The Internet Yellow Pages	Hahn/Stout	1994	$27.95	P3
0-13-065541-4	Exploring Windows 3.1	Grauer/Barber	1994	$24.95	P4
0-13-138686-7	COBOL: From Micro to Mainframe/2e	Grauer/Villar	1994	$52.95	P4
0-13-503328-4	Exploring PowerPoint 7.0	Grauer/Barber	1996	$28.85	P4
0-13-503393-4	Exploring Access 7.0	Grauer/Barber	1996	$28.85	P4
0-13-503401-9	Exploring Excel 7.0	Grauer/Barber	1996	$28.85	P4
0-13-504044-2	Exploring Word 7.0	Grauer/Barber	1996	$28.85	P4
0-13-504051-5	Exploring the Internet	Marks	1996	$28.85	P4
0-13-504069-8	Exploring Office 95	Grauer/Barber	1996	$34.95	P4
0-13-504077-9	Exploring Windows 95	Grauer/Barber	1996	$28.95	P4
0-672-30306-X	Memory Management for All of Us	Goodman	1993	$39.95	P8
0-672-30362-0	Navigating the Internet	Gibbs/Smith	1993	$24.95	P8
0-88022-761-3	Speed Up Your Computer Book	Reed/Nance	1992	$29.95	P5
0-940087-32-4	Looking Good in Print	Parker	1990	$23.95	P6
0-940087-37-5	The Presentation Design Book	Rabb	1990	$24.95	P6
1-56205-306-X	New Riders Internet Yellow Pages	Maxwell/Grycx	1994	$29.95	P7
1-56276-095-5	Using the World Wide Web	Eager	1994	$27.99	P5
1-56604-229-1	HTML Publishing on the Internet	Heslop/Budnick	1995	$49.95	P6
1-56686-127-6	The Hardware Bible	Rosch	1994	$35.00	P2
1-56884-453-0	Windows 95 Secrets	Livingston/Straub	1995	$39.95	P1

(a) Books Table

PublisherID	Publisher Name	Address	City	State	Zipcode	Phone
P1	IDG Books Worldwide	919 E. Hillsdale Blvd.	Foster City	CA	94404	(800)762-2974
P2	Macmillan Publishing	201 West 103 Street	Indianapolis	IN	46290	(317)871-6724
P3	Osborne-McGraw Hill	2600 Tenth Street	Berkeley	CA	94710	(800)338-3987
P4	Prentice Hall	1 Lake Street	Upper Saddle River	NJ	07458	(800)526-0485
P5	Que Corporation	201 West 103 Street	Indianapolis	IN	46290	(317)581-3500
P6	Ventana Press	P.O. Box 2468	Chapel Hill	NC	27515	(800)743-5369
P7	New Riders Publishing	201 West 103 Street	Indianapolis	IN	46290	(317)581-3500
P8	Sams Publishing	11711 N. College Ave.	Carmel	IN	46032	(800)526-0465

(b) Publishers Table

OrderID	Date	PublisherID
O1	1/12/96	P4
O2	3/15/96	P5
O3	11/15/95	P4
O4	2/3/96	P3
O5	1/15/96	P2
O6	12/16/95	P1
O7	3/30/96	P4
O8	11/11/95	P6
O9	12/15/95	P8
O10	2/2/96	P6

(c) Orders Table

OrderID	ISBN	Quantity
O1	0-13-504077-9	200
O1	0-13-503393-4	200
O2	1-56276-095-5	35
O3	0-13-503393-4	450
O3	0-13-503401-9	450
O3	0-13-504044-2	450
O4	0-07-881980-6	50
O4	0-07-882023-5	75
O5	1-56686-127-6	25
O6	1-56884-453-0	30
O7	0-13-503328-4	60
O7	0-13-503401-9	60
O7	0-13-504044-2	60
O7	0-13-504069-8	350
O8	0-940087-32-4	75
O8	1-56604-229-1	125
O9	0-672-30362-0	150
O10	1-56604-229-1	50

(d) Order Details Table

FIGURE 1.7   The Bookstore Database

Query: What is the publisher and address associated with order number O4?
Answer: Osborne-McGraw Hill at 2600 Tenth Street, Berkeley, CA 94710.

To determine the publisher's address, Access first has to identify the publisher. Thus it would search the Orders table (Figure 1.7c) for the specific order (order number O4 in this example) to obtain the corresponding PublisherID (P3). It would then search the Publishers table for the matching PublisherID and return the publisher's name and address.

You probably have no trouble recognizing the need for the Books, Publishers, and Orders tables in Figure 1.7. You may be confused, however, by the presence of the Order Details table, which is made necessary by the ***many-to-many relationship*** between orders and books. One order can specify several books; at the same time, one book can appear in many orders. Consider:

Query: Which books were included in order number O7?
Answer: *Exploring PowerPoint 7.0, Exploring Excel 7.0, Exploring Word 7.0,* and *Exploring Office 95.*

To answer the query, Access would search the Order Details table for all records with an Order ID of O7. Access would then take the ISBN number found in each of these records and search the Books table for the records with matching ISBN numbers. Can you answer the next query, which is also based on the many-to-many relationship between books and orders?

Query: How many copies of *Exploring Access 7.0* were ordered?
Answer: A total of 650 copies.

This time, Access searches the Books table to obtain the ISBN number for *Exploring Access 7.0,* then searches the Order Details table for all records with this ISBN number (0-13-503393-4). It finds two such records (associated with orders 1 and 3), then it adds these quantities (200 and 450) to obtain the total number of copies that were ordered.

We trust that you were able to answer our queries by intuitively relating the tables to one another. Eventually, you will learn how to do this automatically in Access, but you must first gain a solid understanding of how to work with one table at a time. This is the focus of Chapters 2 and 3.

THE INTERNATIONAL STANDARD BOOK NUMBER

The International Standard Book Number (ISBN) is an internationally recognized number that uniquely identifies a book. The first part of the ISBN indicates the publisher; for example, every book published by Prentice Hall begins with 0-13. The founder of Prentice Hall was very superstitious and the selection of the number 13 was not an accident. Prentice Hall was founded in 1913, its first office was on 13th Street in New York City, and its first phone number ended in 1300. The original name of the company included a hyphen. "Prentice-Hall" (including the hyphen) is thirteen characters.

A database consists of multiple tables that are related to each other. Each table in the database is composed of records, and each record is in turn composed of fields. Every record in a given table has the same fields in the same order.

An Access database has six types of objects—tables, forms, queries, reports, macros, and modules. The database window displays these objects and enables you to open an existing object or create a new object.

A table is displayed in one of two views—the Design view or the Datasheet view. The Design view is used to define the table initially and to specify the fields it will contain. The Datasheet view is the view you use to add, edit, or delete records.

A record selector symbol is displayed next to the current record and signifies the status of that record. A triangle indicates that the record has been saved. A pencil indicates that the record has not been saved and that you are in the process of entering (or changing) the data. An asterisk appears next to the blank record present at the end of every table, where you add a new record to the table.

Access automatically saves any changes in the current record as soon as you move to the next record or when you close the table. The Undo Current Record command cancels (undoes) the changes to the previously saved record.

No system, no matter how sophisticated, can produce valid output from invalid input. Data validation is thus a critical part of any system. Access automatically imposes certain types of data validation during data entry. Additional checks can be implemented by the user.

A relational database contains multiple tables and enables you to extract information from multiple tables at the same time. The tables in the database are connected to one another through a one-to-many or many-to-many relationship.

The Office Assistant is new to Office 97 and is activated by clicking the Office Assistant button on the Standard toolbar, by pulling down the Help menu and requesting Word help, or by pressing the F1 function key. The Assistant enables you to ask a question in English, then it returns a series of topics that attempt to answer your question.

KEY WORDS AND CONCEPTS

Asterisk (record selector) symbol	Form	Primary key
AutoCorrect	GIGO (garbage in, garbage out)	Query
Current record	Insertion point	Record
Data validation	Macro	Record selector symbol
Database	Many-to-many relationship	Relational database
Database window	Microsoft Access	Replace command
Datasheet view	Module	Report
Design view	One-to-many relationship	Table
Field	Pencil (record selector) symbol	Triangle (record selector) symbol
Field name		Undo command
Find command		

MULTIPLE CHOICE

1. Which sequence represents the hierarchy of terms, from smallest to largest?
   - (a) Database, table, record, field
   - (b) Field, record, table, database
   - (c) Record, field, table, database
   - (d) Field, record, database, table

2. Which of the following is true regarding movement within a record (assuming you are not in the first or last field of that record)?
   - (a) Press Tab or the right arrow key to move to the next field
   - (b) Press Shift+Tab or the left arrow key to return to the previous field
   - (c) Both (a) and (b)
   - (d) Neither (a) nor (b)

3. You're performing routine maintenance on a table within an Access database. When should you execute the Save command?
   - (a) Immediately after you add, edit, or delete a record
   - (b) Periodically during a session—for example, after every fifth change
   - (c) Once at the end of a session
   - (d) None of the above since Access automatically saves the changes as they are made

4. Which of the following objects are contained within an Access database?
   - (a) Tables and forms
   - (b) Queries and reports
   - (c) Macros and modules
   - (d) All of the above

5. Which of the following is true about the objects in an Access database?
   - (a) Every database must contain at least one object of every type
   - (b) A database may contain at most one object of each type
   - (c) Both (a) and (b)
   - (d) Neither (a) nor (b)

6. Which of the following is true of an Access database?
   - (a) Every record in a table has the same fields as every other record in that table
   - (b) Every table contains the same number of records as every other table
   - (c) Both (a) and (b)
   - (d) Neither (a) nor (b)

7. Which of the following is a *false* statement about the Open Database command?
   - (a) It can be executed from the File menu
   - (b) It can be executed by clicking the Open button on the Database toolbar
   - (c) It loads a database from disk into memory
   - (d) It opens the selected table from the Database window

8. Which of the following is true regarding the record selector symbol?
   (a) A pencil indicates that the current record has already been saved
   (b) A triangle indicates that the current record has not changed
   (c) An asterisk indicates the first record in the table
   (d) All of the above

9. Which view is used to add, edit, and delete records in a table?
   (a) The Design view
   (b) The Datasheet view
   (c) Either (a) or (b)
   (d) Neither (a) nor (b)

10. Which of the following is true with respect to a table within an Access database?
    (a) Ctrl+End moves to the last field in the last record of a table
    (b) Ctrl+Home moves to the first field in the first record of a table
    (c) Both (a) and (b)
    (d) Neither (a) nor (b)

11. What does GIGO stand for?
    (a) Gee, I Goofed, OK
    (b) Grand Illusions, Go On
    (c) Global Indexing, Global Order
    (d) Garbage In, Garbage Out

12. The find and replace values in a Replace command must be:
    (a) The same length
    (b) The same case
    (c) Both (a) and (b)
    (d) Neither (a) nor (b)

13. An Access table containing 10 records, and 10 fields per record, requires two pages for printing. What, if anything, can be done to print the table on one page?
    (a) Print in Landscape rather than Portrait mode
    (b) Decrease the left and right margins
    (c) Both (a) and (b)
    (d) Neither (a) nor (b)

14. Which of the following best describes the relationship between publishers and books as implemented in the Bookstore database within the chapter?
    (a) One to one
    (b) One to many
    (c) Many to many
    (d) Impossible to determine

15. Which of the following best describes the relationship between books and orders as implemented in the Bookstore database within the chapter?
    (a) One to one
    (b) One to many
    (c) Many to many
    (d) Impossible to determine

ANSWERS

1. b
2. c
3. d
4. d
5. d
6. a
7. d
8. b
9. b
10. c
11. d
12. d
13. c
14. b
15. c

PRACTICE WITH ACCESS 97

1. Do the two hands-on exercises in the chapter, then modify the Bookstore database to accommodate the following:
   a. Add the book *Welcome to CompuServe* (ISBN: 1-55828-353-6), written by Banks, published in 1994 by MIS Press, and selling for $24.95.
   b. Change the price of *Memory Management for All of Us* to $29.95.
   c. Delete *The Presentation Design Book.*
   d. Print the *All Books Report* after these changes have been made.

2. The table in Figure 1.8 exists within the Employee database on the data disk. Open the table and do the following:
   a. Add a new record for yourself. You have been hired as a trainee earning $25,000 in Boston.
   b. Delete the record for Kelly Marder.
   c. Change Pamela Milgrom's salary to $59,500.
   d. Use the Replace command to change all occurrences of "Manager" to "Supervisor".
   e. Print the table after making the changes in parts a through d.
   f. Print the Employee Census Report after making the changes in parts a through d.
   g. Create a cover page (in Microsoft Word), then submit the output from parts e and f to your instructor.

Employees : Table

SocialSecurityNumber	LastName	FirstName	Location	Title	Salary	Sex
000-01-0000	Milgrom	Pamela	Boston	Manager	$57,500.00	F
000-02-2222	Adams	Jennifer	Atlanta	Trainee	$19,500.00	F
111-12-1111	Johnson	James	Chicago	Account Rep	$47,500.00	M
123-45-6789	Coulter	Tracey	Atlanta	Manager	$100,000.00	F
222-23-2222	Marlin	Billy	Miami	Manager	$125,000.00	M
222-52-5555	James	Mary	Chicago	Account Rep	$42,500.00	F
333-34-3333	Manin	Ann	Boston	Account Rep	$49,500.00	F
333-43-4444	Smith	Frank	Atlanta	Account Rep	$65,000.00	M
333-66-1234	Brown	Marietta	Atlanta	Trainee	$18,500.00	F
444-45-4444	Frank	Vernon	Miami	Manager	$75,000.00	M
555-22-3333	Rubin	Patricia	Boston	Account Rep	$45,000.00	F
555-56-5555	Charles	Kenneth	Boston	Account Rep	$40,000.00	M
776-67-6666	Adamson	David	Chicago	Manager	$52,000.00	M
777-78-7777	Marder	Kelly	Chicago	Account Rep	$38,500.00	F

Record: 1 of 14

FIGURE 1.8 Screen for Practice Exercise 2

3. Figure 1.9 displays a table from the United States (USA) database that is one of our practice files. The database contains statistical data about all 50 states and enables you to produce various reports such as the 10 largest states in terms of population.

   a. Open the USA database, then open the USstates table. Click anywhere in the Population field, then click the Sort Descending button to list the states in descending order. Click and drag to select the first ten records so that you have selected the ten most populous states.

   b. Pull down the File menu, click the Print command, then click the option button to print the selected records. Be sure to print in Landscape mode so that all of the data fits on one page. (Use the Page Setup command in the File menu prior to printing.)

   c. Repeat the procedure in steps a and b, but this time print the ten states with the largest area.

   d. Repeat the procedure once again to print the first thirteen states admitted to the Union. (You have to sort in ascending rather than descending sequence.)

   e. Submit all three pages together with a title page (created in Microsoft Word) to your instructor.

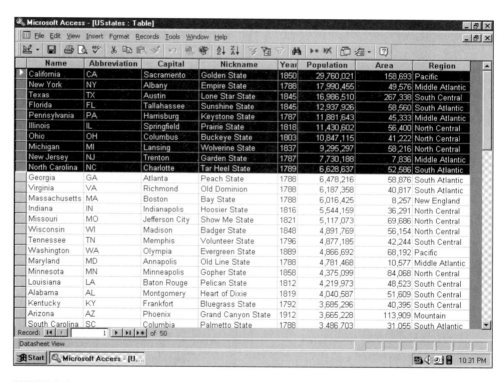

FIGURE 1.9   Screen for Practice Exercise 3

4. Filtering and Sorting: A filter is a set of criteria that is applied to a table in order to display a subset of that table. Access has four types of filters, the easiest of which, Filter by Selection, is illustrated in Figure 1.10.

   a. Open the Super Bowl database on the data disk and display the table in Figure 1.10. Our data stops with the 1996 Super Bowl and is no longer current. Thus, the first thing you need to do is update our table.

b. Pull down the View menu, click Toolbars, then toggle the Web toolbar on. Enter the address of the NFL home page (www.nfl.com) in the Address bar, then click the link to the Super Bowl. Follow the links that will allow you to determine the teams and score of any game(s) not included in our table.

c. Click the New Record button and enter the additional data in the table. The additional data will be entered at the end of the table, and hence you need to sort the data after it is entered. Click anywhere in the Year field, then click the Descending Sort button to display the most recent Super Bowl first.

d. Select the winner in any year (e.g., NFC in 1996 as shown in Figure 1.10). Click the Filter by Selection button to display only those records (i.e., the years in which the NFC won the game). Print these records.

e. Click the Remove Filter button. Select any year in which the AFC won, then click the Filter by Selection button to display the years in which the AFC won. Print these records. Remove the filter.

f. Create one additional filter (e.g., the years in which your team won the big game). Print these records as well.

g. Create a cover sheet, then submit all three reports to your instructor.

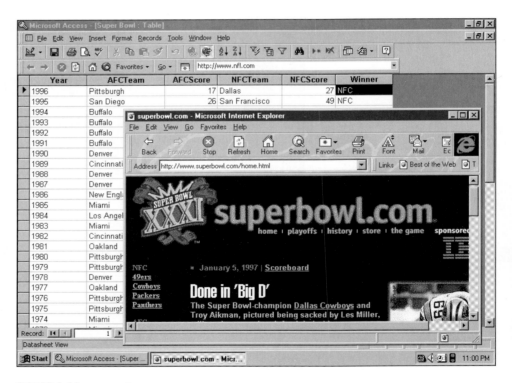

FIGURE 1.10   Screen for Practice Exercise 4

5. This problem is different from the other exercises in that it does not require you to work with a specific database. Instead, we ask you to use the Help facility to review the conceptual information in the chapter.

a. Start the Office Assistant and ask the question, "What is a database?" Select the topic, "Databases: What they are and how they work", to display the screen in Figure 1.11

b. Click the numbers in the upper left corner to read the additional help pages as shown on the screen of Figure 1.11. This will review (and extend) the information about a relational database that was presented at the end of the chapter. The help topic contains a total of seven screens, all of which present helpful information.

c. Was this a useful review? Did you learn anything new that was not covered directly in the chapter? Bring your comments to the next class to discuss your impression with your instructor and classmates.

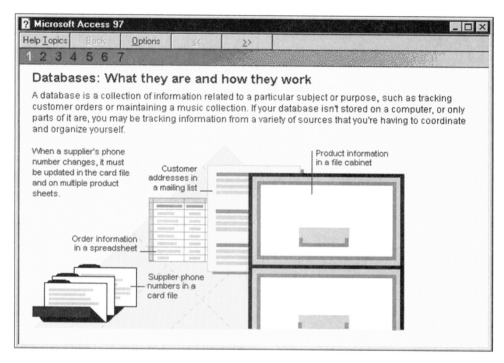

FIGURE 1.11   Screen for Practice Exercise 5

CASE STUDIES

Planning for Disaster

This case has nothing to do with databases per se, but it is perhaps the most important case of all, as it deals with the question of backup. Do you have a backup strategy? Do you even know what a backup strategy is? Now is a good time to learn because sooner or later you will wish you had one. There will come a time when you will accidentally erase a file, be unable to read from a floppy disk, or worse yet, suffer a hardware failure in which you are unable to access the hard drive. The problem always seems to occur the night before an assignment is due. The ultimate disaster is the disappearance of your computer, by theft or natural disaster (e.g., Hurricane Andrew, the floods in the Midwest, or the Los Angeles earthquake). Describe in 250 or fewer words the backup strategy you plan to implement in conjunction with your work in this class.

The Common User Interface

One of the most significant benefits of the Windows environment is the common user interface, which provides a sense of familiarity when you go from one application to another—for example, when you go from Excel to Access. How many similarities can you find between these two applications? Which menus are common to both? Which keyboard shortcuts? Which formatting conventions? Which toolbar icons? Which shortcut menus?

Garbage In, Garbage Out

Your excellent work in this class has earned you an internship in the registrar's office. Your predecessor has created a student database that appears to work well, but in reality has several problems in that many of its reports do not produce the expected information. One problem came to light in conjunction with a report listing business majors: the report contained far fewer majors than were expected. Open the GIGO database on the data disk and see if you can find and correct the problem.

The Database Consultant

The university's bookstore manager has asked your instructor for help in improving the existing database. The manager needs to know which books are used in which courses. One course may require several books, and the same book is often used in many courses. A book may be required in one course and merely recommended in a different course. The manager also needs to be able to contact the faculty coordinator in charge of each course. Which additional table(s) should be added to the database in Figure 1.7 on page 27 to provide this information? Which fields should be present in those tables?

Microsoft Online

Help for Microsoft Access is available from a variety of sources. You can consult the Office Assistant or you can pull down the Help menu to display the Help Contents and Index. Both techniques were illustrated in the chapter. In addition, you can go to the Microsoft Web site to obtain more recent, and often more detailed, information. You will find the answer to the most frequently asked questions and you can access the same knowledge base used by Microsoft support engineers. Experiment with various sources of help, then submit a summary of your findings to your instructor. Try to differentiate between the various techniques and suggest the most appropriate use for each.

2

TABLES AND FORMS: DESIGN, PROPERTIES, VIEWS, AND WIZARDS

OBJECTIVES

After reading this chapter you will be able to:

1. Describe in general terms how to design a table; discuss three guidelines you can use in the design process.
2. Describe the data types and properties available within Access and the purpose of each; set the primary key for a table.
3. Use the Table Wizard to create a table; add and delete fields in an existing table.
4. Discuss the importance of data validation and how it is implemented in Access.
5. Use the Form Wizard to create one of several predefined forms.
6. Distinguish between a bound control, an unbound control, and a calculated control; explain how each type of control is entered on a form.
7. Modify an existing form to include a combo box, command buttons, and color.
8. Switch between the Form view, Design view, and Datasheet view; use a form to add, edit, and delete records in a table.

OVERVIEW

This chapter introduces a new case study, that of a student database, which we use to present the basic principles of table and form design. Tables and forms are used to input data into a system from which information can be produced. The value of that information depends entirely on the quality of the underlying data, which must be both complete and accurate. We begin, therefore, with a conceptual discussion emphasizing the importance of proper design and develop essential guidelines that are used throughout the book.

After the design has been developed, we turn our attention to implementing that design in Access. We show you how to create a table using the Table Wizard, then show you how to refine its design by changing the properties of various fields within the table. We also stress the importance of data validation during data entry.

The second half of the chapter introduces forms as a more convenient way to enter and display data. We introduce the Form Wizard to create a basic form, then show you how to modify that form to include command buttons, a list box, a check box, and an option group.

As always, the hands-on exercises in the chapter enable you to apply the conceptual material at the computer. This chapter contains three exercises, after which you will be well on your way toward creating a useful database in Access.

CASE STUDY: A STUDENT DATABASE

As a student you are well aware that your school maintains all types of data about you. They have your social security number. They have your name and address and phone number. They know whether or not you are receiving financial aid. They know your major and the number of credits you have completed.

Think for a moment about the information your school requires, then write down all of the data needed to produce that information. This is the key to the design process. You must visualize the output the end user will require to determine the input to produce that output. Think of the specific fields you will need. Try to characterize each field according to the type of data it contains (such as text, numbers, or dates) as well as its size (length).

Our solution is shown in Figure 2.1, which may or may not correspond to what you have written down. The order of the fields within the table is not significant. Neither are the specific field names. What is important is that the table contain all necessary fields so that the system can perform as intended.

Field Name	Type
SSN	Text
FirstName	Text
LastName	Text
Address	Text
City	Text
State	Text
PostalCode	Text
PhoneNumber	Text
Major	Text
BirthDate	Date/Time
FinancialAid	Yes/No
Gender	Text
Credits	Number
QualityPoints	Number

FIGURE 2.1   The Students Table

Figure 2.1 may seem obvious upon presentation, but it does reflect the results of a careful design process based on three essential guidelines:

1. Include all of the necessary data
2. Store data in its smallest parts
3. Do not use calculated fields

Each guideline is discussed in turn. As you proceed through the text, you will be exposed to many applications that help you develop the experience necessary to design your own systems.

Include the Necessary Data

How do you determine the necessary data? The best way is to create a rough draft of the reports you will need, then design the table so that it contains the fields necessary to create those reports. In other words, ask yourself what information will be expected from the system, then determine the data required to produce that information.

Consider, for example, the type of information that can and cannot be produced from the table in Figure 2.1:

■ You can contact a student by mail or by telephone. You cannot, however, contact the student's parents if the student lives on campus or has an address different from his or her parents.

■ You can calculate a student's grade point average (GPA) by dividing the quality points by the number of credits. You cannot produce a transcript listing the courses a student has taken.

■ You can calculate a student's age from his or her date of birth. You cannot determine how long the student has been at the university because the date of admission is not in the table.

Whether or not these omissions are important depends on the objectives of the system. Suffice it to say that you must design a table carefully, so that you are not disappointed when it is implemented. *You must be absolutely certain that the data entered into a system is sufficient to provide all necessary information;* otherwise the system is almost guaranteed to fail.

DESIGN FOR THE NEXT 100 YEARS

Your system will not last 100 years, but it is prudent to design as though it will. It is a fundamental law of information technology that systems evolve continually and that information requirements will change. Try to anticipate the future needs of the system, then build in the flexibility to satisfy those demands. Include the necessary data at the outset and be sure that the field sizes are large enough to accommodate future expansion.

Store Data in Its Smallest Parts

Figure 2.1 divides a student's name into two fields (first name and last name) to reference each field individually. You might think it easier to use a single field consisting of both the first and last name, but that approach is inadequate. Consider, for example, the following list in which the student's name is stored as a single field:

Allison Foster
Brit Reback
Carrie Graber
Danielle Ferrarro

The first problem in this approach is one of flexibility, in that you cannot separate a student's first name from her last name. You could not, for example, create a salutation of the form "Dear Allison" or "Dear Ms. Foster" because the first and last name are not accessible individually.

A second difficulty is that the list of students cannot be put into alphabetical order because the last name begins in the middle of the field. Indeed, whether you realize it or not, the names in the list are already in alphabetical order (according to the design criteria of a single field) because sorting always begins with the leftmost position in a field. Thus the "A" in Allison comes before the "B" in Brit, and so on. The proper way to sort a file is on the last name, which can be done only if the last name is stored as a separate field.

CITY, STATE, AND ZIP CODE: ONE FIELD OR THREE?

The city, state, and zip code should always be stored as separate fields. Any type of mass mailing requires you to sort on zip code to take advantage of bulk mail. Other applications may require you to select records from a particular state or zip code, which can be done only if the data is stored as separate fields. The guideline is simple—store data in its smallest parts.

Avoid Calculated Fields

A *calculated field* is a field whose value is derived from a formula or function that references an existing field or combination of fields. Calculated fields should not be stored in a table because they are subject to change, waste space, and are otherwise redundant.

The Grade Point Average (GPA) is an example of a calculated field as it is computed by dividing the number of quality points by the number of credits. It is both unnecessary and undesirable to store GPA in the Students table, because the table contains the fields on which the GPA is based. In other words, Access is able to calculate the GPA from these fields whenever it is needed, which is much more efficient than doing it manually. Imagine, for example, having to manually recalculate the GPA for 10,000 students each semester.

BIRTHDATE VERSUS AGE

A person's age and date of birth provide equivalent information, as one is calculated from the other. It might seem easier, therefore, to store the age rather than the birth date, and thus avoid the calculation. That would be a mistake because age changes continually (and would need to be updated continually), whereas the date of birth remains constant. Similar reasoning applies to an employee's length of service versus date of hire.

There are two ways to create a table. The easier way is to use the **Table Wizard,** an interactive coach that lets you choose from several predefined tables. The Table Wizard asks you questions about the fields you want to include in your table, then creates the table for you. Alternatively, you can create a table yourself by defining every field in the table. Regardless of how a table is created, you can modify it to include a new field or to delete an existing field.

Every field has a **field name** to identify the data that is entered into the field. The field name should be descriptive of the data and can be up to 64 characters in length, including letters, numbers, and spaces. We do not, however, use spaces in our field names, but use uppercase letters to distinguish the first letter of a new word. This is consistent with the default names provided by Access in its predefined tables.

Every field also has a **data type** that determines the type of data that can be entered and the operations that can be performed on that data. Access recognizes nine data types: Number, Text, Memo, Date/Time, Currency, Yes/No, OLE Object, AutoNumber, and Hyperlink.

- A **Number field** contains a value that can be used in a calculation such as the number of quality points or credits a student has earned. The contents of a number field are restricted to numbers, a decimal point, and a plus or minus sign.

- A **Text field** stores alphanumeric data such as a student's name or address. It can contain alphabetic characters, numbers, and/or special characters (e.g., an apostrophe in O'Malley). Fields that contain only numbers but are not used in a calculation (e.g., social security number, telephone number, or zip code) should be designated as text fields for efficiency purposes. A text field can hold up to 255 characters.

- A **Memo field** can be up to 64,000 characters long. Memo fields are used to hold descriptive data (several sentences or paragraphs).

- A **Date/Time field** holds formatted dates or times (e.g., mm/dd/yy) and allows the values to be used in date or time arithmetic.

- A **Currency field** can be used in a calculation and is used for fields that contain monetary values.

- A **Yes/No field** (also known as a Boolean or Logical field) assumes one of two values such as Yes or No, or True or False.

- An **OLE field** contains an object created by another application. OLE objects include pictures, sounds, or graphics.

- An **AutoNumber field** is a special data type that causes Access to assign the next consecutive number each time you add a record. The value of an AutoNumber field is unique for each record in the file, and thus AutoNumber fields are frequently used as the primary key.

- A **Hyperlink field** stores a Web address (URL). All Office 97 documents are Web-enabled so that you can click a hyperlink within an Access database and display the associated Web page, provided that you have access to the Internet.

Primary Key

The **primary key** is a field (or combination of fields) that uniquely identifies a record. There can be only one primary key per table and, by definition, every record in the table must have a different value for the primary key.

A person's name is not used as the primary key because names are not unique. A social security number, on the other hand, is unique and is a frequent choice for the primary key as in the Students table in this chapter. The primary key emerges naturally in many applications such as a part number in an inventory system, or the ISBN in the Books table of Chapter 1. If there is no apparent primary key, a new field can be created with the AutoNumber field type.

Views

A table has two views—the Datasheet view and the Design view. The Datasheet view is the view you used in Chapter 1 to add, edit, and delete records. The Design view is the view you will use in this chapter to create (and modify) a table.

Figure 2.2a shows the Datasheet view corresponding to the table in Figure 2.1. (Not all of the fields are visible.) The *Datasheet view* displays the record selector symbol for the current record (a pencil or a triangle). It also displays an asterisk in the record selector column next to the blank record at the end of the table.

Figure 2.2b shows the Design view of the same table. The *Design view* displays the field names in the table, the data type of each field, and the properties of the selected field. The Design view also displays a key indicator next to the field (or combination of fields) designated as the primary key.

Current record

Blank record

(a) Datasheet View

Key indicates the primary key

Properties of the selected field

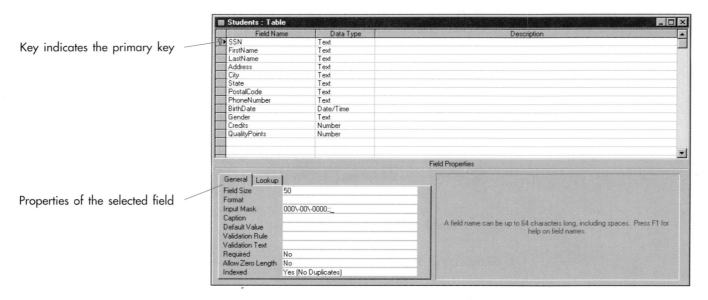

(b) Design View

FIGURE 2.2   The Views of a Table

Properties

A **property** is a characteristic or attribute of an object that determines how the object looks and behaves. Every Access object (tables, forms, queries, and reports) has a set of properties that determine the behavior of that object. The properties for an object are displayed and/or changed in a **property sheet,** which is described in more detail later in the chapter.

Each field has its own set of properties that determine how the data in the field are stored and displayed. The properties are set to default values according to the data type, but can be modified as necessary. The properties are displayed in the Design view and described briefly below:

- The **Field Size property** adjusts the size of a text field or limits the allowable value in a number field. Microsoft Access uses only the amount of space it needs even if the field size allows a greater number.
- The **Format property** changes the way a field is displayed or printed, but does not affect the stored value.
- The **Input Mask property** facilitates data entry by displaying characters, such as hyphens in a social security number or slashes in a date. It also imposes data validation by ensuring that the data entered by the user fits within the mask.
- The **Caption property** specifies a label other than the field name for forms and reports.
- The **Default Value property** automatically assigns a designated (default) value for the field in each record that is added to the table.
- The **Validation Rule property** rejects any record where the data does not conform to the specified rules for data entry.
- The **Validation Text property** specifies the error message that is displayed when the validation rule is violated.
- The **Required property** rejects any record that does not have a value entered for this field.
- The **Allow Zero Length property** allows text or memo strings of zero length.
- The **Indexed property** increases the efficiency of a search on the designated field. (The primary key in a table is always indexed.)

The following exercise has you create a table using the Table Wizard and then modify the table by including additional fields. It also has you change the properties for various fields within the table.

CHANGE THE DEFAULT FOLDER

The default folder is the folder Access uses to retrieve (and save) a database unless it is otherwise instructed. To change the default folder, pull down the Tools menu, click Options, then click the General tab in the Options dialog box. Enter the name of the default database folder (e.g., C:\Exploring Access), then click OK to accept the settings and close the Options dialog box. The next time you access the File menu the default folder will reflect the change.

Creating a Table

Objective: To use the Table Wizard to create a table; to add and delete fields in an existing table; to change the primary key of an existing table; to establish an input mask and validation rule for fields within a table; to switch between the Design and Datasheet views of a table. Use Figure 2.3 as a guide.

STEP 1: Create a New Database

➤ Click the **Start button** to display the Start menu. Click (or point to) the **Programs menu,** then click **Microsoft Access** to start the program.

➤ You should see the Microsoft Access dialog box. Click the option button to create a new database using a **Blank Database.** Click **OK.** You should see the File New Database dialog box shown in Figure 2.3a.

➤ Click the **Details button** to change to the Details view. Click and drag the vertical border between columns to change the size of a column.

➤ Click the **drop-down arrow** on the Save In list box. Click the appropriate drive (e.g., drive C), depending on the location of your data. Double click the **Exploring Access folder** to make it the active folder.

➤ Click in the **File Name text box** and drag to select **db1.** Type **My First Database** as the name of the database you will create. Click the **Create button.**

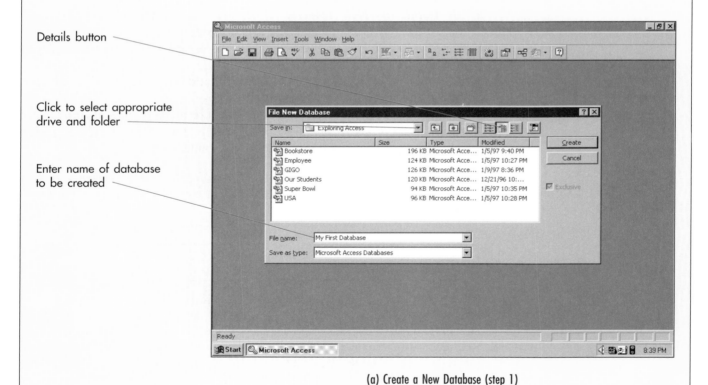

Details button

Click to select appropriate drive and folder

Enter name of database to be created

(a) Create a New Database (step 1)

FIGURE 2.3   Hands-on Exercise 1

STEP 2: Create the Table

➤ The Database window for My First Database should appear on your monitor. The **Tables tab** is selected by default.

➤ Click and drag an edge or border of the Database window to change its size to match that in Figure 2.3b. Click and drag the title bar of the Database window to change its position on the desktop.

➤ Click the **New command button** to display the New Table dialog box shown in Figure 2.3b. Click (select) **Table Wizard** in the New Table dialog box, then click **OK** to start the Table Wizard.

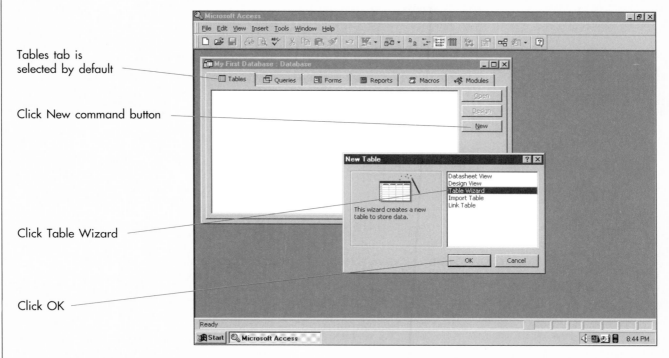

(b) The Table Wizard (step 2)

FIGURE 2.3   Hands-on Exercise 1 (continued)

STEP 3: The Table Wizard

➤ If necessary, click the **Business option button.** Click the **down arrow** on the **Sample Tables list box** to scroll through the available business tables. Click (select) **Students** within the list of sample tables. The tables are *not* in alphabetical order, and the Students table is found near the very bottom of the list.

➤ The **StudentID field** is already selected in the Sample Fields list box. Click the > **button** to enter this field in the list of fields for the new table as shown in Figure 2.3c.

➤ Enter the additional fields for the new table by selecting the field and clicking the > **button** (or by double clicking the field). The fields to enter are: **FirstName, LastName, Address, City,** and **StateOrProvince** as shown in the figure.

Enter State as the new name

Click > button to enter
selected field in new table

Selected field is entered in
new table field list

Click Students from
list of sample tables

Click Business option button

Click Rename Field button

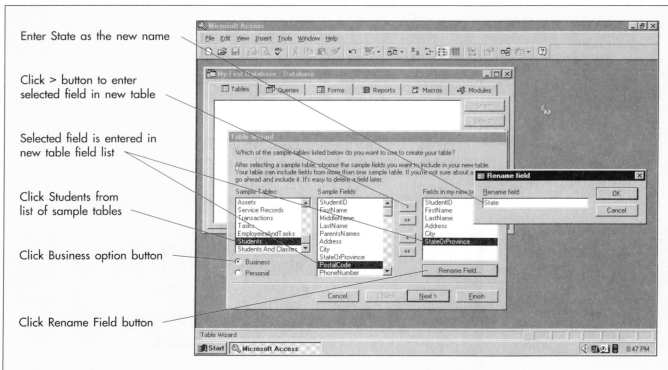

(c) The Table Wizard (step 3)

FIGURE 2.3 Hands-on Exercise 1 (continued)

➤ Click the **Rename Field command button** after adding the StateOrProvince
field to display the Rename Field dialog box. Enter **State** to shorten the name
of this field. Click **OK.**

➤ Add **PostalCode** and **PhoneNumber** as the last two fields in the table. Click
the **Next command button** when you have entered all the fields.

WIZARDS AND BUTTONS

Many Wizards present you with two open list boxes and expect you to
copy some or all fields from the list box on the left to the list box on the
right. The > and >> buttons work from left to right. The < and << buttons work in the opposite direction. The > button copies the selected field
from the list box on the left to the box on the right. The >> button copies
all of the fields. The < button removes the selected field from the list box
on the right. The << removes all of the fields.

STEP 4: The Table Wizard (continued)

➤ The next screen in the Table Wizard asks you to name the table and determine the primary key.

• Accept the Wizard's suggestion of **Students** as the name of the table.

• Make sure that the option button **Yes, set a primary key for me** is selected.

• Click the **Next command button** to accept both of these options.

➤ The final screen in the Table Wizard asks what you want to do next.
  • Click the option button to **Modify the table design.**
  • Click the **Finish command button.** The Students table should appear on your monitor.
➤ Pull down the **File menu** and click **Save** (or click the **Save button** on the Table Design toolbar) to save the table.

STEP 5: Add the Additional Fields

➤ Click the **Maximize button** to give yourself more room to work. Click the cell immediately below the last field in the table (PhoneNumber). Type **Birth-Date** as shown in Figure 2.3d.
➤ Press the **Tab key** to move to the Data Type column. Click the **down arrow** on the drop-down list box. Click **Date/Time** as the data type for the Birth-Date field.
➤ Add the remaining fields with the indicated data types to the Students table:
  • Add **Gender** as a Text field.
  • Add **Credits** as a Number field.
  • Add **QualityPoints** as a Number field. (There is no space in the field name.)
➤ Save the table.

Click drop-down arrow to see list of data types

Enter BirthDate as field name

Select Date/Time as data type

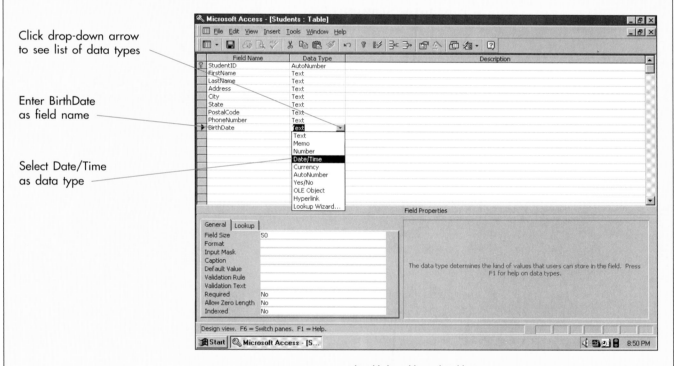

(d) Add the Additional Fields (step 5)

FIGURE 2.3   Hands-on Exercise 1 (continued)

CHOOSING A DATA TYPE

The fastest way to specify the data type is to type the first letter—T for Text, D for Date, N for Number, and Y for Yes/No. Text is the default data type and is entered automatically.

STEP 6: Change the Primary Key

➤ Point to the first row of the table and click the **right mouse button** to display the shortcut menu in Figure 2.3e. Click **Insert Rows.**

➤ Click the **Field Name column** in the newly inserted row. Type **SSN** (for social security number) as the name of the new field. Press **enter.** The data type will be set to Text by default.

➤ Click the **Required box** in the Properties area. Click the drop-down arrow and select **Yes.**

➤ Click in the Field Name column for **SSN,** then click the **Primary Key button** on the Table Design toolbar to change the primary key to social security number. The primary key symbol has moved from the StudentID field to SSN.

➤ Point to the **StudentID field** in the second row. Click the **right mouse button** to display the shortcut menu. Click **Delete Rows** to remove this field from the table definition.

➤ Save the table.

Point to first row and click right mouse button to display the shortcut menu

Click Insert Rows

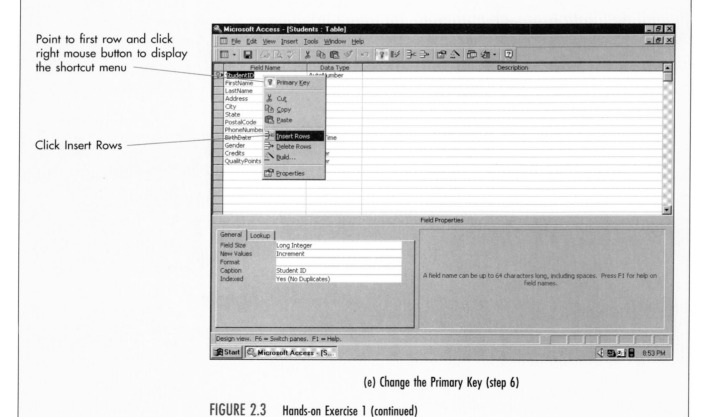

(e) Change the Primary Key (step 6)

FIGURE 2.3   Hands-on Exercise 1 (continued)

INSERTING OR DELETING FIELDS

To insert or delete a field, point to an existing field, then click the right mouse button to display a shortcut menu. Click Insert Row or Delete Row to add or remove a field as appropriate. To insert (or delete) multiple fields, point to the field selector to the left of the field name, click and drag the mouse over multiple rows to extend the selection, then click the right mouse button to display a shortcut menu.

STEP 7: Add an Input Mask

➤ Click the field selector column for **SSN.** Click the **Input Mask box** in the Properties area. (The box is currently empty.)

➤ Click the **Build button** to display the Input Mask Wizard. Click **Social Security Number** in the Input Mask Wizard dialog box as shown in Figure 2.3f.

➤ Click the **Try It** text box and enter a social security number to see how the mask works. If necessary, press the **left arrow key** until you are at the beginning of the text box, then enter a social security number (digits only). Click the **Finish command button** to accept the input mask.

➤ Click the field selector column for **BirthDate,** then follow the steps detailed above to add an input mask. (Choose the **Short Date** format.) Click **Yes** if asked whether to save the table.

➤ Save the table.

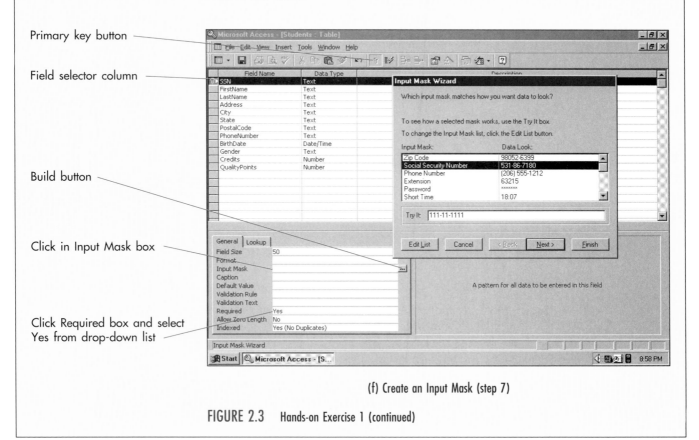

Primary key button

Field selector column

Build button

Click in Input Mask box

Click Required box and select Yes from drop-down list

(f) Create an Input Mask (step 7)

FIGURE 2.3   Hands-on Exercise 1 (continued)

STEP 8: Change the Field Properties

➤ Click the field selector column for the **FirstName** field:
- Click the **Field Size box** in the Properties area and change the field size to **25.** (You can press the F6 key to toggle between the field name and the Properties area.)
- Click the **Required box** in the Properties area. Click the **drop-down arrow** and select **Yes.**

➤ Click the field selector column for the **LastName** field:
- Click the **Field Size box** in the Properties area. Change the field size to **25.**
- Click the **Required box** in the Properties area. Click the **drop-down arrow** and select **Yes.**

➤ Click the field selector column for the **State** field.
- Click the **Field Size box** in the Properties area and change the field size to **2,** corresponding to the accepted abbreviation for a state.
- Click the **Format box** in the Properties area. Type a **> sign** to convert the data to uppercase.

➤ Click the field selector column for the **Credits** field:
- Click the **Field Size box** in the Properties area, click the **drop-down arrow** to display the available field sizes, then click **Integer.**
- Click the **Default Value box** in the Properties area. Delete the **0.**

➤ Click the field selector column for the **QualityPoints** field:
- Click the **Field Size box** in the Properties area, click the **drop-down arrow** to display the available field sizes, then click **Integer.**
- Click the **Default Value box** in the Properties area. Delete the **0.**

➤ Save the table.

THE FIELD SIZE PROPERTY

The field size property for a Text or Number field determines the maximum number of characters that can be stored in that field. The property should be set to the smallest possible setting because smaller data sizes are processed more efficiently. A text field can hold from 0 to 255 characters (50 is the default). Number fields (which do not contain a decimal value) can be set to Byte, Integer, or Long Integer field sizes, which hold values up to 255, or 32,767 or 2,147,483,647, respectively. The Single or Double sizes are required if the field is to contain a decimal value, as they specify the precision with which a value will be stored. (See online Help for details.)

STEP 9: Add a Validation Rule

➤ Click the field selector column for the **Gender** field. Click the **Field Size box** and change the field size to **1** as shown in Figure 2.3g.

➤ Click the **Format box** in the Properties area. Type a **> sign** to convert the data entered to uppercase.

➤ Click the **Validation Rule box.** Type **"M" or "F"** to accept only these values on data entry.

➤ Click the **Validation Text box.** Type **You must specify M or F.**

➤ Save the table.

Save button

View button

Click field selector column for Gender

Click Field Size box and enter 1

Click Format box and enter >

Click and enter validation rule

Click and enter validation text

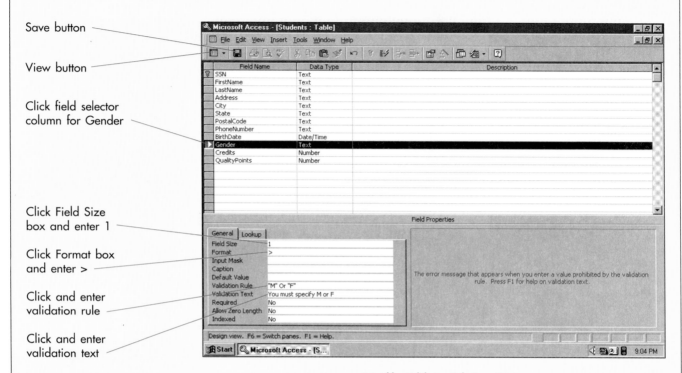

(g) Add a Validation Rule (step 9)

FIGURE 2.3   Hands-on Exercise 1 (continued)

STEP 10: The Datasheet View

➤ Pull down the **View menu** and click **Datasheet View** (or click the **View button** on the toolbar) to change to the Datasheet view as shown in Figure 2.3h.

➤ The insertion point (a flashing vertical line indicating the position where data will be entered) is automatically set to the first field of the first record.

➤ Type **111111111** to enter the social security number for the first record. (The mask will appear as soon as you enter the first digit.)

➤ Press the **Tab key,** the **right arrow key,** or the **enter key** to move to the First-Name field. Enter the data for Ronnie Adili as shown in Figure 2.3h. Make up data for the fields you cannot see.

➤ Scrolling takes place automatically as you move within the record.

CHANGE THE FIELD WIDTH

Drag the border between field names to change the displayed width of a field. Double click the right boundary of a field name to change the width to accommodate the widest entry in that field.

Print button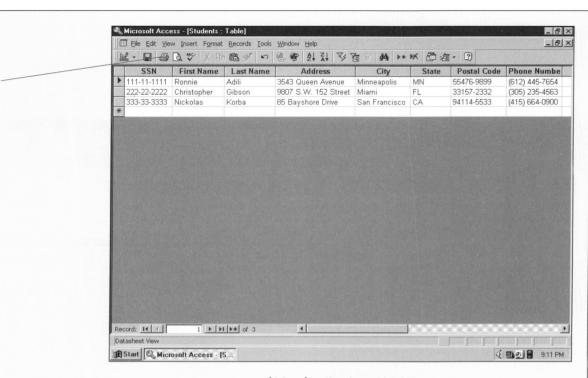

SSN	First Name	Last Name	Address	City	State	Postal Code	Phone Numbe
111-11-1111	Ronnie	Adili	3543 Queen Avenue	Minneapolis	MN	55476-9899	(612) 445-7654
222-22-2222	Christopher	Gibson	9807 S.W. 152 Street	Miami	FL	33157-2332	(305) 235-4563
333-33-3333	Nickolas	Korba	85 Bayshore Drive	San Francisco	CA	94114-5533	(415) 664-0900

(h) Datasheet View (steps 10 & 11)

FIGURE 2.3 Hands-on Exercise 1 (continued)

STEP 11: Enter Additional Data

➤ Enter data for the two additional students shown in the figure, but enter deliberately invalid data to experiment with the validation capabilities built into Access. Here are some of the errors you may encounter:

- The message, *The value you entered isn't valid for this field,* implies that the data type is wrong—for example, alphabetic characters in a numeric field such as Credits.

- The message, *You must specify M or F,* means you entered a letter other than "M" or "F" in the Gender field (or you didn't enter a value at all).

- The message, *The changes you requested to the table were not successful because they would create duplicate values in the index, primary key, or relationship,* indicates that the value of the primary key is not unique.

- The message, *The field 'Students.LastName' can't contain a Null value,* implies that you left a required field blank.

- If you encounter a data validation error, press **Esc** (or click **OK**), then reenter the data.

STEP 12: Print the Students Table

➤ Pull down the **File menu** and click **Print** (or click the **Print button**). Click the **All option button** to print the entire table. Click **OK.** Do not be concerned if the table prints on multiple pages. (You can, however, use the Page Setup command to change the way the data are printed.)

➤ Pull down the **File menu** and click **Close** to close the Students table. Click **Yes** if asked to save the changes to the table.

➤ Pull down the **File menu** and click the **Close** command to close the database and remain in Access.

➤ Pull down the **File menu** a second time and click **Exit** if you do not want to continue with the next exercise at this time.

THE PAGE SETUP COMMAND

The Page Setup command controls the margins and orientation of the printed page and may enable you to keep all fields for a single record on the same page. Pull down the File menu, click Page Setup, click the Margins tab, then decrease the left and right margins (to .5 inch each) to increase the amount of data that is printed on one line. Be sure to check the box to Print Headings so that the field names appear with the table. Click the Page tab, then click the Landscape option button to change the orientation, which further increases the amount of data printed on one line. Click OK to exit the Page Setup dialog box.

FORMS

A *form* provides an easy way to enter and display the data stored in a table. You type data into a form, such as the one in Figure 2.4, and Access stores the data in the corresponding (underlying) table in the database. One advantage of using a form (as opposed to entering records in the Datasheet view) is that you can see all of the fields in a single record without scrolling. A second advantage is that a form can be designed to resemble a paper form, and thus provide a sense of familiarity for the individuals who actually enter the data.

A form has different views, as does a table. The *Form view* in Figure 2.4a displays the completed form and is used to enter or modify the data in the underlying table. The *Design view* in Figure 2.4b is used to create or modify the form.

Controls

All forms consist of *controls* (objects) that accept and display data, perform a specific action, or add descriptive information. There are three types of controls— bound, unbound, and calculated. A *bound control* (such as the text boxes in Figure 2.4a) has a data source (a field in the underlying table) and is used to enter or modify the data in that table. An *unbound control* has no data source. Unbound controls are used to display titles, labels, lines, graphics, or pictures. Note, too, that every bound control (*text box*) in Figure 2.4a is associated with an unbound control (*label*). The bound control for social security number, for example, is preceded by a label (immediately to the left of the control) that indicates to the user the value that is to be entered.

A *calculated control* has as its data source an expression rather than a field. An *expression* is a combination of operators (e.g., +, −, *, and /), field names, constants, and/or functions. A student's Grade Point Average (GPA in Figure 2.4a) is an example of a calculated control, since it is computed by dividing the number of quality points by the number of credits.

Input mask displays
hyphens automatically

Status bar indicates
record 1 of 4

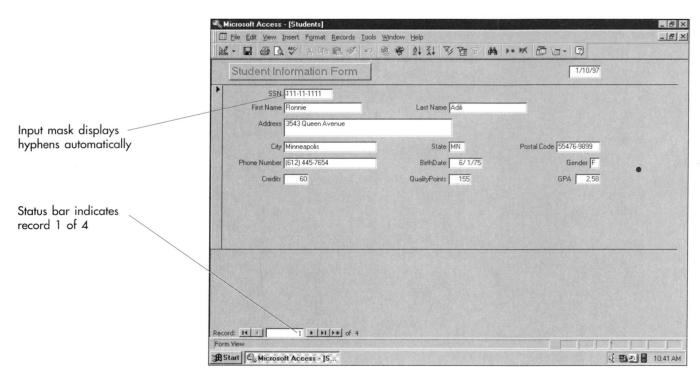

(a) Form View

Bound controls (text boxes)

Unbound controls (labels)

Calculated control (expression)

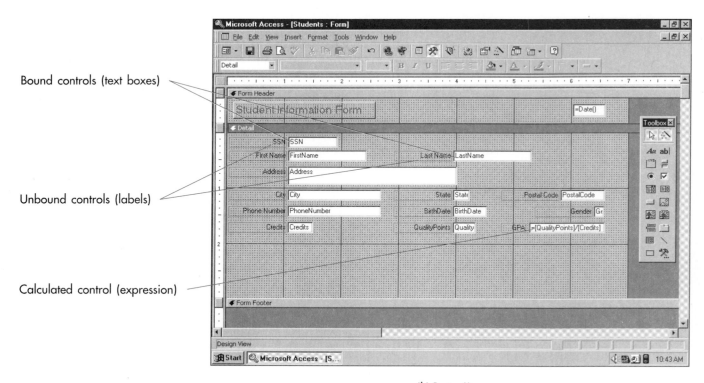

(b) Design View

FIGURE 2.4   Forms

Properties

As previously stated, a *property* is a characteristic or attribute of an object that determines how the object looks and behaves. Each control in a form has its own set of properties, just as every field in a table has its own set of properties. The properties for a control are displayed in a *property sheet,* as shown in Figure 2.5.

Figure 2.5a displays the property sheet for the Form Header Label. There are 32 different properties (note the vertical scroll bar) that control every aspect of the label's appearance. The properties are determined automatically as the object is created; that is, as you move and size the label on the form, the properties related to its size and position (Left, Top, Width, and Height in Figure 2.5a) are established for you.

Other actions, such as various formatting commands, set the properties that determine the font name and size (MS Sans Serif and 14 point in Figure 2.5a). You can change the appearance of an object in two ways—by executing a command to change the object on the form, which in turn changes the property sheet, *or* by changing the property within the property sheet, which in turn changes the object's appearance on the form.

Figure 2.5b displays the property sheet for the bound SSN control. The name of the control is SSN. The source for the control is the SSN field in the Students table. Thus, various properties of the SSN control, such as the input mask, are inherited from the SSN field in the underlying table. Note, too, that the list of properties in Figure 2.5b, which reflects a bound control, is different from the list of properties in Figure 2.5a for an unbound control. Some properties, however (such as left, top, width, and height, which determine the size and position of an object), are present for every control and determine its location on the form.

The Form Wizard

The easiest way to create a form is with the *Form Wizard.* The Form Wizard asks a series of questions, then builds a form according to your answers. You can use the form as is, or you can customize it to better suit your needs.

Figure 2.6 displays the New Form dialog box from which you call the Form Wizard. The Form Wizard, in turn, requires that you specify the table or query on which the form will be based. (Queries are discussed in Chapter 3.) The form in this example will be based on the Students table created in the previous exercise. Once you specify the underlying table, you select one or more fields from that table as shown in Figure 2.6b. Each field that is selected is entered automatically on the form as a bound control. The Form Wizard asks you to select a layout (e.g., Columnar in Figure 2.6c) and a style (e.g., Colorful 1 in Figure 2.6d). The Form Wizard then has all of the information it needs, and creates the form for you. You can enter data immediately, or you can modify the form in the Form Design view.

Scroll bar indicates that more properties exist than can currently be seen

Properties are set as object is moved and sized

Properties are determined as object is formatted

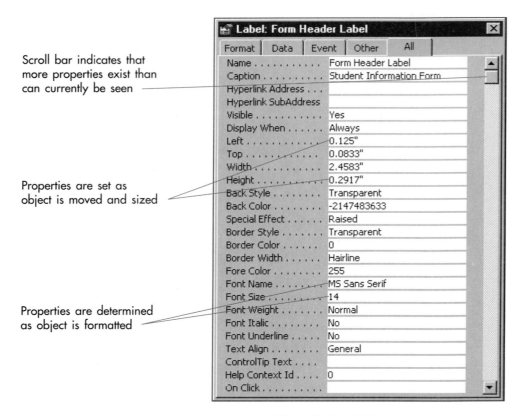

(a) Form Header Label (unbound control)

Name of data source within underlying table

Properties are inherited from underlying table

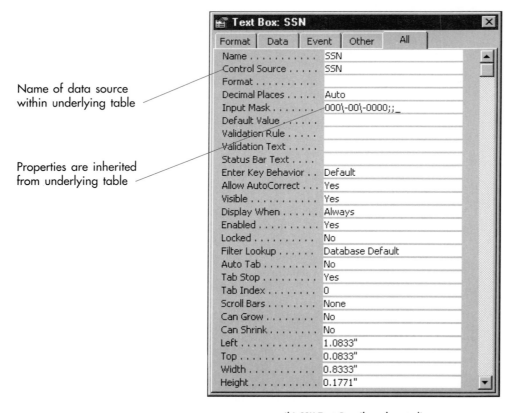

(b) SSN Text Box (bound control)

FIGURE 2.5   Property Sheets

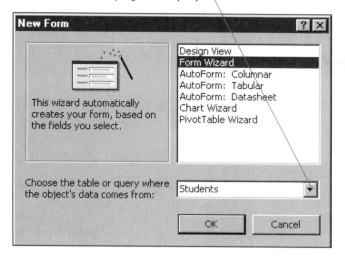

(a) Specify the Underlying Table

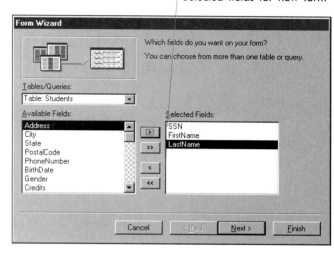

(b) Select the Fields

Selected layout

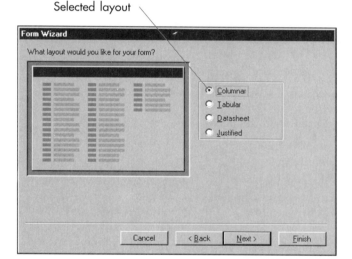

(c) Choose the Layout

Selected style

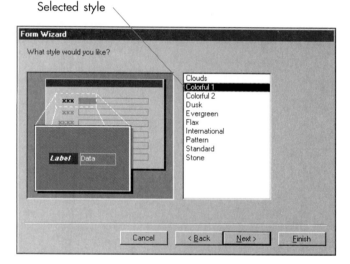

(d) Choose the Style

FIGURE 2.6   The Form Wizard

Modifying a Form

The Form Wizard provides an excellent starting point, but you typically need to customize the form by adding other controls (e.g., the calculated control for GPA) and/or by modifying the controls that were created by the Wizard. Each control is treated as an object, and moved or sized like any other Windows object. In essence, you select the control, then click and drag to resize the control or position it elsewhere on the form. You can also change the properties of the control through buttons on the various toolbars or by displaying the property sheet for the control and changing the appropriate property. Consider:

■ *To select a bound control and its associated label (an unbound control),* click either the control or the label. If you click the control, the control has sizing handles and a move handle, but the label has only a move handle. If you click the label, the opposite occurs; that is, the label will have both sizing handles and a move handle, but the control will have only a move handle.

- *To size a control,* click the control to select the control and display the sizing handles, then drag the sizing handles in the appropriate direction. Drag the handles on the top or bottom to size the box vertically. Drag the handles on the left or right side to size the box horizontally. Drag the handles in the corner to size both horizontally and vertically.

- *To move a control and its label,* click and drag the border of either object. To move either the control or its label, click and drag the move handle (a tiny square in the upper left corner) of the appropriate object.

- *To change the properties of a control,* point to the control, click the right mouse button to display a shortcut menu, then click Properties to display the property sheet. Click the text box for the desired property, make the necessary change, then close the property sheet.

- *To select multiple controls,* press and hold the Shift key as you click each successive control. The advantage of selecting multiple controls is that you can modify the selected controls at the same time rather than working with them individually.

HANDS-ON EXERCISE 2

Creating a Form

Objective: To use the Form Wizard to create a form; to move and size controls within a form; to use the completed form to enter data into the associated table. Use Figure 2.7 as a guide in the exercise.

STEP 1: Open the Existing Database

➤ Start Access as you did in the previous exercise. Select (click) **My First Database** from the list of recently opened databases, then click **OK.** (Click the **Open Database button** on the Database toolbar if you do not see My First Database.)

➤ Click the **Forms tab** in the Database window. Click the **New command button** to display the New Form dialog box as shown in Figure 2.7a.

➤ Click **Form Wizard** in the list box. Click the **drop-down arrow** to display the available tables and queries in the database on which the form can be based.

➤ Click **Students** to select the Students table from the previous exercise. Click **OK** to start the Form Wizard.

THE MOST RECENTLY OPENED FILE LIST

The easiest way to open a recently used database is to select it from the Microsoft Access dialog box that appears when Access is first started. Check to see if your database appears on the list of the four most recently opened databases, and if so, simply double click the database to open it. The list of the most recently opened databases can also be found at the bottom of the File menu.

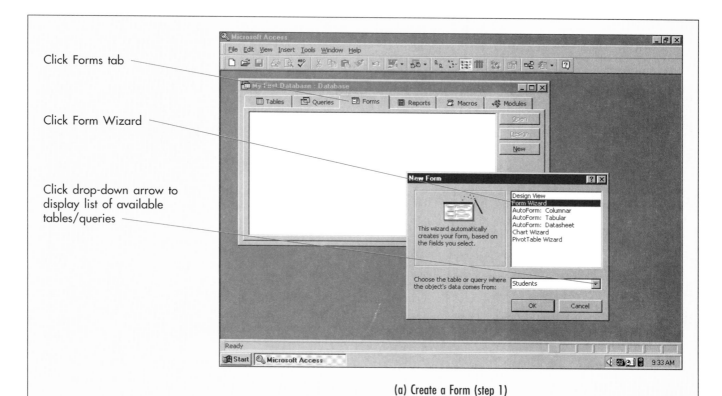

Click Forms tab

Click Form Wizard

Click drop-down arrow to display list of available tables/queries

(a) Create a Form (step 1)

FIGURE 2.7   Hands-on Exercise 2

STEP 2: The Form Wizard

➤ You should see the dialog box in Figure 2.7b, which displays all of the fields in the Students table. Click the **>> button** to enter all of the fields in the table on the form. Click the **Next command button.**

➤ The **Columnar layout** is already selected. Click the **Next command button.**

➤ Click **Standard** as the style for your form. Click the **Next command button.**

➤ The Form Wizard asks you for the title of the form and what you want to do next.

• The Form Wizard suggests **Students** as the title of the form. Keep this entry.

• Click the option button to **Modify the form's design.**

➤ Click the **Finish command button** to display the form in Design view.

FLOATING TOOLBARS

A toolbar is typically docked (fixed) along the edge of the application window, but it can be displayed as a floating toolbar within the application window. To move a docked toolbar, drag the toolbar background. To move a floating toolbar, drag its title bar. To size a floating toolbar, drag any border in the direction you want to go. Double click the background of any toolbar to toggle between a floating toolbar and a docked (fixed) toolbar.

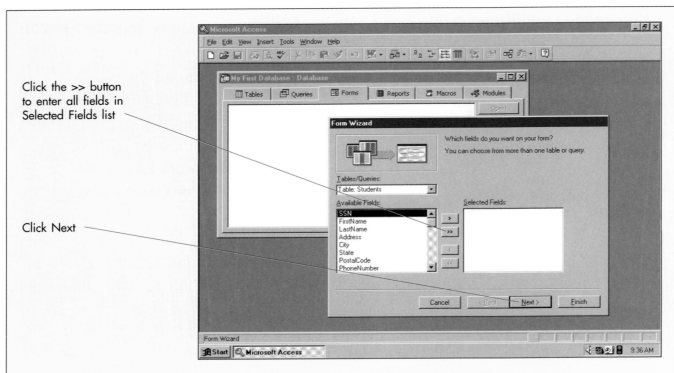

Click the >> button
to enter all fields in
Selected Fields list

Click Next

(b) The Form Wizard (step 2)

FIGURE 2.7   Hands-on Exercise 2 (continued)

STEP 3: Move the Controls

➤ If necessary, click the **Maximize button** so that the form takes the entire screen as shown in Figure 2.7c. The Form Wizard has arranged the controls in columnar format, but you need to rearrange the controls.

➤ Click the **LastName control** to select the control and display the sizing handles. (Be sure to select the text box and *not* the attached label.) Click and drag the **border** of the control (the pointer changes to a hand) so that the LastName control is on the same line as the FirstName control. Use the grid to space and align the controls.

➤ Click and drag the **Address control** under the FirstName control (to take the space previously occupied by the last name).

➤ Click and drag the **border** of the form to **7 inches** so that the City, State, and PostalCode controls will fit on the same line. (Click and drag the title bar of the Toolbox toolbar to move the toolbar out of the way.)

➤ Click and drag the **State control** so that it is next to the City control, then click and drag the **PostalCode control** so that it is on the same line as the other two. Press and hold the **Shift key** as you click the **City, State,** and **PostalCode controls** to select all three, then click and drag the selected controls under the Address control.

➤ Place the controls for **PhoneNumber, BirthDate,** and **Gender** on the same line.

➤ Place the controls for **Credits** and **QualityPoints** on the same line.

➤ Pull down the **File menu** and click **Save** (or click the **Save button**) to save the form.

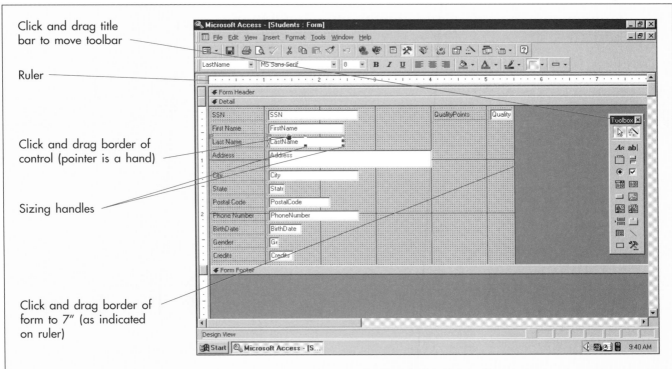

Click and drag title bar to move toolbar

Ruler

Click and drag border of control (pointer is a hand)

Sizing handles

Click and drag border of form to 7" (as indicated on ruler)

(c) Move the Controls (step 3)

FIGURE 2.7   Hands-on Exercise 2 (continued)

THE UNDO COMMAND

The Undo command is invaluable at any time, and is especially useful when moving and sizing controls. Pull down the Edit menu and click Undo (or click the Undo button on the toolbar) immediately to reverse the effects of the last command.

STEP 4: Add a Calculated Control (GPA)

➤ Click the **Text Box tool** in the toolbox as shown in Figure 2.7d. The mouse pointer changes to a tiny crosshair with a text box attached.

➤ Click and drag in the form where you want the text box (the GPA control) to go. Release the mouse. You will see an Unbound control and an attached label containing a field number (e.g., Text24) as shown in Figure 2.7d.

➤ Click in the **text box** of the control. The word Unbound will disappear, and you can enter an expression:

• Enter **=[QualityPoints]/[Credits]** to calculate a student's GPA. Do not be concerned if you cannot see the entire entry as scrolling will take place as necessary.

• You must enter the field names *exactly* as they were defined in the table; that is, do *not* include a space between Quality and Points.

➤ Select the attached label (Text24), then click and drag to select the text in the attached label. Type **GPA** as the label for this control. Size the text box

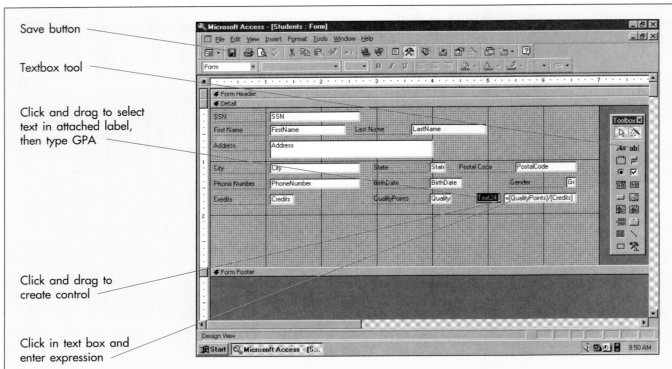

Save button

Textbox tool

Click and drag to select text in attached label, then type GPA

Click and drag to create control

Click in text box and enter expression

(d) Add a Calculated Control (step 4)

FIGURE 2.7   Hands-on Exercise 2 (continued)

appropriately for GPA. Click the **move handle** on the label so that you can move the label closer to the text box.

➤ Click the **Save button.**

SIZING OR MOVING A CONTROL AND ITS LABEL

A bound control is created with an attached label. Select (click) the control, and the control has sizing handles and a move handle, but the label has only a move handle. Select the label (instead of the control), and the opposite occurs; the control has only a move handle, but the label will have both sizing handles and a move handle. To move a control and its label, click and drag the border of either object. To move either the control or its label, click and drag the move handle (a tiny square in the upper left corner) of the appropriate object.

STEP 5: Modify the Property Sheet

➤ Point to the GPA control and click the **right mouse button** to display a shortcut menu. Click **Properties** to display the Properties dialog box.

➤ If necessary, click the **All tab** as shown in Figure 2.7e. The Control Source text box contains the entry =[QualityPoints]/[Credits] from the preceding step.

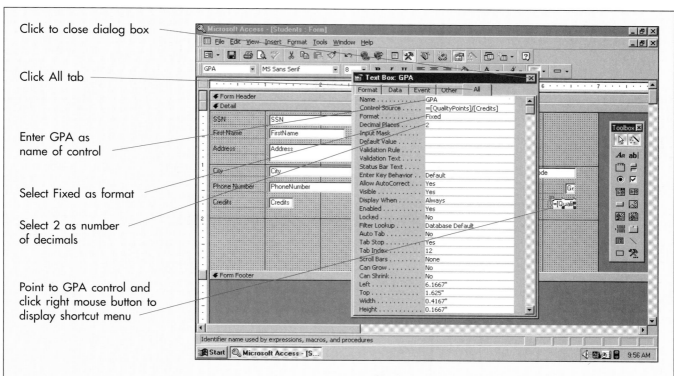

Click to close dialog box

Click All tab

Enter GPA as name of control

Select Fixed as format

Select 2 as number of decimals

Point to GPA control and click right mouse button to display shortcut menu

(e) Modify the Property Sheet (step 5)

FIGURE 2.7 Hands-on Exercise 2 (continued)

➤ Click the **Name text box.** Replace the original name (e.g., Text24) with **GPA.**

➤ Click the **Format box.** Click the **drop-down arrow,** then scroll until you can select **Fixed.**

➤ Click the box for the **Decimal places.** Click the **drop-down arrow** and select **2** as the number of decimal places.

➤ Close the Properties dialog box to accept these settings and return to the form.

USE THE PROPERTY SHEET

You can change the appearance or behavior of a control in two ways—by changing the actual control on the form itself or by changing the underlying property sheet. Anything you do to the control automatically changes the associated property, and conversely, any change to the property sheet is reflected in the appearance or behavior of the control. In general, you can obtain greater precision through the property sheet, but we find ourselves continually switching back and forth between the two techniques.

STEP 6: Align the Controls

➤ Press and hold the **Shift key** as you click the label for each control on the form. This enables you to select multiple controls at the same time in order to apply uniform formatting to the selected controls.

➤ All labels should be selected as shown in Figure 2.7f. Click the **Align Right button** on the Formatting toolbar to move the labels to the right so that each label is closer to its associated control.

➤ Click anywhere on the form to deselect the controls, then fine-tune the form as necessary to make it more attractive. We moved LastName to align it with State. We also made the SSN and PostalCode controls smaller.

Right-align button

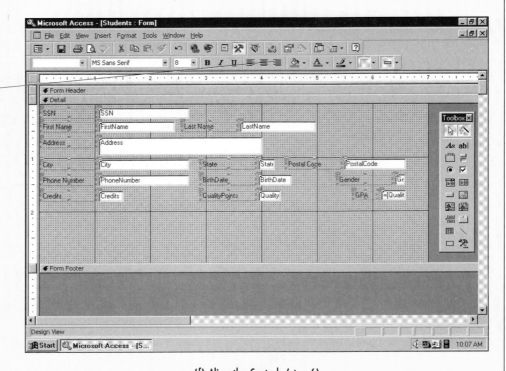

(f) Align the Controls (step 6)

FIGURE 2.7 Hands-on Exercise 2 (continued)

ALIGN THE CONTROLS

To align controls in a straight line (horizontally or vertically), press and hold the Shift key and click the labels of the controls to be aligned. Pull down the Format menu, click Align, then select the edge to align (Left, Right, Top, and Bottom). Click the Undo command if you are not satisfied with the result.

STEP 7: Create the Form Header

➤ Click and drag the line separating the border of the Form Header and Detail to provide space for a header as shown in Figure 2.7g.

➤ Click the **Label tool** on the Toolbox toolbar (the mouse pointer changes to a cross hair combined with the letter A). Click and drag the mouse pointer to create a label within the header. The insertion point (a flashing vertical line) is automatically positioned within the label.

➤ Type **Student Information Form.** Do not be concerned about the size or alignment of the text at this time. Click outside the label when you have completed the entry, then click the control to select it.

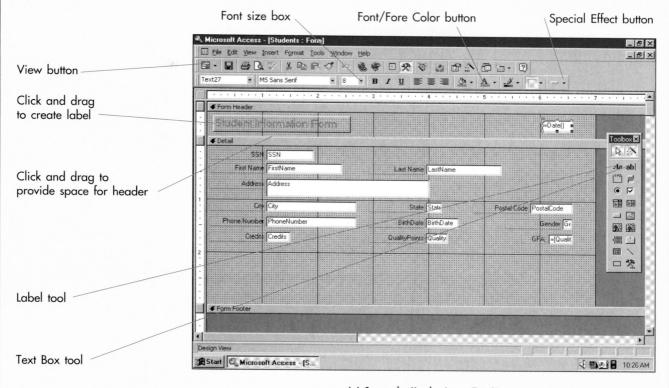

(g) Create the Header (steps 7 & 8)

FIGURE 2.7   Hands-on Exercise 2 (continued)

THE FORMATTING TOOLBAR

The Formatting toolbar contains many of the same buttons that are found on the Formatting toolbars of the other Office applications. These include buttons for boldface, italics, and underlining, as well as left, center, and right alignment. You will find drop-down list boxes to change the font or point size. The Formatting toolbar also contains drop-down palettes to change the foreground or background color, the border color and width, and the special effect.

➤ Click the **drop-down arrow** on the **Font Size list box** on the Formatting tool-bar. Click **14.** The size of the text changes to the larger point size.

➤ Click the **drop-down arrow** next to the **Special Effect button** on the Formatting toolbar to display the available effects. Click the **Raised button** to highlight the label.

➤ Click the **drop-down arrow** next to the **Font/Fore Color button** on the Formatting toolbar. Click **Red.**

➤ Click outside the label to deselect it. Click the **Save button** to save the form.

STEP 8: Add the Date

➤ Click the **Textbox tool** on the Toolbox toolbar. The mouse pointer changes to a tiny crosshair with a text box attached. Click and drag in the form where you want the text box for the date, then release the mouse.

➤ You will see an Unbound control and an attached label containing a number (e.g., Text27). Click in the text box, and the word Unbound will disappear. Type **=Date().** Click the attached label. Press the **Del key** to delete the label.

STEP 9: The Form View

➤ Click the **Form view button** to switch to the Form view. You will see the first record in the table that was created in the previous exercise.

➤ Click the **New Record button** to move to the end of the table to enter a new record as shown in Figure 2.7h. Enter data for yourself:

• The record selector symbol changes to a pencil as you begin to enter data.

• Press the **Tab key** to move from one field to the next within the form. All properties (masks and data validation) have been inherited from the Students table created in the first exercise.

New Record button

Record selector symbol

Enter data for yourself

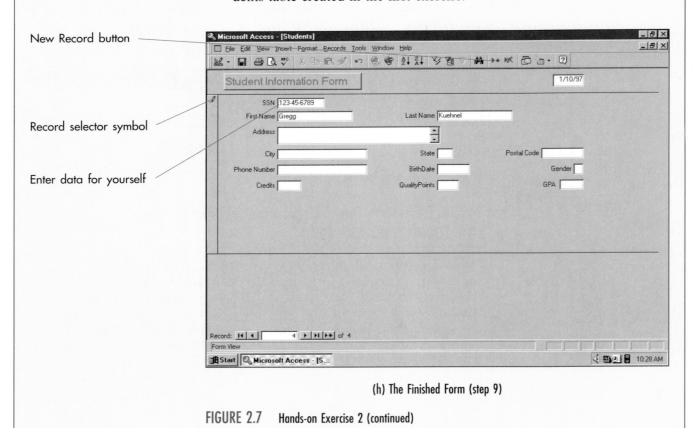

(h) The Finished Form (step 9)

FIGURE 2.7   Hands-on Exercise 2 (continued)

➤ Pull down the **File menu** and click **Close** to close the form. Click **Yes** if asked to save the changes to the form.

➤ Pull down the **File menu** and click **Close** to close the database and remain in Access. Pull down the **File menu** a second time and click **Exit** if you do not want to continue with the next exercise at this time.

ERROR MESSAGES—#NAME? OR #ERROR?

The most common reason for either message is that the control source references a field that no longer exists, or a field whose name is misspelled. Go to the Design view, right click the control, click the Properties command, then click the All tab within the Properties dialog box. Look at the Control Source property and check the spelling of every field. Be sure there are brackets around each field in a calculated control; for example =[QualityPoints]/[Credits].

A MORE SOPHISTICATED FORM

The Form Wizard provides an excellent starting point but stops short of creating the form you really want. The exercise just completed showed you how to add controls to a form that were not in the underlying table, such as the calculated control for the GPA. The exercise also showed how to move and size existing controls to create a more attractive and functional form.

Consider now Figure 2.8, which further improves on the form from the previous exercise. Three additional controls have been added—for major, financial

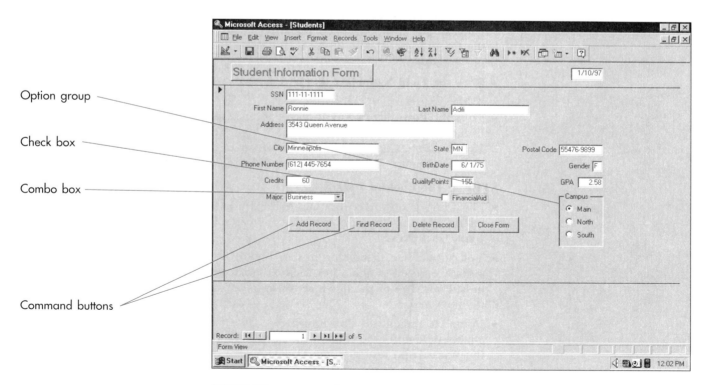

FIGURE 2.8   An Improved Form

aid, and campus—to illustrate other ways to enter data than through a text box. The student's major is selected from a ***drop-down list box.*** The indication of financial aid (a Yes/No field) is entered through a ***check box.*** The student's campus is selected from an ***option group,*** in which you choose one of three mutually exclusive options.

   Command buttons have also been added to the bottom of the form to facilitate the way in which the user carries out certain procedures. To add a record, for example, the user simply clicks the Add Record command button, as opposed to having to click the New Record button on the Database toolbar or having to pull down the Insert menu. The next exercise has you retrieve the form you created in Hands-on Exercise 2 in order to add these enhancements.

HANDS-ON EXERCISE 3

A More Sophisticated Form

Objective: To add fields to an existing table; to use the Lookup Wizard to create a combo box; to add controls to an existing form to demonstrate inheritance; to add command buttons to a form. Use Figure 2.9 as a guide in the exercise.

STEP 1: Modify the Table

➤ Open **My First Database** that we have been using throughout the chapter. If necessary, click the **Tables tab** in the Database window. The **Students table** is already selected since that is the only table in the database.

➤ Click the **Design command button** to open the table in Design view as shown in Figure 2.9a. (The FinancialAid, Campus, and Major fields have not yet been added.) Maximize the window.

➤ Click the **Field Name box** under QualityPoints. Enter **FinancialAid** as the name of the new field. Press the **enter (Tab,** or **right arrow) key** to move to the Data Type column. Type **Y** (the first letter in a Yes/No field) to specify the data type.

➤ Click the **Field Name box** on the next row. Type **Campus.** (There is no need to specify the Data Type since Text is the default.)

➤ Press the **down arrow key** to move to the Field Name box on the next row. Enter **Major.** Press the **enter (Tab,** or **right arrow) key** to move to the Data Type column. Click the **drop-down arrow** to display the list of data types as shown in Figure 2.9a. Click **Lookup Wizard.**

STEP 2: The Lookup Wizard

➤ The first screen in the Lookup Wizard asks how you want to look up the data. Click the option button that indicates **I will type in the values that I want.** Click **Next.**

➤ You should see the dialog box in Figure 2.9b. The number of columns is already entered as one. Click the **text box** to enter the first major. Type **Business.** Press **Tab** or the **down arrow key** (do *not* press the enter key) to enter the next major.

➤ Complete the entries shown in Figure 2.9b. Click **Next.** The Wizard asks for a label to identify the column. (Major is already entered.) Click **Finish** to exit the Wizard and return to the Design View.

➤ Click the **Save button** to save the table. Close the table.

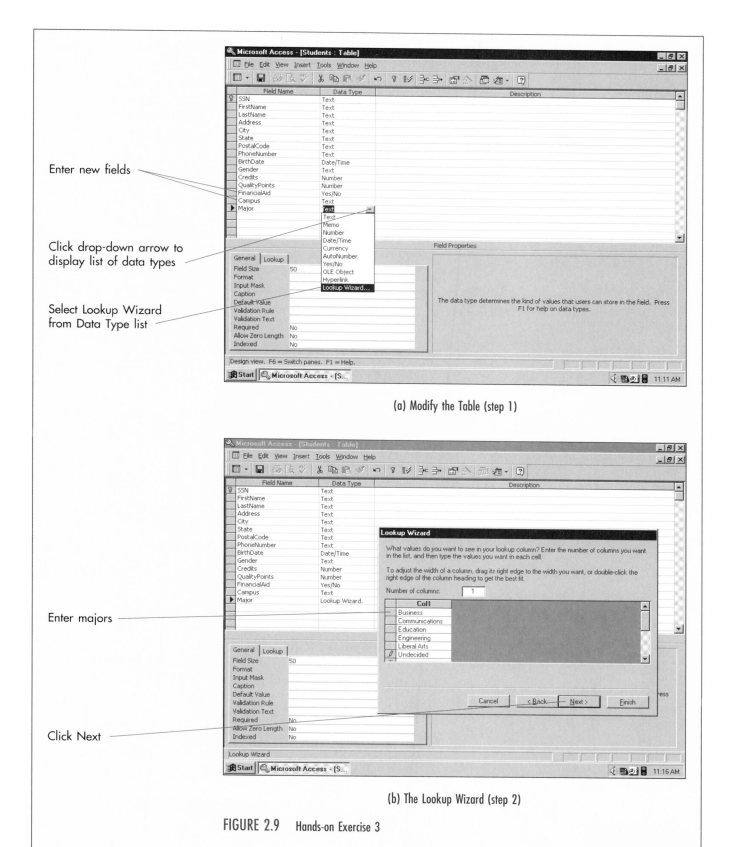

Enter new fields

Click drop-down arrow to display list of data types

Select Lookup Wizard from Data Type list

(a) Modify the Table (step 1)

Enter majors

Click Next

(b) The Lookup Wizard (step 2)

FIGURE 2.9   Hands-on Exercise 3

STEP 3: Add the New Controls

➤ Click the **Forms tab** in the Database window. The Students form is already highlighted since there is only one form in the database.

➤ Click the **Design command button** to open the form from the previous exercise. If necessary, click the **Maximize button** so that the form takes the entire window.

➤ Pull down the **View menu.** Click **Field List** to display the field list for the table on which the form is based. You can move and size the field list just like any other Windows object.

  • Click and drag the **title bar** of the field list to the position in Figure 2.9c.

  • Click and drag a **corner** or **border** of the field list so that you can see all of the fields at the same time.

➤ Fields can be added to the form from the field list in any order. Click and drag the **Major field** from the field list to the form. The Major control is created as a combo box because of the list in the underlying table.

➤ Click and drag the **FinancialAid field** from the list to the form. The FinancialAid control is created as a check box because FinancialAid is a Yes/No field in the underlying table.

➤ Save the form.

INHERITANCE

A bound control inherits the same properties as the associated field in the underlying table. A check box, for example, appears automatically next to any bound control that was defined as a Yes/No field. In similar fashion, a drop-down list will appear next to any bound control that was defined through the Lookup Wizard. Changing the property setting of a field *after* the form has been created will *not* change the property of the associated control. And finally, changing the property setting of a control does *not* change the property setting of the field because the control inherits the properties of the field rather than the other way around.

STEP 4: Create an Option Group

➤ Click the **Option Group button** on the Toolbox toolbar. The mouse pointer changes to a tiny crosshair attached to an option button when you point anywhere in the form. Click and drag in the form where you want the option group to go, then release the mouse.

➤ You should see the Option Group Wizard as shown in Figure 2.9d. Enter **Main** as the label for the first option, then press the **Tab key** to move to the next line. Type **North** and press **Tab** to move to the next line. Enter **South** as the third and last option. Click **Next.**

➤ The option button to select Main (the first label that was entered) as the default is selected. Click **Next.**

➤ Main, North, and South will be assigned the values 1, 2, and 3, respectively. (Numeric entries are required for an option group.) Click **Next.**

➤ Click the **drop-down arrow** to select the field in which to store the value of the option group, then scroll until you can select **Campus.** Click **Next.**

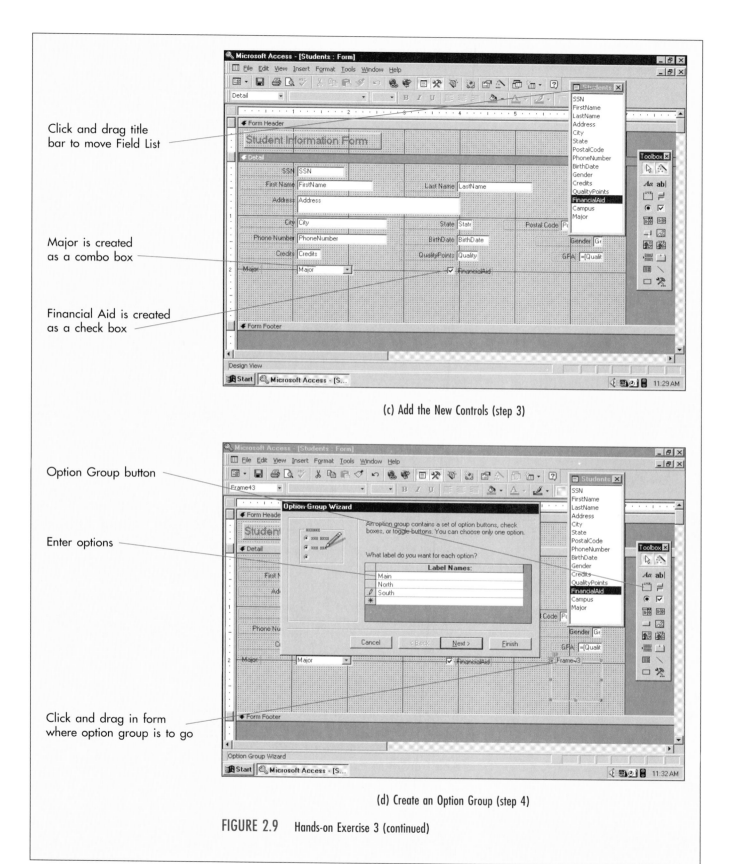

Click and drag title
bar to move Field List

Major is created
as a combo box

Financial Aid is created
as a check box

(c) Add the New Controls (step 3)

Option Group button

Enter options

Click and drag in form
where option group is to go

(d) Create an Option Group (step 4)

FIGURE 2.9   Hands-on Exercise 3 (continued)

- ➤ Make sure the Option button is selected as the type of control.
- ➤ Click the option button for the **Sunken style** to match the other controls on the form. Click **Next.**
- ➤ Enter **Campus** as the caption for the group. Click the **Finish command button** to create the option group on the form. Click and drag the option group to position it on the form under the GPA control.
- ➤ Point to the border of the option group on the form, click the **right mouse button** to display a shortcut menu, and click **Properties.** Click the **All tab.** Change the name to **Campus.** Close the dialog box. Save the form.

MISSING TOOLBARS

The Form Design, Formatting, and Toolbox toolbars appear by default in the Form Design view, but any (or all) of these toolbars may be hidden at the discretion of the user. Point to any visible toolbar, click the right mouse button to display a shortcut menu, then check the name of any toolbar you want to display. You can also click the Toolbox button on the Form Design toolbar to display (hide) the Toolbox toolbar.

STEP 5: Add a Command Button

- ➤ Click the **Command Button tool.** The mouse pointer changes to a tiny crosshair attached to a command button when you point anywhere in the form.
- ➤ Click and drag in the form where you want the button to go, then release the mouse. This draws a button and simultaneously opens the Command Button Wizard as shown in Figure 2.9e. (The number in your button may be different from ours.)
- ➤ Click **Record Operations** in the Categories list box. Choose **Add New Record** as the operation. Click **Next.**
- ➤ Click the **Text option button** in the next screen. Click **Next.**
- ➤ Type **Add Record** as the name of the button, then click the **Finish command button.** The completed command button should appear on your form. Save the form.

STEP 6: Create the Additional Command Buttons

- ➤ Click the **Command Button tool.** Click and drag on the form where you want the second button to go.
- ➤ Click **Record Navigation** in the Categories list box. Choose **Find Record** as the operation. Click the **Next command button.**
- ➤ Click the **Text option button.** Click the **Next command button.**
- ➤ Type **Find Record** as the name of the button, then click the **Finish command button.** The completed command button should appear on the form.
- ➤ Repeat these steps to add the command buttons to delete a record (Record Operations) and close the form (Form Operations).
- ➤ Save the form.

Choose Add New Record

Click Record Operations

Command Button tool

Click and drag to
create command button

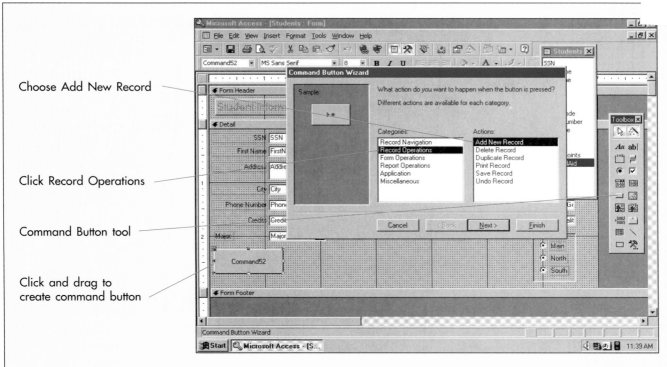

(e) Add a Command Button (step 5)

FIGURE 2.9   Hands-on Exercise 3 (continued)

STEP 7: Align the Command Buttons

➤ Select the four command buttons by pressing and holding the **Shift key** as you click each button. Release the Shift key when all buttons are selected.

➤ Pull down the **Format menu.** Click **Size** to display the cascade menu shown in Figure 2.9f. Click **to Widest** to set a uniform width.

➤ Pull down the **Format menu** a second time, click **Size,** then click **to Tallest** to set a uniform height.

➤ Pull down the **Format menu** again, click **Horizontal Spacing,** then click **Make Equal** so that each button is equidistant from the other buttons.

➤ Pull down the **Format menu** a final time, click **Align,** then click **Bottom** to complete the alignment. Drag the buttons to the center of the form.

MULTIPLE CONTROLS AND PROPERTIES

Press and hold the Shift key as you click one control after another to select multiple controls. To view or change the properties for the selected controls, click the right mouse button to display a shortcut menu, then click Properties to display a property sheet. If the value of a property is the same for all selected controls, that value will appear in the property sheet; otherwise the box for that property will be blank. Changing a property when multiple controls are selected changes the property for all selected controls.

Click Size

Click to Widest

Select all four
command buttons

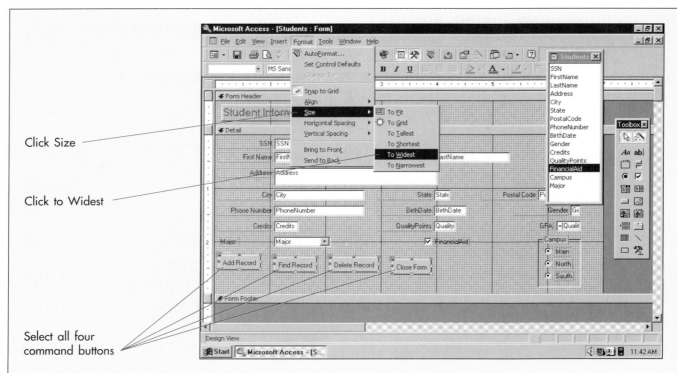

(f) Align the Buttons (step 7)

FIGURE 2.9   Hands-on Exercise 3 (continued)

STEP 8: Reset the Tab Order

➤ Click anywhere in the Detail section. Pull down the **View menu.** Click **Tab Order** to display the Tab Order dialog box in Figure 2.9g.

➤ Click the **AutoOrder command button** so that the tab key will move to fields in left-to-right, top-to-bottom order as you enter data in the form. Click **OK** to close the Tab Order dialog box.

➤ Check the form one more time in order to make any last-minute changes.

➤ Save the form.

CHANGE THE TAB ORDER

The Tab key provides a shortcut in the finished form to move from one field to the next; that is, you press Tab to move forward to the next field and Shift+Tab to return to the previous field. The order in which fields are selected corresponds to the sequence in which the controls were entered onto the form, and need not correspond to the physical appearance of the actual form. To restore a left-to-right, top-to-bottom sequence, pull down the View menu, click Tab Order, then select AutoOrder. Alternatively, you can specify a custom sequence by clicking the selector for the various controls within the Tab Order dialog box, then moving the row up or down within the list.

View button

Click Auto Order

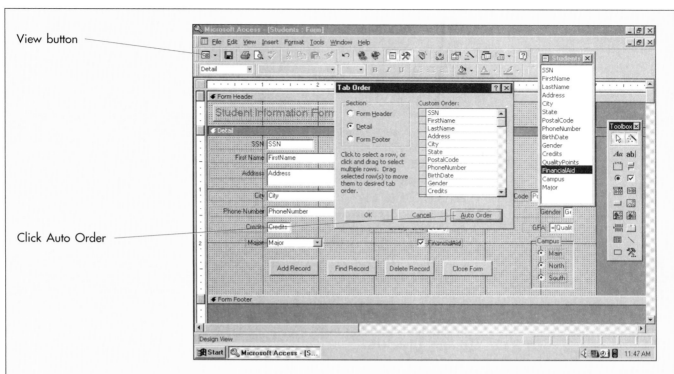

(g) Modify the Tab Order (step 8)

FIGURE 2.9 Hands-on Exercise 3 (continued)

STEP 9: The Page Setup Command

➤ Point to any blank area in the Detail section of the form. Click the **right mouse button** to display a shortcut menu, then click **Properties** to display the Properties dialog box for the Detail section. Click the **All tab.**

➤ Click the text box for **Height.** Enter **3.5** to change the height of the Detail section to three and one-half inches. Close the Properties dialog box.

➤ If necessary, click and drag the **right border** of the form so that all controls are fully visible. Do *not* exceed a width of 7 inches for the entire form.

➤ Pull down the **File menu.** Click **Page Setup** to display the Page Setup dialog box. If necessary, click the **Margins tab.**

➤ Change the left and right margins to **.75** inch. Click **OK** to accept the settings and close the Page Setup dialog box.

CHECK YOUR NUMBERS

The width of the form, plus the left and right margins, cannot exceed the width of the printed page. Thus increasing the width of a form may require a corresponding decrease in the left and right margins or a change to landscape (rather than portrait) orientation. Pull down the File menu and choose the Page Setup command to modify the dimensions of the form prior to printing.

STEP 10: The Completed Form

➤ Click the **View button** to switch to the Form view and display the first record in the table.

➤ Complete the record by adding appropriate data (choose any values you like) for the Major, FinancialAid, and Campus fields that were added to the form in this exercise.

➤ Click the **Add Record command button** to create a new record. Click the text box for **Social Security Number.** Add the record shown in Figure 2.9h. The record selector changes to a pencil as soon as you begin to enter data to indicate the record has not been saved.

➤ Press the **Tab key** or the **enter key** to move from field to field within the record. Click the **arrow** on the drop-down list box to display the list of majors, then click the desired major. Complete all of the information in the form.

➤ Click the **selection area** (the thin vertical column to the left of the form) to select only the current record. The record selector changes from a pencil to an arrow. The selection area is shaded to indicate that the record has been selected.

➤ Pull down the **File menu.** Click **Print** to display the Print dialog box. Click the option button to **print Selected Records**—that is, to print only the one record. Click **OK.**

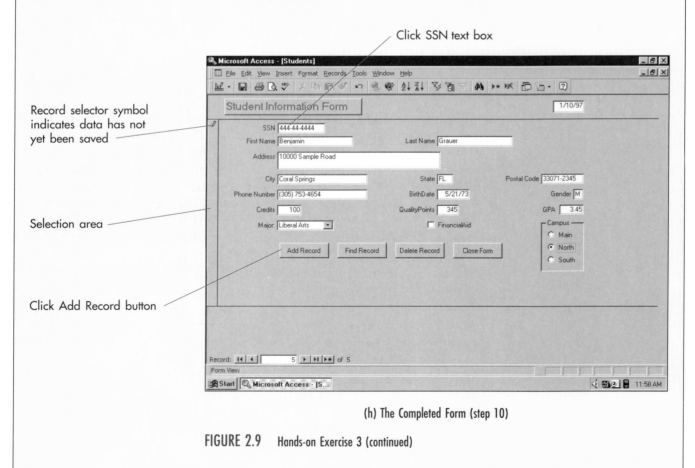

(h) The Completed Form (step 10)

FIGURE 2.9   Hands-on Exercise 3 (continued)

➤ Examine your printed output to be sure that the form fits on a single page. It if doesn't, you need to adjust the margins of the form itself and/or change the margins using the Page Setup command in the File menu, then print the form a second time.

KEYBOARD SHORTCUTS

Press Tab to move from one field to the next in a finished form. Press Shift+Tab to return to the previous field. Type the first letter of an item's name to select the first item in a drop-down list beginning with that letter; for example, type "B" to select the first item in Major beginning with that letter. Type the first two letters quickly—for example, Bu—and you will go directly to Business. Press the space bar to toggle a check box on and off. Press the down arrow key to move from one option to the next within an option group.

STEP 11: Exit Access

➤ Click the **Close Form command button** when you have completed the record. Click **Yes** if you see a message asking to save changes to the form.

➤ Pull down the **File menu.** Click **Exit** to leave Access. Congratulations on a job well done.

SUMMARY

The information produced by a system depends entirely on the underlying data. The design of the database is of critical importance and must be done correctly. Three guidelines were suggested. These are to include the necessary data, to store data in its smallest parts, and to avoid the use of calculated fields in a table.

The Table Wizard is the easiest way to create a table. It lets you choose from a series of business or personal tables, asks you questions about the fields you want, then creates the table for you.

A table has two views—the Design view and the Datasheet view. The Design view is used to create the table and display the fields within the table, as well as the data type and properties of each field. The Datasheet view is used after the table has been created to add, edit, and delete records.

A form provides a user-friendly way to enter and display data, in that it can be made to resemble a paper form. The Form Wizard is the easiest way to create a form. The Design view enables you to modify an existing form.

A form consists of objects called controls. A bound control has a data source such as a field in the underlying table. An unbound control has no data source. A calculated control contains an expression. Controls are selected, moved, and sized the same way as any other Windows object.

A property is a characteristic or attribute of an object that determines how the object looks and behaves. Every Access object (e.g., tables, fields, forms, and controls) has a set of properties that determine the behavior of that object. The properties for an object are displayed in a property sheet.

Allow Zero Length property	Drop-down list box	Page Setup
AutoNumber field	Expression	Primary key
AutoOrder	Field name	Print Preview
Bound control	Field Size property	Property
Calculated control	Form	Property sheet
Calculated field	Form view	Required property
Caption property	Form Wizard	Selection area
Check box	Format property	Tab Order
Combo box	Hyperlink field	Table Wizard
Command button	Indexed property	Text box
Control	Inheritance	Text field
Currency field	Input Mask property	Toolbox toolbar
Data type	Label	Unbound control
Datasheet view	Lookup Wizard	Validation Rule property
Date/Time field	Memo field	Validation Text property
Default Value property	Number field	
Design view	OLE field	Yes/No field
	Option group	

MULTIPLE CHOICE

1. Which of the following is true?
   (a) The Table Wizard must be used to create a table
   (b) The Form Wizard must be used to create a form
   (c) Both (a) and (b)
   (d) Neither (a) nor (b)

2. Which of the following is implemented automatically by Access?
   (a) Rejection of a record with a duplicate value of the primary key
   (b) Rejection of numbers in a text field
   (c) Both (a) and (b)
   (d) Neither (a) nor (b)

3. Social security number, phone number, and zip code should be designated as:
   (a) Number fields
   (b) Text fields
   (c) Yes/No fields
   (d) Any of the above depending on the application

4. Which of the following is true of the primary key?
   (a) Its values must be unique
   (b) It must be defined as a text field
   (c) It must be the first field in a table
   (d) It can never be changed

5. Social security number rather than name is used as a primary key because:
   (a) The social security number is numeric, whereas the name is not
   (b) The social security number is unique, whereas the name is not
   (c) The social security number is a shorter field
   (d) All of the above

6. Which of the following is true regarding buttons within the Form Wizard?
   (a) The > button copies a selected field from a table onto a form
   (b) The < button removes a selected field from a form
   (c) Both (a) and (b)
   (d) Neither (a) nor (b)

7. Which of the following was *not* a suggested guideline for designing a table?
   (a) Include all necessary data
   (b) Store data in its smallest parts
   (c) Avoid calculated fields
   (d) Designate at least two primary keys

8. Which of the following are valid parameters for use with a form?
   (a) Portrait orientation, a width of 6 inches, left and right margins of 1¼ inch
   (b) Landscape orientation, a width of 9 inches, left and right margins of 1 inch
   (c) Both (a) and (b)
   (d) Neither (a) nor (b)

9. Which view is used to add, edit, or delete records in a table?
   (a) The Datasheet view
   (b) The Form view
   (c) Both (a) and (b)
   (d) Neither (a) nor (b)

10. Which of the following is true?
   (a) Any field added to a table after a form has been created is automatically added to the form as a bound control
   (b) Any calculated control that appears in a form is automatically inserted into the underlying table
   (c) Every bound and unbound control in a form has an underlying property sheet
   (d) All of the above

11. In which view will you see the record selector symbols of a pencil and a triangle?
   (a) Only the Datasheet view
   (b) Only the Form view
   (c) The Datasheet view and the Form view
   (d) The Form view, the Design view, and the Datasheet view

12. To move a control (in the Design view), you select the control, then:
   (a) Point to a border (the pointer changes to an arrow) and click and drag the border to the new position
   (b) Point to a border (the pointer changes to a hand) and click and drag the border to the new position

(c) Point to a sizing handle (the pointer changes to an arrow) and click and drag the sizing handle to the new position

(d) Point to a sizing handle (the pointer changes to a hand) and click and drag the sizing handle to the new position

13. Which fields are commonly defined with an input mask?
    (a) Social security number and phone number
    (b) First name, middle name, and last name
    (c) City, state, and zip code
    (d) All of the above

14. Which data type appears as a check box in a form?
    (a) Text field
    (b) Number field
    (c) Yes/No field
    (d) All of the above

15. Which properties would you use to limit a user's response to two characters, and automatically convert the response to uppercase?
    (a) Field Size and Format
    (b) Input Mask, Validation Rule, and Default Value
    (c) Input Mask and Required
    (d) Field Size, Validation Rule, Validation Text, and Required

ANSWERS

1. d	**6.** c	**11.** c
2. a	**7.** d	**12.** b
3. b	**8.** c	**13.** a
4. a	**9.** c	**14.** c
5. b	**10.** c	**15.** a

PRACTICE WITH ACCESS 97

1. Modify the Student form created in the hands-on exercises to match the form in Figure 2.10. (The form contains three additional controls that must be added to the Students table.)

   a. Add the DateAdmitted and EmailAddress as a date and a text field, respectively, in the Students table. Add a Yes/No field to indicate whether or not the student is an International student.

   b. Add controls for the additional fields as shown in Figure 2.10.

   c. Modify the State field in the underlying Students table to use the Lookup Wizard, and set CA, FL, NJ, and NY as the values for the list box. (These are the most common states in the Student population.) The control in the form will not, however, inherit the list box because it was added to the table after the form was created. Hence you have to delete the existing control in the form, display the field list, then click and drag the State field from the field list to the form.

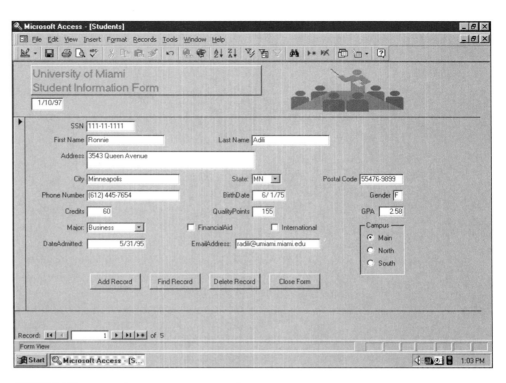

FIGURE 2.10   Screen for Practice Exercises 1 and 2

d. Resize the control in the Form Header so that *University of Miami Student Information Form* takes two lines. Press Ctrl+Enter to force a line break within the control. Resize the Form Header.

e. Change the tab order to reflect the new fields in the form.

f. Add a graphic as described in problem 2.

2. This exercise is a continuation of problem 1 and describes how to insert a graphic created by another application onto an Access form. (The faster your machine, the more you will enjoy the exercise.)

a. Open the Students form in My First Database in the Design view. Move the date in the header under the label.

b. Click the Unbound Object Frame tool on the toolbox. (If you are unsure as to which tool to click, just point to the tool to display the name of the tool.)

c. Click and drag in the Form Header to size the frame, then release the mouse to display an Insert Object dialog box.

d. Click the Create New option button. Select the Microsoft Clip Gallery as the object type. Click OK.

e. Click the Clip Art tab in the Microsoft Clip Gallery dialog box. Choose the category and picture you want from within the Clip Gallery. Click the Insert button to insert the picture into the Access form and simultaneously close the Clip Gallery dialog box. Do *not* be concerned if only a portion of the picture appears on the form.

f. Right click the newly inserted object to display a shortcut menu, then click Properties to display the Properties dialog box. Select (click) the Size Mode property and select Stretch from the associated list. Change the Back Style property to Transparent, the Special Effect property to Flat, and the Border Style property to Transparent. Close the Properties dialog box.

g. You should see the entire clip art image, although it may be distorted because the size and shape of the frame you inserted in steps (b) and (c) do not match the image you selected. Click and drag the sizing handles on the frame to size the object so that its proportions are correct. Click anywhere in the middle of the frame (the mouse pointer changes to a hand) to move the frame elsewhere in the form.

h. If you want to display a different object, double click the clip art image to return to the Clip Gallery in order to select another object.

3. Open the Employee database in the Exploring Access folder to create a form similar to the one in Figure 2.11. (This is the same database that was referenced in problem 2 in Chapter 1.)

a. The form was created using the Form Wizard and Colorful1 style. The various controls were then moved and sized to match the arrangement in the figure.

b. The label in the Form Header, date of execution, and command buttons were added after the form was created, using the techniques in the third hands-on exercise.

c. To add lines to the form, click the Line tool in the toolbox, then click and drag on the form to draw the line. To draw a straight line, press and hold the Shift key as you draw the line.

d. You need not match our form exactly, and we encourage you to experiment with a different design.

e. Add a record for yourself (if you have not already done so in Chapter 1), then print the form containing your data. Submit the printed form to your instructor as proof you did this exercise.

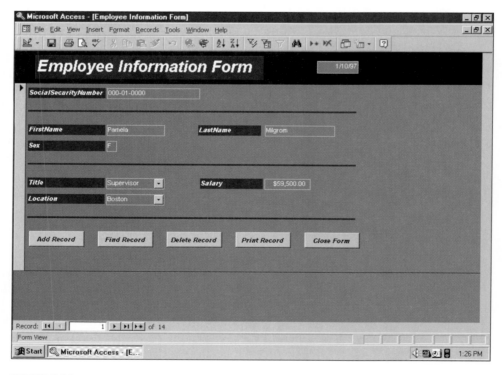

FIGURE 2.11   Screen for Practice Exercise 3

4. Open the USA database found in the Exploring Access folder to create a form similar to the one in Figure 2.12.

   a. The form was created using the Form Wizard and Standard style. The controls were moved and sized to match the arrangement in the figure.

   b. Population density is a calculated control and is computed by dividing the population by the area. Format the density to two decimal places.

   c. You need not match our form exactly, and we encourage you to experiment with different designs.

   d. The Find command can be used after the form has been created to search through the table and answer questions about the United States. The dialog box in Figure 2.12, for example, will identify the Empire State.

   e. Add the graphic, following the steps in the second exercise.

   f. Print the form of your favorite state and submit it to your instructor. Be sure to choose the option to print only the selected record.

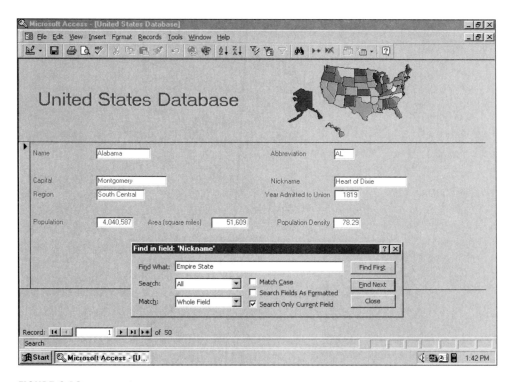

FIGURE 2.12   Screen for Practice Exercise 4

5. Figure 2.13 displays the Design view of a form to maintain an address book of friends and acquaintances. The picture is an added touch and well worth the effort, but it requires you to obtain pictures of your friends in machine-readable form. Each picture is stored initially in its own file (in GIF or JPEG format). The form and underlying table build upon the information in the chapter and should adhere to the following guidelines:

   a. Create an Address Book database containing a table and associated form, using Figure 2.13 as a guide. You can add or delete fields as appropriate with the exception of the FriendID field, which is designated as the primary key. The FriendID should be defined as an AutoNumber field whose value is created automatically each time a record is added to the table.

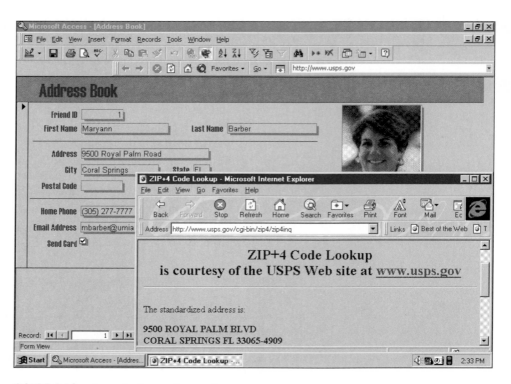

FIGURE 2.13   Screen for Practice Exercise 5

b. Define the postal code as a nine-digit zip code. You can obtain the additional four digits from the U.S. Postal Service as shown in Figure 2.13. Pull down the View menu, click Toolbars, then toggle the Web toolbar on. Enter the address of the Postal Service (www.usps.gov), then click the appropriate link to obtain the complete zip code.

c. Include a logical field (e.g., SendCard) in the underlying table. This will enable you to create a report of those people who are to receive a birthday card (or season's greetings card) once the data have been entered.

d. Include an OLE field in the table, regardless of whether or not you actually have a picture, and be sure to leave space in the form for the picture. Those records that have an associated picture will display the picture in the form; those records that do not have a picture will display a blank space. To insert a picture into the database, open the table, click in the OLE field, pull down the Insert menu, and click the Object command. Click the Create from File option button, click the Browse button in the associated dialog box, then select the appropriate file name and location.

e. Enter data for yourself in the completed form, then print the associated form to submit to your instructor as proof you did this exercise.

6. The potential of Access is limited only by your imagination. Figure 2.14, for example, shows a (partially completed) table to hold statistics for players in the National Basketball Association. The decision on which fields to include is up to you; e.g., you can include statistics for the player's career and/or the current year. We suggest, however, the inclusion of a memo field to add descriptive notes (e.g., career highlights) about each player. You can also include an optional picture field provided you can obtain the player's picture. Design the table, create the associated form, then go the home page of the NBA to obtain statistics for your favorite player. Print the completed form for your player as proof you did this exercise.

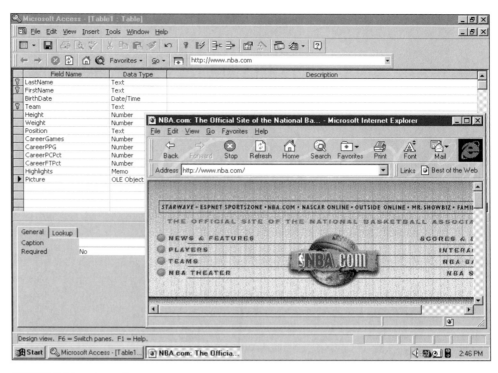

FIGURE 2.14   Screen for Practice Exercise 6

CASE STUDIES

Personnel Management

You have been hired as the Personnel Director for a medium-sized firm (500 employees) and are expected to implement a system to track employee compensation. You want to be able to calculate the age of every employee as well as the length of service. You want to know each employee's most recent performance evaluation. You want to be able to calculate the amount of the most recent salary increase, both in dollars and as a percentage of the previous salary. You also want to know how long the employee had to wait for that increase—that is, how much time elapsed between the present and previous salary. Design a table capable of providing this information.

The Stockbroker

A good friend has come to you for help. He is a new stockbroker whose firm provides computer support for existing clients, but does nothing in the way of data management for prospective clients. Your friend wants to use a PC to track the clients he is pursuing. He wants to know when he last contacted a person, how the contact was made (by phone or through the mail), and how interested the person was. He also wants to store the investment goals of each prospect, such as growth or income, and whether a person is interested in stocks, bonds, and/or a retirement account. And finally, he wants to record the amount of money the person has to invest. Design a table suitable for the information requirements.

Metro Zoo

Your job as Director of Special Programs at the Metro Zoo has put you in charge of this year's fund-raising effort. You have decided to run an "Adopt an Animal" campaign and are looking for contributions on three levels: $25 for a reptile, $50 for a bird, and $100 for a mammal. Adopting "parents" will receive a personalized adoption certificate, a picture of their animal, and educational information about the zoo. You already have a great mailing list—the guest book that is maintained at the zoo entrance. Your main job is to computerize that information and to store additional information about contributions that are received. Design a table that will be suitable for this project.

Form Design

Collect several examples of such real forms as a magazine subscription, auto registration, or employment application. Choose the form you like best and implement the design in Access. Start by creating the underlying table (with some degree of validation), then use the Form Wizard to create the form. How closely does the form you create resemble the paper form with which you began?

File Compression

Photographs add significantly to the value of a database, but they also add to its size. Accordingly, you might want to consider acquisition of a file compression program to facilitate copying large documents to a floppy disk in order to transport your documents to and from school, home, or work. You can download an evaluation copy of the popular WinZip program at www.winzip.com. Investigate the subject of file compression, then submit a summary of your findings to your instructor.

Copyright Infringement

It's fun to download images from the Web for inclusion into a database, but is it legal? Copyright protection (infringement) is one of the most pressing legal issues on the Web. Search the Web for sites that provide information on current copyright law. One excellent site is the copyright page at the Institute for Learning Technologies at www.ilt.columbia.edu/projects/copyright. Another excellent reference is the page at www.benedict.com. Research these and other sites, then summarize your findings in a short note to your instructor.

The Digital Camera

The art of photography is undergoing profound changes with the introduction of the digital camera. The images are stored on disk rather than traditional film and are available instantly. Search the Internet for the latest information on digital cameras and report back to the class with the results of your research. Perhaps one of your classmates has access to a digital camera, in which case you can take pictures of the class for inclusion in an Access database.

3

INFORMATION FROM THE DATABASE: REPORTS AND QUERIES

OBJECTIVES

After reading this chapter you will be able to:

1. Describe the various types of reports available through the Report Wizard.
2. Describe the various views in the Report Window and the purpose of each.
3. Describe the similarities between forms and reports with respect to bound, unbound, and calculated controls.
4. List the sections that may be present in a report and explain the purpose of each.
5. Differentiate between a query and a table; explain how the objects in an Access database (tables, forms, queries, and reports) interact with one another.
6. Use the design grid to create and modify a select query.
7. Explain the use of multiple criteria rows within the design grid to implement AND and OR conditions in a query.
8. Describe the various views in the Query window and the purpose of each.

OVERVIEW

Data and information are not synonymous. Data refers to a fact or facts about a specific record, such as a student's name, major, quality points, or number of completed credits. Information can be defined as data that has been rearranged into a more useful format. The individual fields within a student record are considered data. A list of students on the Dean's List, however, is information that has been produced from the data about the individual students.

Chapters 1 and 2 described how to enter and maintain data through the use of tables and forms. This chapter shows how to convert the data to information through queries and reports. Queries enable you to ask questions about the database. Reports provide presentation quality output and display detail as well as summary information about the records in a database.

As you read the chapter, you will see that the objects in an Access database (tables, forms, reports and queries) have many similar characteristics. We use these similarities to build on what you have learned in previous chapters. You already know, for example, that the controls in a form inherit their properties from the corresponding fields in a table. The same concept applies to the controls in a report. And since you know how to move and size controls within a form, you also know how to move and size the controls in a report. As you read the chapter, look for these and other similarities to apply your existing knowledge to the new material.

REPORTS

A *report* is a printed document that displays information from a database. Figure 3.1 shows several sample reports, each of which will be created in this chapter. The reports were created with the Report Wizard and are based on the Students table that was presented in Chapter 2. (The table has been expanded to 24 records.) As you view each report, ask yourself how the data in the table was rearranged to produce the information in the report.

The *columnar (vertical) report* in Figure 3.1a is the simplest type of report. It lists every field for every record in a single column (one record per page) and typically runs for many pages. The records in this report are displayed in the same sequence (by social security number) as the records in the table on which the report is based.

The *tabular report* in Figure 3.1b displays fields in a row rather than in a column. Each record in the underlying table is printed in its own row. Unlike the previous report, only selected fields are displayed, so the tabular report is more concise than the columnar report of Figure 3.1a. Note, too, that the records in the report are listed in alphabetical order rather than by social security number.

The report in Figure 3.1c is also a tabular report, but it is very different from the report in Figure 3.1b. The report in Figure 3.1c lists only a selected set of students (those students with a GPA of 3.50 or higher), as opposed to the earlier reports, which listed every student. The students are listed in descending order according to their GPA.

The report in Figure 3.1d displays the students in groups, according to their major, then computes the average GPA for each group. The report also contains summary information (not visible in Figure 3.1d) for the report as a whole, which computes the average GPA for all students.

DATA VERSUS INFORMATION

Data and information are not synonymous although the terms are often interchanged. Data is the raw material and consists of the table (or tables) that compose a database. Information is the finished product. Data is converted to information by selecting records, performing calculations on those records, and/or changing the sequence in which the records are displayed. Decisions in an organization are made on the basis of information rather than raw data.

Student Roster

SSN	111-11-1111
FirstName	Jared
LastName	Berlin
Address	900 Main Highway
City	Charleston
State	SC
PostalCode	29410-0560
PhoneNumber	(803) 223-7868
BirthDate	1/15/72
Gender	M
Credits	100
QualityPoints	250
FinancialAid	Yes
Campus	1
Major	Engineering

Saturday, January 11, 1997 — Page 1 of 24

(a) Columnar Report

Student Master List

Last Name	First Name	Phone Number	Major
Adili	Ronnie	(612) 445-7654	Business
Berlin	Jared	(803) 223-7868	Engineering
Camejo	Oscar	(716) 433-3321	Liberal Arts
Coe	Bradley	(415) 235-6543	Undecided
Cornell	Ryan	(404) 755-4490	Undecided
DiGiacomo	Kevin	(305) 531-7652	Business
Faulkner	Eileen	(305) 489-8876	Communications
Frazier	Steven	(410) 995-8755	Undecided
Gibson	Christopher	(305) 235-4563	Business
Heltzer	Peter	(305) 753-4533	Engineering
Huerta	Carlos	(212) 344-5654	Undecided
Joseph	Cedric	(404) 667-8955	Communications
Korba	Nickolas	(415) 664-0900	Education
Ortiz	Frances	(303) 575-3211	Communications
Parulis	Christa	(410) 877-6565	Liberal Arts
Price	Lori	(310) 961-2323	Communications
Ramsay	Robert	(212) 223-9889	Business
Slater	Erica	(312) 545-6978	Communications
Solomon	Wendy	(305) 666-4532	Engineering
Watson	Ana	(305) 595-7877	Liberal Arts
Watson	Ana	(305) 561-2334	Business
Weissman	Kimberly	(904) 388-8605	Liberal Arts
Zacco	Michelle	(617) 884-3434	Undecided
Zimmerman	Kimberly	(713) 225-3434	Education

Saturday, January 11, 1997 — Page 1 of 1

(b) Tabular Report

Dean's List

First Name	Last Name	Major	Credits	Quality Points	GPA
Peter	Heltzer	Engineering	25	100	4.00
Cedric	Joseph	Communications	45	170	3.78
Erica	Slater	Communications	105	390	3.71
Kevin	DiGiacomo	Business	105	375	3.57
Wendy	Solomon	Engineering	50	175	3.50

Saturday, January 11, 1997 — Page 1 of 1

(c) Dean's List

GPA by Major

Major	Last Name	First Name	GPA
Business			
	Adili	Ronnie	2.58
	Cornell	Ryan	1.78
	DiGiacomo	Kevin	3.57
	Gibson	Christopher	1.71
	Ramsay	Robert	3.24
	Watson	Ana	2.50
	Average GPA for Major		2.56
Communications			
	Faulkner	Eileen	2.67
	Joseph	Cedric	3.78
	Ortiz	Frances	2.14
	Price	Lori	1.75
	Slater	Erica	3.71
	Average GPA for Major		2.81
Education			
	Korba	Nickolas	1.66
	Zimmerman	Kimberly	3.29
	Average GPA for Major		2.48
Engineering			
	Berlin	Jared	2.50
	Heltzer	Peter	4.00
	Solomon	Wendy	3.50
	Average GPA for Major		3.33
Liberal Arts			
	Camejo	Oscar	2.80
	Parulis	Christa	1.80
	Watson	Ana	2.79
	Weissman	Kimberly	2.63
	Average GPA for Major		2.51

Saturday, January 11, 1997 — Page 1 of 2

(d) Summary Report

FIGURE 3.1   Report Types

Anatomy of a Report

All reports are based on an underlying table or query within the database. (Queries are discussed later in the chapter, beginning on page 102.) A report, however, displays the data or information in a more attractive fashion because it contains various headings and/or other decorative items that are not present in either a table or a query.

The easiest way to learn about reports is to compare a printed report with its underlying design. Consider, for example, Figure 3.2a, which displays the tabular report, and Figure 3.2b, which shows the underlying design. The latter shows how a report is divided into sections, which appear at designated places when the report is printed. There are seven types of sections, but a report need not contain all seven.

The *report header* appears once, at the beginning of a report. It typically contains information describing the report, such as its title and the date the report was printed. (The report header appears above the page header on the first page of the report.) The *report footer* appears once at the end of the report, above the page footer on the last page of the report, and displays summary information for the report as a whole.

The *page header* appears at the top of every page in a report and can be used to display page numbers, column headings, and other descriptive information. The *page footer* appears at the bottom of every page and may contain page numbers (when they are not in the page header) or other descriptive information.

A *group header* appears at the beginning of a group of records to identify the group. A *group footer* appears after the last record in a group and contains summary information about the group. Group headers and footers are used only when the records in a report are sorted (grouped) according to a common value in a specific field. These sections do not appear in the report of Figure 3.2, but were shown earlier in the report of Figure 3.1d.

The *detail section* appears in the main body of a report and is printed once for every record in the underlying table (or query). It displays one or more fields for each record in columnar or tabular fashion, according to the design of the report.

The Report Wizard

The *Report Wizard* is the easiest way to create a report, just as the Form Wizard is the easiest way to create a form. The Report Wizard asks you questions about the report you want, then builds the report for you. You can accept the report as is, or you can customize it to better suit your needs.

Figure 3.3a displays the New Report dialog box, from which you can select the Report Wizard. The Report Wizard, in turn, requires you to specify the table or query on which the report will be based. The report in this example will be based on an expanded version of the Students table that was created in Chapter 2.

After you specify the underlying table, you select one or more fields from that table, as shown in Figure 3.3b. The Report Wizard then asks you to select a layout (e.g., Tabular in Figure 3.3c.) and a style (e.g., Soft Gray in Figure 3.3d). This is all the information the Report Wizard requires, and it proceeds to create the report for you. The controls on the report correspond to the fields you selected and are displayed in accordance with the specified layout.

Apply What You Know

The Report Wizard provides an excellent starting point, but typically does not create the report exactly as you would like it to be. Accordingly, you can modify a

Report header ————————

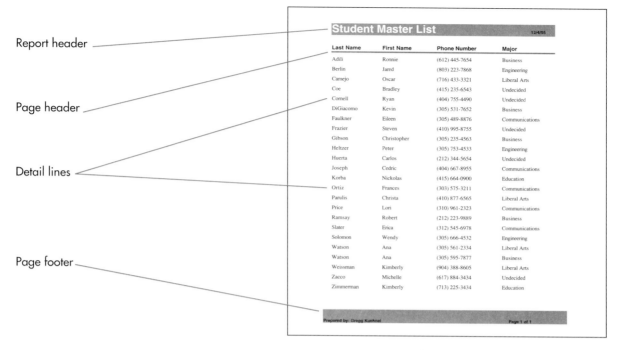

Page header ————————

Detail lines ————————

Page footer ————————

(a) The Printed Report

Report header (title and date)

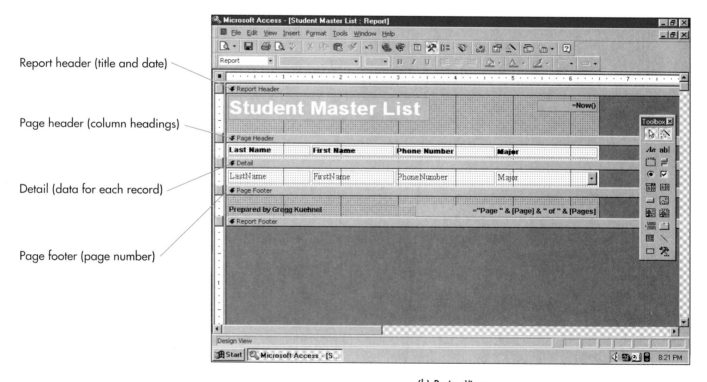

Page header (column headings)

Detail (data for each record)

Page footer (page number)

(b) Design View

FIGURE 3.2   Anatomy of a Report

Select the underlying table/query

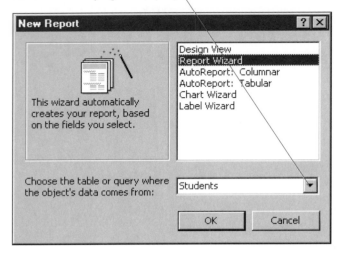

(a) Select the Underlying Table

Selected fields for report

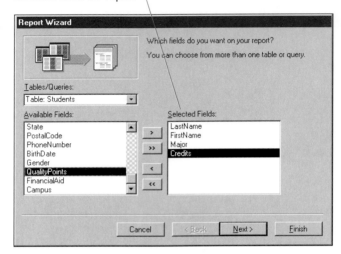

(b) Select the Fields

Selected layout and orientation

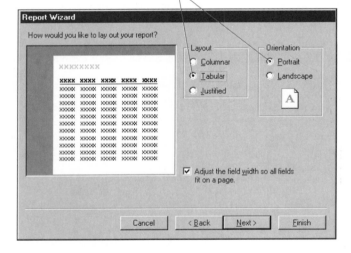

(c) Choose the Layout

Selected style

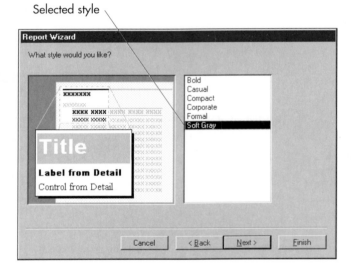

(d) Choose the Style

FIGURE 3.3 The Report Wizard

report created by the Report Wizard, just as you can modify a form created by the Form Wizard. The techniques are the same, and you should look for similarities between forms and reports so that you can apply what you already know. Knowledge of one is helpful in understanding the other.

Controls appear in a report just as they do in a form, and the same definitions apply. A **bound control** has as its data source a field in the underlying table. An **unbound control** has no data source and is used to display titles, labels, lines, rectangles, and graphics. A **calculated control** has as its data source an expression rather than a field. A student's Grade Point Average is an example of a calculated control since it is computed by dividing the number of quality points by the number of credits. The means for selecting, sizing, moving, aligning, and deleting controls are the same, regardless of whether you are working on a form or a report. Thus:

- To select a control, click anywhere on the control. To select multiple controls, press and hold the Shift key as you click each successive control.
- To size a control, click the control to select it, then drag the sizing handles. Drag the handles on the top or bottom to size the box vertically. Drag the handles on the left or right side to size the box horizontally. Drag the handles in the corner to size both horizontally and vertically.
- To move a control, point to any border, but not to a sizing handle (the mouse pointer changes to a hand), then click the mouse and drag the control to its new position.
- To change the properties of a control, point to the control, click the right mouse button to display a shortcut menu, then click Properties to display the property sheet. Click the text box for the desired property, make the necessary change, then close the property sheet.

INHERITANCE

A bound control inherits the same property settings as the associated field in the underlying table. Changing the property setting for a field after the report has been created does *not*, however, change the property of the corresponding control in the report. In similar fashion, changing the property setting of a control in a report does *not* change the property setting of the field in the underlying table.

HANDS-ON EXERCISE 1

The Report Wizard

Objective: To use the Report Wizard to create a new report; to modify an existing report by adding, deleting, and/or modifying its controls. Use Figure 3.4 as a guide in the exercise.

STEP 1: Open the Our Students Database

➤ Start Access. You should see the Microsoft Access dialog box with the option button to **Open an Existing Database** already selected.
➤ Double click the **More Files** selection to display the Open dialog box. Click the **drop-down arrow** on the Look In list box, click the drive containing the **Exploring Access folder,** then open that folder.

THE OUR STUDENTS DATABASE

The Our Students database has the identical design as the database you created in Chapter 2. We have, however, expanded the Students table so that it contains 24 records. The larger table enables you to create more meaningful reports and to obtain the same results as we do in the hands-on exercise.

> Click the **down scroll arrow,** if necessary, and select the **Our Students** database. Click the **Open command button** to open the database.
> Click the **Reports tab** in the database window, then click the **New command button** to display the New Report dialog box in Figure 3.4a. Select the **Report Wizard** as the means of creating the report.
> Click the **drop-down arrow** to display the tables and queries in the database in order to select the one on which the report will be based. Click **Students** (the only table in the database). Click **OK** to start the Report Wizard.

Click Reports tab

Click Report Wizard

Click drop-down arrow to see list of available tables and queries

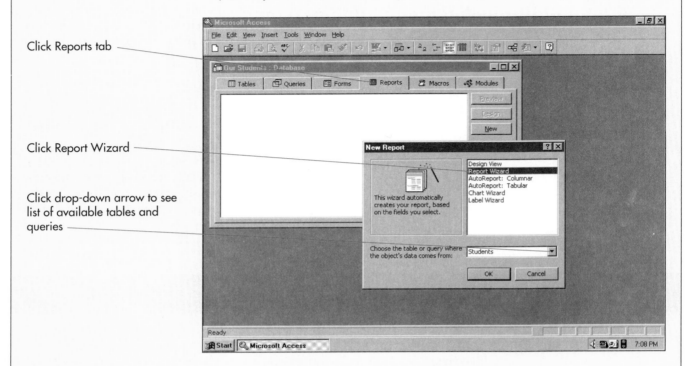

(a) Create a Report (step 1)

FIGURE 3.4   Hands-on Exercise 1

STEP 2: The Report Wizard
> You should see the dialog box in Figure 3.4b, which displays all of the fields in the Students table. Click the **LastName field** in the Available Fields list box, then click the **> button** to enter this field in the Selected Fields list, as shown in Figure 3.4b.
> Enter the remaining fields (FirstName, PhoneNumber, and Major) one at a time, by selecting the field name, then clicking the **> button.** Click the **Next command button** when you have entered all fields.

WHAT THE REPORT WIZARD DOESN'T TELL YOU

The fastest way to select a field is by double clicking; that is, double click a field in the Available Fields list box, and it is automatically moved to the Selected Fields list for inclusion in the report. The process also works in reverse; that is, you can double click a field in the Selected Fields list to remove it from the report.

Click the > button to move selected field from Available Fields list to Selected Fields list

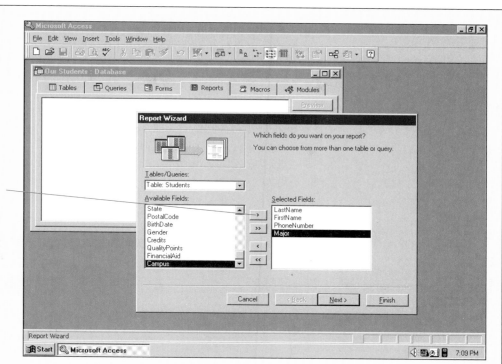

(b) The Report Wizard

FIGURE 3.4   Hands-on Exercise 1 (continued)

STEP 3: The Report Wizard (continued)

➤ The Report Wizard displays several additional screens asking about the report you want to create. The first screen asks whether you want to choose any grouping levels. Click **Next** without specifying a grouping level.

➤ The next screen asks whether you want to sort the records. Click the **drop-down arrow** to display the available fields, then select **LastName.** Click **Next.**

➤ The **Tabular layout** is selected, as is **Portrait orientation.** Be sure the box is checked to **Adjust field width so all fields fit on a page.** Click **Next.**

➤ Choose **Soft Gray** as the style. Click **Next.**

➤ Enter **Student Master List** as the title for your report. The option button to **Preview the Report** is already selected. Click the **Finish command button** to exit the Report Wizard and view the report.

AUTOMATIC SAVING

The Report Wizard automatically saves a report under the name you supply for the title of the report. To verify that a report has been saved, change to the Database window by pulling down the Window menu or by clicking the Database Window button that appears on every toolbar. Once you are in the Database window, click the Reports tab to see the list of existing reports. Note, however, that any subsequent changes must be saved explicitly by clicking the Save button in the Report Design view, or by clicking Yes in response to the warning prompt should you attempt to close the report without saving the changes.

STEP 4: Preview the Report

➤ Click the **Maximize button** so the report takes the entire window as shown in Figure 3.4c. Note the report header at the beginning of the report, the page header (column headings) at the top of the page, and the page footer at the bottom of the page.

➤ Click the **drop-down arrow** on the Zoom Control box so that you can view the report at **75%.** Click the **scroll arrows** on the vertical scroll bar to view the names of additional students.

➤ Click the **Close button** to close the Print Preview window and change to the Report Design view.

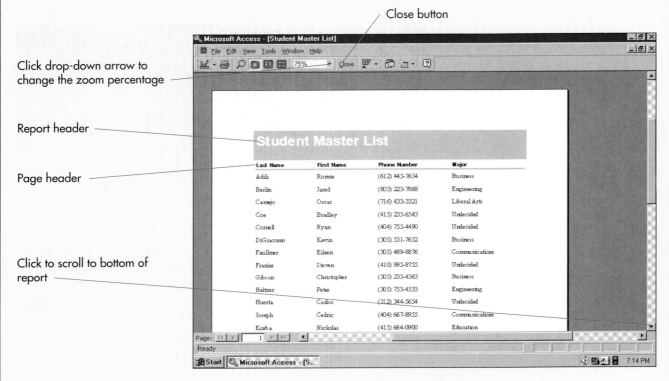

(c) The Initial Report (step 4)

FIGURE 3.4   Hands-on Exercise 1 (continued)

THE PRINT PREVIEW WINDOW

The Print Preview window enables you to preview a report in various ways. Click the One Page, Two Page, or Multiple Page buttons for different views of a report. Use the Zoom button to toggle between the full page and zoom (magnified) views, or use the Zoom Control box to choose a specific magnification. The Navigation buttons at the bottom of the Print Preview window enable you to preview a specific page, while the vertical scroll bar at the right side of the window lets you scroll within a page.

STEP 5: Modify an Existing Control

➤ Click and drag the control containing the **Now function** from the report footer to the report header as shown in Figure 3.4d. Size the control as necessary, then check that the control is still selected and click the **Align Right button** on the Formatting toolbar.

➤ Point to the control, then click the **right mouse button** to display a shortcut menu and click **Properties** to display the Properties sheet.

➤ Click the **Format tab** in the Properties sheet, click the **Format property,** then click the **drop-down arrow** to display the available formats. Click **Short Date,** then close the Properties sheet.

➤ Pull down the **File menu** and click **Save** (or click the **Save button**) to save the modified design

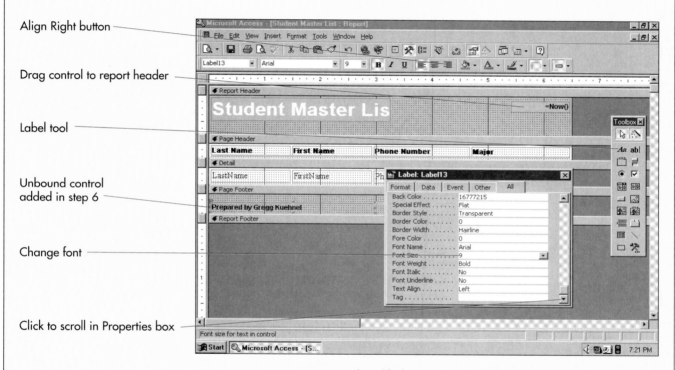

Align Right button

Drag control to report header

Label tool

Unbound control added in step 6

Change font

Click to scroll in Properties box

(d) Modify the Report (steps 5 & 6)

FIGURE 3.4   Hands-on Exercise 1 (continued)

ACCESS FUNCTIONS

Access contains many built-in functions, each of which returns a specific value or the result of a calculation. The Now function, for example, returns the current date and time. The Page and Pages functions return the specific page number and total number of pages, respectively. The Report Wizard automatically adds these functions at appropriate places in a report. You can also add these (or other) functions explicitly, by creating a text box, then replacing the default unbound control by an equal sign, followed by the function name (and associated arguments if any)—for example, =Now( ) to insert the current date and time.

STEP 6: Add an Unbound Control

➤ Click the **Label tool** on the Toolbox toolbar, then click and drag in the report footer where you want the label to go and release the mouse. You should see a flashing insertion point inside the label control. (If you see the word *Unbound* instead of the insertion point, it means you selected the Text box tool rather than the Label tool; delete the text box and begin again.)

➤ Type **Prepared by** followed by your name as shown in Figure 3.4d. Press **enter** to complete the entry and also select the control. Point to the control, click the **right mouse button** to display the shortcut menu, then click **Properties** to display the Properties dialog box.

➤ Click the **down arrow** on the scroll bar, then scroll until you see the Font Size property. Click in the **Font Size box,** click the **drop-down arrow,** then scroll until you can change the font size to **9.** Close the Property sheet.

MISSING TOOLBARS

The Report Design, Formatting, and Toolbox toolbars appear by default in the Report Design view, but any (or all) of these toolbars may be hidden at the discretion of the user. If any of these toolbars do not appear, point to any visible toolbar, click the right mouse button to display a shortcut menu, then click the name of the toolbar you want to display. You can also click the Toolbox button on the Report Design toolbar to display (hide) the Toolbox toolbar.

STEP 7: Change the Sort Order

➤ Pull down the **View menu.** Click **Sorting and Grouping** to display the Sorting and Grouping dialog box. The students are currently sorted by last name.

➤ Click the **drop-down arrow** in the Field Expression box. Click **Major.** (The ascending sequence is selected automatically.)

➤ Click on the next line in the Field Expression box, click the **drop-down arrow** to display the available fields, then click **LastName** to sort the students alphabetically within major as shown in Figure 3.4e.

➤ Close the Sorting and Grouping dialog box. Save the report.

STEP 8: View the Modified Report

➤ Click the **Print Preview button** to preview the finished report. If necessary, click the **Zoom button** on the Print Preview toolbar so that the display on your monitor matches Figure 3.4f. The report has changed so that:

• The date appears in the report header (as opposed to the report footer). The format of the date has changed to a numbered month, and the day of the week has been eliminated.

• The students are listed by major and, within each major, alphabetically according to last name.

• Your name appears in the Report Footer. Click the **down arrow** on the vertical scroll bar to move to the bottom of the page to see your name.

➤ Click the **Print button** to print the report and submit it to your instructor. Click the **Close button** to exit the Print Preview window.

➤ Click the **Close button** in the Report Design window. Click **Yes** if asked whether to save the changes to the Student Master List report.

Print Preview button

Click to close dialog box

Select Major from drop-down list

Select LastName from drop-down list

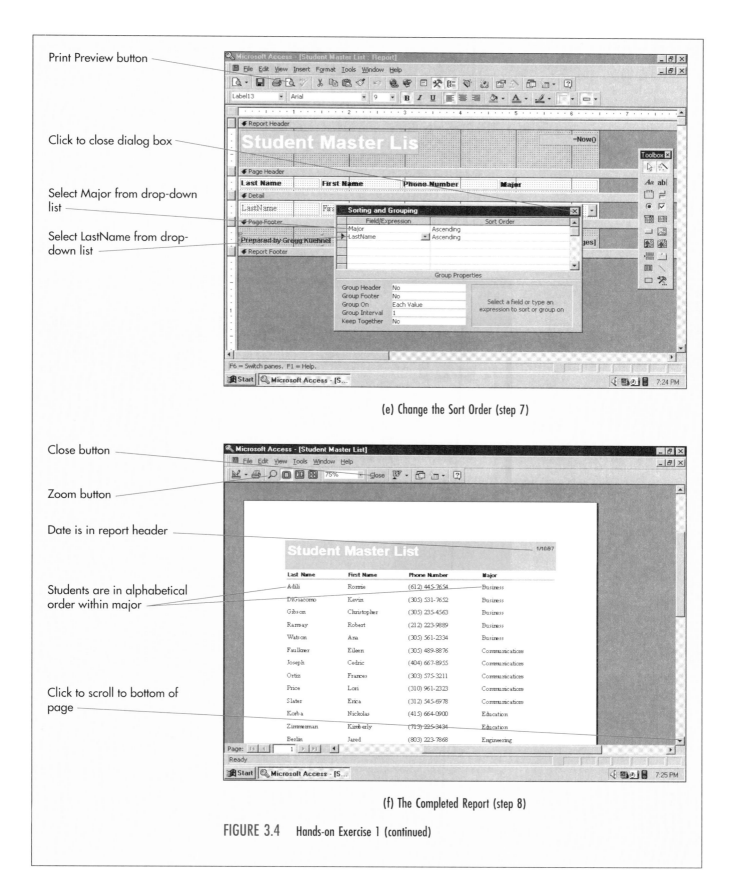

(e) Change the Sort Order (step 7)

Close button

Zoom button

Date is in report header

Students are in alphabetical order within major

Click to scroll to bottom of page

(f) The Completed Report (step 8)

FIGURE 3.4   Hands-on Exercise 1 (continued)

STEP 9: Report Properties

➤ The Database window for the Our Students database should be displayed on the screen as shown in Figure 3.4g. Click the **Restore button** to restore the window to its earlier size.

➤ The **Reports tab** is already selected. Point to the **Student Master List** (the only report in the database), click the **right mouse button** to display a shortcut menu, then click **Properties** to display the Properties dialog box as shown in Figure 3.4g.

➤ Click the **Description text box,** then enter the description shown in the figure. Click **OK** to close the Properties dialog box.

➤ Close the database. Exit Access if you do not wish to continue with the next exercise at this time.

Point to report and click right mouse button to display shortcut menu

Enter report description

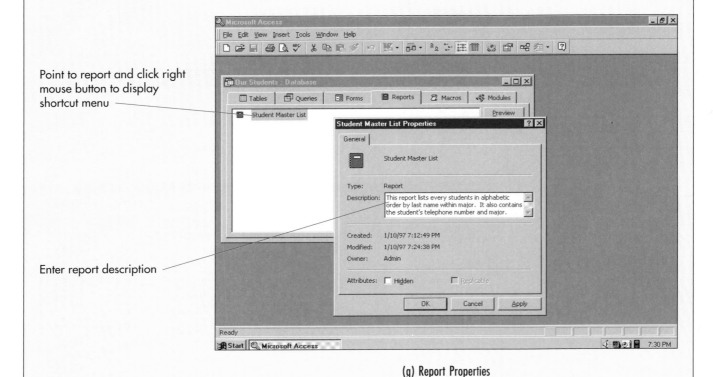

(g) Report Properties

FIGURE 3.4   Hands-on Exercise 1 (continued)

DESCRIBE YOUR OBJECTS

A working database will contain many different objects of the same type, making it all too easy to forget the purpose of the individual objects. It is important, therefore, to use meaningful names for the objects themselves, and further to take advantage of the Description property to enter additional information about the object. Once a description has been created, you can right click any object in the Database window, then click the Properties command from the shortcut menu to display the Properties dialog box with the description of the object.

The report you just created displayed every student in the underlying table. What if, however, we wanted to see just the students who are majoring in Business? Or the students who are receiving financial aid? Or the students who are majoring in Business *and* receiving financial aid? The ability to ask questions such as these, and to see the answers to those questions, is provided through a query. Queries represent the real power of a database.

A *query* lets you see the data you want in the sequence that you want it. It lets you select specific records from a table (or from several tables) and show some or all of the fields for the selected records. It also lets you perform calculations to display data that is not explicitly stored in the underlying table(s), such as a student's GPA.

A query represents a question and an answer. The question is developed by using a graphical tool known as the *design grid.* The answer is displayed in a *dynaset,* which contains the records that satisfy the criteria specified in the query.

A dynaset looks and acts like a table, but it isn't a table; it is a *dyna*mic sub*set* of a table that selects and sorts records as specified in the query. A dynaset is similar to a table in appearance and, like a table, it enables you to enter a new record or modify or delete an existing record. Any changes made in the dynaset are automatically reflected in the underlying table.

Figure 3.5a displays the Students table we have been using throughout the chapter. (We omit some of the fields for ease of illustration.) Figure 3.5b contains the design grid used to select students whose major is "Undecided" and further, to list those students in alphabetical order. (The design grid is explained in the next section.) Figure 3.5c displays the answer to the query in the form of a dynaset.

The table in Figure 3.5a contains 24 records. The dynaset in Figure 3.5c has only five records, corresponding to the students who are undecided about their major. The table in Figure 3.5a has 15 fields for each record (some of the fields are hidden). The dynaset in Figure 3.5c has only four fields. The records in the table are in social security number order (the primary key), whereas the records in the dynaset are in alphabetical order by last name.

The query in Figure 3.5 is an example of a *select query,* which is the most common type of query. A select query searches the underlying table (Figure 3.5a in the example) to retrieve the data that satisfies the query. The data is displayed in a dynaset (Figure 3.5c), which you can modify to update the data in the underlying table(s). The specifications for selecting records and determining which fields will be displayed for the selected records, as well as the sequence of the selected records, are established within the design grid of Figure 3.5b.

The design grid consists of columns and rows. Each field in the query has its own column and contains multiple rows. The *Field row* displays the field name. The *Sort row* enables you to sort in *ascending* or *descending sequence.* The *Show row* controls whether or not the field will be displayed in the dynaset. The *Criteria row(s)* determine the records that will be selected, such as students with an undecided major.

REPORTS, QUERIES, AND TABLES

Every report is based on either a table or a query. The design of the report may be the same with respect to the fields that are included, but the actual reports will be very different. A report based on a table contains every record in the table and is in sequence by the primary key. A report based on a query contains only the records that satisfy the criteria in the query in the specified sequence.

Records in table are in order by SSN

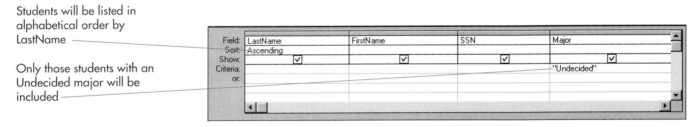

SSN	First Name	Last Name	Major	BirthDate	Gender	Credits	QualityPoints
111-11-1111	Jared	Berlin	Engineering	1/15/72	M	100	250
111-22-3333	Christopher	Gibson	Business	3/12/73	M	35	60
112-12-1212	Peter	Heltzer	Engineering	3/8/73	M	25	100
222-22-2222	Cedric	Joseph	Communications	4/12/74	M	45	170
223-34-2323	Kimberly	Zimmerman	Education	4/18/70	F	120	395
233-33-4444	Robert	Ramsay	Business	5/1/74	M	50	162
333-22-1111	Steven	Frazier	Undecided	9/9/68	M	35	45
333-33-3333	Kimberly	Weissman	Liberal Arts	11/11/74	F	63	166
334-44-4444	Christa	Parulis	Liberal Arts	7/15/72	F	50	90
444-44-4444	Oscar	Camejo	Liberal Arts	3/10/75	M	100	280
445-55-4444	Ronnie	Adili	Business	6/1/75	F	60	155
446-66-7777	Ana	Watson	Business	4/18/75	F	30	75
555-55-5555	Ana	Watson	Liberal Arts	8/1/75	F	70	195
556-66-7777	Frances	Ortiz	Communications	2/3/74	F	28	60
666-33-1111	Bradley	Coe	Undecided	8/22/71	M	52	143
666-66-6666	Nickolas	Korba	Education	11/11/71	M	100	166
666-77-7766	Erica	Slater	Communications	5/1/72	F	105	390
777-77-7777	Wendy	Solomon	Engineering	1/31/75	F	50	175
777-88-8888	Ryan	Cornell	Undecided	9/30/74	M	45	80
888-77-7777	Lori	Price	Communications	7/1/72	F	24	42
888-88-8888	Michelle	Zacco	Undecided	10/24/75	F	21	68
888-99-9999	Eileen	Faulkner	Communications	9/12/75	F	30	80
999-11-1111	Kevin	DiGiacomo	Business	5/31/72	M	105	375
999-99-9999	Carlos	Huerta	Undecided	6/18/75	M	15	40

Record: 1 of 24

(a) Students Table

Students will be listed in alphabetical order by LastName

Only those students with an Undecided major will be included

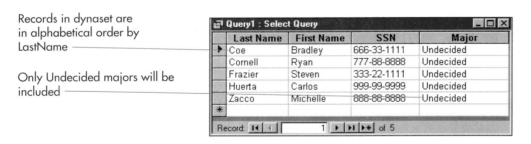

Field:	LastName	FirstName	SSN	Major
Sort:	Ascending			
Show:	☑	☑	☑	☑
Criteria:				"Undecided"
or:				

(b) Design Grid

Records in dynaset are in alphabetical order by LastName

Only Undecided majors will be included

Query1 : Select Query

Last Name	First Name	SSN	Major
Coe	Bradley	666-33-1111	Undecided
Cornell	Ryan	777-88-8888	Undecided
Frazier	Steven	333-22-1111	Undecided
Huerta	Carlos	999-99-9999	Undecided
Zacco	Michelle	888-88-8888	Undecided

Record: 1 of 5

(c) Dynaset

FIGURE 3.5   Queries

Query Window

The **Query window** has three views. The **Design view** is displayed by default and is used to create (or modify) a select query. The **Datasheet view** displays the resulting dynaset. The **SQL view** enables you to use SQL (Structured Query Language) statements to modify the query and is beyond the scope of the present

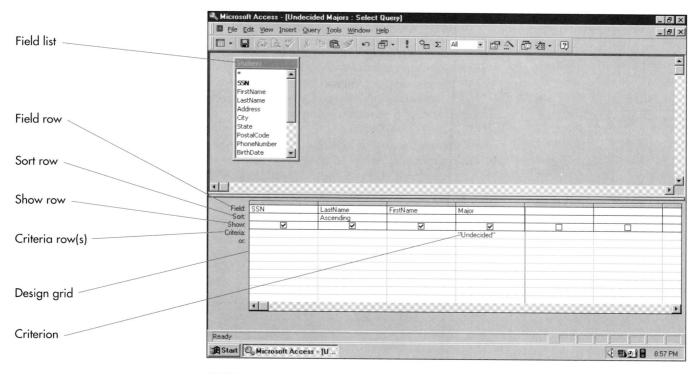

Field list

Field row

Sort row

Show row

Criteria row(s)

Design grid

Criterion

FIGURE 3.6   Query Design View

discussion. The Query Design toolbar contains the buttons to display all three views.

A select query is created in the Design view as shown in Figure 3.6a. The upper portion of the Design view window contains the field list for the table(s) on which the query is based (the Students table in this example). The lower portion of the window displays the design grid, which is where the specifications for the select query are entered. A field is added to the design grid by dragging it from the field list.

The data type of a field determines the way in which the criteria are specified for that field. The criterion for a text field is enclosed in quotation marks. The criteria for number, currency, and counter fields are shown as digits with or without a decimal point. (Commas and dollar signs are not allowed.) Dates are enclosed in pound signs and are entered in the mm/dd/yy format. The criterion for a Yes/No field is entered as Yes (or True) or No (or False).

CONVERSION TO STANDARD FORMAT

Access accepts values for text and date fields in the design grid in multiple formats. The value for a text field can be entered with or without quotation marks (Undecided or "Undecided"). A date can be entered with or without pound signs (1/1/97 or #1/1/97#). Access converts your entries to standard format as soon as you move to the next cell in the design grid. Thus, text entries are always shown in quotation marks, and dates are enclosed in pound signs.

Selection Criteria

To specify selection criteria in the design grid, enter a value or expression in the Criteria row of the appropriate column. Figure 3.7 contains several examples of simple criteria and provides a basic introduction to select queries.

The criterion in Figure 3.7a selects the students majoring in Business. The criteria for text fields are case-insensitive. Thus, *"Business"* is the same as *"business"* or *"BUSINESS"*.

Values entered in multiple columns of the same Criteria row implement an **AND condition** in which the selected records must meet *all* of the specified criteria. The criteria in Figure 3.7b select students who are majoring in Business *and* who are from the state of Florida. The criteria in Figure 3.7c select Communications majors who are receiving financial aid.

Values entered in different Criteria rows are connected by an **OR condition** in which the selected records may satisfy *any* of the indicated criteria. The criteria in Figure 3.7d select students who are majoring in Business *or* who are from Florida or both.

Field:	LastName	State	Major	BirthDate	FinancialAid	Credits
Sort:						
Show:	☑	☑	☑	☑	☑	☑
Criteria:			"Business"			
or:						

(a) Business Majors

Field:	LastName	State	Major	BirthDate	FinancialAid	Credits
Sort:						
Show:	☑	☑	☑	☑	☑	☑
Criteria:		"FL"	"Business"			
or:						

(b) Business Majors from Florida

Field:	LastName	State	Major	BirthDate	FinancialAid	Credits
Sort:						
Show:	☑	☑	☑	☑	☑	☑
Criteria:			"Communications"		Yes	
or:						

(c) Communications Majors Receiving Financial Aid

Field:	LastName	State	Major	BirthDate	FinancialAid	Credits
Sort:						
Show:	☑	☑	☑	☑	☑	☑
Criteria:		"FL"				
or:			"Business"			

(d) Business Majors or Students from Florida

FIGURE 3.7   Criteria

Relational operators (>, <, >=, <=, =, and <>) are used with date or number fields to return records within a designated range. The criteria in Figure 3.7e select Engineering majors with fewer than 60 credits. The criteria in Figure 3.7f select Communications majors who were born on or after April 1, 1974.

Field:	LastName	State	Major	BirthDate	FinancialAid	Credits
Sort:						
Show:	☑	☑	☑	☑	☑	☑
Criteria:			"Engineering"			<60
or:						

(e) Engineering Majors with Fewer than 60 Credits

Field:	LastName	State	Major	BirthDate	FinancialAid	Credits
Sort:						
Show:	☑	☑	☑	☑	☑	☑
Criteria:			"Communications"	>=#4/1/74#		
or:						

(f) Communications Majors Born on or after April 1, 1974

Field:	LastName	State	Major	BirthDate	FinancialAid	Credits
Sort:						
Show:	☑	☑	☑	☑	☑	☑
Criteria:			"Engineering"			<60
or:			Communications	>=#4/1/74#		

(g) Engineering Majors with Fewer than 60 Credits or Communications Majors Born on or after April 1, 1974

Field:	LastName	State	Major	BirthDate	FinancialAid	Credits
Sort:						
Show:	☑	☑	☑	☑	☑	☑
Criteria:						Between 60 and 90
or:						

(h) Students with between 60 and 90 Credits

Field:	LastName	State	Major	BirthDate	FinancialAid	Credits
Sort:						
Show:	☑	☑	☑	☑	☑	☑
Criteria:			Not "Liberal Arts"			
or:						

(i) Students with Majors Other Than Liberal Arts

FIGURE 3.7   Criteria (continued)

Criteria can grow more complex by combining multiple AND and OR conditions. The criteria in Figure 3.7g select Engineering majors with fewer than 60 credits *or* Communications majors who were born on or after April 1, 1974.

Other functions enable you to impose still other criteria. The ***Between function*** selects records that fall within a range of values. The criterion in Figure 3.7h selects students who have between 60 and 90 credits. The ***NOT function*** selects records that do not contain the designated value. The criterion in Figure 3.7i selects students with majors other than Liberal Arts.

WILD CARDS

Select queries recognize the question mark and asterisk wild cards that enable you to search for a pattern within a text field. A question mark stands for a single character in the same position as the question mark; thus H?ll will return Hall, Hill, and Hull. An asterisk stands for any number of characters in the same position as the asterisk; for example, S*nd will return Sand, Stand, and Strand.

HANDS-ON EXERCISE 2

Creating a Select Query

Objective: To create a select query using the design grid; to show how changing values in a dynaset changes the values in the underlying table; to create a report based on a query. Use Figure 3.8 as a guide in the exercise.

STEP 1: Open the Existing Database

➤ Start Access as you did in the previous exercise. Our Students (the database you used in the previous exercise) should appear within the list of recently opened databases.

➤ Select (click) **Our Students,** then click **OK** (or simply double click the name of the database) to open the database and display the database window.

➤ Click the **Queries tab** in the database window. Click the **New command button** to display the New Query dialog box as shown in Figure 3.8a.

➤ **Design View** is already selected as the means of creating a query. Click **OK** to begin creating the query.

THE SIMPLE QUERY WIZARD

The Simple Query Wizard is exactly what its name implies—simple. It lets you select fields from an underlying table, but it does not let you enter values or a sort sequence. We prefer, therefore, to bypass the Wizard and to create the query entirely from the Query Design window.

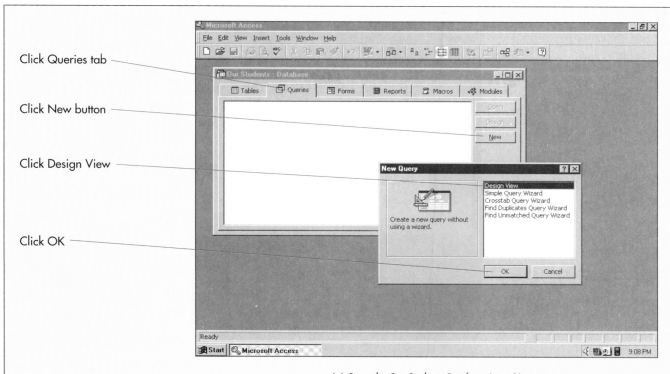

Click Queries tab

Click New button

Click Design View

Click OK

(a) Open the Our Students Database (step 1)

FIGURE 3.8   Hands-on Exercise 2

STEP 2: Add the Students Table

➤ The Show Table dialog box appears as shown in Figure 3.8b, with the **Tables tab** already selected.

➤ Click the **Add button** to add the Students table to the query. (You can also double click the Students table.)

➤ The field list should appear within the Query Design window. Click **Close** to close the Show Table dialog box.

➤ Click the **Maximize button** so that the Query Design window takes up the entire screen.

CUSTOMIZE THE QUERY WINDOW

The Query window displays the field list and design grid in its upper and lower halves, respectively. To increase (decrease) the size of either portion of the window, drag the line dividing the upper and lower sections. Drag the title bar to move a field list. You can also size a field list by dragging a border just as you would size any other window. Press the F6 key to toggle between the upper and lower halves of the Design window.

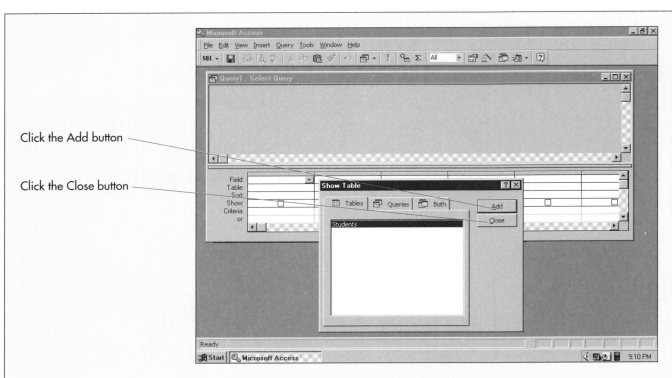

Click the Add button

Click the Close button

(b) Add the Students Table (step 2)

FIGURE 3.8 Hands-on Exercise 2 (continued)

STEP 3: Create the Query

➤ Click and drag the **LastName field** from the Students field list to the Field row in the first column of the QBE grid as shown in Figure 3.8c.

➤ Click and drag the **FirstName, PhoneNumber, Major,** and **Credits fields** (in that order) in similar fashion, dragging each field to the next available column in the Field row.

➤ A check appears in the Show row under each field name to indicate that the field will be displayed in the dynaset. (The show box functions as a toggle switch; thus, you can click the box to clear the check and hide the field in the dynaset. Click the box a second time to display the check and show the field.)

ADDING AND DELETING FIELDS

The fastest way to add a field to the design grid is to double click the field name in the field list. To add more than one field at a time, press and hold the Ctrl key as you click the fields within the field list, then drag the group to a cell in the Field row. To delete a field, click the column selector above the field name to select the column, then press the Del key.

STEP 4: Specify the Criteria

➤ Click the **Criteria row** for Major. Type **Undecided.**

➤ Click the **Sort row** under the LastName field, click the **drop-down arrow,** then select **Ascending** as the sort sequence.

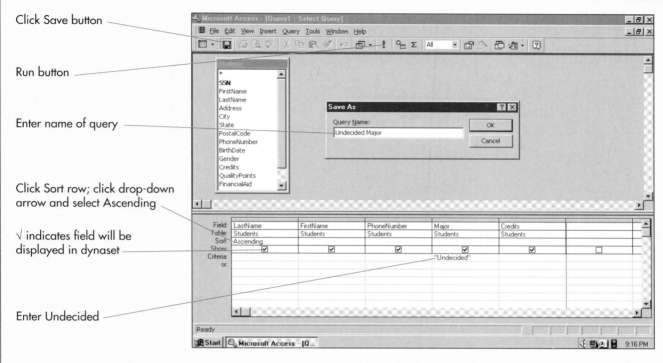

Click Save button

Run button

Enter name of query

Click Sort row; click drop-down arrow and select Ascending

√ indicates field will be displayed in dynaset

Enter Undecided

(c) Create the Query (steps 3 & 4)

FIGURE 3.8   Hands-on Exercise 2 (continued)

➤ Pull down the **File menu** and click **Save** (or click the **Save button**) to display the dialog box in Figure 3.8c.

➤ Type **Undecided Major** as the query name. Click **OK.**

FLEXIBLE CRITERIA

Access offers a great deal of flexibility in the way you enter the criteria for a text field. Quotation marks and/or an equal sign are optional. Thus "Undecided", Undecided, =Undecided, or ="Undecided" are all valid, and you may choose any of these formats. Access will convert your entry to standard format ("Undecided" in this example) after you have moved to the next cell.

STEP 5: Run the Query

➤ Pull down the **Query menu** and click **Run** (or click the **Run button**) to run the query and change to the Datasheet view.

➤ You should see the five records in the dynaset of Figure 3.8d. Change Ryan Cornell's major to Business by clicking in the **Major field,** clicking the **drop-down arrow,** then choosing **Business** from the drop-down list.

➤ Click the **View button** to change the query.

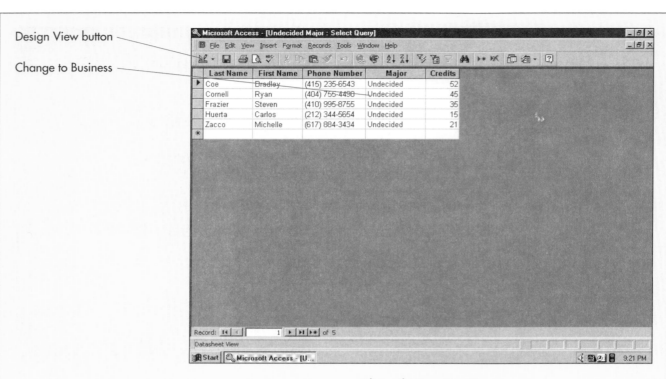

Design View button

Change to Business

(d) Run the Query (step 5)

FIGURE 3.8   Hands-on Exercise 2 (continued)

STEP 6: Modify the Query

➤ Click the **Show check box** in the Major field to remove the check as shown in Figure 3.8e.

➤ Click the **Criteria row** under credits. Type **>30** to select only the Undecided majors with more than 30 credits.

➤ Click the **Save button** to save the revised query. Click the **Run button** to run the revised query. This time there are only two records (Bradley Coe and Steven Frazier) in the dynaset, and the major is no longer displayed.

  • Ryan Cornell does not appear because he has changed his major.

  • Carlos Huerta and Michelle Zacco do not appear because they do not have more than 30 credits.

STEP 7: Create a Report

➤ Pull down the **Window menu** and click **1 Our Students: Database** (or click the **Database window button** on the toolbar). You will see the Database window in Figure 3.8f.

➤ Click the **Reports tab,** then click the **New button** to create a report based on the query you just created. Select **Report Wizard** as the means of creating the report.

➤ Select **Undecided Major** from the drop-down list as shown in Figure 3.8f. Click **OK** to begin the Report Wizard.

➤ You should see the Report Wizard dialog box, which displays all of the visible fields (Major has been hidden) in the Undecided Major query. Click the **>>** **button** to select all of the fields from the query for the report. Click **Next.**

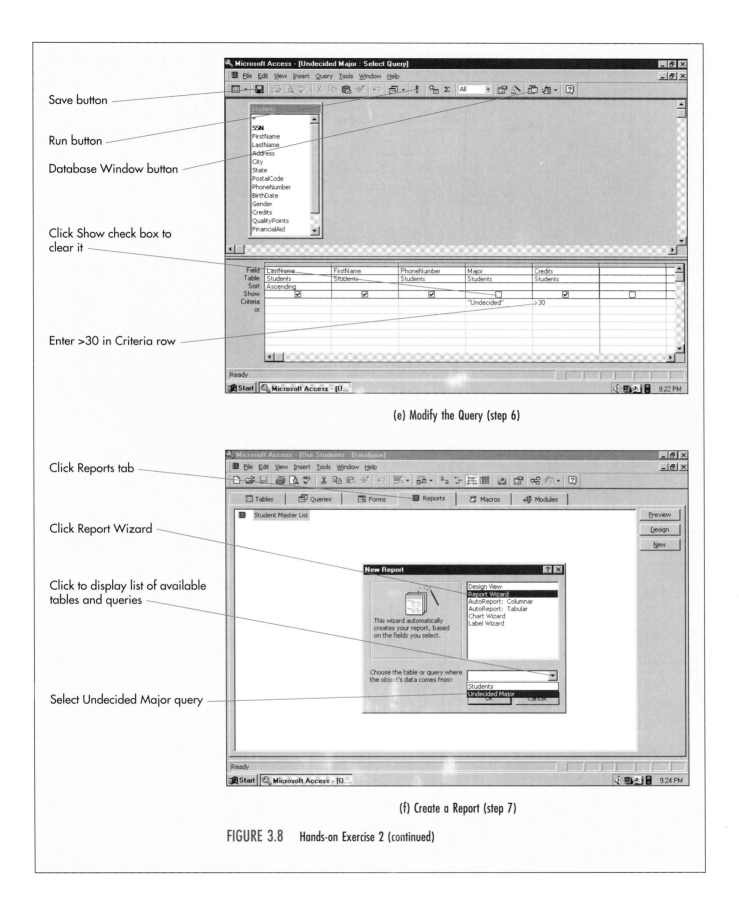

Save button

Run button

Database Window button

Click Show check box to clear it

Enter >30 in Criteria row

(e) Modify the Query (step 6)

Click Reports tab

Click Report Wizard

Click to display list of available tables and queries

Select Undecided Major query

(f) Create a Report (step 7)

FIGURE 3.8   Hands-on Exercise 2 (continued)

➤ You do not want to choose additional grouping levels. Click **Next** to move to the next screen.

➤ There is no need to specify a sort sequence. Click **Next.**

➤ The **Tabular layout** is selected, as is **Portrait orientation.** Be sure the box is checked to **Adjust field width so all fields fit on a page.** Click **Next.**

➤ Choose **Soft Gray** as the style. Click **Next.**

➤ If necessary, enter **Undecided Major** as the title for your report. The option button to **Preview the Report** is already selected. Click the **Finish command button** to exit the Report Wizard and view the report.

THE BACK BUTTON

The Back button is present on every screen within the Report Wizard and enables you to recover from mistakes or simply to change your mind about how you want the report to look. Click the Back button at any time to return to the previous screen, then click it again if you want to return to the screen before that, and continue, if necessary, all the way back to the beginning.

STEP 8: View the Report

➤ If necessary, click the **Maximize button** to see the completed report as shown in Figure 3.8g. Click the **Zoom button** to see the full page.

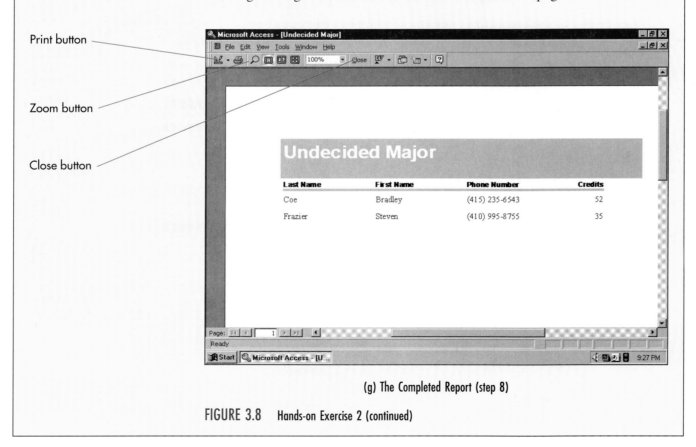

Print button

Zoom button

Close button

(g) The Completed Report (step 8)

FIGURE 3.8   Hands-on Exercise 2 (continued)

➤ Click the **Print button** to print the report and submit it to your instructor. Click the **Close button** to exit the Print Preview window.

➤ Click the **Close button** in the Report Design window.

➤ If necessary, click the **Database Window button** on the toolbar to return to the Database window. Click the **Maximize button**:

- Click the **Queries tab** to display the names of the queries in the Our Students database. You should see the *Undecided Major* query created in this exercise.

- Click the **Reports tab.** You should see two reports: *Student Master List* (created in the previous exercise) and *Undecided Major* (created in this exercise).

- Click the **Forms tab.** You should see the *Students* form corresponding to the form you created in Chapter 2.

- Click the **Tables tab.** You should see the *Students* table, which is the basis of all other objects in the database.

➤ Close the **Our Students database** and exit Access if you do not wish to continue with the next exercise. Click **Yes** if asked to save changes to any of the objects in the database.

DATABASE PROPERTIES

The tabs within the Database window display the objects within a database, but show only one type of object at a time. You can, for example, see all of the reports or all of the queries, but you cannot see the reports and queries at the same time. There is another way. Pull down the File menu, click Database Properties, then click the Contents tab to display the contents (objects) in the database. You cannot, however, use the Database Properties dialog box to open those objects.

GROUPING RECORDS

The records in a report are often grouped according to the value of a specific field. The report in Figure 3.9a, for example, groups students according to their major, sorts them alphabetically according to last name within each major, then calculates the average GPA for all students in each major. A group header appears before each group of students to identify the group and display the major. A group footer appears at the end of each group and displays the average GPA for students in that major

Figure 3.9b displays the Design view of the report in Figure 3.9a, which determines the appearance of the printed report. Look carefully at the design to relate each section to the corresponding portion of the printed report:

■ The report header contains the title of the report and appears once, at the beginning of the printed report.

■ The page header contains the column headings that appear at the top of each page. The column headings are labels (or unbound controls) and are formatted in bold.

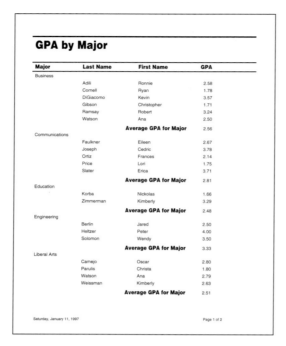
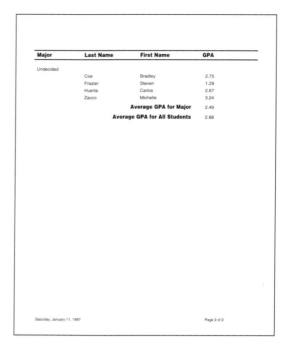

(a) The Printed Columnar Report

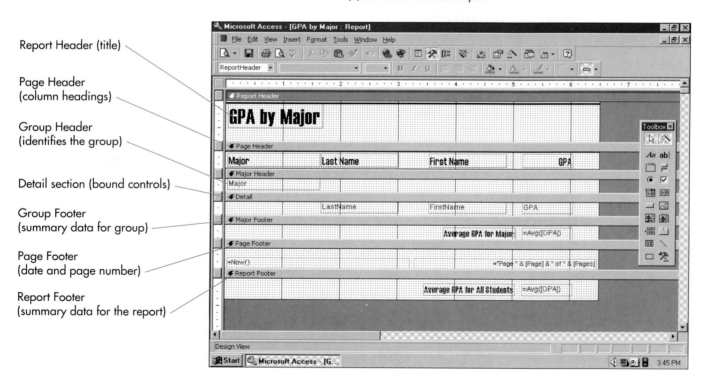

Report Header (title)

Page Header (column headings)

Group Header (identifies the group)

Detail section (bound controls)

Group Footer (summary data for group)

Page Footer (date and page number)

Report Footer (summary data for the report)

(b) Design View

FIGURE 3.9   Summary Reports

- The group header consists of a single bound control that displays the value of the major field prior to each group of detail records.
- The detail section consists of bound controls that appear directly under the corresponding heading in the page header. The detail section is printed once for each record in each group.

- The group footer appears after each group of detail records. It consists of an unbound control (Average GPA for Major:) followed by a calculated control that computes the average GPA for each group of students.
- The page footer appears at the bottom of each page and contains the date, page number, and total number of pages in the report.
- The report footer appears at the end of the report. It consists of an unbound control (Average GPA for All Students:) followed by a calculated control that computes the average GPA for all students.

Grouping records within a report enables you to perform calculations on each group of records as was done in the group footer of Figure 3.9. The calculations in our example made use of the *Avg function,* but other types of calculations are possible:

- The *Sum function* computes the total of a specific field for all records in the group.
- The *Min function* determines the minimum value for all records in the group.
- The *Max function* determines the maximum value for all records in the group.
- The *Count function* counts the number of records in the group.

The following exercise has you create the report in Figure 3.9. The report is based on a query containing a calculated control, GPA, which is computed by dividing the QualityPoints field by the Credits field. The Report Wizard is used to design the basic report, but additional modifications are necessary to create the group header and group footer.

HANDS-ON EXERCISE 3

Grouping Records

Objective: To create a query containing a calculated control, then create a report based on that query; to use the Sorting and Grouping command to add a group header and group footer to a report. Use Figure 3.10 as a guide.

STEP 1: Create the Query

➤ Start Access and open the **Our Students database** from the previous exercise.

➤ Click the **Queries tab** in the database window, then click the **New command button** to display the New Query dialog box. **Design View** is already selected as the means of creating a query. Click **OK** to begin creating the query.

➤ The Show Table dialog box appears; the **Tables tab** is already selected, as is the **Students table.**

➤ Click the **Add button** to add the table to the query (the field list should appear within the Query window). Click **Close** to close the Show Table dialog box.

➤ Click the **Maximize button** so that the window takes up the entire screen as shown in Figure 3.10a. Drag the border between the upper and lower portions of the window to give yourself more room in the upper portion. Make the field list larger, to display more fields at one time.

➤ Scroll (if necessary) within the field list, then click and drag the **Major field** from the field list to the query. Click and drag the **LastName, FirstName, QualityPoints,** and **Credits fields** (in that order) in similar fashion.

Click drop-down arrow and
Select Ascending

Click Sort row, then select
Ascending from drop-down list

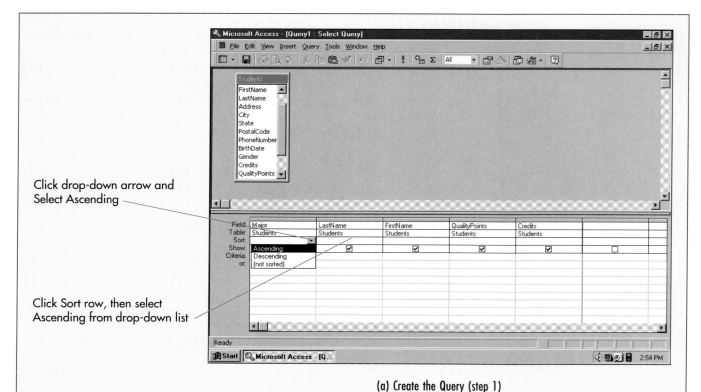

(a) Create the Query (step 1)

FIGURE 3.10   Hands-on Exercise 3

➤ Click the **Sort row** for the Major field. Click the **down arrow** to open the drop-down list box. Click **Ascending.**

➤ Click the **Sort row** for the LastName field. Click the **down arrow** to open the drop-down list box. Click **Ascending.**

SORTING ON MULTIPLE FIELDS

You can sort a query on more than one field, but you must be certain that the fields are in the proper order within the design grid. Access sorts from left to right (the leftmost field is the primary sort key), so the fields must be arranged in the desired sort sequence. To move a field within the design grid, click the column selector above the field name to select the column, then drag the column to its new position.

STEP 2: Add a Calculated Control

➤ Click in the first blank column in the Field row. Enter the expression **=[QualityPoints]/[Credits].** Do not be concerned if you cannot see the entire expression.

➤ Press **enter.** Access has substituted Expr1: for the equal sign you typed initially. Drag the **column selector boundary** so that the entire expression is visible as in Figure 3.10b. (You may have to make some of the columns narrower to see all of the fields in the design grid.)

➤ Pull down the **File menu** and click **Save** (or click the **Save button**) to display the dialog box in Figure 3.10b. Enter **GPA By Major** for the Query Name. Click **OK.**

USE DESCRIPTIVE NAMES

An Access database contains multiple objects—tables, forms, queries, and reports. It is important, therefore, that the name assigned to each object be descriptive of its function so that you can select the proper object from the Database window. The name of an object can contain up to 64 characters and can include any combination of letters, numbers, and spaces. (Names may not, however, include leading spaces, a period, an exclamation mark, or brackets ([ ]).

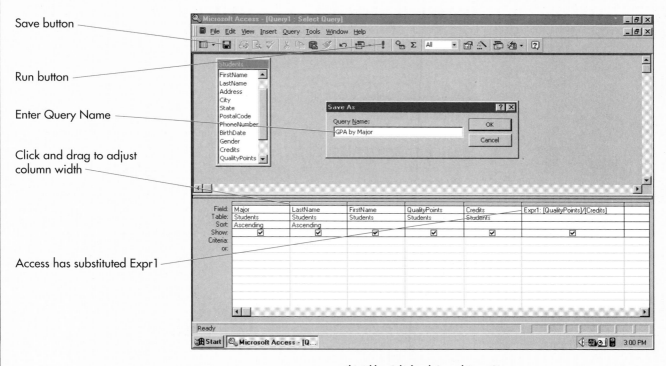

(b) Add a Calculated Control (step 2)

FIGURE 3.10   Hands-on Exercise 3 (continued)

STEP 3: Run the Query

➤ Pull down the **Query menu** and click **Run** (or click the **Run button** on the Query Design toolbar). You will see the dynaset in Figure 3.10c:

- Students are listed by major and alphabetically by last name within major.
- The GPA is calculated to several places (you may not even see the number to the left of the decimal) and appears in the Expr1 field.

➤ Click the **View button** in order to modify the query.

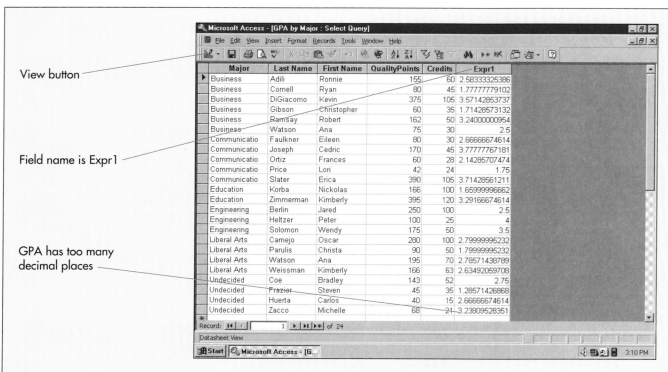

View button

Field name is Expr1

GPA has too many
decimal places

(c) Run the Query (step 3)

FIGURE 3.10   Hands-on Exercise 3 (continued)

ADJUST THE COLUMN WIDTH

Point to the right edge of the column you want to resize, then drag the
mouse in the direction you want to go; drag to the right to make the column wider or to the left to make it narrower. Alternatively, you can double click the column selector line (right edge) to fit the longest entry in
that column. Adjusting the column width in the Design view does not
affect the column width in the Datasheet view, but you can use the same
technique in both views.

STEP 4: Modify the Query

➤ Click and drag to select **Expr1** in the Field row for the calculated field. (Do
not select the colon). Type **GPA** to substitute a more meaningful field name.

➤ Point to the column and click the **right mouse button** to display a shortcut
menu. Click **Properties** to display the Field Properties dialog box in Figure
3.10d. Click the **General tab** if necessary:

• Click the **Description text box.** Enter **GPA** as shown in Figure 3.10d.

• Click the **Format text box.** Click the **drop-down arrow** to display the available formats. Click **Fixed.**

• Close the Field Properties dialog box.

➤ Click the **Save button** to save the modified query.

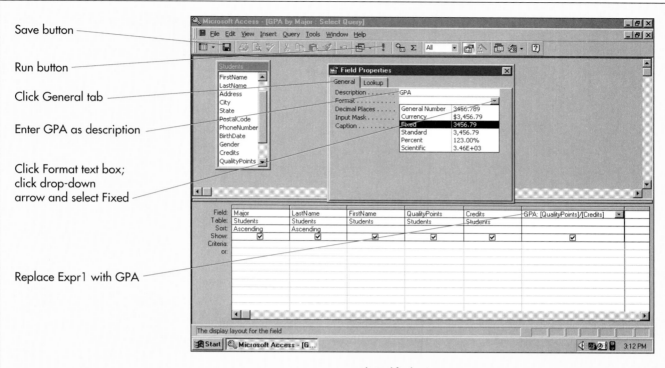

Save button

Run button

Click General tab

Enter GPA as description

Click Format text box;
click drop-down
arrow and select Fixed

Replace Expr1 with GPA

(d) Modify the Query (step 4)

FIGURE 3.10   Hands-on Exercise 3 (continued)

THE TOP VALUES PROPERTY

Can you create a query that lists only the five students with the highest or lowest GPA? It's easy, if you know about the Top Values property. First, sort the query according to the desired sequence—for example, students in descending order by GPA to see the students with the highest GPA. (Remove all other sort keys within the query.) Point anywhere in the gray area in the upper portion of the Query window, click the right mouse button to display a shortcut menu, then click Properties to display the Query Properties sheet. Click the Top Values box and enter the desired number of students (e.g., 5 for five students, or 5% for the top five percent). When you run the query you will see only the top five students. (You can see the bottom five instead if you specify ascending rather than descending as the sort sequence.)

STEP 5: Rerun the Query

➤ Click the **Run button** to run the modified query. You will see a new dynaset corresponding to the modified query as shown in Figure 3.10e. Resize the column widths (as necessary) within the dynaset.

• Students are still listed by major and alphabetically within major.

• The GPA is calculated to two decimal places and appears under the GPA field.

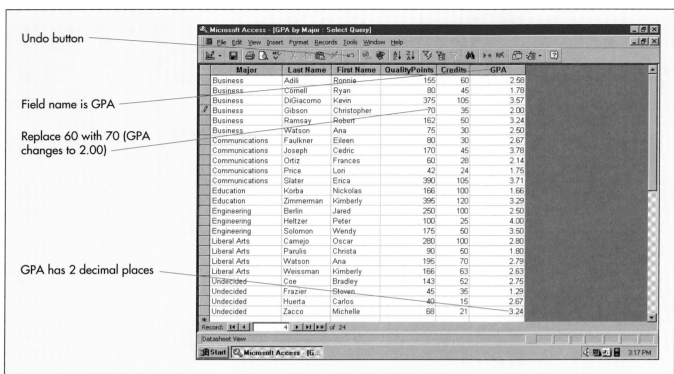

Undo button

Field name is GPA

Replace 60 with 70 (GPA changes to 2.00)

GPA has 2 decimal places

(e) Rerun the Query (step 5)

FIGURE 3.10 Hands-on Exercise 3 (continued)

➤ Click the **QualityPoints field** for Christopher Gibson. Replace 60 with **70**. Press **enter.** The GPA changes automatically to 2.

➤ Pull down the **Edit menu** and click **Undo Current Field/Record** (or click the **Undo button** on the Query toolbar). The GPA returns to its previous value.

➤ Tab to the **GPA field** for Christopher Gibson. Type **2.** Access will beep and prevent you from changing the GPA because it is a calculated field as indicated on the status bar.

➤ Click the **Close button** to close the query and return to the Database window. Click **Yes** if asked whether to save the changes.

THE DYNASET

A query represents a question and an answer. The question is developed by using the design grid in the Query Design view. The answer is displayed in a dynaset that contains the records that satisfy the criteria specified in the query. A dynaset looks and acts like a table but it isn't a table; it is a dynamic subset of a table that selects and sorts records as specified in the query. A dynaset is like a table in that you can enter a new record or modify or delete an existing record. It is dynamic because the changes made to the dynaset are automatically reflected in the underlying table.

STEP 6: The Report Wizard

➤ You should see the Database window. Click the **Reports tab,** then click the **New button** to create a report based on the query you just created. Select **Report Wizard** as the means of creating the report.

➤ Select **GPA By Major** from the drop-down list at the bottom of the dialog box. Click **OK** to begin the Report Wizard. You should see the Report Wizard dialog box, which displays all of the fields in the GPA by Major query.

  • Click the **Major field** in the Available fields list box. Click the **> button.**

  • Add the **LastName, FirstName,** and **GPA fields** one at a time.

  • Do not include the QualityPoints or Credits fields. Click **Next.**

➤ You should see the screen asking whether you want to group the fields. Click (select) the **Major field,** then click the **> button** to display the screen in Figure 3.10f. The Major field appears above the other fields to indicate that the records will be grouped according to the value of the Major field. Click **Next.**

➤ The next screen asks you to specify the order for the detail records. Click the **drop-down arrow** on the list box for the first field. Click **LastName** to sort the records alphabetically by last name within each major. Click **Next.**

➤ The **Stepped Option button** is already selected for the report layout, as is **Portrait orientation.** Be sure the box is checked to **Adjust field width so all fields fit on a page.** Click **Next.**

➤ Choose **Compact** as the style. Click **Next.**

➤ **GPA By Major** (which corresponds to the name of the underlying query) is already entered as the name of the report. Click the Option button to **Modify the report's design.** Click **Finish** to exit the Report Wizard.

Click Reports tab

Major field appears above other fields to indicate that records will be grouped by Major

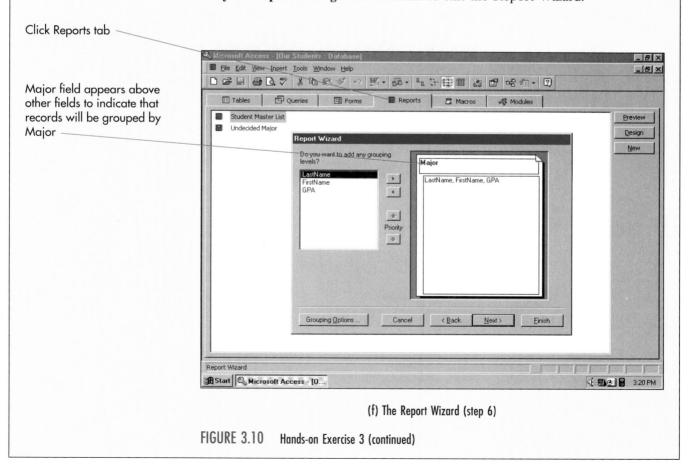

(f) The Report Wizard (step 6)

FIGURE 3.10   Hands-on Exercise 3 (continued)

STEP 7: Sorting and Grouping

➤ You should see the Report Design view as shown in Figure 3.10g. (The Sorting and Grouping dialog box is not yet visible.)

➤ Maximize the Report window (if necessary) so that you have more room in which to work.

➤ Move, size, and align the column headings and bound controls as shown in Figure 3.10g. We made GPA (label and bound control) smaller. We also moved FirstName (label and bound control) to the right.

➤ Pull down the **View menu.** Click **Sorting and Grouping** to display the Sorting and Grouping dialog box.

Save button

Click Group Footer property; click drop-down arrow and select Yes

Click and drag to extend Report Footer section

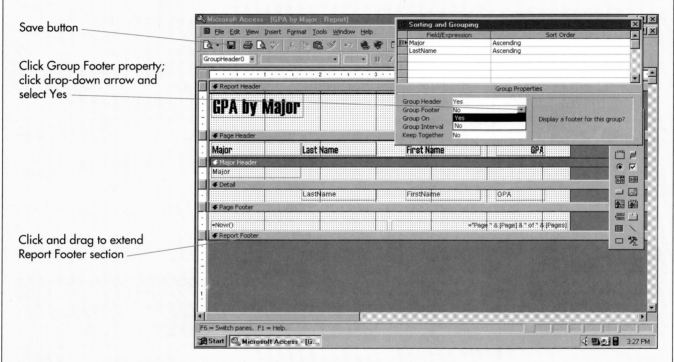

(g) Sorting and Grouping (step 7)

FIGURE 3.10   Hands-on Exercise 3 (continued)

SELECTING MULTIPLE CONTROLS

Select (click) a column heading in the page header, then press and hold the Shift key as you select the corresponding bound control in the Detail section. This selects both the column heading and the bound control and enables you to move and size the objects in conjunction with one another. Continue to work with both objects selected as you apply formatting through various buttons on the Formatting toolbar, or change properties through the property sheet. Click anywhere on the report to deselect the objects when you are finished.

➤ The **Major field** should already be selected. Click the **Group Footer** property, click the **drop-down arrow,** then click **Yes** to create a group footer for the Major field.

➤ Close the dialog box. The Major footer has been added to the report. Click the Save button to save the modified report.

STEP 8: Create the Group Footer

➤ Click the **Text Box button** on the Toolbox toolbar. The mouse pointer changes to a tiny crosshair with a text box attached.

➤ Click and drag in the group footer where you want the text box (which will contain the average GPA) to go. Release the mouse. You will see an Unbound control and an attached label containing a field number (e.g., Text 14).

➤ Click in the **text box** of the control (Unbound will disappear). Enter **=Avg(GPA)** to calculate the average of the GPA for all students in this group as shown in Figure 3.10h.

➤ Click in the attached unbound control, click and drag to select the text (Text14), then type **Average GPA for Major** as the label for this control. Size, move, and align the label as shown in the figure. (See the boxed tip on sizing or moving a control and its label.)

➤ Point to the **Average GPA control,** click the **right mouse button** to display a shortcut menu, then click **Properties** to display the Properties dialog box. If necessary, click the **All tab,** then scroll to the top of the list to view and/or modify the existing properties:

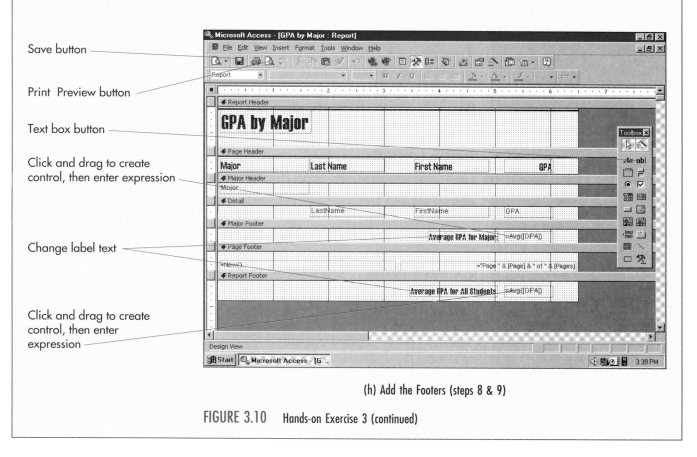

Save button

Print Preview button

Text box button

Click and drag to create control, then enter expression

Change label text

Click and drag to create control, then enter expression

(h) Add the Footers (steps 8 & 9)

FIGURE 3.10   Hands-on Exercise 3 (continued)

- The Control Source text box contains the entry =Avg([GPA]) from the preceding step.
- Click the **Name text box.** Replace the original name (e.g., Text14) with **Average GPA for Major.**
- Click the **Format box.** Click the **drop-down arrow** and select **Fixed.**
- Click the box for the **Decimal places.** Click the **drop-down arrow** and select (click) **2.**
- Close the Properties dialog box to accept these settings and return to the report.

➤ Click the **Save button** on the toolbar.

SIZING OR MOVING A BOUND CONTROL AND ITS LABEL

A bound control is created with an attached label. Select (click) the control, and the control has sizing handles and a move handle, but the label has only a move handle. Select the label (instead of the control), and the opposite occurs: the control has only a move handle, but the label will have both sizing handles and a move handle. To move a control and its label, click and drag the border of either object. To move either the control or its label (but not both), click and drag the move handle (a tiny square in the upper left corner) of the appropriate object. (Use the Undo command if the result is not what you expect; then try again.)

STEP 9: Create the Report Footer

➤ The report footer is created in similar fashion to the group footer. Click and drag the bottom of the report footer to extend the size of the footer as shown in Figure 3.10h.

➤ Click the **Text Box button** on the Toolbox toolbar, then click and drag in the report footer where you want the text box to go. Release the mouse. You will see an Unbound control and an attached label containing a field number (e.g., Text16).

➤ Click in the **text box** of the control (Unbound will disappear). Enter **=Avg(GPA)** to calculate the average of the grade point averages for all students in the report.

➤ Click in the attached label, click and drag to select the text (Text16), then type **Average GPA for All Students** as the label for this control. Move, size, and align the label appropriately.

➤ Size the text box, then format the control:
- Point to the control, click the **right mouse button** to display a shortcut menu, then click **Properties** to display the Properties dialog box. Change the properties to **Fixed Format** with **2 decimal places.** Change the name to **Average GPA for All Students.**
- Close the Properties dialog box to accept these settings and return to the report.

➤ Click the **Save button** on the toolbar.

SECTION PROPERTIES

Each section in a report has properties that control its appearance and behavior. Point to the section header, click the right mouse button to display a shortcut menu, then click Properties to display the property sheet and set the properties. You can hide the section by changing the Visible property to No. You can also change the Special Effect property to Raised or Sunken.

STEP 10: View the Report

➤ Click the **Print Preview button** to view the completed report as shown in Figure 3.10i. The status bar shows you are on page 1 of the report.

➤ Click the **Zoom button** to see the entire page. Click the **Zoom button** a second time to return to the higher magnification, which lets you read the report.

➤ Click the **Navigation button** to move to the next page (page 2). Click the **Navigation button** to return to page 1.

➤ Be sure that you are satisfied with the appearance of the report and that all controls align properly with their associated labels. If necessary, return to the Design view to modify the report.

➤ Pull down the **File menu** and click **Print** (or click the **Print button**) to display the Print dialog box. The **All option button** is already selected under Print Range. Click **OK** to print the report.

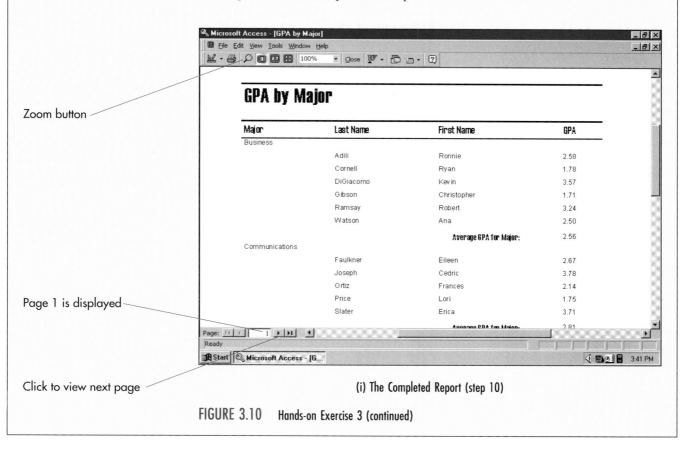

Zoom button

Page 1 is displayed

Click to view next page

(i) The Completed Report (step 10)

FIGURE 3.10   Hands-on Exercise 3 (continued)

THE BORDER PROPERTY

The Border property enables you to display a border around any type of control. Point to the control (in the Design view), click the right mouse button to display a shortcut menu, then click Properties to display the Properties dialog box. Select the Format tab, click the Border Style property, then choose the type of border you want (e.g., solid to display a border or transparent to suppress a border). Use the Border Color and Border Width properties to change the appearance of the border.

STEP 11: Exit Access

➤ Pull down the **File menu** and click **Close** to close the GPA by Major report. Click **Yes** if asked to save design changes to the report.

➤ Close the **Our Students database** and exit Access.

COMPACTING A DATABASE

The size of an Access database is quite large even if the database contains only a limited number of records. It is not surprising to see simple databases, such as the Our Students database in this chapter, grow to 500KB or more. You can, however, reduce the storage requirements by compacting the database, a practice we highly recommend. See the case study at the end of the chapter.

SUMMARY

Data and information are not synonymous. Data refers to a fact or facts about a specific record. Information is data that has been rearranged into a more useful format. Data may be viewed as the raw material, whereas information is the finished product.

A report is a printed document that displays information from the database. Reports are created through the Report Wizard, then modified as necessary in the Design view. A report is divided into sections. The report header (footer) occurs at the beginning (end) of the report. The page header (footer) appears at the top (bottom) of each page. The detail section is found in the main body of the report and is printed once for each record in the report.

Each section is comprised of objects known as controls. A bound control has a data source such as a field in the underlying table. An unbound control has no data source. A calculated control contains an expression. Controls are selected, moved, and sized the same way as any other Windows object.

Every report is based on either a table or a query. A report based on a table contains every record in that table. A report based on a query contains only the records satisfying the criteria in the query.

A query enables you to select records from a table (or from several tables), display the selected records in any order, and perform calculations on fields within the query. A select query is the most common type of query and is created using the design grid. A select query displays its output in a dynaset that can be used to update the data in the underlying table(s).

The records in a report are often grouped according to the value of a specific field within the record. A group header appears before each group to identify the group. A group footer appears at the end of each group and can be used to display the summary information about the group.

All objects (tables, forms, queries, and reports) in an Access database are named according to the same rules. The name can contain up to 64 characters (letters or numbers) and can include spaces. A form and/or a report can have the same name as the table or query on which it is based to emphasize the relationship between the two.

KEY WORDS AND CONCEPTS

AND condition	Dynaset	Relational operators
Ascending sequence	Field row	Report
Avg function	Group footer	Report footer
Between function	Group header	Report header
Bound control	Inheritance	Report Wizard
Calculated control	Label tool	Select query
Columnar report	Max function	Show row
Compacting	Min function	Sort row
Count function	NOT function	Sorting and Grouping
Criteria row	Now function	Sum function
Database Properties	OR condition	Tabular report
Datasheet view	Page footer	Text box tool
Descending sequence	Page header	Top Values property
Design grid	Print Preview	Unbound control
Design view	Query	Wild card
Detail section	Query window	

MULTIPLE CHOICE

1. Which of the following is a reason for basing a report on a query rather than a table?
   (a) To limit the report to selected records
   (b) To include a calculated field in the report
   (c) Both (a) and (b)
   (d) Neither (a) nor (b)

2. An Access database may contain:
   (a) One or more tables
   (b) One or more queries
   (c) One or more reports
   (d) All of the above

3. Which of the following is true regarding the names of objects within an Access database?
   (a) A form or report may have the same name as the underlying table
   (b) A form or report may have the same name as the underlying query
   (c) Both (a) and (b)
   (d) Neither (a) nor (b)

4. The dynaset created by a query may contain:
   (a) A subset of records from the associated table but must contain all of the fields for the selected records
   (b) A subset of fields from the associated table but must contain all of the records
   (c) Both (a) and (b)
   (d) Neither (a) nor (b)

5. Which toolbar contains a button to display the properties of a selected object?
   (a) The Query Design toolbar
   (b) The Report Design toolbar
   (c) Both (a) and (b)
   (d) Neither (a) nor (b)

6. Which of the following does *not* have both a Design view and a Datasheet view?
   (a) Tables
   (b) Forms
   (c) Queries
   (d) Reports

7. Which of the following is true regarding the wild card character within Access?
   (a) A question mark stands for a single character in the same position as the question mark
   (b) An asterisk stands for any number of characters in the same position as the asterisk
   (c) Both (a) and (b)
   (d) Neither (a) nor (b)

8. Which of the following will print at the top of every page?
   (a) Report header
   (b) Group header
   (c) Both (a) and (b)
   (d) Neither (a) nor (b)

9. A query, based on the Our Students database within the chapter, contains two fields from the Student table (QualityPoints and Credits) as well as a calculated field (GPA). Which of the following is true?
   (a) Changing the value of Credits or QualityPoints in the query's dynaset automatically changes these values in the underlying table
   (b) Changing the value of GPA automatically changes its value in the underlying table
   (c) Both (a) and (b)
   (d) Neither (a) nor (b)

10. Which of the following must be present in every report?
    (a) A report header and a report footer
    (b) A page header and a page footer
    (c) Both (a) and (b)
    (d) Neither (a) nor (b)

11. Which of the following may be included in a report as well as in a form?
    (a) Bound control
    (b) Unbound control
    (c) Calculated control
    (d) All of the above

12. The navigation buttons ▶ and ◀ will:
    (a) Move to the next or previous record in a table
    (b) Move to the next or previous page in a report
    (c) Both (a) and (b)
    (d) Neither (a) nor (b)

13. Assume that you created a query based on an Employee table, and that the query contains fields for Location and Title. Assume further that there is a single criteria row and that New York and Manager have been entered under the Location and Title fields, respectively. The dynaset will contain:
    (a) All employees in New York
    (b) All managers
    (c) Only the managers in New York
    (d) All employees in New York and all managers

14. You have decided to modify the query from the previous question to include a second criteria row. The Location and Title fields are still in the query, but this time New York and Manager appear in *different* criteria rows. The dynaset will contain:
    (a) All employees in New York
    (b) All managers
    (c) Only the managers in New York
    (d) All employees in New York and all managers

15. Which of the following is true about a query that lists employees by city and alphabetically within city?
    (a) The design grid should specify a descending sort on both city and employee name
    (b) The City field should appear to the left of the employee name in the design grid
    (c) Both (a) and (b)
    (d) Neither (a) nor (b)

ANSWERS

1. c	**6.** d	**11.** d
2. d	**7.** c	**12.** c
3. c	**8.** d	**13.** c
4. d	**9.** a	**14.** d
5. d	**10.** d	**15.** b

1. Use the Our Students database as the basis for the following queries and reports:

   a. Create a select query for students on the Dean's List (GPA >= 3.50). Include the student's name, major, quality points, credits, and GPA. List the students alphabetically.

   b. Use the Report Wizard to prepare a tabular report based on the query in part a. Include your name in the report header as the academic advisor.

   c. Create a select query for students on academic probation (GPA < 2.00). Include the same fields as the query in part a. List the students in alphabetical order.

   d. Use the Report Wizard to prepare a tabular report similar to the report in part b.

   e. Print both reports and submit them to your instructor as proof that you did this exercise.

2. Use the Employee database in the Exploring Access folder to create the reports listed below. (This is the same database that was used earlier in Chapters 1 and 2.)

   a. A report containing all employees in sequence by location and alphabetically within location. Show the employee's last name, first name, location, title, and salary. Include summary statistics to display the total salaries in each location as well as for the company as a whole.

   b. A report containing all employees in sequence by title and alphabetically within title. Show the employee's last name, first name, location, title, and salary. Include summary statistics to show the average salary for each title as well as the average salary in the company.

   c. Add your name to the report header in the report so that your instructor will know the reports came from you. Print both reports and submit them to your instructor.

3. Use the United States database in the Exploring Access folder to create the report shown in Figure 3.11. (This is the same database that was used in Chapters 1 and 2.) The report lists states by geographic region, and alphabetically within region. It includes a calculated field, Population Density, which is computed by dividing a state's population by its area. Summary statistics are also required as shown in the report.

   Note that the report header contains a map of the United States that was taken from the Microsoft Clip Gallery. The instructions for inserting an object can be found on page 81 in conjunction with an earlier problem. Be sure to include your name in the report footer so that your instructor will know that the report comes from you.

4. Use the Bookstore database in the Exploring Access folder to create the report shown in Figure 3.12. (This is the same database that was used in the hands-on exercises in Chapter 1.)

   The report header in Figure 3.12 contains a graphic object that was taken from the Microsoft Clip Gallery. You are not required to use this specific image, but you are required to insert a graphic. The instructions for inserting an object can be found on page 81 in conjunction with an earlier problem. Be sure to include your name in the report header so that your instructor will know that the report comes from you.

United States By Region

Region	Name	Capital	Population	Area	Population Density
Middle Atlantic					
	Delaware	Dover	666,168	2,057	323.85
	Maryland	Annapolis	4,781,468	10,577	452.06
	New Jersey	Trenton	7,730,188	7,836	986.50
	New York	Albany	17,990,455	49,576	362.89
	Pennsylvania	Harrisburg	11,881,643	45,333	262.10
	Total for Region:		43,049,922	115,379	
	Average for Region:		8,609,984.40	23,075.80	477.48
Mountain					
	Arizona	Phoenix	3,665,228	113,909	32.18
	Colorado	Denver	3,294,394	104,247	31.60
	Idaho	Boise	1,006,749	83,557	12.05
	Montana	Helena	799,065	147,138	5.43
	Nevada	Carson City	1,201,833	110,540	10.87
	New Mexico	Santa Fe	1,515,069	121,666	12.45
	Utah	Salt Lake City	1,722,850	84,916	20.29
	Wyoming	Cheyenne	453,588	97,914	4.63
	Total for Region:		13,658,776	863,887	
	Average for Region:		1,707,347.00	107,985.88	16.19
New England					
	Connecticut	Hartford	3,287,116	5,009	656.24
	Maine	Augusta	1,227,928	33,215	36.97
	Massachusetts	Boston	6,016,425	8,257	728.65
	New	Concord	1,109,252	9,304	119.22
	Rhode Island	Providence	1,003,464	1,214	826.58
	Vermont	Montpellier	562,758	9,609	58.57
	Total for Region:		13,206,943	66,608	
	Average for Region:		2,201,157.17	11,101.33	404.37

Saturday, January 11, 1997   Page 1 of 3

FIGURE 3.11   Screen for Practice Exercise 3

University of Miami Book Store

Publisher	ISBN Number	Author	Title	List Price
IDG Books Worldwide				
	1-56884-453-0	Livingston/Straub	Windows 95 Secrets	$39.95
			Number of Books:	1
			Average List Price:	$39.95
Macmillan Publishing				
	1-56686-127-6	Rosch	The Hardware Bible	$35.00
			Number of Books:	1
			Average List Price:	$35.00
MIS Press				
	1-55828-353-6	Banks	Welcome to CompuServe	$24.95
			Number of Books:	1
			Average List Price:	$24.95
New Riders Publishing				
	1-56205-306-X	Maxwell/Grycz	New Riders Internet Yellow Pages	$29.95
			Number of Books:	1
			Average List Price:	$29.95
Osborne-McGraw Hill				
	0-07-882023-5	Hahn/Stout	The Internet Yellow Pages	$27.95
	0-07-881980-6	Hahn/Stout	The Internet Complete Reference	$29.95
			Number of Books:	2
			Average List Price:	$28.95
Prentice Hall				
	0-13-754235-6	Grauer/Barber	Exploring PowerPoint 97	$30.95
	0-13-065541-4	Grauer/Barber	Exploring Windows 3.1	$24.95

Saturday, January 11, 1997   Page 1 of 2

FIGURE 3.12   Screen for Practice Exercise 4

Super Bowl

http://www.nfl.com

Year	AFC Team	AFC Score	NFC Team	NFC Score
1997	New England	21	Green Bay	35
1996	Pittsburgh	17	Dallas	27
1995	San Diego	26	San Francisco	49
1994	Buffalo	13	Dallas	30
1993	Buffalo	17	Dallas	52
1992	Buffalo	24	Washington	37
1991	Buffalo	19	Giants	20
1990	Denver	10	San Francisco	55
1989	Cincinnati	16	San Francisco	20
1988	Denver	10	Washington	42
1987	Denver	20	Giants	39
1986	New England	10	Chicago	46
1985	Miami	16	San Francisco	38
1984	Los Angeles	38	Washington	9
1983	Miami	17	Washington	27
1982	Cincinnati	21	San Francisco	26
1981	Oakland	27	Philadelphia	10
1980	Pittsburgh	31	Los Angeles	19
1979	Pittsburgh	35	Dallas	31
1978	Denver	10	Dallas	27
1977	Oakland	32	Minnesota	14
1976	Pittsburgh	21	Dallas	17
1975	Pittsburgh	16	Minnesota	6
1974	Miami	24	Minnesota	7
1973	Miami	14	Washington	7
1972	Miami	3	Dallas	24
1971	Baltimore	16	Dallas	13

Saturday, January 11, 1997   Page 1 of 2

FIGURE 3.13   Screen for Practice Exercise 5

5. Use the Super Bowl database in the Exploring Access folder to create the report in Figure 3.13, which lists the participants and scores in every game played to date. It also displays the Super Bowl logo, which we downloaded from the home page of the NFL (www.nfl.com). Be sure to include your name in the report footer so that your instructor will know that the report comes from you. (See the Super Bowl case study for suggestions on additional reports or queries that you can create from this database.)

6. There are many sources of help for Access as well as every Office application. You can use the regular Help facility or you can go to the Microsoft web site to obtain the latest information. Start Access, pull down the Help menu, click Microsoft on the Web, then click online support to go to the home page for Microsoft Access. Explore the various options that are available, then write a short summary of your findings and submit it to your instructor as proof you did this exercise. Figure 3.14 displays the feature articles that were available when this book went to press and provides an indication of what you can expect to find.

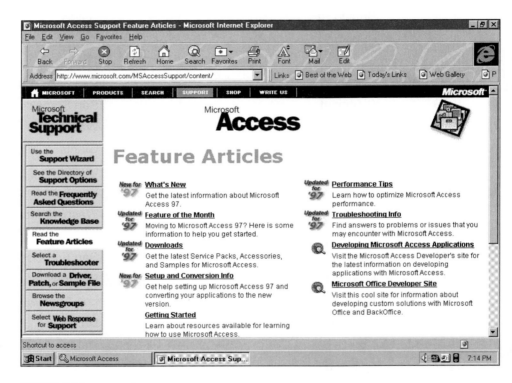

FIGURE 3.14   Screen for Practice Exercise 6

CASE STUDIES

The Fortune 500

Research the Fortune 500 (or a similar list) to obtain the gross revenue and net income for the present and previous year for the 20 largest corporations. Create an Access database to hold a table for this data and an associated form to enter the data. Validate your data carefully, then produce at least three reports based on the data. An alternative to entering the data manually is to use your favorite search engine to locate the home page of *Fortune* magazine. Once there, you will find a link to the *Fortune 500*, from where you can download an Excel workbook with current information. You then have to copy that information into an Access table. (Use online Help to find out how.)

The United States of America

What is the total population of the United States? What is its area? Can you name the 13 original states or the last five states admitted to the Union? Do you know the 10 states with the highest population or the five largest states in terms of area? Which states have the highest population density (people per square mile)?

The answers to these and other questions can be obtained from the United States database that is available on the data disk. The key to the assignment is to use the Top Values property within a query that limits the number of records returned in the dynaset. Use the database to create several reports that you think will be of interest to the class.

The Super Bowl (continued)

How many times has the NFC won the Super Bowl? When was the last time the AFC won? What was the largest margin of victory? What was the closest game? What is the most points scored by two teams in one game? How many times have the Miami Dolphins appeared? How many times did they win? Use the data in the Super Bowl database to create a trivia sheet on the Super Bowl, then incorporate your analysis into a letter addressed to NBC Sports. Convince them you are a super fan and that you merit two tickets to next year's game. Go to the home page of the National Football League (www.nfl.com) to obtain score(s) from the most recent game(s) to update our table if necessary.

Mail Merge

A mail merge takes the tedium out of sending form letters, as it creates the same letter many times, changing the name, address, and other information as appropriate from letter to letter. The form letter is created in a word processor (e.g., Microsoft Word), but the data file may be taken from an Access table or query. Use the Our Students database as the basis for two different form letters sent to two different groups of students. The first letter is to congratulate students on the Dean's list (GPA of 3.50 or higher). The second letter is a warning to students on academic probation (GPA of less than 2.00).

Compacting versus Compressing

An Access database becomes fragmented, and thus unnecessarily large, as objects (e.g., reports and forms) are modified or deleted. It is important, therefore, to periodically compact a database to reduce its size (enabling you to back it up on a floppy disk). Choose a database with multiple objects; e.g., the Our Students database used in this chapter. Use the Windows Explorer to record the file size of the database as it presently exists. Start Access, open the database, pull down the Tools menu and select Database Utilities to compact the database, then record the size of the database after compacting. You can also compress a compacted database (using a standard Windows utility such as WinZip) to further reduce the requirement for disk storage. Summarize your findings in a short report to your instructor. Try compacting and compressing at least two different databases to better appreciate these techniques.

4

ONE-TO-MANY RELATIONSHIPS: SUBFORMS AND MULTIPLE TABLE QUERIES

OBJECTIVES

After reading this chapter you will be able to:

1. Explain how a one-to-many relationship is essential in the design of a database; differentiate between a primary key and a foreign key.

2. Use the Relationships window to implement a one-to-many relationship within an Access database.

3. Define referential integrity; explain how the enforcement of referential integrity maintains consistency within a database.

4. Distinguish between a main form and a subform; explain how a subform is used in conjunction with a one-to-many relationship.

5. Create a query based on multiple tables, then create a report based on that query.

6. Create a main form containing two subforms linked to one another

OVERVIEW

The Our Students database in earlier chapters presented the different types of objects in an Access database: tables, forms, queries, and reports. It was, however, a simple database because it contained only one table. The real power of Access stems from its use as a relational database, which contains multiple tables.

This chapter presents a new case study that focuses on a relational database. The case is that of a consumer loan system within a bank. The database contains two tables, one for customers and one for loans. There is a one-to-many relationship between the tables, in that one customer can have many loans, but a loan is tied to only one customer.

The case solution includes a discussion of database concepts. It reviews the definition of a primary key and explains how the primary key of one table exists as a foreign key in a related table. It also introduces the concept of referential integrity, which ensures that the tables within the database are consistent with one another. And most important, it shows how to implement these concepts in an Access database.

The chapter builds on what you already know by expanding the earlier material on forms, queries, and reports. It describes how to create a main form and a corresponding subform that contains data from a related table. It develops a query that contains data from multiple tables, then creates a report based on that query.

Suffice it to say that this is a critically important chapter because it is built around a relational database, as opposed to a single table. Thus, when you complete the chapter, you will have a much better appreciation of what can be accomplished within Access. As always, the hands-on exercises are essential to your understanding of the material.

CASE STUDY: CONSUMER LOANS

Let us assume that you are in the Information Systems department of a commercial bank and are assigned the task of implementing a system for consumer loans. The bank needs complete data about every loan (the amount, interest rate, term, and so on). It also needs data about the customers holding those loans (name, address, telephone, etc.)

The problem is how to structure the data so that the bank will be able to obtain all of the information it needs from its database. The system must be able to supply the name and address of the person associated with a loan. The system must also be able to retrieve all of the loans for a specific individual.

The solution calls for a database with two tables, one for loans and one for customers. To appreciate the elegance of this approach, consider first a single table containing a combination of loan and customer data as shown in Figure 4.1. At first glance this solution appears to be satisfactory. You can, for example, search for a specific loan (e.g., L022) and determine that Lori Sangastiano is the customer associated with that loan. You can also search for a particular customer (e.g., Michelle Zacco) and find all of her loans (L028, L030, and L060).

There is a problem, however, in that the table duplicates customer data throughout the database. Thus, when one customer has multiple loans, the customer's name, address, and other data are stored multiple times. Maintaining the data in this form is a time-consuming and error-prone procedure, because any change to the customer's data has to be made in many places.

A second problem arises when you enter data for a new customer that occurs before a loan has been approved. The bank receives the customer's application data prior to granting a loan, and it wants to retain the customer data even if a loan is turned down. Adding a customer to the database in Figure 4.1 is awkward, however, because it requires the creation of a "dummy" loan record to hold the customer data.

The deletion (payoff) of a loan creates a third type of problem. What happens, for example, when Ted Myerson pays off loan L020? The loan record would be deleted, but so too would Ted's data as he has no other outstanding loans. The bank might want to contact Mr. Myerson about another loan in the future, but it would lose his data with the deletion of the existing loan.

The database in Figure 4.2 represents a much better design because it eliminates all three problems. It uses two different tables, a Loans table and a Customers table. Each record in the Loans table has data about a specific loan (LoanID, Date, Amount, Interest Rate, Term, Type, and CustomerID). Each record in the Customers table has data about a specific customer (CustomerID, First Name, Last Name, Address, City, State, Zip Code, and Phone Number). Each record in the Loans table is associated with a matching record in the Cus-

LoanID	Loan Data (Date, Amount, Interest Rate...)	Customer Data (First Name, Last Name, Address...)
L001	Loan Data for Loan L001	Customer data for Wendy Solomon
L004	Loan Data for Loan L004	Customer data for Wendy Solomon
L010	Loan Data for Loan L010	Customer data for Alex Rey
L014	Loan Data for Loan L014	Customer data for Wendy Solomon
L020	Loan Data for Loan L020	Customer data for Matt Hirsch
L022	Loan Data for Loan L022	Customer data for Lori Sangastiano
L026	Loan Data for Loan L026	Customer data for Matt Hirsch
L028	Loan Data for Loan L028	Customer data for Michelle Zacco
L030	Loan Data for Loan L030	Customer data for Michelle Zacco
L031	Loan Data for Loan L031	Customer data for Eileen Faulkner
L032	Loan Data for Loan L032	Customer data for Scott Wit
L033	Loan Data for Loan L033	Customer data for Alex Rey
L039	Loan Data for Loan L039	Customer data for David Powell
L040	Loan Data for Loan L040	Customer data for Matt Hirsch
L047	Loan Data for Loan L047	Customer data for Benjamin Grauer
L049	Loan Data for Loan L049	Customer data for Eileen Faulkner
L052	Loan Data for Loan L052	Customer data for Eileen Faulkner
L053	Loan Data for Loan L053	Customer data for Benjamin Grauer
L054	Loan Data for Loan L054	Customer data for Scott Wit
L057	Loan Data for Loan L057	Customer data for Benjamin Grauer
L060	Loan Data for Loan L060	Customer data for Michelle Zacco
L062	Loan Data for Loan L062	Customer data for Matt Hirsch
L100	Loan Data for Loan L100	Customer data for Benjamin Grauer
L109	Loan Data for Loan L109	Customer data for Wendy Solomon
L120	Loan Data for Loan L120	Customer data for Lori Sangastiano

FIGURE 4.1   Single Table Solution

tomers table through the CustomerID field common to both tables. This solution may seem complicated, but it is really quite simple and elegant.

Consider, for example, how easy it is to change a customer's address. If Michelle Zacco were to move, you would go into the Customers table, find her record (Customer C08), and make the necessary change. You would not have to change any of the records in the Loans table, because they do not contain customer data, but only a CustomerID that indicates who the customer is. In other words, you would change Michelle's address in only one place, and the change would be automatically reflected for every associated loan.

The addition of a new customer is done directly in the Customers table. This is much easier than the approach of Figure 4.1, which required an existing loan in order to add a new customer. And finally, the deletion of an existing loan is also easier than with the single table organization. A loan can be deleted from the Loans table without losing the corresponding customer data.

The database in Figure 4.2 is composed of two tables in which there is a **one-to-many relationship** between customers and loans. One customer (Michelle Zacco) can have many loans (Loan numbers L028, L030, and L060), but a specific loan (L028) is associated with only one customer (Michelle Zacco). The tables are related to one another by a common field (CustomerID) that is present in both the Customers and the Loans table.

Access enables you to create the one-to-many relationship between the tables, then uses that relationship to answer questions about the database. It can retrieve information about a specific loan, such as the name and address of the customer holding that loan. It can also find all of the loans for a particular customer, as illustrated in the queries that follow.

LoanID	Date	Amount	Interest Rate	Term	Type	CustomerID
L001	1/15/97	$475,000	6.90%	15	M	C04
L004	1/23/97	$35,000	7.20%	5	C	C04
L010	1/25/97	$10,000	5.50%	3	C	C05
L014	1/31/97	$12,000	9.50%	10	O	C04
L020	2/8/97	$525,000	6.50%	30	M	C06
L022	2/12/97	$10,500	7.50%	5	O	C07
L026	2/15/97	$35,000	6.50%	5	O	C10
L028	2/20/97	$250,000	8.80%	30	M	C08
L030	2/21/97	$5,000	10.00%	3	O	C08
L031	2/28/97	$200,000	7.00%	15	M	C01
L032	3/1/97	$25,000	10.00%	3	C	C02
L033	3/1/97	$20,000	9.50%	5	O	C05
L039	3/3/97	$56,000	7.50%	5	C	C09
L040	3/10/97	$129,000	8.50%	15	M	C10
L047	3/11/97	$200,000	7.25%	15	M	C03
L049	3/21/97	$150,000	7.50%	15	M	C01
L052	3/22/97	$100,000	7.00%	30	M	C01
L053	3/31/97	$15,000	6.50%	3	O	C03
L054	4/1/97	$10,000	8.00%	5	C	C02
L057	4/15/97	$25,000	8.50%	4	C	C03
L060	4/18/97	$41,000	9.90%	4	C	C08
L062	4/22/97	$350,000	7.50%	15	M	C10
L100	5/1/97	$150,000	6.00%	15	M	C03
L109	5/3/97	$350,000	8.20%	30	M	C04
L120	5/8/97	$275,000	9.20%	15	M	C07

(a) Loans Table

CustomerID	First Name	Last Name	Address	City	State	Zip Code	Phone Number
C01	Eileen	Faulkner	7245 NW 8 Street	Minneapolis	MN	55346	(612) 894-1511
C02	Scott	Wit	5660 NW 175 Terrace	Baltimore	MD	21224	(410) 753-0345
C03	Benjamin	Grauer	10000 Sample Road	Coral Springs	FL	33073	(305) 444-5555
C04	Wendy	Solomon	7500 Reno Road	Houston	TX	77090	(713) 427-3104
C05	Alex	Rey	3456 Main Highway	Denver	CO	80228	(303) 555-6666
C06	Ted	Myerson	6545 Stone Street	Chapel Hill	NC	27515	(919) 942-7654
C07	Lori	Sangastiano	4533 Aero Drive	Santa Rosa	CA	95403	(707) 542-3411
C08	Michelle	Zacco	488 Gold Street	Gainesville	FL	32601	(904) 374-5660
C09	David	Powell	5070 Battle Road	Decatur	GA	30034	(301) 345-6556
C10	Matt	Hirsch	777 NW 67 Avenue	Fort Lee	NJ	07624	(201) 664-3211

(b) Customers Table

FIGURE 4.2   Multiple Table Solution

Query: What are the name, address, and phone number of the customer associated with loan number L010?

Answer: Alex Rey, at 3456 Main Highway is the customer associated with loan L010. His phone number is (303) 555-6666.

To determine the answer, Access searches the Loans table for loan L010 to obtain the CustomerID (C05 in this example). It then searches the Customers table for the customer with the matching CustomerID and retrieves the name, address, and phone number. Consider a second example:

Query: What loans are associated with Wendy Solomon?

Answer: Wendy Solomon has four loans: loan L001 for $475,000, loan L004 for $35,000, loan L014 for $12,000, and loan L109 for $350,000.

This time Access begins in the Customers table and searches for Wendy Solomon to determine the CustomerID (C04). It then searches the Loans table for all records with a matching CustomerID.

PEDAGOGY VERSUS REALITY

Our design requires that the CustomerID and LoanID begin with the letters C and L, respectively, to emphasize the tables in which these fields are found and to facilitate data entry in the hands-on exercises. This convention places artificial limits on the number of customers and loans at 100 and 1000, respectively. (CustomerID goes from C00 to C99, and LoanID goes from L000 to L999.)

Implementation in Access

An Access database contains multiple tables. Each table stores data about a specific subject, such as customers or loans. Each table has a ***primary key,*** which is a field (or combination of fields) that uniquely identifies each record. CustomerID is the primary key in the Customers table. LoanID is the primary key in the Loans table.

A one-to-many relationship uses the primary key of the "one" table as a ***foreign key*** in the "many" table, and it is through the foreign key that the relationship is established. (A foreign key is simply the primary key of the related table.) The CustomerID appears in both the Customers table and the Loans table. It is the primary key in the Customers table, where its values are unique; it is a foreign key in the Loans table, where its values are not unique. Thus, multiple records in the Loans table can have the same CustomerID to implement the one-to-many relationship between customers and loans.

To create a one-to-many relationship, you open the ***Relationships window*** in Figure 4.3 and add the necessary tables. You then drag the field on which the relationship is built, from the field list of the "one" table (Customers) to the matching field in the ***related table*** (Loans). Once the relationship has been established, you will see a ***relationship line*** connecting the tables, which indicates the "one" and "many" sides of the relationship. The line extends from the primary key in the "one" table to the foreign key in the "many" table and uses the symbols 1 and ∞, respectively.

RELATED FIELDS AND DATA TYPES

The related fields must have the same data type—both text or both number. In addition, number fields must also have the same field size. The exception is an AutoNumber field in the primary table, which is related to a Number field with a Long Integer field size in the related table. AutoNumber fields are discussed in the next chapter.

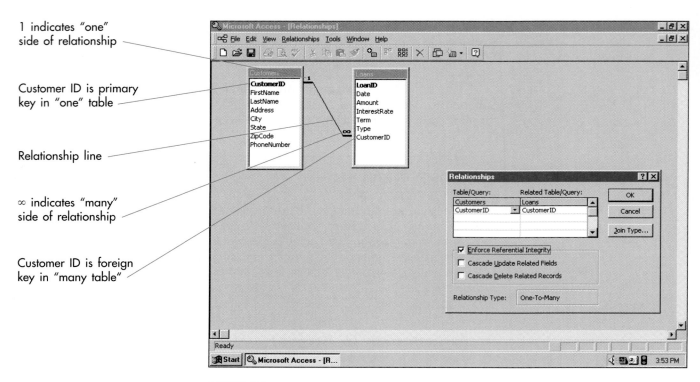

1 indicates "one" side of relationship

Customer ID is primary key in "one" table

Relationship line

∞ indicates "many" side of relationship

Customer ID is foreign key in "many table"

FIGURE 4.3   The Relationships Window

Referential Integrity

Referential integrity ensures that the records in related tables are consistent with one another. When enforcement of referential integrity is in effect, Access will prevent you from adding a record to the related table if that record contains an invalid foreign key. In other words, you cannot add a record to the Loans table if that record contains an invalid customer number. (Access will, however, let you leave the customer number blank unless it is specified as a required field or another validation rule is in effect.)

Enforcement of referential integrity will also prevent you from deleting a record in the primary (Customers) table if there is a corresponding record in the related (Loans) table. (Thus, to delete a customer, you would first have to delete all loans for that customer.) In similar fashion, you cannot change the primary key of a Customer record when there are matching Loan records. (These restrictions are relaxed if you check the Cascade Delete Related Records or Cascade Update Related Fields option in the Relationships dialog box. These options are discussed further in the next chapter.)

HANDS-ON EXERCISE 1

One-to-Many Relationships

Objective: To create a one-to-many relationship between existing tables in a database; to demonstrate referential integrity between the tables in a one-to-many relationship. Use Figure 4.4 as a guide in the exercise.

STEP 1: Open the National Bank Database

➤ Start Access. Open the **National Bank database** in the **Exploring Access folder.** The database contains three tables: for Customers, Loans, and Payments. (The Payments table will be used later in the chapter.)

➤ Pull down the **Tools menu** and click **Relationships** to open the Relationships window as shown in Figure 4.4a. (The Customers and Loans tables are not yet visible.) If you do not see the Show Table dialog box, pull down the **Relationships menu** and click the **Show Table command.**

➤ The **Tables tab** is selected within the Show Table dialog box. Click (select) the **Customers table,** then click the **Add Command button** to add the table to the Relationships window.

➤ Click the **Loans table,** then click the **Add Command button** (or simply double click the **Loans table**) to add this table to the Relationships window.

➤ Do *not* add the Payments table at this time. Click the **Close button** to close the Show Table dialog box.

Click to maximize window

Customers and Loans tables are added to Relationships window

Click Loans table

Click Add button

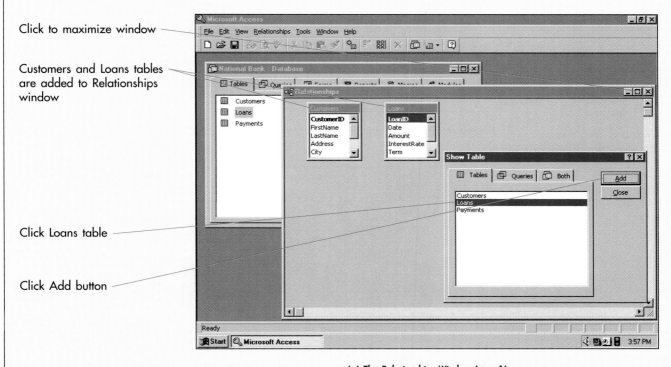

(a) The Relationships Window (step 1)

FIGURE 4.4   Hands-on Exercise 1

STEP 2: Create the Relationships

➤ Maximize the Relationships window so that you have more room in which to work. Point to the bottom border of the **Customers field list** (the mouse pointer changes to a double arrow), then click and drag the border until all of the fields are visible.

➤ Click and drag the bottom border of the **Loans field list** until all of the fields are visible.

➤ Click and drag the title bar of the **Loans field list** so that it is approximately one inch away from the Customers field list.

➤ Click and drag the **CustomerID field** in the Customers field list to the **CustomerID field** in the Loans field list. You will see the Relationships dialog box in Figure 4.4b.

➤ Check the **Enforce Referential Integrity** check box. (If necessary, clear the check boxes to Cascade Update Related Fields and Delete Related Records.)

➤ Click the **Create Command button** to establish the relationship and close the Relationships dialog box. You should see a line indicating a one-to-many relationship between the Customers and Loans tables.

THE RELATIONSHIPS ARE VISUAL

Access displays a relationship line between related tables to indicate the relationship between those tables. It uses the number 1 and the infinity symbol (∞) to indicate a one-to-many relationship in which referential integrity is enforced. The 1 appears at the end of the relationship line near the primary (one) table. The infinity symbol appears at the end nearest the related (many) table. Access shows the primary keys in each table in bold.

Click and drag title bar to move field list

Click and drag CustomerID to CustomerID field in Loans table

Click and drag bottom border until all fields are visible

Click check box to Enforce Referential Integrity

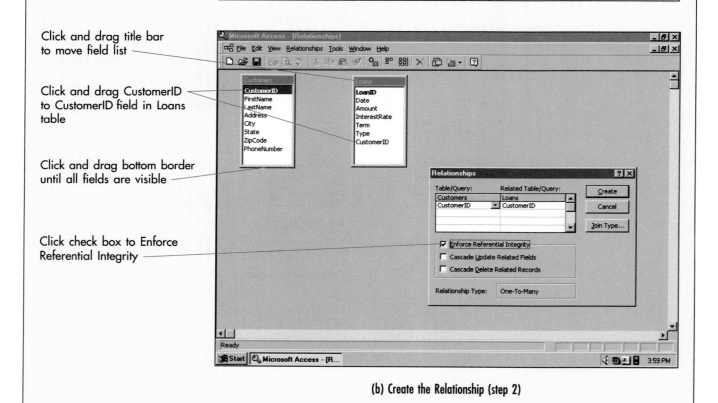

(b) Create the Relationship (step 2)

FIGURE 4.4   Hands-on Exercise 1 (continued)

STEP 3: Deleting a Relationship

➤ Point to the line indicating the relationship between the tables, then click the **right mouse button** to select the relationship and display a shortcut menu.

➤ Click the **Delete command.** You will see the dialog box in Figure 4.4c, asking whether you want to delete the relationship. Click **No** since you do *not* want to delete the relationship.

➤ Close the Relationships window. Click **Yes** when asked whether to save the layout changes.

Click to close Relationships window

Point to relationship line and click right mouse button to display shortcut menu

Click No

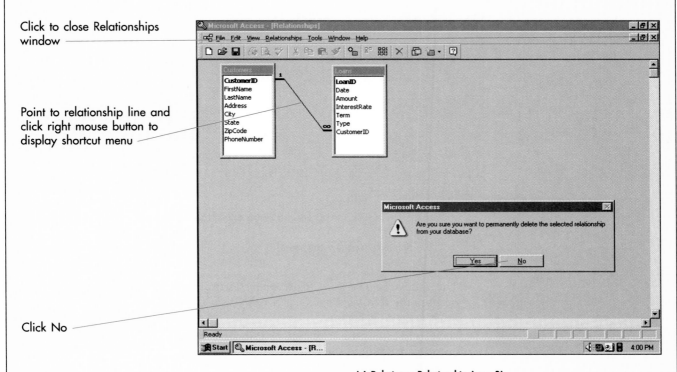

(c) Deleting a Relationship (step 3)

FIGURE 4.4   Hands-on Exercise 1 (continued)

STEP 4: Add a Customer Record

➤ The Database window is again visible with the Tables tab selected. Open the **Customers table.** If necessary, click the **Maximize button** to give yourself additional room when adding a record. Widen the fields as necessary to see the data.

➤ Click the **New Record button** on the toolbar. The record selector moves to the last record (record 11).

➤ Enter **C11** as the CustomerID as shown in Figure 4.4d. The record selector changes to a pencil as soon as you enter the first character.

➤ Enter data for yourself as the new customer. Data validation has been built into the Customers table, so you must enter the data correctly, or it will not be accepted.

• The message, *Customer ID must begin with the letter C followed by a two-digit number,* indicates that the CustomerID field is invalid.

New Record button

Database Window button

Enter C11 as Customer ID,
then enter data for yourself

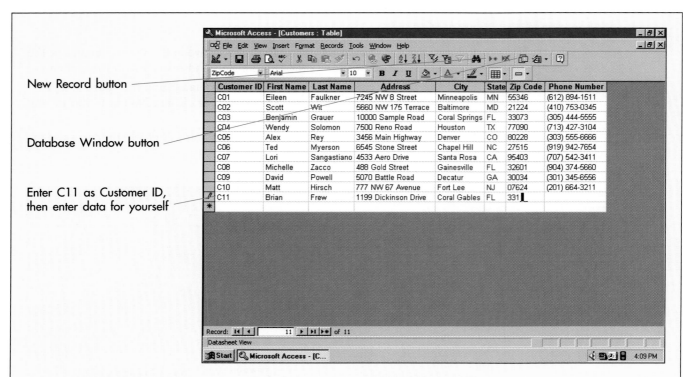

(d) Add a Customer Record (step 4)

FIGURE 4.4   Hands-on Exercise 1 (continued)

- The message, *The field 'Customers.LastName' can't contain a Null value because the Required property for this field is set to True*, indicates that you must enter a last name.
- A beep in either the ZipCode or PhoneNumber field indicates that you are entering a nonnumeric character.
- If you encounter a data validation error, press **Esc** (or Click **OK**), then reenter the data.

➤ Press **enter** when you have completed your record. Remember your CustomerID (C11) because you will need to enter it in the corresponding loan records.

THE RECORD SELECTOR

The record selector symbol indicates the status of the record. A triangle means the data in the current record has not changed. A pencil indicates you are in the process of entering (or changing) the data. An asterisk appears next to the blank record at the end of every table.

STEP 5: Add a Loan Record

➤ Click the **Database Window button** on the toolbar, then open the **Loans table.** Maximize the window containing the Loans table to give yourself additional room when adding a record.

➤ Click the **New Record button** on the toolbar. The record selector moves to the blank record at the end of the table. Add a new loan record as shown in Figure 4.4e.

• Use **L121** for the LoanID and enter the terms of the loan as you see fit.

• Data validation has been built into the Loans table so you will have to enter data correctly for it to be accepted. The term of the loan, for example, cannot exceed 30 years. The date of the loan cannot be set to a future date. The interest rate must be entered as a decimal. The type of the loan must be C, M, or O for Car, Mortgage, or Other. Enter **C** for a car loan.

• Be sure to enter **C11** as the CustomerID field. (This is your CustomerID from step 4.).

➤ Press **enter** when you have completed the loan record.

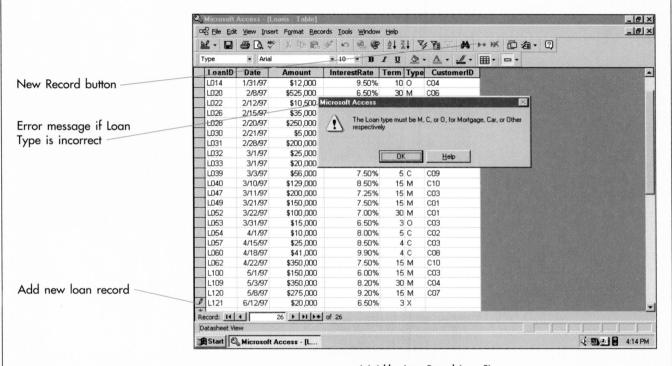

New Record button

Error message if Loan Type is incorrect

Add new loan record

(e) Add a Loan Record (step 5)

FIGURE 4.4   Hands-on Exercise 1 (continued)

GARBAGE IN, GARBAGE OUT

The information produced by a system depends entirely on the quality of the data. It is important, therefore, that you validate data as it is being entered to ensure that the data is as accurate as possible. A well-designed system will anticipate errors that a user may make during data entry and will include data validation checks that will prevent invalid data from being accepted into the system.

STEP 6: Referential Integrity

➤ Pull down the **Window menu.** Click **Cascade** to cascade the open windows (the Database window, the Customers table, and the Loans table.)

➤ Click the **Database window,** then click the **Minimize button** to minimize this window. Move and size the Customers and Loans windows so that your desktop matches ours in Figure 4.4f.

➤ Click in the **Loans window.** Click the **CustomerID field** of your loan record and (attempt to) replace the CustomerID (C11) with **C88.** Press **enter.** You will see the dialog box in Figure 4.4f, indicating that referential integrity has been violated because there is no related record in the Customers table.

➤ Click **OK.** Reenter **C11** as the valid CustomerID. Press **enter.**

➤ Click the window for the **Customers table.** Click the **row selector** to select the first record (Customer C01). Press the **Del key** (in an attempt) to delete this record.

➤ Access indicates that you cannot delete this record because related records exist in the Loans table. Click **OK.**

Dialog box indicates referential integrity has been violated

Enter C88 as Customer ID

Database window has been minimized

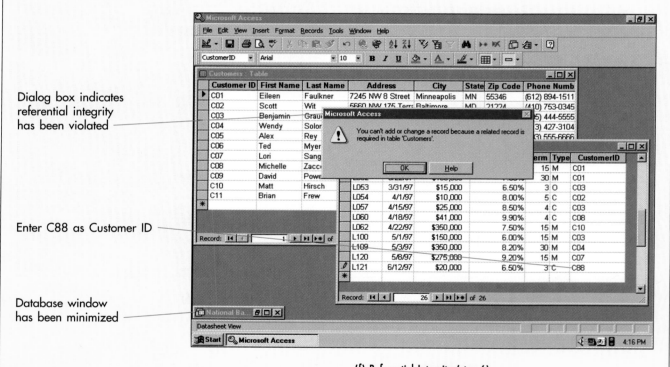

(f) Referential Integrity (step 6)

FIGURE 4.4   Hands-on Exercise 1 (continued)

STEP 7: Close the Database

➤ Close the Customers table. Close the Loans table.

➤ Close the Database window if you do not want to continue with the next hands-on exercise at this time.

SUBFORMS

A *subform* is a form within a form. It appears inside a main form to display records from a related table. A main form and its associated subform, to display the loans for one customer, are shown in Figure 4.5. The *main form* (also known as the primary form) is based on the *primary table* (the Customers table). The subform is based on the related table (the Loans table).

The main form and the subform are linked to one another so that the subform displays only the records related to the record currently displayed in the main form. The main form shows the "one" side of the relationship (the customer). The subform shows the "many" side of the relationship (the loans). The main form displays the customer data for one record (Eileen Faulkner with CustomerID C01). The subform shows the loans for that customer. The main form is displayed in the *Form view,* whereas the subform is displayed in the *Datasheet view.* (A subform can also be displayed in the Form view, in which case it would show one loan at a time.)

Each form in Figure 4.5a has its own status bar and associated navigation buttons. The status bar for the main form indicates that the active record is record 1 of 11 records in the Customers table. The status bar for the subform indicates record 1 of 3 records. (The latter shows the number of loans for this customer rather than the number of loans in the Loans table.) Click the navigation button to move to the next customer record, and you will automatically see the loans associated with that customer. If, for example, you were to move to the last customer record (C11, which contains the data you entered in the first hands-on exercise), you would see your loan information.

The Loans form also contains a calculated control, the payment due, which is based on the loan parameters. Loan L031, for example (a $200,000 mortgage with a 15-year term), has a monthly payment of $1,797.66. The amount of the payment is calculated using a predefined function, as will be described in the next hands-on exercise.

Figure 4.5b displays the Design view of the Customers form in Figure 4.5a. The Loans subform control is an object on the Customers form and can be moved and sized (or deleted) just like any other object. It should also be noted that the Loans subform is a form in and of itself, and can be opened in either the Datasheet

Calculated control

Main form is based on primary table

Subform is based on related table and displays only records related to current record in main form

Status bar for subform

Status bar for main form

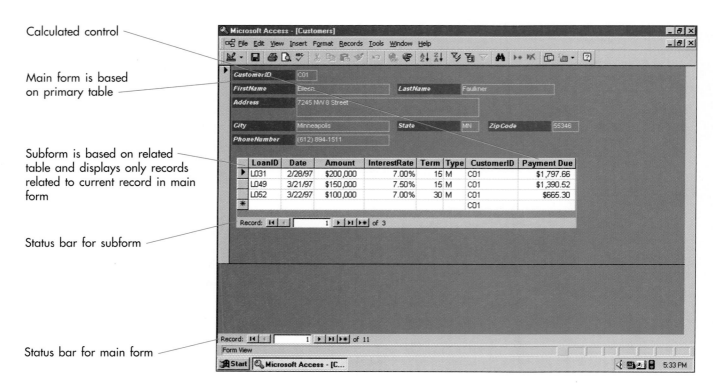

(a) Form View

Loans subform control

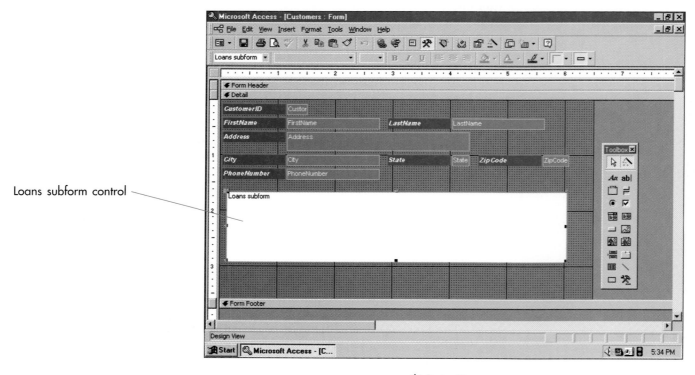

(b) Design View

FIGURE 4.5   A Main Form and a Subform

view or the Form view. It can also be opened in the Design view (to modify its appearance) as will be done in the next hands-on exercise.

THE PMT FUNCTION

The Pmt function is one of several predefined *functions* built into Access. It calculates the payment due on a loan based on the principal, interest rate, and term and is similar to the PMT function in Excel. The Pmt function is reached most easily through the Expression Builder and can be entered onto any form, query, or report. (See step 7 in the hands-on exercise.)

The Subform Wizard

A subform can be created as a separate form, then dragged onto the main form. It can also be created directly on the main form by selecting the Subform/Subreport button, then clicking and dragging on the main form to size and position the subform. This in turn opens the **Subform Wizard** as shown in Figure 4.6. You specify whether to build the subform from an existing form or from a table or query

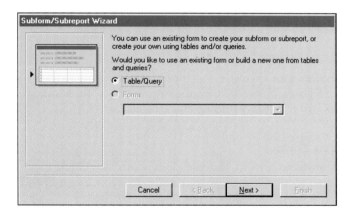

(a) Use an Existing Table/Query

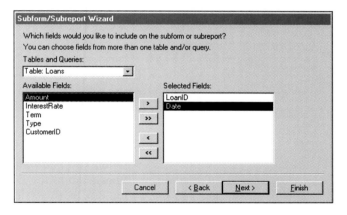

(b) Select the Fields

(c) Create the Link

(d) Save the Subform

FIGURE 4.6   The Subform Wizard

as shown in Figure 4.6a, then you select the desired fields in Figure 4.6b. Next, you specify the relationship between the main form and the subform as shown in Figure 4.6c. The subform in this example will show all of the loans for a particular customer. And finally, you specify the name for the subform as in Figure 4.6d to save the subform as an object within the database.

The Subform Wizard provides an excellent starting point, but as with the Form Wizard and a regular form, you usually need to customize the subform so that it meets your requirements. This is done using the identical techniques that were presented in Chapter 2 to move and size the controls and/or to modify their properties.

THE POWER OF SUBFORMS

A subform exists as a separate object within the database and can be opened or modified just like any other form. A main form can have any number of subforms, and a subform in turn can have its own subform. (See Hands-on Exercise 4 at the end of the chapter.)

HANDS-ON EXERCISE 2

Creating a Subform

Objective: To create a subform that displays the many records in a one-to-many relationship; to move and size controls in an existing form; to enter data in a subform. Use Figure 4.7 as a guide in doing the exercise.

STEP 1: Create the Customers Form

➤ Open the **National Bank database** from the previous exercise. Click the **Forms tab** in the Database window. Click **New** to display the New Form dialog box as shown in Figure 4.7a. Click **Form Wizard** in the list box.

➤ Click the **drop-down arrow** to display the available tables and queries in the database on which the form can be based. Click **Customers** to select the Customers table, then click **OK** to start the Form Wizard.

STEP 2: The Form Wizard

➤ You should see the dialog box in Figure 4.7b, which displays all of the fields in the Customers table. Click the **>> button** to enter all of the fields in the table on the form. Click **Next.**

➤ The **Columnar layout** is already selected. Click **Next.**

➤ Click **Colorful 1** as the style for your form. Click **Next.**

➤ The Form Wizard suggests **Customers** as the title of the form. (Keep this entry.) Click the option button to **Modify the form's design,** then click the **Finish Command button** to create the form and exit the Form Wizard.

Click Forms tab

Click Form Wizard

Click drop-down arrow

Click Customers

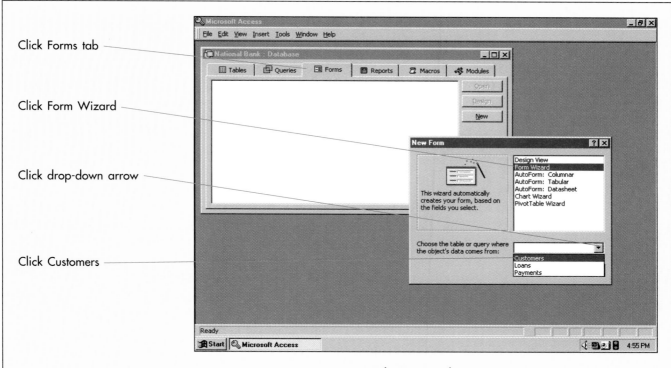

(a) The Form Wizard (step 1)

Click >> button to
select all fields

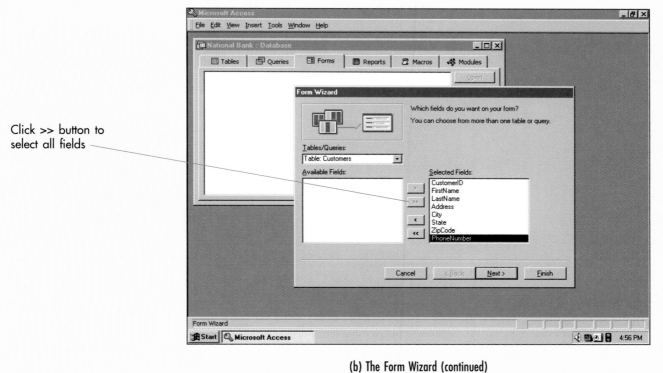

(b) The Form Wizard (continued)

FIGURE 4.7   Hands-on Exercise 2

THE NAME'S THE SAME

The Form Wizard automatically assigns the name of the underlying table (or query) to each form (subform) it creates. The Report Wizard works in similar fashion. The intent of the similar naming convention is to help you select the proper object from the Database window when you want to subsequently open the object. This becomes increasingly important in databases that contain a large number of objects.

STEP 3: Modify the Customers Form

➤ You should see the Customers form in Figure 4.7c. Maximize the window. Click and drag the right edge of the form to widen the form to **6½ inches.**

➤ Click the control for **LastName** to select the control and display the sizing handles, then drag the **LastName control** so that it is next to the FirstName control.

➤ Click and drag the other controls to complete the form:

  • Click and drag the **Address control** under the control for FirstName.

  • Place the controls for **City, State,** and **ZipCode** on the same line, then move these controls under the Address control.

  • Move the control for **PhoneNumber** under the control for City.

➤ Click the **Save button** to save the form.

Save button

Drag last name control next to first name control

Click and drag right edge of form to 6½ inches

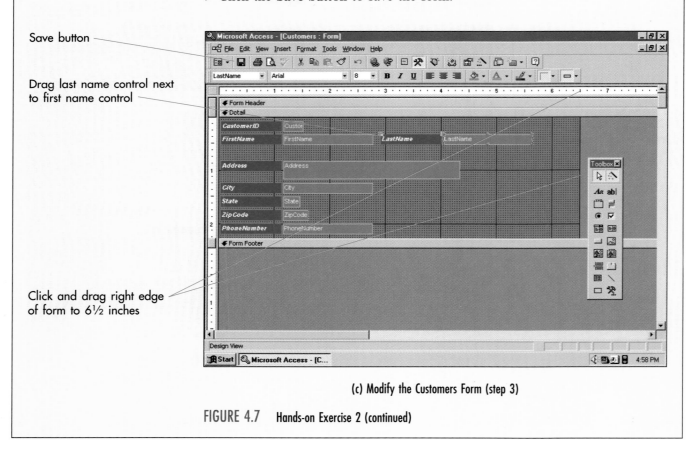

(c) Modify the Customers Form (step 3)

FIGURE 4.7   Hands-on Exercise 2 (continued)

ALIGN THE CONTROLS

To align labels or controls in a straight line (horizontally or vertically), press and hold the Shift key as you click the labels or the controls to be aligned. Pull down the Format menu and select the edge to align (Left, Right, Top, or Bottom). Click the Undo button if you are not satisfied with the result.

STEP 4: Create the Loans Subform

➤ Click and drag the bottom edge of the **Detail section** so that you have approximately 2 inches of blank space in the Detail section as shown in Figure 4.7d. (This is where the subform will go.)

➤ Click the **Subform/Subreport button** on the Toolbox toolbar, then click and drag in the Customers form where you want the subform to go. Release the mouse to start the Subform/Subreport Wizard.

➤ The **Table/Query Option button** is selected, indicating that we will build the subform from a table or query. Click **Next**.

➤ You should see the Subform/Subreport Wizard dialog box in Figure 4.7d. Click the **down arrow** on the Tables and Queries list box to select the **Loans table.** Click the **>> button** to enter all of the fields in the Loans table onto the subform. Click **Next**.

Subform/Subreport Wizard button

Click >> button to select all fields

Click and drag bottom edge of Detail section

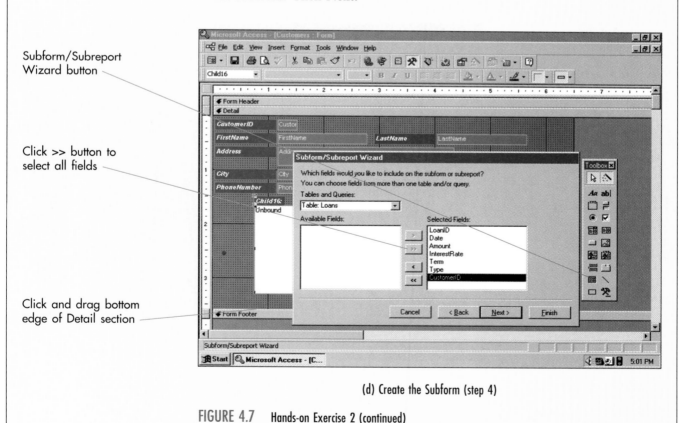

(d) Create the Subform (step 4)

FIGURE 4.7   Hands-on Exercise 2 (continued)

➤ The next step asks you to define the fields that link the main form to the sub-form. The option button to **Choose from a list** is selected. The selected link will **Show Loans for each record in Customers using CustomerID.** Click **Next.**

➤ The Wizard suggests **Loans subform** as the name of the subform. Click **Finish** to exit the Subform/Subreport wizard.

STEP 5: The Loans Subform (Datasheet view)

➤ You should be in the Design view for the Customers form, which contains a white rectangular area indicating the position of the Loans subform control. Maximize the window.

➤ Click the label attached to the subform control and press the **Del key.** Be sure you delete only the label and not the control for the subform.

➤ You need to open the Loans subform to check the column width of its fields. This is done in one of two ways:

  • Deselect the Loans subform (by clicking anywhere in the main form), then double click the **Loans subform** to open it. Change to the **Datasheet view,** *or*

  • Pull down the **Window menu** to change to the **Database window,** click the **Forms tab,** and open the **Loans subform.**

➤ You should see the Datasheet view of the Loans subform as shown in Figure 4.7e. Click and drag the various column headings to the approximate sizes shown in the figure so that you can see the complete field names.

➤ Save the Loans subform. Close the Loans subform.

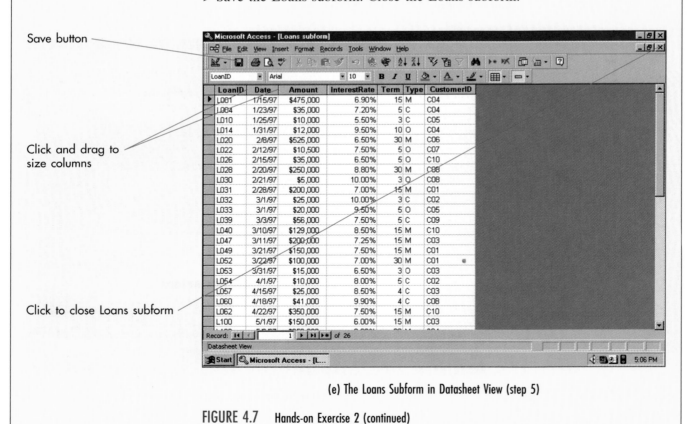

(e) The Loans Subform in Datasheet View (step 5)

FIGURE 4.7   Hands-on Exercise 2 (continued)

CHANGE THE VIEW

A subform can be displayed in either the Datasheet view or the Form view. To change the default view, open the subform in Design view, point to the Form Selection box in the upper-left corner, click the right mouse button to display a shortcut menu, and click Properties. Click the Default View box, click the drop-drop arrow, select the desired view, and close the Properties dialog box.

STEP 6: View the Customers Form

➤ You are either in the Database window or the Customers form, depending on how you opened the Loans subform. Use the **Window menu** to change to the Customers form (if necessary), then click the **Maximize button** so that the form takes the entire window.

➤ Change to the **Form view** as shown in Figure 4.7f. You may have to return to the Design view of the Customers form to increase the space allotted for the Loans subform. Size and/or move the subform control as necessary, then save the form. You may also have to reopen the Loans subform in the Datasheet view to adjust the column widths.

➤ Note the following:
  • The customer information for the first customer (C01) is displayed in the main portion of the form. The loans for that customer are displayed in the subform.

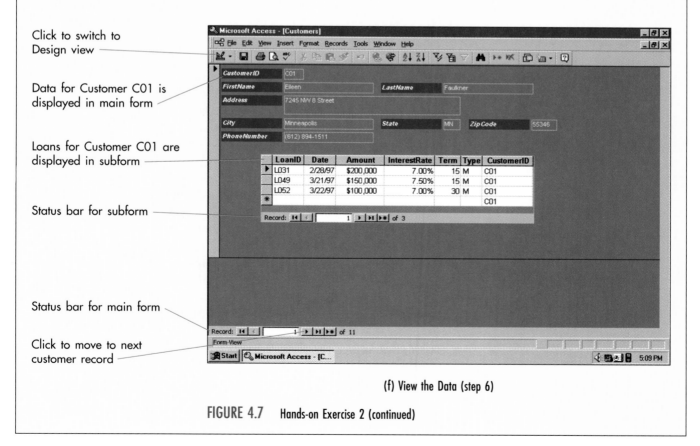

Click to switch to Design view

Data for Customer C01 is displayed in main form

Loans for Customer C01 are displayed in subform

Status bar for subform

Status bar for main form

Click to move to next customer record

(f) View the Data (step 6)

FIGURE 4.7   Hands-on Exercise 2 (continued)

- The status bar at the bottom of the window (corresponding to the main form) displays record 1 of 11 records (you are looking at the first record in the Customers table).
- The status bar for the subform displays record 1 of 3 records (you are on the first of three loan records for this customer).

➤ Click the ▶ **button** on the status bar for the main form to move to the next customer record. The subform is updated automatically to display the two loans belonging to this customer.

➤ Press the **PgDn key** to move through the customer records until you come to your record in the Customers table.

WHY IT WORKS

The main form (Customers) and subform (Loans) work in conjunction with one another so that you always see all of the loans for a given customer. The link between the forms is established through a common field as described at the beginning of the chapter. To see how the link is actually implemented, change to the Design view of the Customers form and point anywhere inside the Loans subform. Click the right mouse button to display a shortcut menu, click Properties to display the Subform/Subreport properties dialog box, and if necessary, click the All tab within the dialog box. You should see CustomerID next to two properties (Link Child Fields and Link Master Fields), which define how the main and subforms are linked to one another.

STEP 7: Add the Payment Amount

➤ Click the **Database Window button,** click the **Forms tab,** select the **Loans subform,** then click the **Design button.** The Loans subform is open in the Design view as shown in Figure 4.7g. (The dialog boxes are not yet visible.)

➤ If necessary, maximize the window. Click and drag the right edge of the form to **6½ inches** to make room for a new control and its associated label.

➤ Click the **Label button,** then click and drag in the **Form Header** to create an unbound control. Enter **Payment Due** as the text for the label as shown in Figure 4.7g. Size and align the control to match the other labels.

➤ Click the **Textbox button** on the Toolbox toolbar, then click and drag in the **Detail section** to create an unbound control that will contain the amount of the monthly payment. Click the label for the control (e.g., Text 15), then press the **Del key** to delete the label.

➤ Point to the unbound control, click the **right mouse button** to display a shortcut menu, then click **Properties** to open the properties dialog box. Click the **All tab** to view all existing properties.

➤ Click the **Name property.** Enter **Payment Due** in place of the existing label (e.g., Text 15).

➤ Click the **Control Source property,** then click the **Build (...) button** to display the Expression Builder dialog box.

- Double click **Functions** (if there is a plus sign in its button), then click **Built-In Functions.** Click **Financial** in the second column, then double click **Pmt** to enter the Pmt function in the Expression Builder.

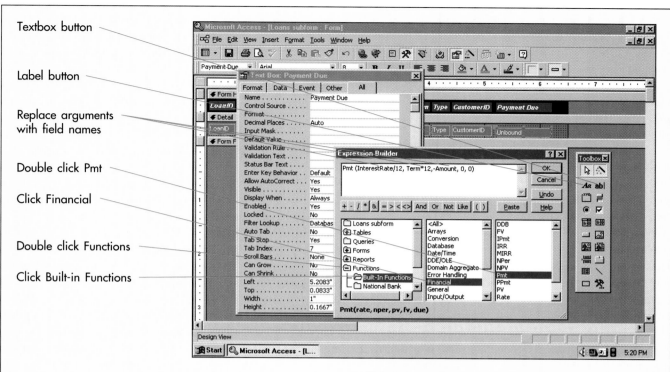

Textbox button

Label button

Replace arguments with field names

Double click Pmt

Click Financial

Double click Functions

Click Built-in Functions

(g) Add the Payment Function (step 7)

FIGURE 4.7   Hands-on Exercise 2 (continued)

- You need to replace each of the arguments in the Pmt function with the appropriate field names from the Loans table. Select the arguments one at a time and enter the replacement for that argument exactly as shown in Figure 4.7g. Click **OK** when finished.
- ➤ Click the **Format property,** click the **down arrow,** and specify **Currency** (scrolling if necessary). Click the **Decimal Places property,** click the **down arrow,** and select **2.**
- ➤ Close the Properties dialog box. Size and align the control. Change to the Datasheet view and check the column widths, making adjustments as necessary. Close the Loans subform. Click **Yes** to save the changes.

THE ZOOM WINDOW

Trying to enter or edit a long expression directly in the Control Source properties box can be confusing in that you may not be able to see the entire expression. Access anticipates the situation and provides a Zoom window to increase the space in which you can work. Press Shift+F2 to open the Zoom window, enter or edit the expression as necessary, then click OK to accept the changes and close the Zoom window.

STEP 8: Enter a New Loan

➤ Pull down the **Window menu** and click **Customers** to return to the **Customers form** in the Form view as shown in Figure 4.7h. You may have to return to the Design view of the Customers form to increase the space allotted for the Loans subform. You may also have to reopen the Loans subform to adjust the column widths.

➤ Click the ▶| on the status bar of the main form to move to the last record (customer C11), which is the record you entered in the previous exercise. (Click the **PgUp key** if you are on a blank record.)

➤ Click the **LoanID field** next to the asterisk in the subform. The record selector changes to a triangle. Enter data for the new loan as shown in Figure 4.7h:

- The record selector changes to a pencil as soon as you begin to enter data.
- The payment due will be computed automatically as soon as you complete the Term field.
- You do *not* have to enter the CustomerID since it appears automatically due to the relationship between the Customers and Loans tables.

➤ Press the **down arrow** when you have entered the last field (Type), which saves the data in the current record. (The record selector symbol changes from a pencil to a triangle.)

Print Preview button

Selection area for current record

Enter data for new loan

Payment due is computed automatically

Click to move to last customer record (your record)

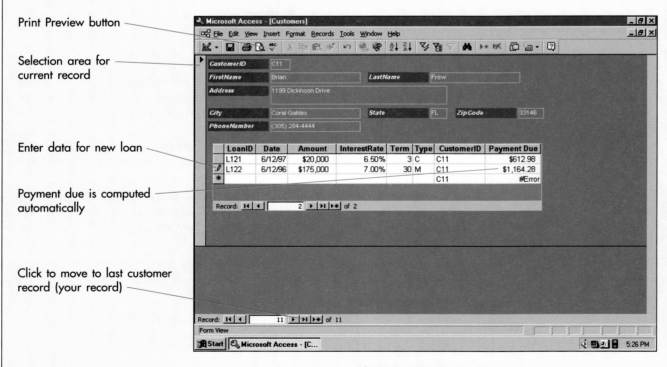

(h) Enter a New Loan (step 8)

FIGURE 4.7   Hands-on Exercise 2 (continued)

#ERROR AND HOW TO AVOID IT

A #Error message will be displayed if the Pmt function is unable to compute a periodic payment—for example, in a new record prior to entering the term of the loan. You can, however, suppress the display of the message by using the IIf (Immediate If) function to test for a null argument. In other words, if the term of the loan has not been entered, do not display anything, otherwise compute the payment in the usual way. This is accomplished by using the IIf function =IIf([Term] Is Null,"",Pmt([InterestRate]/12,[Term]*12,-[Amount],)) as the control source for the payment amount. Use Help for additional information.

STEP 9: Print the Form

➤ Click the **Print Preview button** to view the form prior to printing to be sure that the form fits within the width of the page. (See boxed tip on the Page Setup command if the form does not fit.) Click the **Close button** to return to the Form view.

➤ Check that you are still on the record for customer 11 (the record containing your data), then click the **selection area** at the left of the form to select this record.

➤ Pull down the **File menu** and click **Print** to display the Print dialog box. Click the **Selected Record(s) option button.** Click **OK** to print the selected form.

➤ Close the Customers form. Click **Yes** if asked to save the changes to the form.

➤ Close the National Bank database and exit Access if you do not want to continue with the next hands-on exercise at this time.

THE PAGE SETUP COMMAND

The Page Setup command controls the appearance of the printed page in Access just as it does in other applications. Pull down the File menu and click Page Setup. You can change the orientation from Landscape to Portrait. You can also change the top, bottom, left, and right margins to fit more or less on a page.

MULTIPLE TABLE QUERIES

A relational database consists of multiple tables, each dealing with a specific subject. The related data can be displayed in a main form/subform combination as was done in the preceding exercise. It can also be displayed in a select query that is developed from multiple tables.

The real power of a select query is its ability to include fields from several tables. If, for example, you wanted the name and address of all customers holding a certain type of loan, you would need data from both the Customers table and the Loans table. Thus, you create the select query using the data from both tables. You would select the customer's name and address fields from the Customers table, and the various loan parameters from the Loans table.

Figure 4.8a shows the Design view of a query to select the 15-year mortgages (the term is 15 and the loan type is "M") issued after April 1, 1997. Figure 4.8b displays the resulting dynaset. You should recognize the design grid and the Field, Sort, Show, and Criteria rows from our earlier discussion. The *Table row* is new and displays the name of the table containing the field.

In Figure 4.8a the LastName and the FirstName fields are taken from the Customers table. All of the other fields are from the Loans table. The one-to-many relationship between the Customers table and the Loans table is shown graphically within the Query window. The tables are related through the CustomerID field, which is the primary key in the Customers table and a foreign key in the Loans table. The line between the two field lists is called a join line and tells Access how to relate the data in the tables.

Return for a moment to the discussion at the beginning of the chapter, where we asked the name and address of the customer holding loan L010 (Alex Rey at

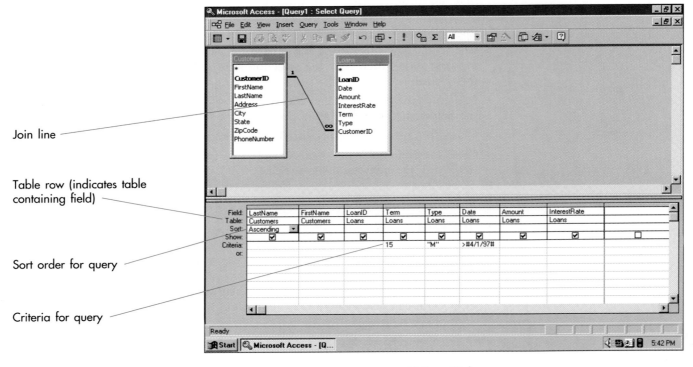

(a) Query Window

	Last Name	First Name	LoanID	Term	Type	Date	Amount	InterestRate
▶	Grauer	Benjamin	L100	15	M	5/1/97	$150,000	6.00%
	Hirsch	Matt	L062	15	M	4/22/97	$350,000	7.50%
	Sangastiano	Lori	L120	15	M	5/8/97	$275,000	9.20%
*								

(b) Dynaset

FIGURE 4.8   A Multitable Query

3456 Main Highway). Look at the data in Figure 4.2 at the beginning of the chapter and see how you have to consult both tables to answer the query. You do it intuitively; Access does it using a query containing fields from both tables.

Forms and reports become more interesting and contain more useful information when they are based on multiple table queries. The following exercise has you create a query similar to the one in Figure 4.8, then create a report based on that query.

THE JOIN LINE

Access joins the tables in a query automatically if a relationship exists between the tables. Access will also join the tables (even if no relationship exists) if both tables have a field with the same name and data type, and if one of the fields is a primary key. You can also create the join yourself by dragging a field from one table to the other, but this type of join applies only to the query in which it was created.

HANDS-ON EXERCISE 3

Queries and Reports

Objective: To create a query that relates two tables to one another, then create a report based on that query. Use Figure 4.9 as a guide in the exercise.

STEP 1: Create a Select Query

➤ Open the **National Bank database** from the previous exercise.

➤ Click the **Queries tab** in the Database window. Click the **New Command button** to display the New Query dialog box. **Design View** is already selected as the means of creating a query. Click **OK** to begin creating the query.

➤ The Show Table dialog box appears as shown in Figure 4.9a, with the Tables tab already selected. Click the **Customers table,** then click the **Add button** (or double click the **Customers table**) to add the Customers table to the query (the field list should appear within the Query window).

➤ Double click the **Loans table** to add the Loans table to the query.

➤ Click **Close** to close the Show Table dialog box.

ADDING AND DELETING TABLES

To add a table to an existing query, pull down the Query menu, click Show Table, then double click the name of the table from the Table/Query list. To delete a table, click anywhere in its field list and press the Del key, or pull down the Query menu and click Remove Table.

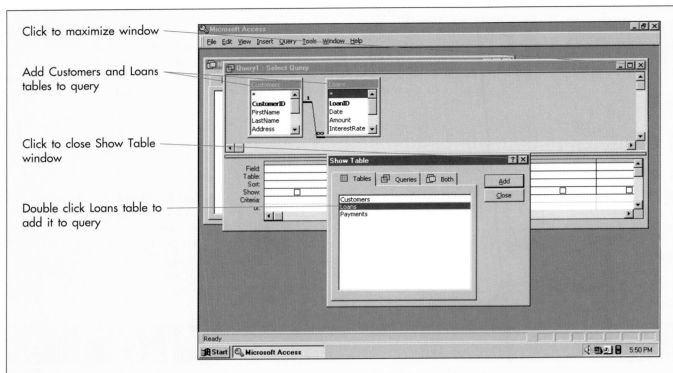

Click to maximize window

Add Customers and Loans tables to query

Click to close Show Table window

Double click Loans table to add it to query

(a) Add the Tables (step 1)

FIGURE 4.9   Hands-on Exercise 3

STEP 2: Move and Size the Field Lists

➤ Click the **Maximize button** so that the Query Design window takes the entire desktop.

➤ Point to the line separating the field lists from the design grid (the mouse pointer changes to a cross), then click and drag in a downward direction. This gives you more space to display the field lists for the tables in the query as shown in Figure 4.9b.

➤ Click and drag the bottom of the **Customers table field list** until you can see all of the fields in the Customers table. Click and drag the bottom of the **Loans table field list** until you can see all of the fields in the Loans table.

➤ Click and drag the title bar of the **Loans table** to the right until you are satisfied with the appearance of the line connecting the tables.

CONVERSION TO STANDARD FORMAT

Access is flexible in accepting text and date expressions in the Criteria row of a select query. A text entry can be entered with or without quotation marks (e.g., M or "M"). A date entry can be entered with or without pound signs (you can enter 1/1/96 or #1/1/96#). Access does, however, convert your entries to standard format as soon you move to the next cell in the design grid. Thus, text entries are always displayed in quotation marks, and dates are always enclosed in pound signs.

Click and drag title bar to move field list

Click and drag bottom border of field list so all field names are visible

Click and drag to increase size of upper portion of window

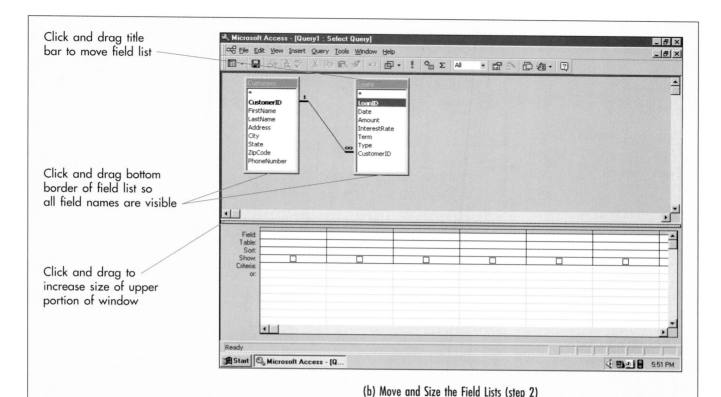

(b) Move and Size the Field Lists (step 2)

FIGURE 4.9   Hands-on Exercise 3 (continued)

STEP 3: Create the Query

➤ The Table row should be visible within the design grid. If not, pull down the **View menu** and click **Table Names** to display the Table row in the design grid as shown in Figure 4.9c.

➤ Double click the **LastName** and **FirstName fields,** in that order, from the Customers table to add these fields to the design grid. Double click the **title bar** of the Loans table to select all of the fields, then drag the selected group of fields to the design grid.

➤ Enter the selection criteria (scrolling if necessary) as follows:

• Click the **Criteria row** under the **Date field.** Type **Between 1/1/97 and 3/31/97.** (You do not have to type the pound signs.)

• Click the **Criteria row** for the **Amount field.** Type **>200000.**

• Type **M** in the Criteria row for the **Type field.** (You do not have to type the quotation marks.)

➤ Select all of the columns in the design grid by clicking the column selector in the first column, then pressing and holding the **Shift key** as you scroll to the last column and click its column selector. Double click the right edge of any column selector to adjust the column width of all the columns simultaneously.

➤ Click the **Sort row** under the LastName field, then click the **down arrow** to open the drop-down list box. Click **Ascending.**

➤ Click the **Save button** on the Query Design toolbar. Save the query as **First Quarter 1997 Jumbo Loans.**

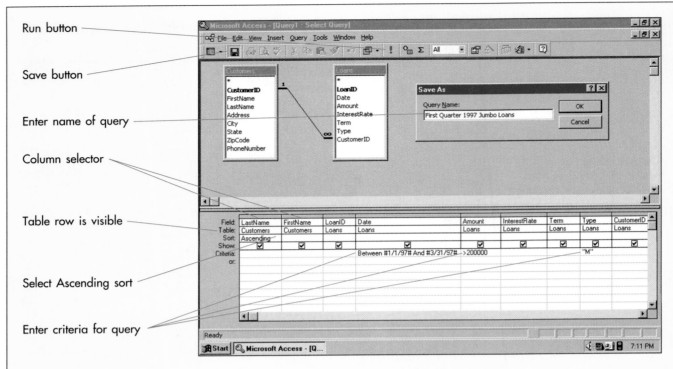

Run button

Save button

Enter name of query

Column selector

Table row is visible

Select Ascending sort

Enter criteria for query

(c) Create the Query (step 3)

FIGURE 4.9   Hands-on Exercise 3 (continued)

SORTING ON MULTIPLE FIELDS

A query can be sorted on more than one field, but you must be certain that the fields are in the proper order within the design grid. Access sorts from left to right (the leftmost field is the primary key), so the fields must be arranged in the desired sort sequence. To move a field within the design grid, click the column selector above the field name to select the column, then drag the column to its new position.

STEP 4: Run the Query

➤ Click the **Run button** (the exclamation point) to run the query and create the dynaset in Figure 4.9d. Three jumbo loans are listed.

➤ Click the **Amount field** for loan L028. Enter **100000** as the corrected amount and press **enter.** (This will reduce the number of jumbo loans in subsequent reports to two.)

➤ Click the **Close button** to close the query. Click **Yes** if asked whether to save the changes to the query.

Click to close query —————

Change Loan Amount
to 100000 ——————————

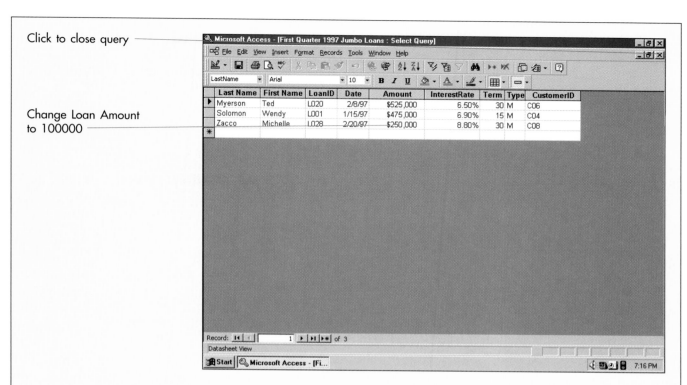

(d) The Dynaset (step 4)

FIGURE 4.9   Hands-on Exercise 3 (continued)

DATA TYPE MISMATCH

The data type determines the way in which criteria appear in the design grid. A text field is enclosed in quotation marks. Number, currency, and counter fields are shown as digits with or without a decimal point. Dates are enclosed in pound signs. A Yes/No field is entered as Yes or No without quotation marks. Entering criteria in the wrong form produces a Data Type Mismatch error when attempting to run the query.

STEP 5: Create a Report

➤ The National Bank database should still be open (although the size of your window may be different from the one in the figure).

➤ Click the **Reports tab** in the Database window, then click the **New command button** to display the New Report dialog box as shown in Figure 4.9e. Select the **Report Wizard** as the means of creating the report.

➤ Click the **drop-down arrow** to display the tables and queries in the database in order to select the one on which the report will be based. Select **First Quarter 1997 Jumbo Loans** (the query you just created) as the basis of your report. Click **OK** to start the Report Wizard.

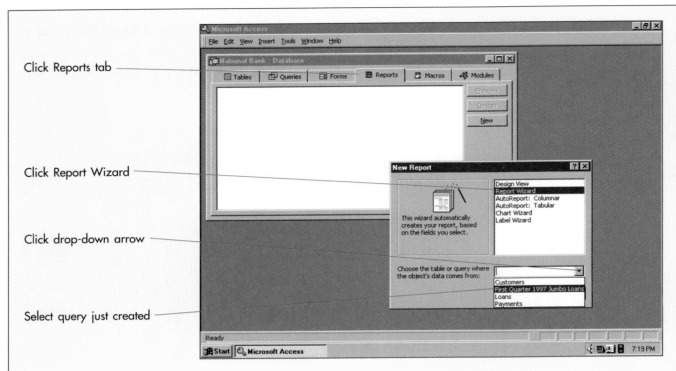

Click Reports tab

Click Report Wizard

Click drop-down arrow

Select query just created

(e) Create a Report (step 5)

FIGURE 4.9 Hands-on Exercise 3 (continued)

REPORTS WITHOUT QUERIES

You can create a report containing fields from multiple tables or queries without having to first create the underlying query. Use the Report Wizard as the basis for your design, and select fields from the first table or query in normal fashion. Click the down arrow in the Table/Query list box, select the next table or query, and enter the appropriate fields. Click the down arrow to select additional tables or queries as necessary, and continue in this fashion until you have selected all of the necessary fields.

STEP 6: The Report Wizard

➤ Double click **LoanID** from the Available Fields list box to add this field to the report. Add the **LastName, FirstName, Date,** and **Amount** fields as shown in Figure 4.9f. Click **Next.**

➤ The **by Loans option** is selected as the means of viewing your report. (This means that the report will display the loans in sequence by the LoanID field.) Click **Next.**

➤ There is no need to group the records. Click **Next.**

➤ There is no need to sort the records. Click **Next.**

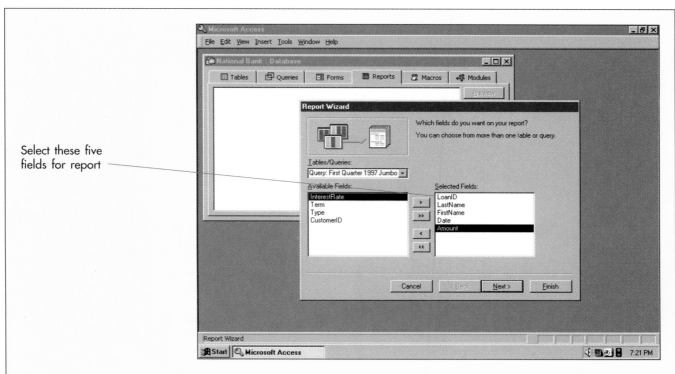

Select these five fields for report

(f) The Report Wizard (step 6)

FIGURE 4.9   Hands-on Exercise 3 (continued)

➤ The **Tabular layout** is selected, as is **Portrait orientation.** Be sure the box is checked to **Adjust field width so all fields fit on a page.** Click **Next.**

➤ Choose **Soft Gray** as the style. Click **Next.**

➤ Enter **First Quarter 1997 Jumbo Loans** as the title for your report. The option button to **Preview the Report** is already selected.

➤ Click the **Finish Command button** to exit the Report Wizard and preview the report.

STEP 7: Print the Completed Report

➤ Click the **Maximize button.** If necessary, click the **Zoom button** in the Print Preview window so that you can see the whole report as in Figure 4.9g.

➤ The report is based on the query created earlier. Michelle Zacco is *not* in the report because the amount of her loan was updated in the query's dynaset in step 4.

➤ Click the **Print button** to print the report. Close the Preview window, then close the Report window. Click **Yes** if asked to save the changes.

➤ Close the National Bank database and exit Access if you do not want to continue with the next exercise at this time.

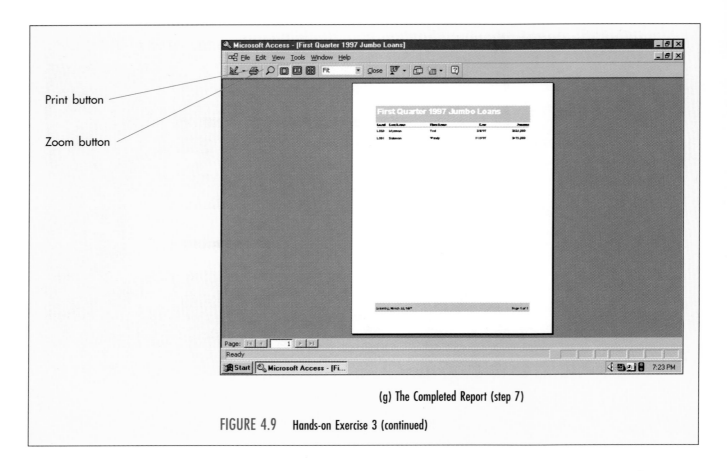

Print button

Zoom button

(g) The Completed Report (step 7)

FIGURE 4.9   Hands-on Exercise 3 (continued)

EXPANDING THE DATABASE

One of the advantages of a relational database is that it can be easily expanded to include additional tables without disturbing the existing tables. The database used throughout the chapter consisted of two tables: a Customers table and a Loans table. Figure 4.10 extends the database to include a partial listing of the Payments table containing the payments received by the bank. Each record in the Payments table has four fields: LoanID, PaymentNumber, Date (the date the payment was received), and PaymentReceived (the amount sent in).

The original database had a one-to-many relationship between customers and loans. One customer may have many loans, but a given loan is associated with only one customer. The expanded database contains a second one-to-many relationship between loans and payments. One loan has many payments, but a specific payment is associated with only one loan. Thus, the primary key of the Loans table (LoanID) appears as a foreign key in the Payments table.

Look carefully at the Payments table and note that it contains multiple records with the same payment number (e.g., every loan has a payment number 1). In similar fashion, there are multiple records with the same LoanID. Loan L001, for example, has five payments. The combination of LoanID and Payment-Number is unique, however (there is only one payment 1 for loan L001), and thus the combination of the two fields serves as the primary key in the Payments table.

We began the chapter by showing you hypothetical records in the database and asking you to answer queries based on that data. We end the chapter the same way, by asking you to reference one or more tables in Figure 4.10. As you consider each query, think of how it would appear in the design grid.

(a) Customers Table

CustomerID	First Name	Last Name	Address	City	State	Zip Code	Phone Number
C01	Eileen	Faulkner	7245 NW 8 Street	Minneapolis	MN	55346	(612) 894-1511
C02	Scott	Wit	5660 NW 175 Terrace	Baltimore	MD	21224	(410) 753-0345
C03	Benjamin	Grauer	10000 Sample Road	Coral Springs	FL	33073	(305) 444-5555
C04	Wendy	Solomon	7500 Reno Road	Houston	TX	77090	(713) 427-3104
C05	Alex	Rey	3456 Main Highway	Denver	CO	80228	(303) 555-6666
C06	Ted	Myerson	6545 Stone Street	Chapel Hill	NC	27515	(919) 942-7654
C07	Lori	Sangastiano	4533 Aero Drive	Santa Rosa	CA	95403	(707) 542-3411
C08	Michelle	Zacco	488 Gold Street	Gainesville	FL	32601	(904) 374-5660
C09	David	Powell	5070 Battle Road	Decatur	GA	30034	(301) 345-6556
C10	Matt	Hirsch	777 NW 67 Avenue	Fort Lee	NJ	07624	(201) 664-3211

(a) Customers Table

(b) Loans Table

LoanID	Date	Amount	Interest Rate	Term	Type	CustomerID
L001	1/15/97	$475,000	6.90%	15	M	C04
L004	1/23/97	$35,000	7.20%	5	C	C04
L010	1/25/97	$10,000	5.50%	3	C	C05
L014	1/31/97	$12,000	9.50%	10	O	C04
L020	2/8/97	$525,000	6.50%	30	M	C06
L022	2/12/97	$10,500	7.50%	5	O	C07
L026	2/15/97	$35,000	6.50%	5	O	C10
L028	2/20/97	$250,000	8.80%	30	M	C08
L030	2/21/97	$5,000	10.00%	3	O	C08
L031	2/28/97	$200,000	7.00%	15	M	C01
L032	3/1/97	$25,000	10.00%	3	C	C02
L033	3/1/97	$20,000	9.50%	5	O	C05
L039	3/3/97	$56,000	7.50%	5	C	C09
L040	3/10/97	$129,000	8.50%	15	M	C10
L047	3/11/97	$200,000	7.25%	15	M	C03
L049	3/21/97	$150,000	7.50%	15	M	C01
L052	3/22/97	$100,000	7.00%	30	M	C01
L053	3/31/97	$15,000	6.50%	3	O	C03
L054	4/1/97	$10,000	8.00%	5	C	C02
L057	4/15/97	$25,000	8.50%	4	C	C03
L060	4/18/97	$41,000	9.90%	4	C	C08
L062	4/22/97	$350,000	7.50%	15	M	C10
L100	5/1/97	$150,000	6.00%	15	M	C03
L109	5/3/97	$350,000	8.20%	30	M	C04
L120	5/8/97	$275,000	9.20%	15	M	C07

(b) Loans Table

(c) Payments Table (partial list)

LoanID	Payment Number	Date	Payment Received
L001	1	2/15/97	$4,242.92
L001	2	3/15/97	$4,242.92
L001	3	4/15/97	$4,242.92
L001	4	5/15/97	$4,242.92
L001	5	6/15/97	$4,242.92
L004	1	2/23/97	$696.35
L004	2	3/23/97	$696.35
L004	3	4/23/97	$696.35
L004	4	5/23/97	$696.35
L004	5	6/23/97	$696.35
L010	1	2/25/97	$301.96
L010	2	3/25/97	$301.96
L010	3	4/25/97	$301.96
L010	4	5/25/97	$301.96
L010	5	6/25/97	$301.96
L014	1	2/28/97	$155.28
L014	2	3/31/97	$155.28
L014	3	4/30/97	$155.28
L014	4	5/30/97	$155.28
L014	5	6/30/97	$155.28
L020	1	3/8/97	$3,318.36
L020	2	4/8/97	$3,318.36
L020	3	5/8/97	$3,318.36
L020	4	6/8/97	$3,318.36
L022	1	3/12/97	$210.40
L022	2	4/12/97	$210.40
L022	3	5/12/97	$210.40
L022	4	6/12/97	$210.40
L026	1	3/15/97	$684.82
L026	2	4/15/97	$684.82
L026	3	5/15/97	$684.82
L026	4	6/15/97	$684.82
L028	1	3/20/97	$1,975.69
L028	2	4/20/97	$1,975.69
L028	3	5/20/97	$1,975.69
L028	4	6/20/97	$1,975.69
L030	1	3/21/97	$161.34
L030	2	4/21/97	$161.34
L030	3	5/21/97	$161.34
L030	4	6/21/97	$161.34

(c) Payments Table (partial list)

FIGURE 4.10   Expanding the Database

Query: How many payments have been received for loan L022? What was the date of the most recent payment?

Answer: Four payments have been received for loan L022. The most recent payment was received on 6/12/97.

The query can be answered with reference to just the Payments table by finding all payments for loan L022. To determine the most recent payment, you would retrieve the records in descending order by Date and retrieve the first record.

Query: How many payments have been received from Michelle Zacco since May 1, 1997?

Answer: Four payments have been received. Two of the payments were for loan L028 on May 20th and June 20th. Two were for loan L030 on May 21st and June 21st.

To answer this query, you would look in the Customers table to determine the CustomerID for Ms. Zacco, search the Loans table for all loans for this customer, then retrieve the corresponding payments from the Payments table. (Michelle is also associated with loan L060. The Payments table, however, is truncated in Figure 4.10, and hence the payments for this loan are not visible.)

Multiple Subforms

Subforms were introduced earlier in the chapter as a means of displaying data from related tables. Figure 4.11 continues the discussion by showing a main form with two levels of subforms. The main (Customers) form has a one-to-many relationship with the first (Loans) subform. The Loans subform in turn has a one-to-many relationship with the second (Payments) subform. The Customers form and the Loans subform are the forms you created in the second hands-on exercise. (The Loans subform is displayed in the Form view as opposed to the Data sheet view.) The Payments subform is new and will be developed in our next exercise.

The records displayed in the three forms are linked to one another according to the relationships within the database. There is a one-to-many relationship between customers and loans so that the first subform displays all of the loans for one customer. There is also a one-to-many relationship between loans and payments so that the second subform (Payments) displays all of the payments for the selected loan. Click on a different loan (for the same customer), and the Payments subform is updated automatically to show all of the payments for that loan.

The status bar for the main form indicates record 5 of 11, meaning that you are viewing the fifth of 11 Customer records. The status bar for the Loans subform indicates record 2 of 2, corresponding to the second of two loan records for the fifth customer. The status bar for the Payments subform indicates record 1 of 3, corresponding to the first of three Payment records for this loan for this customer.

The three sets of navigation buttons enable you to advance to the next record(s) in any of the forms. The records move in conjunction with one another. Thus, if you advance to the next record in the Customers form you will automatically display a different set of records in the Loans subform, as well as a different set of Payment records in the Payments subform.

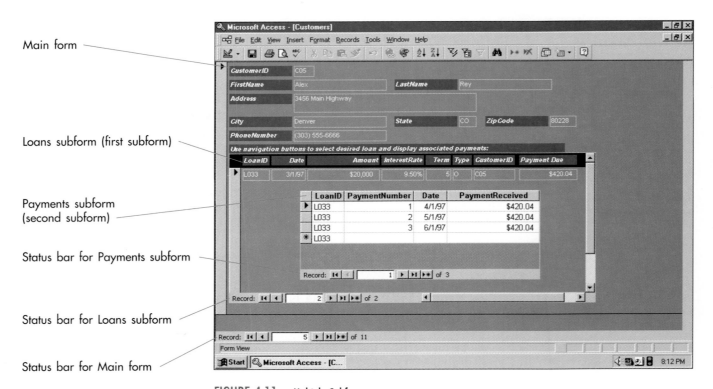

FIGURE 4.11   Multiple Subforms

Linked Subforms

Objective: To create a main form with two levels of subforms; to display a subform in Form view or Datasheet view. Use Figure 4.12 as a guide.

STEP 1: Add a Relationship

➤ Open the **National Bank database.** Pull down the **Tools menu.** Click **Relationships** to open the Relationships window as shown in Figure 4.12a. Maximize the Relationships window.

➤ Pull down the **Relationships menu.** Click **Show Table** to display the Show Table dialog box.

➤ The **Tables tab** is selected within the Show Table dialog box. Double click the **Payments table** to add the table to the Relationships window. Close the Show Table dialog box.

➤ Click and drag the title bar of the **Payments Field list** so that it is positioned approximately one inch from the Loans table.

➤ Click and drag the **LoanID field** in the Loans field list to the **LoanID field** in the Payments field list. You will see the Relationships dialog box.

➤ Check the **Enforce Referential Integrity** check box. (If necessary, clear the check boxes to Cascade Update Related Fields and Delete Related Records.)

Save button

Click and drag LoanID field to LoanID field in Payments table

Select check box to enforce referential integrity

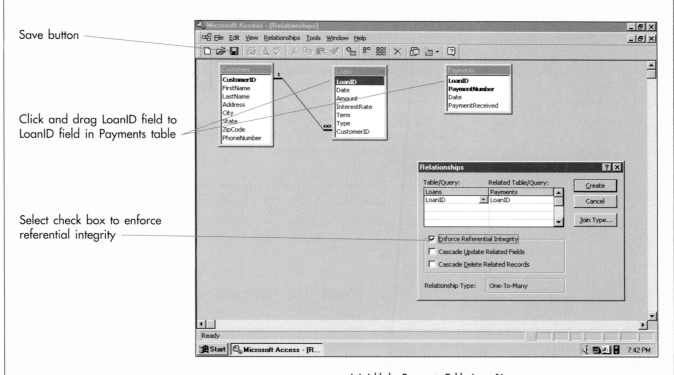

(a) Add the Payments Table (step 1)

FIGURE 4.12 Hands-on Exercise 4

➤ Click the **Create button** to establish the relationship. You should see a line indicating a one-to-many relationship between the Loans and Payments tables.

➤ Click the **Save button** to save the Relationships window, then close the Relationships window.

A CONCATENATED PRIMARY KEY

The primary key is defined as the field, or combination of fields, that is unique for every record in a table. The Payments table contains multiple records with the same payment number (i.e., every loan has a payment number 1, 2, 3, and so on) as well as multiple payments for the same LoanID. The combination of LoanID and PaymentNumber is unique, however, and serves as the primary key for the Payments table.

STEP 2: Create the Payments Subform

➤ You should be back in the Database window. Click the **Forms tab,** then open the **Loans subform** (from the second exercise) in Design view as shown in Figure 4.12b. If necessary, maximize the Form Design window.

➤ Click and drag the bottom edge of the **Details section** so that you have approximately 2 to 2½ inches of blank space in the Detail section. (This is where the Payments subform will go.)

➤ Click the **Subform/Subreport button** on the Toolbox toolbar, then click and drag in the Loans form to create the Payments subform. Release the mouse to begin the Subform/Subreport Wizard.

➤ The **Table/Query Option button** is selected, indicating that we will build the subform from a table or query. Click **Next.** You should see the Subform/Subreport dialog box in Figure 4.12b.

➤ Click the **drop-down arrow** on the Tables and Queries list box to select the **Payments table.** Click the **>> button** to add all of the fields in the Payments table to the subform. Click **Next.**

➤ The Subform Wizard asks you to define the fields that link the main form to the subform. The option button to **Choose from a list** is selected, as is **Show Payments for each record in <SQL Statement> using LoanID.** Click **Next.**

➤ The Wizard suggests **Payments subform** as the name of the subform. Click **Finish** to exit the Subform/Subreport wizard.

LINKING FIELDS, FORMS, AND SUBFORMS

Linking fields do not have to appear in the main form and subform but must be included in the underlying table or query. The LoanID, for example, is used to link the Loans form and the Payments form and need not appear in either form. We have, however, chosen to display the LoanID in both forms to emphasize the relationship between the corresponding tables.

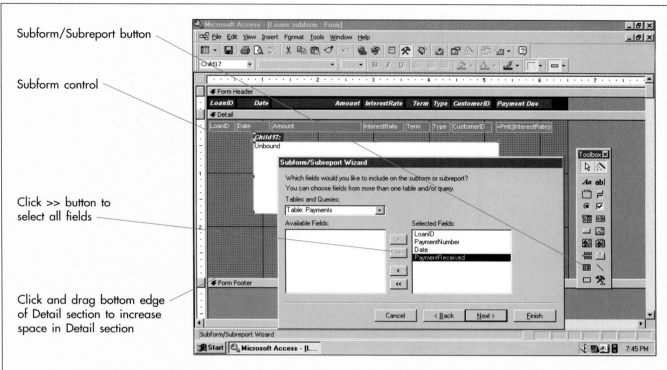

Subform/Subreport button

Subform control

Click >> button to select all fields

Click and drag bottom edge of Detail section to increase space in Detail section

(b) Create the Payments Subform (step 2)

FIGURE 4.12   Hands-on Exercise 4 (continued)

STEP 3: Change the Default View

➤ Maximize the window. Point to the **Form Selector box** in the upper-left corner of the Design window, click the **right mouse button** to display a shortcut menu, and click **Properties** to display the Form Properties dialog box in Figure 4.12c.

➤ Click in the **Default View box,** click the **drop-down arrow** to display the views, then click **Single Form.** Close the Properties dialog box.

➤ Select the label for the Payments subform control, then press the **Del key** to delete the label. Save the form.

THE DEFAULT VIEW PROPERTY

The Default View property determines how a form is dislayed initially and is especially important when working with multiple forms. In general, the highest level form(s) is (are) displayed in the Single Form view and the lowest level in the Datasheet view. In this example, the Customers and Loans forms are both set to the Single Form view, whereas the Payment form is set to the Datasheet view.

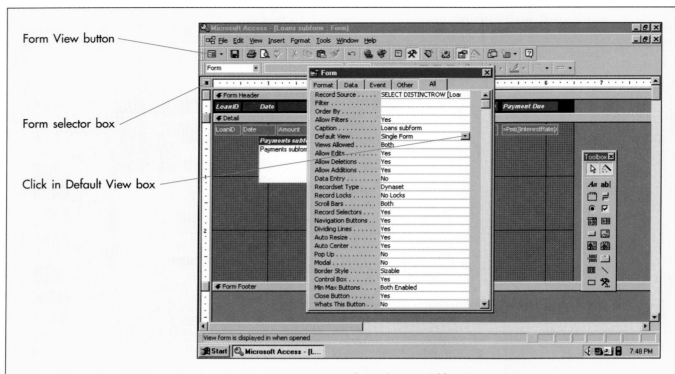

Form View button

Form selector box

Click in Default View box

(c) Change the Loans Subform View (step 3)

FIGURE 4.12   Hands-on Exercise 4 (continued)

STEP 4: The Loans Subform in Form View

➤ Click the **Form View button** to switch to the Form view for the Loans subform as shown in Figure 4.12d.

➤ Do not be concerned if the size and/or position of your form is different from ours as you can return to the Design view in order to make the necessary changes.

• The status bar of the Loans form indicates record 1 of 27, meaning that you are positioned on the first of 27 records in the Loans table.

• The status bar for the Payments subform indicates record 1 of 5, corresponding to the first of five payment records for this loan.

➤ Change to the **Design view** to adjust the column widths within the Payments subform. This is accomplished by opening the subform in the Datasheet view (see boxed tip on page 177 on modifying a subform) and adjusting the column headings.

➤ You will most likely have to size and/or move the Payments subform control within the Loans subform. Click and drag the subform control as necessary.

➤ Save, then close, the Loans subform.

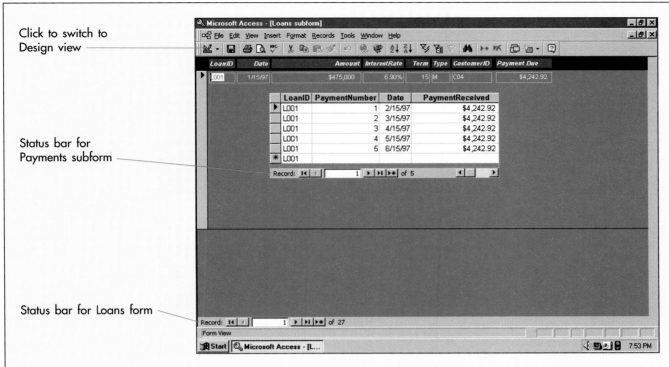

Click to switch to Design view

Status bar for Payments subform

Status bar for Loans form

(d) The Form View (step 4)

FIGURE 4.12   Hands-on Exercise 4 (continued)

STEP 5: The Customers Form

➤ You should be back in the Database window. Click the **Forms tab** (if necessary), then open the **Customers form** as shown in Figure 4.12e. Do not be concerned if the size of the Loans or Payments subforms are different from ours as you can return to the Design view to make the necessary changes.

• The status bar of the Customers form indicates record 1 of 11, meaning that you are positioned on the first of 11 records in the Customers table.

• The status bar for the Loans subform indicates record 1 of 3, corresponding to the first of three records for this customer.

• The status bar for the Payments subform indicates record 1 of 4, corresponding to the first of four payments for this loan.

➤ Change to the **Design view** to move and/or size the control for the Loans subform. You may also need to open the subform in the Datasheet view to adjust the column widths.

MODIFYING A SUBFORM

The Payment subform appears as an object in the Design view of the Loans form, but it can be opened and modified as an independent form. To open a subform, click outside the subform to deselect it, then double click the subform to open it.

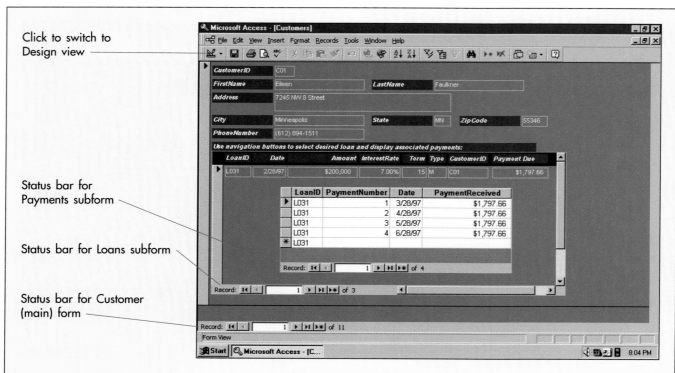

Click to switch to
Design view

Status bar for
Payments subform

Status bar for Loans subform

Status bar for Customer
(main) form

(e) The Customers Form (step 5)

FIGURE 4.12   Hands-on Exercise 4 (continued)

STEP 6: The Finishing Touches

➤ Point to the **Label tool,** then click and drag in the **Customers form** to create an unbound control as shown in Figure 4.12f.

➤ Release the mouse, then enter **Use navigation buttons to select desired loan and display associated payments.** Click outside the control when you have completed the text.

➤ Click the **Save button** to save the Customers form, which contains the two subforms.

USER-FRIENDLY FORMS

The phrase *user friendly* appears so frequently that we tend to take it for granted. The intention is clear, however, and you should strive to make your forms as clear as possible so that the user is provided with all the information he or she may need. It may be obvious to the designer that one has to click the Navigation buttons to move to a new loan, but a user unfamiliar with Access may not know that. Adding a descriptive label to the form goes a long way toward making the system successful.

Click to switch to Form view

Label tool

Create unbound control

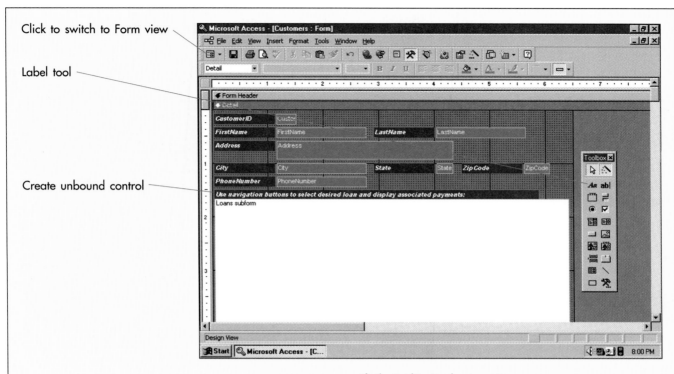

(f) The Finishing Touches (step 6)

FIGURE 4.12   Hands-on Exercise 4 (continued)

STEP 7: Make Your Payments

➤ Change to the **Form view.** Click the ▶| on the status bar for the Customers form to move to the last record as shown in Figure 4.12g. This should be Customer C11 (your record) that you entered in the earlier exercises in this chapter. You currently have two loans, L121 and L122, the first of which is displayed.

➤ Click in the **Payments subform.** Enter the payment number, press **Tab,** enter the date of your first payment, press **Tab,** then enter the amount paid. Press **enter** to move to the next payment record and enter this payment as well. Press **enter** and enter a third payment.

➤ Click the **selection area** at the left of the form to select this record. Pull down the **File menu** and click **Print** to display the Print dialog box. Click the **Selected Records Option button.** Click **OK** to print the selected form.

➤ Close the Customers form. Click **Yes** if asked to save the changes to the form.

➤ Close the National Bank database and exit Access.

THREE SETS OF NAVIGATION BUTTONS

Each form or subform has its own set of navigation buttons. Thus you are looking at record 11 of 11 in the Customers form, loan 1 of 2 in the Loans form for this customer, and payment 3 of 3 in the Payments form for this loan.

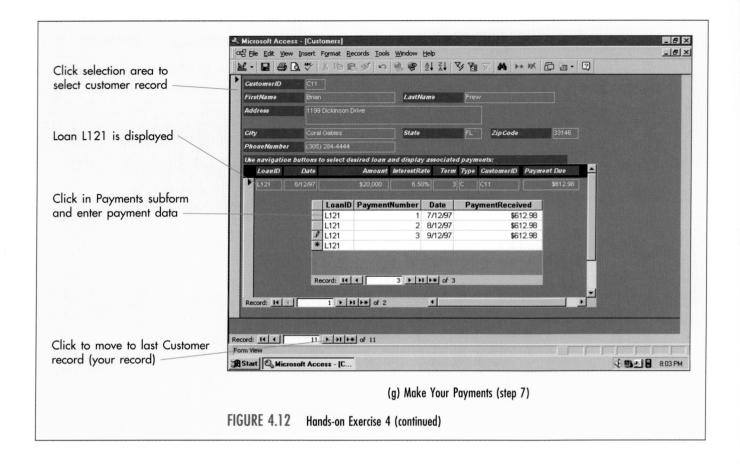

Click selection area to select customer record

Loan L121 is displayed

Click in Payments subform and enter payment data

Click to move to last Customer record (your record)

(g) Make Your Payments (step 7)

FIGURE 4.12   Hands-on Exercise 4 (continued)

SUMMARY

An Access database may contain multiple tables. Each table stores data about a specific subject. Each table has a primary key, which is a field (or combination of fields) that uniquely identifies each record.

A one-to-many relationship uses the primary key of the "one" table as a foreign key in the "many" table. (A foreign key is simply the primary key of the related table.) The Relationships window enables you to graphically create a one-to-many relationship by dragging the join field from one table to the other.

Referential integrity ensures that the tables in a database are consistent with one another. When referential integrity is enforced, Access prevents you from adding a record to a related table if that record contains an invalid foreign key. It also prevents you from deleting a record in the primary table if there is a corresponding record in the related table.

A subform is a form within a form and is used to display data from a related table. It is created most easily with the Form Wizard, then modified in the Form Design view just as any other form. A main form can have any number of subforms. Subforms can extend to two levels, enabling a subform to be created within a subform.

The power of a select query lies in its ability to include fields from several tables. The query shows the relationships that exist between the tables by drawing a join line that indicates how to relate the data. The Tables row displays the name of the table containing the corresponding field. Once created, a multiple table query can be the basis for a form or report.

Tables can be added to a relational database without disturbing the data in existing tables. A database can have several one-to-many relationships.

Build button
Control Source
    property
Datasheet view
Foreign key
Form view
Function

Main form
One-to-many
    relationship
Primary key
Primary table
Referential integrity
Related table

Relationship line
Relationships window
Subform
Subform Wizard
Table row

MULTIPLE CHOICE

1. Which of the following will cause a problem of referential integrity when there is a one-to-many relationship between customers and loans?
    (a) The deletion of a customer record that has corresponding loan records
    (b) The deletion of a customer record that has no corresponding loan records
    (c) The deletion of a loan record with a corresponding customer record
    (d) All of the above

2. Which of the following will cause a problem of referential integrity when there is a one-to-many relationship between customers and loans?
    (a) The addition of a new customer prior to entering loans for that customer
    (b) The addition of a new loan that references an invalid customer
    (c) Both (a) and (b)
    (d) Neither (a) nor (b)

3. Which of the following is true about a database that monitors players and the teams to which those players are assigned?
    (a) The PlayerID will be defined as a primary key within the Teams table
    (b) The TeamID will be defined as a primary key within the Players table
    (c) The PlayerID will appear as a foreign key within the Teams table
    (d) The TeamID will appear as a foreign key within the Players table

4. Which of the following best expresses the relationships within the expanded National Bank database as it appeared at the end of the chapter?
    (a) There is a one-to-many relationship between customers and loans
    (b) There is a one-to-many relationship between loans and payments
    (c) Both (a) and (b)
    (d) Neither (a) nor (b)

5. A database has a one-to-many relationship between branches and employees (one branch can have many employees). Which of the following is true?
    (a) The EmployeeID will be defined as a primary key within the Branches table
    (b) The BranchID will be defined as a primary key within the Employees table
    (c) The EmployeeID will appear as a foreign key within the Branches table
    (d) The BranchID will appear as a foreign key within the Employees table

6. Every table in an Access database:
   (a) Must be related to every other table
   (b) Must have one or more foreign keys
   (c) Both (a) and (b)
   (d) Neither (a) nor (b)

7. Which of the following is true of a main form and subform that are created in conjunction with the one-to-many relationship between customers and loans?
   (a) The main form should be based on the Customers table
   (b) The subform should be based on the Loans table
   (c) Both (a) and (b)
   (d) Neither (a) nor (b)

8. Which of the following is true regarding the navigation buttons for a main form and its associated subform?
   (a) The navigation buttons pertain to just the main form
   (b) The navigation buttons pertain to just the subform
   (c) There are separate navigation buttons for each form
   (d) There are no navigation buttons at all

9. How do you open a subform?
   (a) Go to the Design view of the associated main form, click anywhere in the main form to deselect the subform, then double click the subform
   (b) Go to the Database window, select the subform, then click the Open or Design buttons, depending on the desired view
   (c) Both (a) and (b)
   (d) Neither (a) nor (b)

10. Which of the following is true?
    (a) A main form may contain multiple subforms
    (b) A subform may contain another subform
    (c) Both (a) and (b)
    (d) Neither (a) nor (b)

11. Which command displays the open tables in an Access database in equal-sized windows one on top of another?
    (a) The Tile command in the Window menu
    (b) The Cascade command in the Window menu
    (c) The Tile command in the Relationships menu
    (d) The Cascade command in the Relationships menu

12. Which of the following describes how to move and size a field list within the Relationships window?
    (a) Click and drag the title bar to size the field list
    (b) Click and drag a border or corner to move the field list
    (c) Both (a) and (b)
    (d) Neither (a) nor (b)

13. Which of the following is true regarding entries in a Criteria row of a select query?
    (a) A text field may be entered with or without quotation marks
    (b) A date field may be entered with or without surrounding number (pound) signs
    (c) Both (a) and (b)
    (d) Neither (a) nor (b)

14. Which of the following is true about a select query?

    (a) It may reference fields in one or more tables

    (b) It may have one or more criteria rows

    (c) It may sort on one or more fields

    (d) All of the above

15. A report may be based on:

    (a) A table

    (b) A query

    (c) Both (a) and (b)

    (d) Neither (a) nor (b)

ANSWERS

1. a	**6.** d	**11.** b
2. b	**7.** c	**12.** d
3. d	**8.** c	**13.** c
4. c	**9.** c	**14.** d
5. d	**10.** c	**15.** c

PRACTICE WITH ACCESS 97

1. Figure 4.13 contains a modified version of the Customers form and its associated subforms. Complete the hands-on exercises in the chapter, then modify the completed Customers form so that it matches Figure 4.13. (The easiest way to add the label at the top of the form is to create a form header.) Follow the steps below to add the clip art image. (The faster your machine, the more you will enjoy the exercise.)

    a. Open the Customers form in the Design view. Double click the Loans subform control to open the Loans subform in the Design view. Move the control for the Payments subform to the left to allow room for the OLE object.

    b. Click the Unbound Object Frame tool on the toolbox. (If you are unsure as to which tool to click, just point to the tool to display the name of the tool.)

    c. Click and drag in the Loans subform to size the frame, then release the mouse to display an Insert Object dialog box.

    d. Click the Create New Option button. Select the Microsoft Clip Gallery as the object type. Click OK.

    e. Click the ClipArt tab. Choose the category and picture you want from within the Clip Gallery. Click the Insert button to insert the picture into the Access form and simultaneously close the Clip Gallery dialog box. Do *not* be concerned if only a portion of the picture appears on the form.

    f. Right click the newly inserted object to display a shortcut menu, then click Properties to display the Properties dialog box. Click the Format tab, then select (click) the Size Mode property and select Stretch from the associated list. Change the Back Style property to Transparent, the Special Effect property to Flat, and the Border Style property to Transparent. Close the Properties dialog box.

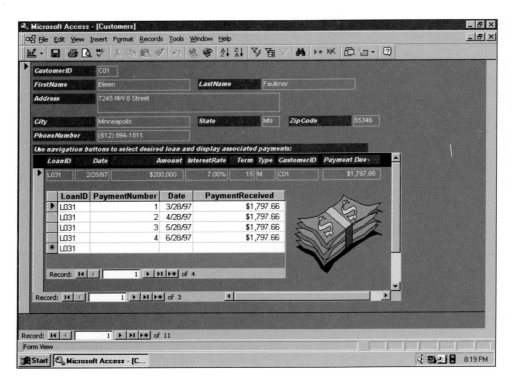

FIGURE 4.13   Screen for Practice Exercise 1

g. You should see the entire clip art image, although it may be distorted because the size and shape of the frame you inserted in steps (a) and (b) does not match the image you selected. Click and drag the sizing handles on the frame to size the object so that its proportions are correct. Click anywhere in the middle of the frame (the mouse pointer changes to a hand) to move the frame elsewhere in the form.

h. If you want to display a different object, double click the clip art image to return to the Clip Gallery in order to select another object. View the completed form, then make any final changes.

i. Print the completed form with your customer information. Remember to click the selection area prior to printing. (You are still customer C11.)

2. Interest rates have come down and National Bank has decided to run a promotion on car loans. The loan officer would like to contact all existing customers with a car loan to inform them of their new rates. Create a report similar to the one in Figure 4.14 in response to the request from the loan officer.

The report may be based on a query that contains fields from both the Customers and the Loans tables, or it may be created directly in the Report Wizard. Note, too, the clip art image, which is required in the Report heading and which can be added using the techniques described in the previous problem. Be sure to add your name to the heading so that your instructor will know the report came from you.

3. Use the Employee database in the Exploring Access folder on the data disk to create the main form and subform combination shown in Figure 4.15. There is a one-to-many relationship between locations and employees (one location contains many employees), and you need to define this relationship prior to creating the form.

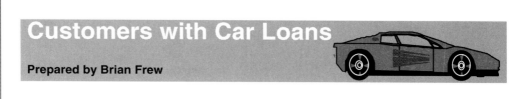

Customers with Car Loans

Prepared by Brian Frew

Last Name	First	Address	Phone Number
Frew	Brian	1199 Dickinson Drive Coral Gables FL 33146	(305) 284-4444
Grauer	Benjamin	10000 Sample Road Coral Springs FL 33073	(305) 444-5555
Powell	David	5070 Battle Road Decatur GA 30034	(301) 345-6556
Rey	Alex	3456 Main Highway Denver CO 80228	(303) 555-6666
Solomon	Wendy	7500 Reno Road Houston TX 77090	(713) 427-3104
Wit	Scott	5660 NW 175 Terrace Baltimore MD 21224	(410) 753-0345
Wit	Scott	5660 NW 175 Terrace Baltimore MD 21224	(410) 753-0345
Zacco	Michelle	488 Gold Street Gainesville FL 32601	(904) 374-5660

Thursday, June 10, 1997   Page 1 of 1

FIGURE 4.14   Report for Practice Exercise 2

You also need to modify the underlying Employee table to use a Location code rather than the Location name. (The change in design was requested by the end-user after the initial database was completed. This is not a trivial task, and you will see how important it is to arrive at a satisfactory design as early as possible in a project.)

In creating the form we used the Colorful 2 style, but you are free to use any style you like. You can create the forms using the techniques in the second hands-on exercise. Alternatively, you can access the Subform/Subreport Wizard directly from the Form Wizard by following the steps on the next page.

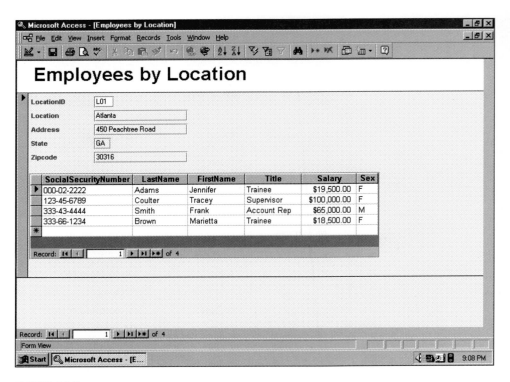

FIGURE 4.15   Screen for Practice Exercise 3

a. Click the Forms tab in the Database window, click New to display the New Form dialog box, then click Form Wizard as the means of creating the form. Select Locations as the table on which to base the main form, and click OK to start the Form Wizard.

b. Click the >> button to select all of the fields in the Locations table for the form. Do *not,* however, click Next at this time as you will select additional fields from the Employees table for inclusion on the form.

c. Click the drop-down arrow on the Tables/Queries list box, select the Employees table, then add all of the fields in the Employees table except Location ID. Click Next.

d. View your data by Locations and be sure the Form with subform(s) option button is selected. Click Next.

e. Choose the Datasheet layout for your subform, then answer the remaining questions to complete the forms.

f. Add your name as an Account Rep in Miami at a salary of $50,000. Print the location form for the Miami location only, and submit it to your instructor as proof you did this exercise.

4. The Titles form in Figure 4.16 is based on the Employees database referenced in problem 3. Open the Employee database and add the one-to-many relationship between titles and employees, then create the form in Figure 4.16. As in the previous exercise, you will need to change the Employees table to accommodate a Title code rather than a Title description.

   Use the technique described in problem 1 to add a clip art logo of your choice to the form. (You can download additional clipart from the site www.clipart.com).

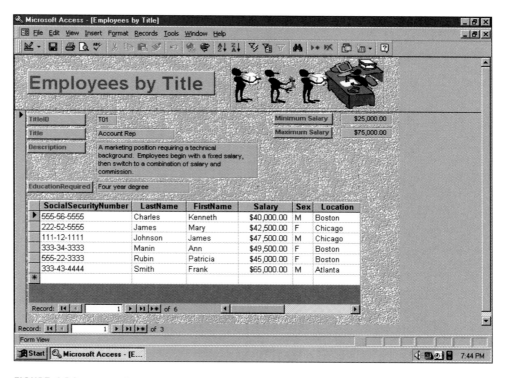

FIGURE 4.16   Report for Practice Exercise 4

CASE STUDIES

Recreational Sports League

Design a database for a recreational sports league that will monitor players, coaches, and sponsors. There may be any number of teams in the league, with each team having any number of players. A player is associated with only one team.

Each team has at least one coach. The league also imposes the rule that a person may not coach more than one team. Each team has a sponsor such as a local business. One sponsor can be associated with multiple teams.

Your solution should make the system as realistic as possible. The player table, for example, requires not only the identifying information for each player (name, address, phone, and so on) but additional fields such as birth date (to implement age limits on various teams), ability ratings, and so on. Your system should be capable of producing reports that will display all information about a specific team, such as its players, coach, and sponsor. The league administrators would also like master lists of all teams, players, coaches, and sponsors.

Show the required tables in the database, being sure to indicate the primary key and foreign keys in each table. Indicate one or two other fields in each table (you need not list them all).

The Personnel Director

You have been hired as a personnel director for a medium-sized company with offices in several cities. You require the usual personal data for each employee (birth date, hire date, home address, and so on.) You also need to reach an employee at work, and must be able to retrieve the office address, office phone number, and office fax number for each employee. Each employee is assigned to only one branch office.

Your duties also include the administration of various health plans offered by the company. Each employee is given his or her choice of several health plans. Each plan has a monthly premium and deductible amount. Once the deductible is reached, each plan pays a designated percentage of all subsequent expenses.

Design a database that will include the necessary data to provide all of the information you need. Show the required tables in the database, being sure to indicate the primary key and foreign keys in each table. Indicate one or two other fields in each table (you need not list them all).

The Franchise

The management of a national restaurant chain is automating its procedure for monitoring its restaurants, restaurant owners (franchisees), and the contracts that govern the two. Each restaurant has one owner (franchisee). There is no limit on the number of restaurants an individual may own, and franchisees are encouraged to apply for multiple restaurants.

The payment from the franchisee to the company varies according to the contract in effect for the particular restaurant. The company offers a choice of contracts, which vary according to the length of the contract, the franchise fee, and the percentage of the restaurant's sales paid to the company for marketing and royalty fees. Each restaurant has one contract, but a given contract may pertain to many restaurants.

The company needs a database capable of retrieving all data for a given restaurant, such as its annual sales, location, phone number, owner, and type of contract in effect. It would also like to know all restaurants owned by one person as well as all restaurants governed by a specific contract type.

Widgets of America

Widgets of America gives its sales staff exclusive rights to specific customers. Each sales person has many customers, but a specific customer always deals with the same sales representative. The company needs to know all of the orders placed by a specific customer as well as the total business generated by each sales representative. The data for each order includes the date the order was placed and the amount of the order. Design a database capable of producing the information required by the company.

Show the required tables in the database, being sure to indicate the primary key and foreign keys in each table. Indicate one or two other fields in each table (you need not list them all).

5

MANY-TO-MANY RELATIONSHIPS: A MORE COMPLEX SYSTEM

OBJECTIVES

After reading this chapter you will be able to:

1. Define a many-to-many relationship and explain how it is implemented in Access.
2. Use the Cascade Update and Cascade Delete options in the Relationships window to relax enforcement of referential integrity.
3. Explain how the AutoNumber field type simplifies the entry of a primary key for a new record.
4. Create a main and subform based on a query; discuss the advantage of using queries rather than tables as the basis for a form or report.
5. Create a parameter query; explain how a parameter query can be made to accept multiple parameters.
6. Use aggregate functions in a select query to perform calculations on groups of records.
7. Use the Get External Data command to add external tables to an existing database.

OVERVIEW

This chapter introduces a new case study to give you additional practice in database design. The system extends the concept of a relational database that was introduced in the previous chapter to include both a one-to-many and a many-to-many relationship. The case solution reviews earlier material on establishing relationships in Access and the importance of referential integrity. Another point of particular interest is the use of an AutoNumber field to facilitate the addition of new records.

The chapter extends what you already know about subforms and queries, and uses both to present information from related tables. The

189

forms created in this chapter are based on multiple table queries rather than tables. The queries themselves are of a more advanced nature. We show you how to create a parameter query, where the user is prompted to enter the criteria when the query is run. We also show you how to create queries that use the aggregate functions built into Access to perform calculations on groups of records.

The chapter contains four hands-on exercises to implement the case study. We think you will be pleased with what you have accomplished by the end of the chapter, working with a sophisticated system that is typical of real-world applications.

CASE STUDY: THE COMPUTER SUPER STORE

The case study in this chapter is set within the context of a computer store that requires a database for its customers, products, and orders. The store maintains the usual customer data (name, address, phone, etc.). It also keeps data about the products it sells, storing for each product a product ID, description, quantity on hand, quantity on order, and unit price. And finally, the store has to track its orders. It needs to know the date an order was received, the customer who placed it, the products that were ordered, and the quantity of each product ordered.

Think, for a moment, about the tables that are necessary and the relationships between those tables, then compare your thoughts to our solution in Figure 5.1. You probably have no trouble recognizing the need for the Customers, Products, and Orders tables. Initially, you may be puzzled by the Order Details table, but you will soon appreciate why it is there and how powerful it is.

You can use the Customers, Products, and Orders tables individually to obtain information about a specific customer, product, or order, respectively. For example:

Query: What is Jeffrey Muddell's phone number?
Answer: Jeffrey Muddell's phone is (305) 253-3909.

Query: What is the price of a Pentium laptop/133? How many are in stock?
Answer: A Pentium laptop/133 sells for $2,599. Fifteen systems are in stock.

Query: When was order O0003 placed?
Answer: Order O0003 was placed on April 18, 1997.

Other queries require you to relate the tables to one another. There is, for example, a *one-to-many relationship* between customers and orders. One customer can place many orders, but a specific order can be associated with only one customer. The tables are related through the CustomerID, which appears as the *primary key* in the Customers table and as a *foreign key* in the Orders table. Consider:

Query: What is the name of the customer who placed order number O0003?
Answer: Order O0003 was placed by Jeffrey Muddell.

Query: How many orders were placed by Jeffrey Muddell?
Answer: Jeffrey Muddell placed five orders: O0003, O0014, O0016, O0024, and O0025.

These queries require you to use two tables. To answer the first query, you would search the Orders table to find order O0003 and obtain the CustomerID (C0006 in this example). You would then search the Customers table for the customer with this CustomerID and retrieve the customer's name. To answer the

Customer ID	First Name	Last Name	Address	City	State	Zip Code	Phone Number
C0001	Benjamin	Lee	1000 Call Street	Tallahassee	FL	33340	(904) 327-4124
C0002	Eleanor	Milgrom	7245 NW 8 Street	Margate	FL	33065	(305) 974-1234
C0003	Neil	Goodman	4215 South 81 Street	Margate	FL	33065	(305) 444-5555
C0004	Nicholas	Colon	9020 N.W. 75 Street	Coral Springs	FL	33065	(305) 753-9887
C0005	Michael	Ware	276 Brickell Avenue	Miami	FL	33131	(305) 444-3980
C0006	Jeffrey	Muddell	9522 S.W. 142 Street	Miami	FL	33176	(305) 253-3909
C0007	Ashley	Geoghegan	7500 Center Lane	Coral Springs	FL	33070	(305) 753-7830
C0008	Serena	Sherard	5000 Jefferson Lane	Gainesville	FL	32601	(904) 375-6442
C0009	Luis	Couto	455 Bargello Avenue	Coral Gables	FL	33146	(305) 666-4801
C0010	Derek	Anderson	6000 Tigertail Avenue	Coconut Grove	FL	33120	(305) 446-8900
C0011	Lauren	Center	12380 S.W. 137 Avenue	Miami	FL	33186	(305) 385-4432
C0012	Robert	Slane	4508 N.W. 7 Street	Miami	FL	33131	(305) 635-3454

(a) Customers Table

Product ID	Product Name	Units In Stock	Units On Order	Unit Price
P0001	Pentium desktop/166 with MMX	50	0	$1,899.00
P0002	Pentium desktop/200 with MMX	25	5	$1,999.00
P0003	Pentium Pro desktop/180	125	15	$2,099.00
P0004	Pentium Pro desktop/200	25	50	$2,299.00
P0005	Pentium laptop/133	15	25	$2,599.00
P0006	15" SVGA Monitor	50	0	$499.00
P0007	17" SVGA Monitor	25	10	$899.00
P0008	20" Multisync Monitor	50	20	$1,599.00
P0009	2.5 Gb IDE Hard Drive	15	20	$399.00
P0010	2 Gb SCSI Hard Drive	25	15	$799.00
P0011	4 Gb SCSI Hard Drive	10	0	$1,245.00
P0012	CD-ROM: 8X	40	0	$249.00
P0013	CD-ROM: 12X	50	15	$449.95
P0014	HD Floppy Disks	500	200	$9.99
P0015	HD Data Cartridges	100	50	$14.79
P0016	2 Gb Tape Backup	15	3	$179.95
P0017	Serial Mouse	150	50	$69.95
P0018	Trackball	55	0	$59.95
P0019	Joystick	250	100	$39.95
P0020	Fax/Modem 56 Kbps	35	10	$189.95
P0021	Fax/Modem 33.6 Kbps	20	0	$65.95
P0022	Laser Printer	100	15	$1,395.00
P0023	Ink Jet Printer	50	50	$249.95
P0024	Color Ink Jet Printer	125	25	$569.95
P0025	Windows 95	400	200	$95.95
P0026	Norton Anti-Virus	150	50	$75.95
P0027	Norton Utilities	150	50	$115.95
P0028	Microsoft Scenes Screen Saver	75	25	$29.95
P0029	Microsoft Bookshelf	250	100	$129.95
P0030	Microsoft Cinemania	25	10	$59.95
P0031	Professional Photos on CD-ROM	15	0	$45.95

(b) Products Table

Order ID	Customer ID	Order Date
O0001	C0004	4/15/97
O0002	C0003	4/18/97
O0003	C0006	4/18/97
O0004	C0007	4/18/97
O0005	C0001	4/20/97
O0006	C0001	4/21/97
O0007	C0002	4/21/97
O0008	C0002	4/22/97
O0009	C0001	4/22/97
O0010	C0002	4/22/97
O0011	C0001	4/24/97
O0012	C0007	4/24/97
O0013	C0004	4/24/97
O0014	C0006	4/25/97
O0015	C0009	4/25/97
O0016	C0006	4/26/97
O0017	C0011	4/26/97
O0018	C0011	4/26/97
O0019	C0012	4/27/97
O0020	C0012	4/28/97
O0021	C0010	4/29/97
O0022	C0010	4/29/97
O0023	C0008	4/30/97
O0024	C0006	5/1/97
O0025	C0006	5/1/97

(c) Orders Table

Order ID	Product ID	Quantity
O0001	P0013	1
O0001	P0014	4
O0001	P0027	1
O0002	P0001	1
O0002	P0006	1
O0002	P0020	1
O0002	P0022	1
O0003	P0005	1
O0003	P0020	1
O0003	P0022	1
O0004	P0003	1
O0004	P0010	1
O0004	P0022	2
O0005	P0003	2
O0005	P0012	2
O0005	P0016	2
O0006	P0007	1
O0006	P0014	10
O0007	P0028	1
O0007	P0030	3
O0008	P0001	1
O0008	P0004	3
O0008	P0008	4
O0008	P0011	2
O0008	P0012	1
O0009	P0006	1
O0010	P0002	2
O0010	P0022	1
O0010	P0023	1
O0011	P0016	2
O0011	P0020	2
O0012	P0021	10
O0012	P0029	10
O0012	P0030	10
O0013	P0009	4
O0013	P0016	10
O0013	P0024	2
O0014	P0019	2
O0014	P0028	1
O0015	P0018	1
O0015	P0020	1
O0016	P0029	2
O0017	P0019	2
O0018	P0009	1
O0018	P0025	2
O0018	P0026	2
O0019	P0014	25
O0020	P0024	1
O0021	P0004	1
O0022	P0027	1
O0023	P0021	1
O0023	P0028	1
O0023	P0029	1
O0024	P0007	1
O0024	P0013	5
O0024	P0014	3
O0024	P0016	1
O0025	P0012	2
O0025	P0029	2

(d) Order Details Table

FIGURE 5.1   Super Store Database

second query, you would begin in the Customers table and search for Jeffrey Mud-dell to determine the CustomerID (C0006), then search the Orders table for all records with this CustomerID.

The system is more complicated than earlier examples in that there is a *many-to-many relationship* between orders and products. One order can include many products, and at the same time a specific product can appear in many orders. The implementation of a many-to-many relationship requires an additional table, the Order Details table, containing (at a minimum) the primary keys of the individual tables.

The Order Details table will contain many records with the same OrderID, because there is a separate record for each product in a given order. It will also contain many records with the same ProductID, because there is a separate record for every order containing that product. However, the *combination* of OrderID and ProductID is unique, and this **combined key** becomes the primary key in the Order Details table. The Order Details table also contains an additional field (Quantity) whose value depends on the primary key (the *combination* of OrderID and ProductID). Thus:

Query: How many units of product P0014 were included in order O0001?
Answer: Order O0001 included four units of product P0014. (The order also included one unit of Product P0013 and one unit of P0027.)

The Order Details table has four records with a ProductID of P0014. It also has three records with an OrderID of O0001. There is, however, only one record with a ProductID P0014 *and* an OrderID O0001, which is for four units.

The Order Details table makes it possible to determine all products in one order or all orders for one product. You can also use the Products table in conjunction with the Order Details table to determine the names of those products. Consider:

Query: Which orders include a Pentium desktop/166 with MMX?
Answer: A Pentium desktop/166 with MMX is found in orders O0002 and O0008.

Query: Which products were included in Order O0003?
Answer: Order O0003 consisted of products P0005 (a Pentium laptop/133), P0020 (a 56Kbps fax/modem), and P0022 (a laser printer).

To answer the first query, you would begin in the Products table to find the ProductID for a Pentium desktop/166 with MMX (P0001). You would then search the Order Details table for records containing a ProductID of P0001, which in turn identifies orders O0002 and O0008. The second query is processed in similar fashion except that you would search the Order Details table for an OrderID of O0003. This time you would find three records with ProductIDs P0005, P0020, and P0022, respectively. You would then go to the Products table to look up the ProductIDs to return the name of each product.

We've emphasized that the power of a relational database comes from the inclusion of multiple tables and the relationships between those tables. As you already know, you can use data from several tables to compute the answer to more complex queries. For example:

Query: What is the total cost of order O0006?
Answer: Order O0006 costs $998.90.

To determine the cost of an order, you must first identify all of the products associated with that order, the quantity of each product, and the price of each product. The previous queries have shown how you would find the products in an order and the associated quantities. The price of a specific product is obtained from the Products table, which enables you to compute the invoice by multiplying the price of each product by the quantity. Thus, the total cost of order O0006 is $998.90. (One unit of P0007 at $899.00 and ten units of product P0014 at $9.99.)

PRACTICE WITH DATABASE DESIGN

An Access database consists of multiple tables, each of which stores data about a specific subject. To use Access effectively, you must be able to relate the tables to one another, which in turn requires a knowledge of database design. Appendix B provides additional examples that enable you to master the principles of a relational database.

The AutoNumber Field Type

Look carefully at the Customer, Order, and Product numbers in their respective tables and note that each set of numbers is consecutive. This is accomplished by specifying the *AutoNumber field* type for each of these fields in the design of the individual tables. The AutoNumber specification automatically assigns the next sequential number to the primary key of a new record. If, for example, you were to add a new customer to the existing Customers table, that customer would be assigned the number 13. In similar fashion, the next order will be order number 26, and the next product will be product number 32. (Deleting a record does not, however, renumber the remaining records in the table; that is, once a value is assigned to a primary key, the primary key will always retain that value.)

The C, O, and P that appear as the initial character of each field, as well as the high-order zeros, are *not* part of the fields themselves, but are displayed through the *Format property* associated with each field. In other words, the internal value of the first CustomerID is the number 1 (not C0001). The letters function as a prefix and identify the table to which the field belongs; for example, C0001, O0001, and P0001 correspond to the first record in the Customers, Orders, and Products tables, respectively. The zeros provide a uniform appearance for that field throughout the table.

SIMPLIFIED DATA ENTRY

The AutoNumber field type is often assigned to the primary key of a table to ensure a unique value (the next consecutive number) in each new record. This simplifies data entry in situations where the user has no knowledge of what the primary key should be, as in the case of a customer number other than a social security number. The Format property can be used in conjunction with an AutoNumber field to improve its appearance through the addition of a letter prefix and/or high-order zeros.

The Relationships Window

The Relationships window in Figure 5.2 shows the Computer Store database as it will be implemented in Access. The database contains the Customers, Orders,

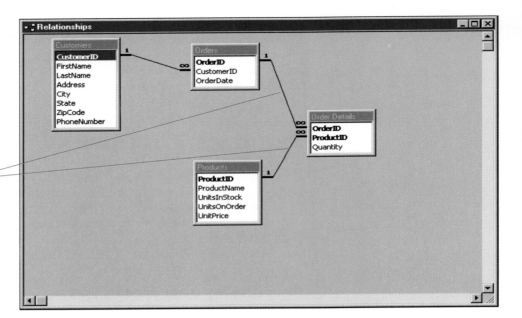

Many-to-many relationship implemented by a pair of one-to-many relationships

FIGURE 5.2   The Relationships Window

Products, and Order Details tables as per the previous discussion. The field lists display the fields within each table, with the primary key shown in bold. The OrderID and ProductID are both shown in bold in the Order Details table, to indicate that the primary key consists of the combination of these fields.

The many-to-many relationship between Orders and Products is implemented by a *pair* of one-to-many relationships. There is a one-to-many relationship between the Orders table and the Order Details table. There is a second one-to-many relationship between the Products table and the Order Details table. In other words, the Orders and Products tables are not related to each other directly, but indirectly through the pair of one-to-many relationships with the Order Details table.

The ***relationship lines*** show the relationships between the tables. The number 1 appears next to the Orders table on the relationship line connecting the Orders table and the Order Details table. The infinity symbol appears at the end of the line next to the Order Details table. The one-to-many relationship between these tables means that each record in the Orders table can be associated with many records in the Order Details table. Each record in the Order Details table, however, can be associated with only one record in the Orders table.

In similar fashion, there is also a one-to-many relationship between the Products table and the Order Details table. The number 1 appears on the relationship line next to the Products table. The infinity symbol appears at the end of the relationship line next to the Order Details table. Each record in the Products table can be associated with many records in the Order Details table, but each record in the Order Details table is associated with only one product.

Referential Integrity

The concept of ***referential integrity,*** which was introduced in the previous chapter, ensures that the records in related tables are consistent with one another. Enforcement of referential integrity prevents you from adding a record to the related table with an invalid foreign key. It means, for example, that you cannot add a record to the Orders table that references a nonexistent customer. Access will, however, let you add an order without referencing a specific customer, unless the CustomerID is a required field or some other validation rule is in effect.

Enforcement of referential integrity will also prevent you from deleting a record in the primary (Customers) table when there are corresponding records in the related (Orders) table. Nor will it let you change the primary key of a record in the primary (Customers) table if there are matching records in the related (Orders) table.

Consider, for example, the application of referential integrity to the one-to-many relationship between the Orders table and the Order Details table. Referential integrity prevents the addition of a record to the related (Order Details) table with a specific value of OrderID unless there is a corresponding record in the primary (Orders) table. It prevents the deletion of a record in the Orders table when there are corresponding records in the Order Details table. And finally, it prevents the modification of the OrderID in any record in the Orders table when there are matching records in the Order Details table.

There may be times, however, when you want to delete an order and simultaneously delete the corresponding records in the Order Details table. This is accomplished by enabling the *cascaded deletion* of related records, so that when you delete a record in the Orders table, Access automatically deletes the associated records in the Order Details table.

You might also want to enable the *cascaded updating* of related fields to correct the value of an OrderID. Enforcement of referential integrity would ordinarily prevent you from changing the value of the OrderID field in the Orders table when there are corresponding records in the Order Details table. You could, however, specify the cascaded updating of related fields so that if you were to change the OrderID in the Orders table, the corresponding fields in the Order Details table would also change.

USE WITH CAUTION

The cascaded deletion of related records relaxes referential integrity and eliminates errors that would otherwise occur during data entry. That does not mean, however, that the option should always be selected, and in fact, most of the time it is disabled. What would happen, for example, in an employee database with a one-to-many relationship between branch offices and employees, if cascade deleted records was in effect and a branch office was eliminated?

HANDS-ON EXERCISE 1

Relationships and Referential Integrity

Objective: To create relationships between existing tables in order to demonstrate referential integrity; to edit an existing relationship to allow the cascaded deletion of related records. Use Figure 5.3 as a guide in the exercise.

STEP 1: Add a Customer (the AutoNumber field type)

➤ Start Access. Open the **Computer Store database** in the **Exploring Access folder.**

➤ The **Tables tab** is already selected in the Database window. Open the **Customers table,** then click the **Maximize button** (if necessary) so that the table takes the entire screen as shown in Figure 5.3a.

➤ Click the **New Record button,** then click in the **First Name field.** Enter the first letter of your first name (e.g., "J" as shown in the figure):

- The record selector changes to a pencil to indicate that you are in the process of entering a record.

- The CustomerID is assigned automatically as soon as you begin to enter data. *Remember your customer number as you will use it throughout the chapter.* (Your CustomerID is 13, not C0013. The prefix and high-order zeros are displayed through the Format property. See boxed tip.)

THE AUTONUMBER FIELD TYPE AND FORMAT PROPERTY

The Format property can enhance the appearance of an AutoNumber field by displaying a prefix and/or high-order zeros. To view (or assign) the Format property of a field, open the table in Design view, select (click) the field name in the upper part of the window, then click the Format property and enter the desired format. Our Customers table, for example, uses the format \C0000, which displays a C in front of the field and pads it with high-order zeros. The Format property determines how a value is displayed, but does not affect how it is stored in the table. The CustomerID of the first customer, for example, is stored as the number 1, rather than C0001.

New Record button

CustomerID assigned automatically as soon as you begin to enter data

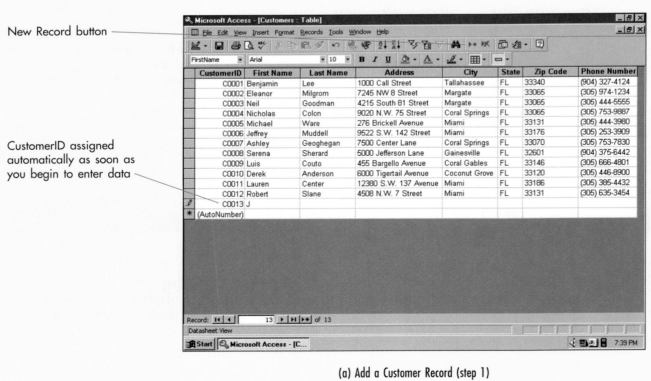

(a) Add a Customer Record (step 1)

FIGURE 5.3 Hands-on Exercise 1

➤ Complete your customer record, pressing the **Tab key** to move from one field to the next. Press **Tab** after you have entered the last field (phone number) to complete the record.

➤ Close the Customers table.

STEP 2: The Relationships Window

➤ Pull down the **Tools menu** and click **Relationships** to open the Relationships window as shown in Figure 5.3b. (The tables are not yet visible.) Maximize the Relationships window so that you have more room in which to work.

➤ Pull down the **Relationships menu** and click **Show Table** (or click the **Show Table button** on the Relationships toolbar) to display the Show Table dialog box.

➤ The **Tables tab** is selected within the Show Table dialog box, and the **Customers table** is selected. Click the **Add Command button** (or double click the **table name**) to add the Customers table to the Relationships window.

➤ Add the **Order Details, Orders,** and **Products** tables in similar fashion. Close the Show Table dialog box.

➤ Point to the bottom border of the **Customers field list** (the mouse pointer changes to a double arrow), then click and drag the border until all of the fields are visible. (The vertical scroll bar will disappear.)

➤ If necessary, click and drag the bottom border of the other tables until all of their fields are visible.

➤ Click and drag the title bars to move the field lists so that they are positioned as in Figure 5.3b.

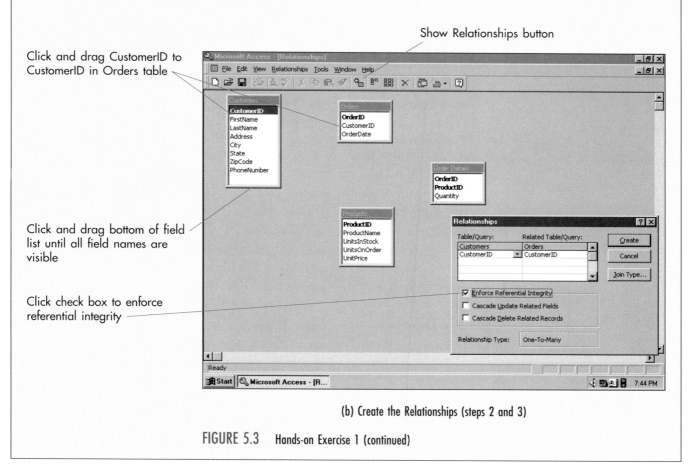

(b) Create the Relationships (steps 2 and 3)

FIGURE 5.3   Hands-on Exercise 1 (continued)

STEP 3: Create the Relationships

➤ Click and drag the **CustomerID field** in the Customers field list to the **CustomerID field** in the Orders field list. You will see the Relationships dialog box in Figure 5.3b when you release the mouse.

➤ Click the **Enforce Referential Integrity** check box. Click the **Create Command button** to establish the relationship and close the Relationships dialog box. You should see a line indicating a one-to-many relationship between the Customers and Orders tables.

➤ Click and drag the **OrderID field** in the Orders field list to the **OrderID field** in the Order Details field list. Click the **Enforce Referential Integrity** check box, then click the **Create Command button.**

➤ Click and drag the **ProductID field** in the Products field list to the **ProductID field** in the Order Details field list. Click the **Enforce Referential Integrity** check box, then click the **Create Command button.**

➤ Click the **Save button** to save the relationships, then close the Relationships window.

RELATED FIELDS AND DATA TYPE

The related fields on both sides of a relationship must be the same data type—for example, both number fields or both text fields. (Number fields must also have the same field size setting.) You cannot, however, specify an AutoNumber field on both sides of a relationship. Accordingly, if the related field in the primary table is an AutoNumber field, the related field in the related table must be specified as a number field, with the Field Size property set to Long Integer.

STEP 4: Open the Orders and Order Details Tables

➤ You should be in the Database window. Click the **Restore button** to return the window to its previous size, then click the **Tables tab** (if necessary) and open the **Orders table.**

➤ Return to the Database window:
- Click in the **Database window** (if it is visible), *or*
- Click the **Database Window button** on the toolbar, *or*
- Pull down the **Window menu** and click **Computer Store: Database.**

➤ Open the **Order Details table.** Your desktop should resemble Figure 5.3c although the precise arrangement of the open windows will be different.

➤ Return to the Database window, then click the **Minimize button** to lessen the clutter on the desktop.

STEP 5: Delete an Order Details Record

➤ Pull down the **Window menu.** Click **Tile Vertically** to display the Orders table and the Order Details table side by side as in Figure 5.3d. (It doesn't matter whether the Orders table appears on the left or right.)

➤ Click the **Order Details window.** Click the row selector column for the last Order Details record for order O0005. You should have selected the record for product **P0016** in order **O0005.**

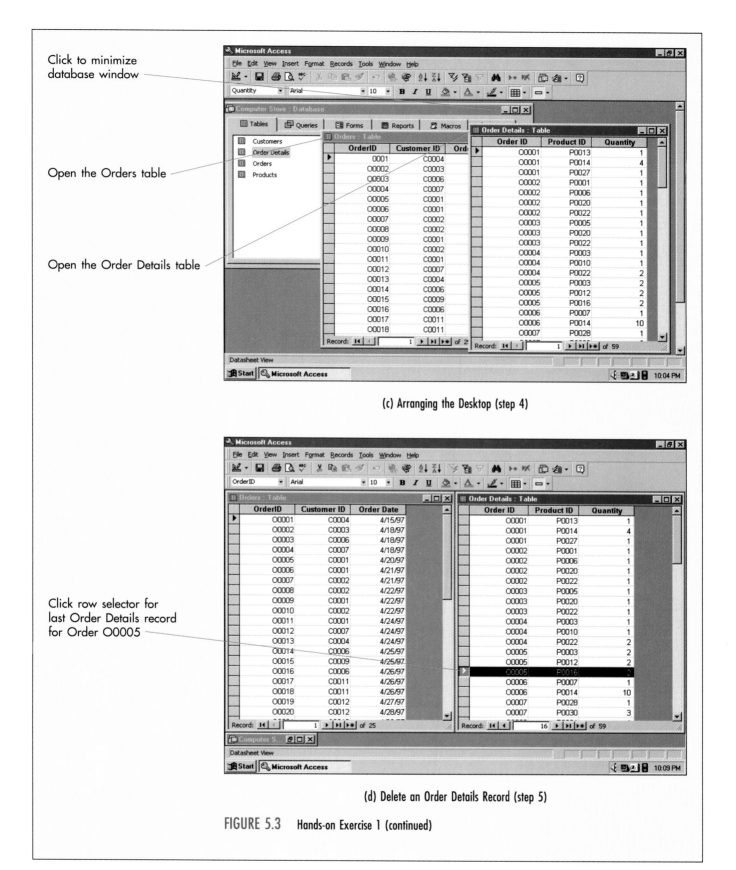

Click to minimize database window

Open the Orders table

Open the Order Details table

(c) Arranging the Desktop (step 4)

Click row selector for last Order Details record for Order O0005

(d) Delete an Order Details Record (step 5)

FIGURE 5.3   Hands-on Exercise 1 (continued)

➤ Press the **Del key.** You will see a message indicating that you have just deleted one record. Click **Yes** to delete the record. The Delete command works because you are deleting a "many record" in a one-to-many relationship.

STEP 6: Referential Integrity

➤ Click the **Orders window.** Click the row selector column for **Order O0005** as shown in Figure 5.3e. Press the **Del key** to (attempt to) delete the record.

➤ You will see the message in Figure 5.3e, indicating that you cannot delete the record. The Delete command does not work because you are attempting to delete the "one record" in a one-to-many relationship. Click **OK.**

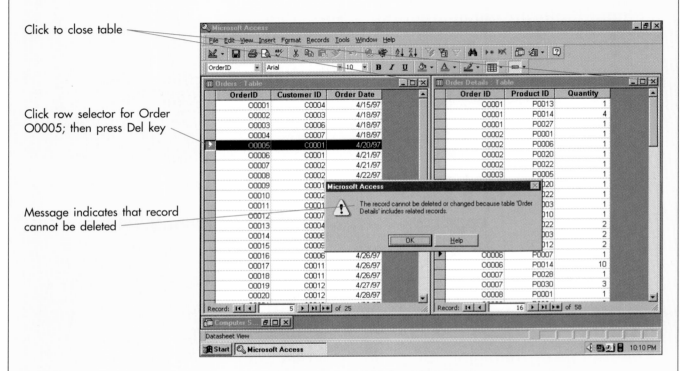

Click to close table

Click row selector for Order O0005; then press Del key

Message indicates that record cannot be deleted

(e) Referential Integrity (step 6)

FIGURE 5.3 Hands-on Exercise 1 (continued)

STEP 7: Edit a Relationship

➤ Close the Orders table. Close the Order Details table. (The tables in a relationship must be closed before the relationship can be edited.)

➤ Pull down the **Tools menu** and click **Relationships** to reopen the Relationships window (or click the **Relationships button** on the toolbar). Maximize the window.

➤ Point to the line connecting the Orders and Order Details tables, then click the **right mouse button** to display a shortcut menu. Click **Edit Relationship** to display the Relationships dialog box in Figure 5.3f.

➤ Check the box to **Cascade Delete Related Records,** then click **OK** to accept the change and close the dialog box.

➤ Click the **Save button** to save the edited relationship. Close the Relationships window.

Save button

Point to relationship line and click right mouse button to display shortcut menu

Click to select check box to Cascade Delete Related Records

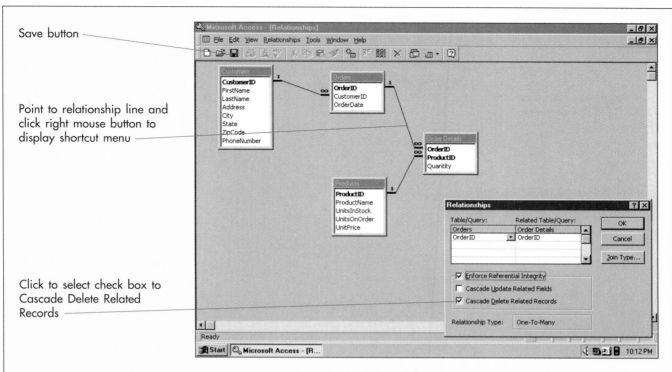

(f) Edit a Relationship (step 7)

FIGURE 5.3   Hands-on Exercise 1 (continued)

TO CLICK OR DOUBLE CLICK

Click the relationship line connecting two tables to select the relationship, then press the Del key to delete the relationship. Double click the relationship line to select the relationship and bring up the Relationships window to edit the relationship.

STEP 8: Delete the Related Records

➤ If necessary, restore the Database window, then open the **Orders table** and the **Order Details table.** Minimize the Database window, then tile the open windows vertically as shown in Figure 5.3g.

➤ Click the **Orders window** and select the record for **Order O0005.** Press the **Del key** to delete the record.

➤ You will see a message about cascaded deletes, indicating that records in the Orders table as well as related tables are about to be deleted. Click **Yes.** Order O0005 is gone from the Orders table.

➤ The related records in the Order Details table have also been deleted but are displayed with the #Deleted indicator as shown in Figure 5.3g. (The records will be gone the next time the Order Details table is opened.)

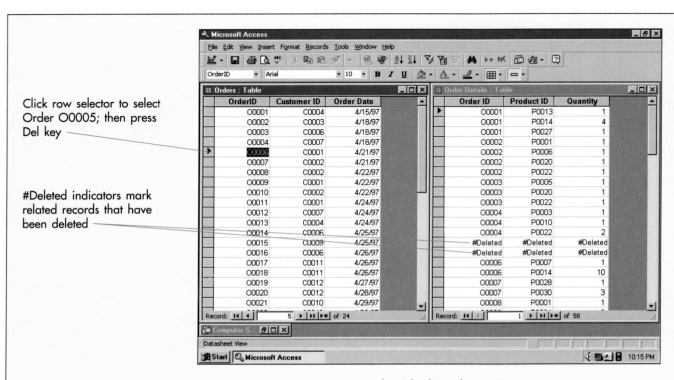

Click row selector to select Order O0005; then press Del key

#Deleted indicators mark related records that have been deleted

(g) Delete Related Records (step 8)

FIGURE 5.3   Hands-on Exercise 1 (continued)

➤ The Delete command works this time (unlike the previous attempt in step 5) because the relationship was changed to permit the deletion of related records.

➤ Close the Orders table. Close the Order Details table.

STEP 9: Document the Relationships

➤ Pull down the **Tools menu,** click (or point to) **Analyze,** then click **Documenter** to display the Database Documenter dialog box.

➤ Click the **Current database tab,** then check the box for **Relationships.** Click **OK.**

➤ Be patient as it takes a little while for Access to check the relationships within the database and to display the Object Definition window in Figure 5.3h. Maximize the window.

➤ Scroll through the report to note the relationship between the Orders and Order Details tables (one-to-many; enforced, cascade deletes), which is consistent with the edited relationship.

➤ Click the **Print button** to print the definition. Close the Object Definition window to continue.

➤ Close the database. Click **Yes** if prompted to save the tables or relationships.

➤ Exit Access if you do not want to continue with the next exercise at this time.

Print button

Close Object
Definition window

Relationship information
is displayed

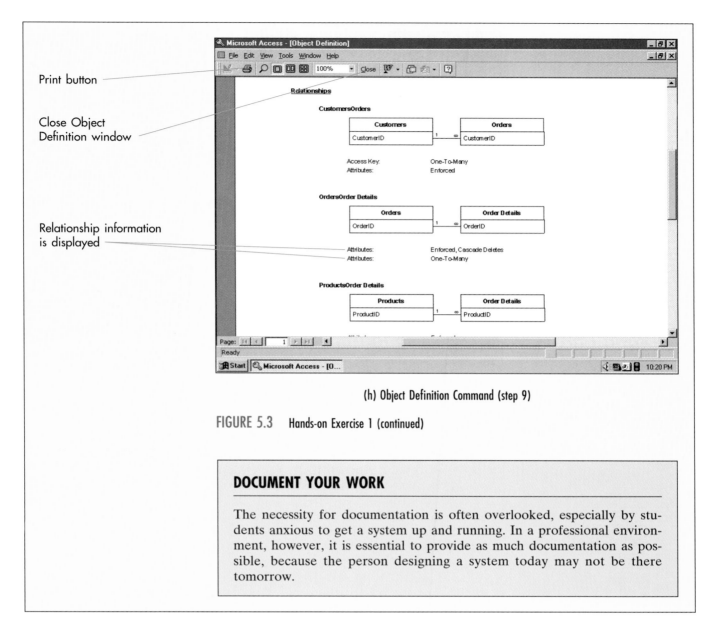

(h) Object Definition Command (step 9)

FIGURE 5.3   Hands-on Exercise 1 (continued)

DOCUMENT YOUR WORK

The necessity for documentation is often overlooked, especially by students anxious to get a system up and running. In a professional environment, however, it is essential to provide as much documentation as possible, because the person designing a system today may not be there tomorrow.

SUBFORMS, QUERIES, AND AUTOLOOKUP

The main and subform combination in Figure 5.4 is used by the store to enter a new order for an existing customer. The forms are based on queries (rather than tables) for several reasons. A query enables you to display data from multiple tables, to display a calculated field, and to take advantage of AutoLookup, a feature that is explained shortly. A query also lets you display records in a sequence other than by primary key.

The main form contains fields from both the Orders table and the Customers table. The OrderID, OrderDate, and CustomerID (the join field) are taken from the Orders table. The other fields are taken from the Customers table. The query is designed so that you do not have to enter any customer information other than the CustomerID; that is, you enter the CustomerID, and Access will automatically look up (**AutoLookup**) the corresponding customer data.

Main form has fields from both
Orders and Customers tables

Subform has fields from both
Products and Order Details tables

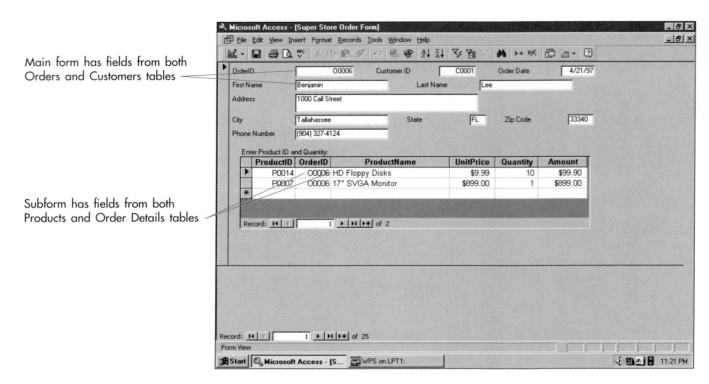

FIGURE 5.4   The Super Store Order Form

The subform is based on a second query containing fields from the Order Details table and the Products table. The OrderID, Quantity, and ProductID (the join field) are taken from the Order Details table. The ProductName and Unit-Price fields are from the Products table. AutoLookup works here as well so that when you enter the ProductID, Access automatically displays the Product Name and Unit Price. You then enter the quantity, and the amount (a calculated field) is determined automatically.

The queries for the main form and subform are shown in Figures 5.5a and 5.5b, respectively. The upper half of the Query window displays the field list for each table and the relationship between the tables. The lower half of the Query window contains the design grid. Any query intended to take advantage of AutoLookup must adhere to the following:

1. The tables in the query must have a one-to-many relationship, such as customers to orders in Figure 5.5a or products to order details in Figure 5.5b.
2. The join field on the "one" side of the relationship must have a unique value in the primary table. The CustomerID in Figure 5.5a and the ProductID in Figure 5.5b are primary keys in their respective tables and therefore unique.
3. The join field in the query must be taken from the "many" side of the relationship. Thus, CustomerID is from the Orders table in Figure 5.5a rather than from the Customers table. In similar fashion, ProductID is taken from the Order Details table in Figure 5.5b, not from the Products table.

The following exercise has you create the main and subform in Figure 5.4. We supply the query for the main form (Figure 5.5a), but we ask you to create the query for the subform (Figure 5.5b).

Join field in "one"
table is unique

Tables have a one-to-many
relationship

Join field in query is
from "many" table

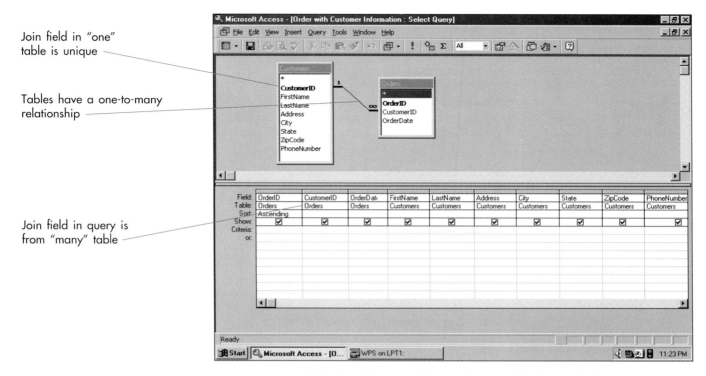

(a) Order with Customer Information Query (used for the main form)

Join field in "one"
table is unique

Tables have a one-to-many
relationship

Join field in query is
from "many" table

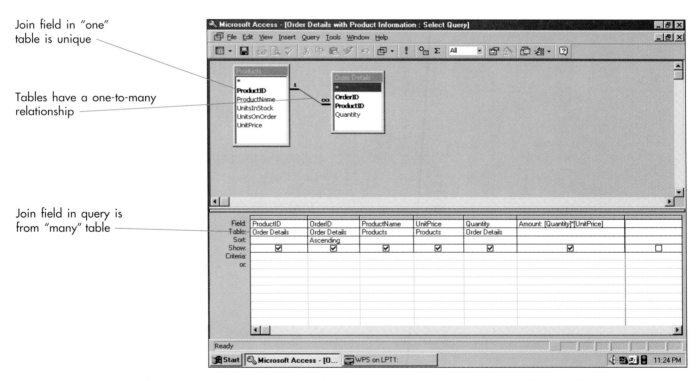

(b) Order Details with Product Information Query (used for the subform)

FIGURE 5.5   Multiple Table Queries

Subforms and Multiple Table Queries

Objective: To use multiple table queries as the basis for a main form and its associated subform; to create the link between a main form and subform manually. Use Figure 5.6 as a guide in the exercise.

STEP 1: Create the Subform Query

➤ Open the **Computer Store database** from the previous exercise. Click the **Queries tab** in the Database window, click **New** to display the New Query dialog box, select **Design View** as the means of creating the query, then click **OK.**

➤ The Show Table dialog box appears in Figure 5.6a with the Tables tab already selected.

➤ Double click the **Products table** to add this table to the query. Double click the **Order Details table** to add this table to the query. A join line showing the one-to-many relationship between the Products and Order Details table appears automatically.

➤ Click **Close** to close the Show Table dialog box. If necessary, click the **Maximize button.**

Double click Order Details table to add it to the query

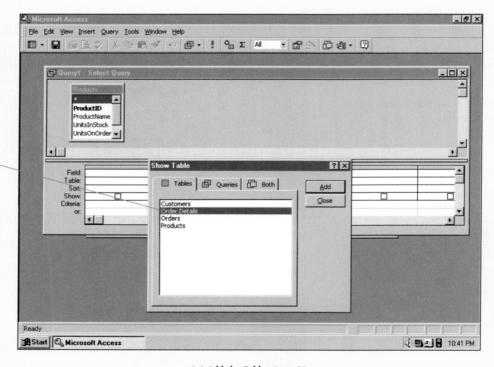

(a) Add the Tables (step 1)

FIGURE 5.6   Hands-on Exercise 2

CUSTOMIZE THE QUERY WINDOW

The Query window displays the field list and design grid in its upper and lower halves, respectively. To increase (decrease) the size of either portion of the window, drag the line dividing the upper and lower sections. Drag the title bar to move a field list. You can also size a field list by dragging a border just as you can size any other window.

STEP 2: Create the Subform Query (continued)

➤ Add the fields to the query as follows:
- Double click the **ProductID** and **OrderID fields** in that order from the Order Details table.
- Double click the **ProductName** and **UnitPrice fields** in that order from the Products table.
- Double click the **Quantity field** from the Order Details table.

➤ Click the **Sort row** under the **OrderID field.** Click the **drop-down arrow,** then specify an **ascending** sequence.

➤ Click the first available cell in the Field row. Type **=[Quantity]*[UnitPrice].** Do not be concerned if you cannot see the entire expression, but be sure you put square brackets around each field name.

➤ Press **enter.** Access has substituted Expr1: for the equal sign you typed. Drag the column boundary so that the entire expression is visible as in Figure 5.6b. (You may need to make the other columns narrower in order to see all of the fields in the design grid.)

➤ Click and drag to select **Expr1.** (Do not select the colon.) Type **Amount** to substitute a more meaningful field name.

➤ Point to the expression and click the **right mouse button** to display a shortcut menu. Click **Properties** to display the Field Properties dialog box in Figure 5.6b.

➤ Click the box for the **Format property.** Click the **drop-down arrow,** then scroll until you can click **Currency.** Close the Properties dialog box.

➤ Save the query as **Order Details with Product Information.** Click the **Run button** to test the query so that you know the query works prior to using it as the basis of a form.

THE ZOOM BOX

Creating a long expression can be confusing in that you cannot see the entire expression as it is entered. Access anticipates the situation and provides a Zoom box to increase the space in which you can work. Press Shift+F2 as you enter the expression (or select Zoom from the shortcut menu) to display the Zoom box. Click OK to close the Zoom box and continue working in the design grid.

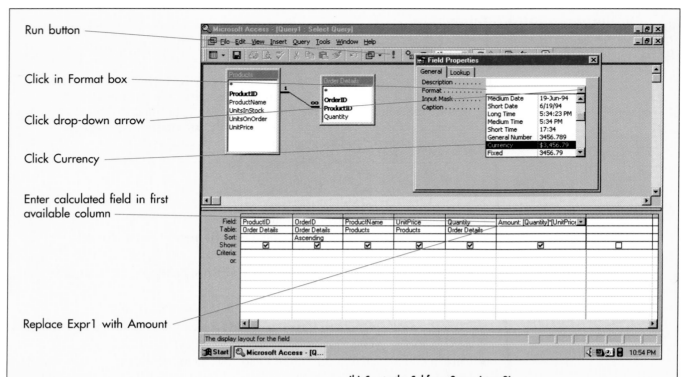

Run button

Click in Format box

Click drop-down arrow

Click Currency

Enter calculated field in first
available column

Replace Expr1 with Amount

(b) Create the Subform Query (step 2)

FIGURE 5.6   Hands-on Exercise 2 (continued)

STEP 3: Test the Query

➤ You should see the dynaset shown in Figure 5.6c. (See the boxed tip below if the dynaset does not appear.)

➤ Enter **1** (not P0001) to change the ProductID to 1 (from 14) in the very first record. (The Format property automatically displays the letter P and the high-order zeros.)

➤ Press **enter.** The Product Name changes to a Pentium desktop/166 with MMX system as you hit the enter key. The unit price also changes, as does the computed amount.

➤ Click the **Undo button** to cancel the change. The ProductID returns to P0014, and the Product Name changes back to HD Floppy Disks. The unit price also changes, as does the computed amount.

➤ Close the query.

A PUZZLING ERROR

If you are unable to run a query, it is most likely because you misspelled a field name in the design grid. Access interprets the misspelling as a parameter query (see page 223) and asks you to enter a parameter value (the erroneous field name is displayed in the dialog box). Press the Esc key to exit the query and return to the Design view. Click the field row for the problem field and make the necessary correction.

Change ProductID to 1

Product data will change when you press enter

Calculated amount will also change

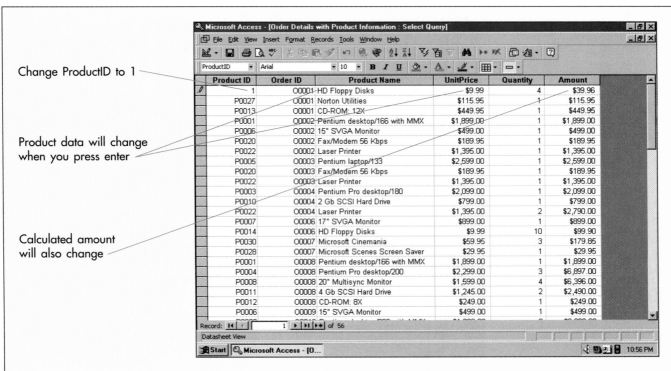

(c) Test the Query (step 3)

FIGURE 5.6   Hands-on Exercise 2 (continued)

STEP 4: Create the Orders Form

➤ You should be back in the Database window. Click the **Forms tab.** Click the **New Command button** to display the New Form dialog box, click **Form Wizard** in the list box, then click the **drop-down arrow** to display the available tables and queries.

➤ Select the **Order with Customer Information query** (the query we provided) as the basis for the form, then click **OK** to start the Form Wizard.

➤ You should see the Form Wizard dialog box, which displays all of the fields in the selected query. Click the **>> button** to enter all of the fields onto the form. Click **Next.**

➤ **By Orders** is selected as the means of viewing your data. Click **Next.** The **Columnar layout** is already selected. Click **Next.** Click **Standard** as the style for your form. Click **Next.**

➤ Save the form as **Super Store Order Form.** Click the option button to **Modify the form's design,** then click the **Finish Command button** to create the form and exit the Form Wizard.

STEP 5: Modify the Orders Form

➤ You should see the Super Store Order Form in Figure 5.6d. Click the **CustomerID control** to select the control and display the sizing handles, then drag the **CustomerID control** so that it is next to the OrderID.

➤ Click and drag the **OrderDate control** so that it is next to the CustomerID. (The width of the form will change automatically, but you will need to extend the width a little further when you release the mouse.)

Save button

Click CustomerID control,
then drag it next to OrderID
control

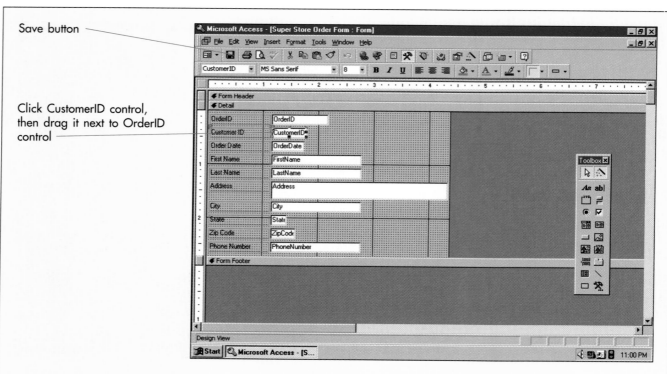

(d) Create the Super Store Order Form (steps 4 and 5)

FIGURE 5.6   Hands-on Exercise 2 (continued)

➤ Click and drag the other controls to complete the form:
  • Click and drag the **LastName control** so that it is next to the FirstName control.
  • Click and drag the **Address control** under the control for FirstName.
  • Place the controls for **City, State,** and **ZipCode** on the same line and move them under the Address control.
  • Move the control for **PhoneNumber** under the control for City.
  • Move all of the controls under the OrderID control.
➤ Click the **Save button** to save the form.

SIZING OR MOVING A CONTROL AND ITS LABEL

A bound control is created with an attached label. Select (click) the control, and the control has sizing handles and a move handle, but the label has only a move handle. Select the label (instead of the control) and the opposite occurs: The control has only a move handle, but the label will have both sizing handles and a move handle. To move a control and its label, click and drag the border of either object. To move either the control or its label, click and drag the move handle (a tiny square in the upper-left corner) of the appropriate object.

STEP 6: Create the Order Details Subform

➤ Click and drag the bottom edge of the **Detail section** so that you have approximately 2 inches of blank space as shown in Figure 5.6e. (This is where the subform will go.)

➤ Click the **Subform/Subreport button** on the Toolbox toolbar, then click and drag in the **Orders form** where you want the subform to go. Release the mouse to begin the Subform/Subreport Wizard.

➤ The **Table/Query option button** is selected, indicating that we will build the subform from a table or query. Click **Next**.

➤ You should see the Subform/Subreport dialog box. Click the **drop-down arrow** on the Tables and Queries list box to select the **Order Details with Product Information query** as shown in Figure 5.6e. (This is the query you created in steps 1 and 2.)

➤ Click the **>> button** to enter all of the fields in the query onto the subform. Click **Next**.

➤ The next step asks you to define the fields that link the main form to the subform: The option button to **Choose from a list** is selected. The selected link will **Show Order Details with Product Information.** Click **Next**.

➤ The Wizard suggests **Order Details with Product Information subform** as the name of the subform. Click **Finish** to exit the Subform/Subreport wizard.

Click Subform/Subreport button

Click drop-down arrow

Select Order Details with Product Information query

Subform control

Click and drag bottom edge of Detail section to increase amount of space in Detail section

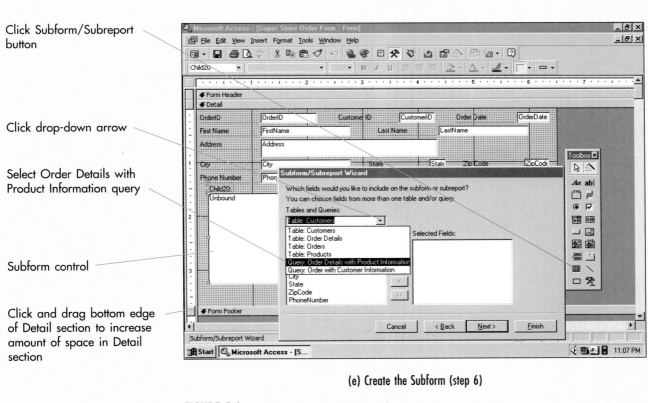

(e) Create the Subform (step 6)

FIGURE 5.6   Hands-on Exercise 2 (continued)

STEP 7: The Order Details Subform (Datasheet view)

➤ You should be in the Design view for the Super Store Order Form. The white rectangular control indicates the position of the Order Details with Product Information subform within the main form. Maximize the window.

➤ You need to open the **Order Details with Product Information subform** to check the column width of its columns. Accordingly:

• Deselect the Order Details subform (by clicking anywhere in the main form), then double click the **Order Details with Product Information subform** to open it. Change to the Datasheet view, *or*

• Change to the **Database window,** click the **Forms tab,** and open the **Order Details subform.**

➤ You should see the Datasheet view of the Order Details with Product Information subform as shown in Figure 5.6f. Click and drag the various column headings until you can read all of the information.

➤ Click the **Save button** to save the new layout, then close the subform. This returns you to the Design view of the Orders form. (Alternatively, you may be back in the Database window, in which case you need to pull down the Window menu to return to the Super Store Order Form.)

➤ Select (click) the label of the **subform control,** then click and drag to select the existing text (Order Details with Product Information subform). Type **Enter Product ID and Quantity** (to provide descriptive help to the user).

➤ Save the completed form.

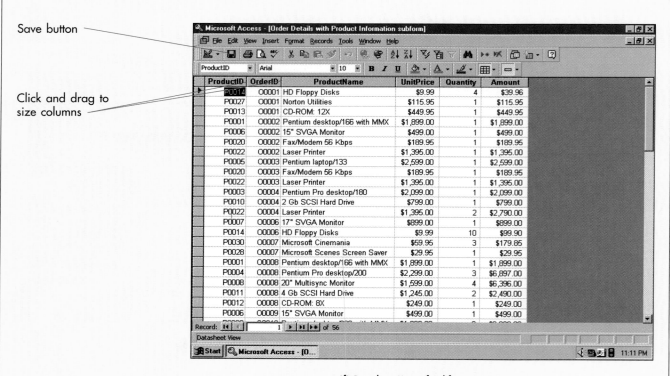

Save button

Click and drag to size columns

(f) Datasheet View of Subform (step 7)

FIGURE 5.6   Hands-on Exercise 2 (continued)

STEP 8: Enter a New Order

➤ Change to the **Form view** of the Orders form as shown in Figure 5.6g. (You will probably need to return to the Design view to move and/or size the subform control.)

➤ Click the **New Record button** to display a blank form so that you can place an order.

➤ Click in the **Customer ID text box.** Enter **13** (your customer number from the first exercise), then press the **Tab** or **enter key** to move to the next field.
- The OrderID is entered automatically as it is an AutoNumber field and assigned the next sequential number.
- All of your customer information (your name, address, and phone number) is entered automatically because of the AutoLookup feature that is built into the underlying query.
- Today's date is entered automatically because of the default value (=Date()) that is built into the Orders table.

➤ Click the **ProductID text box** in the subform. Enter **1** (not P0001) and press the **enter key** to move to the next field. The OrderID (O0026) is entered automatically, as is the Product Name and Unit Price.

➤ Press the **Tab key** three times to move to the Quantity field, enter **1,** and press the **Tab key** twice more to move to the ProductID field for the next item. (The amount is calculated automatically.)

➤ Complete your order as shown in Figure 5.6g. (If necessary, re-open the subform in the Datasheet view as described in step 7 to adjust the column widths.)

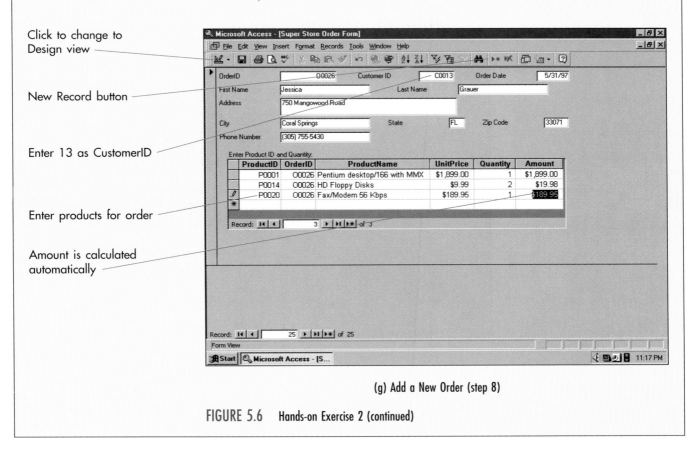

(g) Add a New Order (step 8)

FIGURE 5.6   Hands-on Exercise 2 (continued)

AUTOLOOKUP—WHY IT WORKS

The main form is based on a query containing a one-to-many relationship between Customers and Orders, in which CustomerID is the join field and appears in both tables. The CustomerID is the primary key in the Customers table and is unique in that table. The query, however, must contain the CustomerID field from the Orders table for the AutoLookup feature to take effect. AutoLookup is implemented in similar fashion in the subform, which is based on a query containing a one-to-many relationship between the Products and Order Details tables. The ProductID field is common to both tables and must be taken from the Order Details table (the "many" table) in order for AutoLookup to work.

STEP 9: Print the Completed Order

➤ Click the **Selection Area** to select the current record (the order you just completed). This is done to print only the current record.

➤ Pull down the **File menu.** Click **Page Setup** to display the Page Setup dialog box as shown in Figure 5.6h. Click the **Page tab,** then click the **Landscape option button** so that your form will fit on the page. (Alternatively, you could click the **Margins tab** and decrease the left and right margins.) Click **OK** to close the Page Setup dialog box.

Selection area

Click Page tab

Click Landscape option button

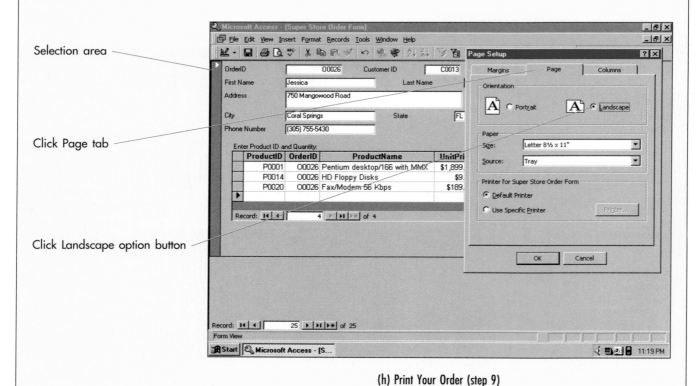

(h) Print Your Order (step 9)

FIGURE 5.6   Hands-on Exercise 2 (continued)

> ➤ Pull down the **File menu,** click **Print** to display the Print dialog box, then click the option button to specify **Selected Record(s)** as the print range. (You cannot click the Print button on the toolbar as that will print every record.)
>
> ➤ Click **OK** to print the form and submit it to your instructor as proof that you did this exercise. Close the form, then close the database. Answer **Yes** if asked to save the changes.
>
> ➤ Exit Access if you do not want to continue with the next exercise at this time.

ADDING CUSTOMERS

The form that you just created enables you to add an order for an existing customer, provided you know the CustomerID. It does not, however, let you add an order for a new customer because the underlying query does not contain the primary key from the Customers table. See practice exercises 3 and 4 at the end of the chapter for instructions on how to overcome these limitations.

ADVANCED QUERIES

A select query, powerful as it is, has its limitations. It requires you to enter the criteria directly in the query, which means you have to change the query every time you vary the criteria. What if you wanted to use a different set of criteria (e.g., a different customer's name) every time you ran the "same" query?

A second limitation of select queries is that they do not produce summary information about groups of records. How many orders have we received this month? What was the largest order? What was the smallest order? This section introduces two additional types of queries to overcome both limitations.

Parameter Queries

A *parameter query* prompts you for the criteria each time you execute the query. It is created in similar fashion to a select query and is illustrated in Figure 5.7. The difference between a parameter query and an ordinary select query is the way in which the criteria are specified. A select query contains the actual criteria. A parameter query, however, contains a *prompt* (message) that will request the criteria when the query is executed.

The design grid in Figure 5.7a creates a parameter query that will display the orders for a particular customer. The query does not contain the customer's name, but a prompt for that name. The prompt is enclosed in square brackets and is displayed in a dialog box in which the user enters the requested data when the query is executed. Thus, the user supplies the customer's name in Figure 5.7b, and the query displays the resulting dynaset in Figure 5.7c. This enables you to run the same query with different criteria; that is, you can enter a different customer name every time you execute the query.

A parameter query may prompt for any number of variables (parameters), which are entered in successive dialog boxes. The parameters are requested in order from left to right, according to the way in which they appear in the design grid.

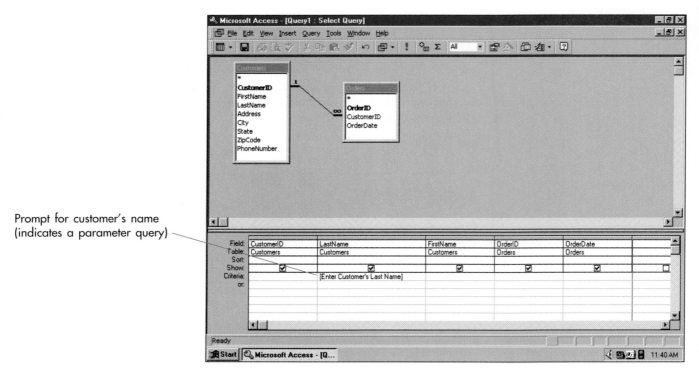

Prompt for customer's name (indicates a parameter query)

(a) Design Grid

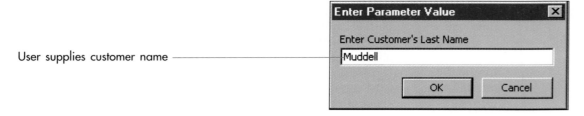

User supplies customer name

(b) Dialog Box

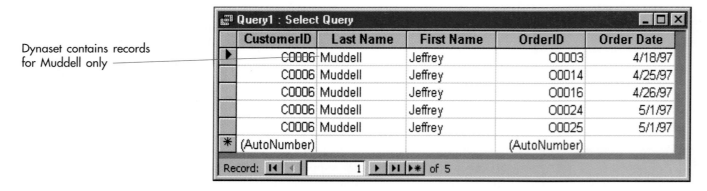

Dynaset contains records for Muddell only

(c) Dynaset

FIGURE 5.7   Parameter Query

Total Queries

A *total query* performs calculations on a *group* of records using one of several summary (aggregate) functions available within Access. These include the Sum, Count, Avg, Max, and Min functions to determine the total, number of, average, maximum, and minimum values, respectively. Figure 5.8 illustrates the use of a total query to compute the total amount for each order.

Figure 5.8a displays the dynaset from a select query with fields from both the Products and Order Details tables. (The dynaset contains one record for each product in each order and enables us to verify the results of the total query in Figure 5.8c.) Each record in Figure 5.8a contains the price of the product, the quantity ordered, and the amount for that product. There are, for example, three products in order O0001. The first product costs $449.95, the second product costs $39.96 (four units at $9.99 each), and the third product costs $115.95. The total for the order comes to $605.86, which is obtained by (manually) adding the amount field in each of the records for this order.

Figure 5.8b shows the Design view of the total query to calculate the cost of each order. The query contains only two fields, OrderID and Amount. The QBE grid also displays a *Total row* in which each field in the query has either a Group By or aggregate entry. The *Group By* entry under OrderID indicates that the records in the dynaset are to be grouped (aggregated) according to the like values of OrderID; that is, there will be one record in the total query for each distinct value of OrderID. The *Sum function* specifies the arithmetic operation to be performed on each group of records.

The dynaset in Figure 5.8c displays the result of the total query and contains *aggregate* records, as opposed to *individual* records. There are, for example, three records for order O0001 in Figure 5.8a, but only one record in Figure 5.8c. This is because each record in a total query contains a calculated result for a group of records.

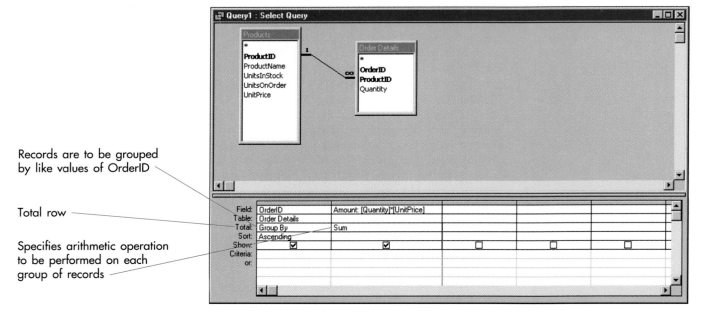

Contains multiple records for order O0001

(a) Order Details with Product Information Dynaset

Records are to be grouped by like values of OrderID

Total row

Specifies arithmetic operation to be performed on each group of records

(b) Design Grid

Reflects the total cost for order O0001

(c) Dynaset

FIGURE 5.8   Total Query

The exercise that follows begins by having you create the report in Figure 5.9. The report is a detailed analysis of all orders, listing every product in every order. The report is based on a query containing fields from the Orders, Customers, Products, and Order Details tables. The exercise also provides practice in creating parameter queries and total queries.

Sales Analysis by Order

Prepared by: Jessica Grauer

			Product Name	Quantity	UnitPrice	Amount
O0001	Colon	4/15/97				
			CD-ROM: 12X	1	$449.95	$449.95
			HD Floppy Disks	4	$9.99	$39.96
			Norton Utilities	1	$115.95	$115.95
					Sum	**$605.86**
O0002	Goodman	4/18/97				
			15" SVGA Monitor	1	$499.00	$499.00
			Fax/Modem 56 Kbps	1	$189.95	$189.95
			Laser Printer	1	$1,395.00	$1,395.00
			Pentium desktop/166 with MMX	1	$1,899.00	$1,899.00
					Sum	**$3,982.95**
O0003	Muddell	4/18/97				
			Fax/Modem 56 Kbps	1	$189.95	$189.95
			Laser Printer	1	$1,395.00	$1,395.00
			Pentium laptop/133	1	$2,599.00	$2,599.00
					Sum	**$4,183.95**
O0004	Geoghegan	4/18/97				
			2 Gb SCSI Hard Drive	1	$799.00	$799.00
			Laser Printer	2	$1,395.00	$2,790.00
			Pentium Pro desktop/180	1	$2,099.00	$2,099.00
					Sum	**$5,688.00**
O0006	Lee	4/21/97				
			17" SVGA Monitor	1	$899.00	$899.00
			HD Floppy Disks	10	$9.99	$99.90
					Sum	**$998.90**
O0007	Milgrom	4/21/97				
			Microsoft Cinemania	3	$59.95	$179.85
			Microsoft Scenes Screen Saver	1	$29.95	$29.95
					Sum	**$209.80**

Saturday, May 31, 1997   **Page 1 of 4**

FIGURE 5.9   Sales Analysis by Order

Advanced Queries

Objective: To copy an existing query; to create a parameter query; to create a total query using the aggregate Sum function. Use Figure 5.10 as a guide.

STEP 1: Create the Query

➤ Open the **Computer Store database** from the previous exercise. Click the **Queries tab** in the Database window, click **New** to display the New Query dialog box, select **Design View,** then click **OK.**

➤ By now you have had sufficient practice creating a query, so we will just outline the steps:

- Add the **Customers, Orders, Products,** and **Order Details** tables. Move and size the field lists within the Query window to match Figure 5.10a. Maximize the window.

- Add the indicated fields to the design grid. Be sure to take each field from the appropriate table.

- Add the calculated field to compute the amount by multiplying the quantity by the unit price. Point to the expression, click the **right mouse button** to display a shortcut menu, then change the Format property to **Currency.**

- Check that your query matches Figure 5.10a. Save the query as **Sales Analysis by Order.**

➤ Click the **Run button** (the exclamation point) to run the query. The dynaset contains one record for every item in every order. Close the query.

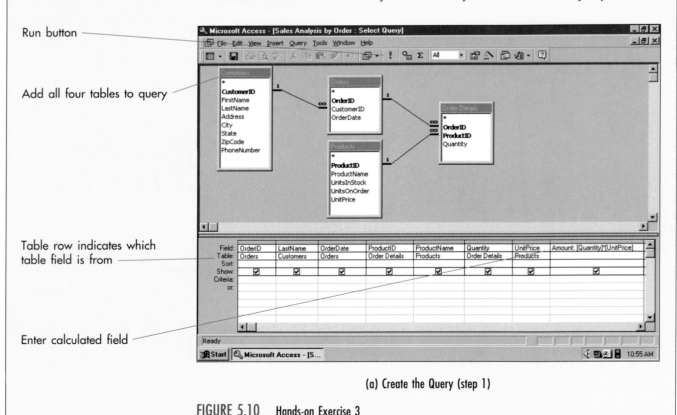

Run button

Add all four tables to query

Table row indicates which table field is from

Enter calculated field

(a) Create the Query (step 1)

FIGURE 5.10   Hands-on Exercise 3

STEP 2: The Report Wizard

➤ Click the **Reports tab** in the Database window, then click the **New Command button** to display the New Report dialog box. Select the **Report Wizard.**

➤ Click the **drop-down arrow** to display the tables and queries in the database, then select **Sales Analysis by Order** (the query you just created). Click **OK.**

➤ By now you have had sufficient practice using the Report Wizard, so we will just outline the steps:

- Select all of the fields in the query *except* the ProductID. Click the **>> button** to move every field in the Available Fields list box to the Selected Fields list, then select the **ProductID field** within the Selected Fields list and click the **< button** to remove this field. Click **Next.**

- Group the report by **OrderID.** Click **Next.**

- Sort the report by **ProductName.** Click the **Summary Options button** to display the Summary Options dialog box in Figure 5.10b. Check **Sum** under the Amount field. The option button to **Show Detail and Summary** is selected. Click **OK** to close the Summary Options dialog box. Click **Next.**

- The **Stepped Layout** is selected, as is **Portrait orientation.** Be sure the box is checked to **Adjust field width so all fields fit on a page.** Click **Next.**

- Choose **Bold** as the style. Click **Next.**

- **Sales Analysis by Order** is entered as the title of the report. The option button to **Preview the Report** is selected. Click **Finish.**

➤ The report you see approximates the finished report, but requires several modifications to improve the formatting. The OrderDate and LastName, for example, are repeated for every product in an order, when they should appear only once in the group (OrderID) header.

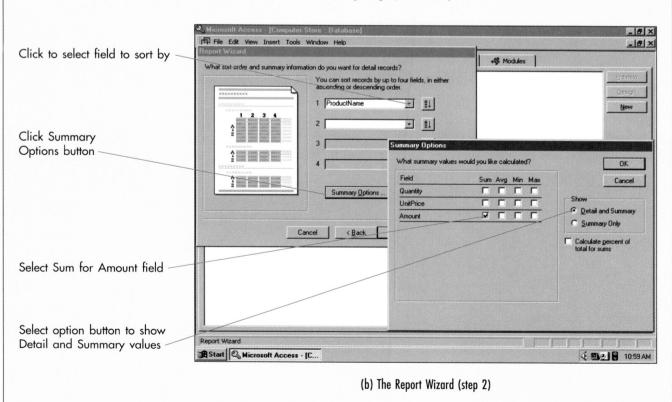

(b) The Report Wizard (step 2)

FIGURE 5.10   Hands-on Exercise 3 (continued)

STEP 3: Modify the Report

➤ Click the **Close button** to change to the Design view to modify the report as shown in Figure 5.10c.

➤ Press and hold the **Shift key** as you click the **OrderDate** and **LastName** controls to select both controls, then drag the controls to the group header next to the OrderID.

➤ Click anywhere in the report to deselect the controls after they have been moved. Press and hold the **Shift key** to select the **OrderID, OrderDate,** and **LastName** labels in the Page Header. Press the **Del key** to delete the labels.

➤ Size the **Quantity, UnitPrice,** and **Amount controls** (and their **labels**). Move the **ProductName control** and its **label** closer to the other controls.

➤ Click the **OrderID control** in the OrderID header. Click the **right mouse button,** click **Properties,** and change the Border Style to **Transparent.** Close the Properties dialog box.

➤ Click the **Label tool,** then click and drag in the report header to create an unbound control under the title of the report. Type **Prepared by:** followed by your name as shown in Figure 5.10c.

➤ Select (click) the first control in the OrderID footer (which begins with "Summary for). Press the **Del key.** Click and drag the unbound control containing the word **Sum** to the right of the group footer so that the label is next to the computed total for each order. Do the same for the Grand Total label in the Report footer.

➤ Click the **Save button** to save the report, then click the **View button** to preview the report.

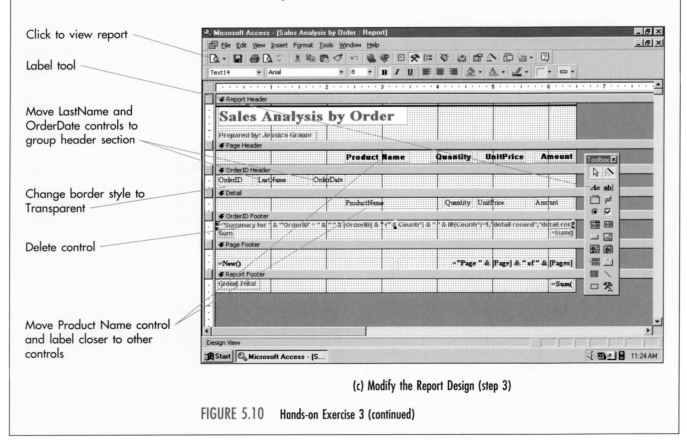

Click to view report

Label tool

Move LastName and OrderDate controls to group header section

Change border style to Transparent

Delete control

Move Product Name control and label closer to other controls

(c) Modify the Report Design (step 3)

FIGURE 5.10   Hands-on Exercise 3 (continued)

STEP 4: Print the Report

➤ You should see the report in Figure 5.10d, which groups the reports by Order ID. The products are in alphabetical order within each order.

➤ Click the **Zoom button** to see the entire page. Click the **Zoom button** a second time to return to the higher magnification.

➤ Click the **Printer button** if you are satisfied with the appearance of the report, or return to the Design view to make any needed changes.

➤ Pull down the **File menu** and click **Close** to close the report. Click **Yes** if asked whether to save the changes.

Zoom button

Report is grouped by OrderID

Products are in alphabetical order

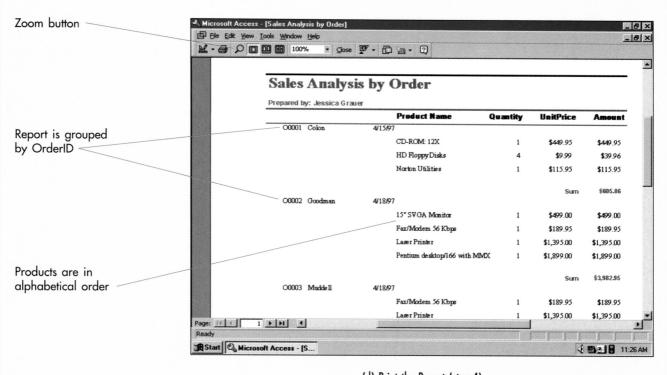

(d) Print the Report (step 4)

FIGURE 5.10   Hands-on Exercise 3 (continued)

STEP 5: Copy a Query

➤ If necessary, return to the Database window, then click the **Queries tab** in the Database window.

➤ Click the **Sales Analysis by Order query** to select the query as shown in Figure 5.10e.

➤ Pull down the **Edit menu.** Click **Copy** to copy the query to the clipboard.

➤ Pull down the **Edit menu.** Click **Paste** to produce the Paste As dialog box in Figure 5.10e. Type **Sales Totals.** Click **OK.** The Database window contains the original query (Sales Analysis by Order) as well as the copied version (Sales Totals) you just created.

COPY, DELETE, OR RENAME A REPORT

The Database window enables you to copy, delete, or rename any object (a table, form, query, or report) in an Access database. To copy an object, select the object, pull down the Edit menu, and click Copy. Pull down the Edit menu a second time, click Paste, then enter the name of the copied object. To delete or rename an object, point to the object, then click the right mouse button to display a shortcut menu, and select the desired operation.

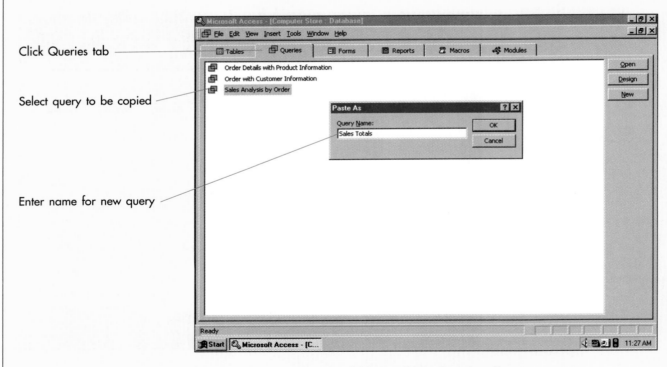

Click Queries tab

Select query to be copied

Enter name for new query

(e) Copy an Existing Query (step 5)

FIGURE 5.10   Hands-on Exercise 3 (continued)

STEP 6: Create a Total Query

➤ Select the newly created **Sales Totals query.** Click the **Design button** to open the Query Design window in Figure 5.10f.

➤ Click the **column selector** for the **OrderDate field** to select the column. Press the **Del key** to delete the field from the query. Delete the **ProductID, ProductName, Quantity,** and **UnitPrice fields** in similar fashion.

➤ Pull down the **View menu** and click **Totals** to display the Total row (or click the **Totals button** on the toolbar).

➤ Click the **Total row** under the Amount field, then click the **drop-down arrow** to display the summary functions. Click **Sum** as shown in the figure.

➤ Save the query.

THE DESCRIPTION PROPERTY

A working database will contain many different objects of the same type, making it all too easy to forget the purpose of the individual objects. The Description property helps you to remember. Point to any object within the Database window, click the right mouse button to display a shortcut menu, click Properties to display the Properties dialog box, enter an appropriate description, then click OK to close the Properties sheet. Once a description has been created, you can right click any object in the Database window, then click the Properties command from the shortcut menu to display the information.

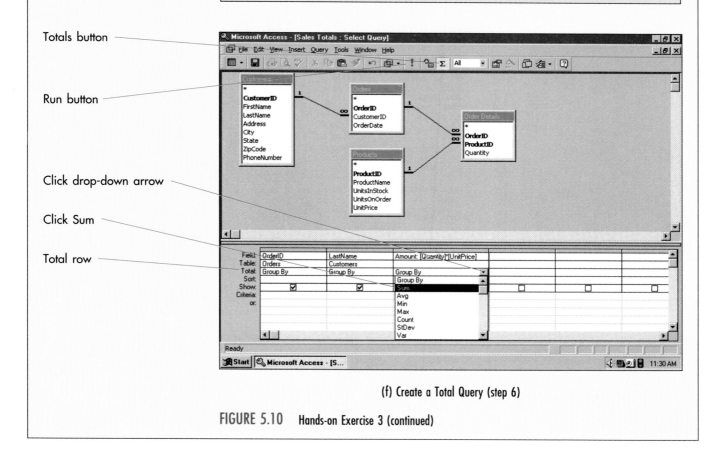

Totals button
Run button
Click drop-down arrow
Click Sum
Total row

(f) Create a Total Query (step 6)

FIGURE 5.10   Hands-on Exercise 3 (continued)

STEP 7: Run the Query

➤ Pull down the **Query menu** and click **Run** (or click the **Run button**) to run the query. You should see the datasheet in Figure 5.10g, which contains one record for each order with the total amount of that order.

➤ Click any field and attempt to change its value. You will be unable to do so as indicated by the beep and the message in the status bar, indicating that the recordset is not updatable.

➤ Click the **Design View button** to return to the Query Design view.

UPDATING THE QUERY

The changes made to a query's dynaset are automatically made in the underlying table(s). Not every field in a query is updatable, however, and the easiest way to determine if you can change a value is to run the query, view the dynaset, and attempt to edit the field. Access will prevent you from updating a calculated field, a field based on an aggregate function (such as Sum or Count), or the join field on the "one side" of a one-to-many relationship. If you attempt to update a field you cannot change, the status bar will display a message indicating why the change is not allowed.

Design View button

Attempt to change any entry

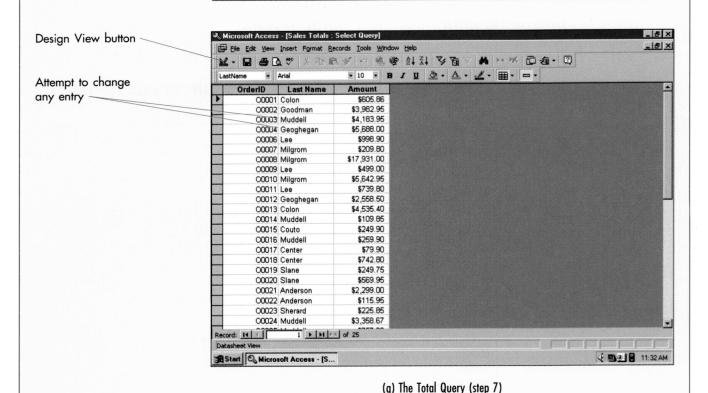

(g) The Total Query (step 7)

FIGURE 5.10   Hands-on Exercise 3 (continued)

STEP 8: Create a Parameter Query

➤ Click the **Criteria row** under **LastName.** Type **[Enter Customer's Last Name].** Be sure to enclose the entry in square brackets.

➤ Pull down the **File menu.** Click **Save As/Export.** Save the query as **Customer Parameter Query.**

➤ Run the query. Access will display the dialog box in Figure 5.10h, asking for the Customer's last name. Type **your name** and press **enter.** Access displays the information for your order(s). Close the query.

THE TOPVALUES PROPERTY

The TopValues property returns a designated number of records rather than the entire dynaset. Open the query in Design view, then click the right mouse button *outside* the design grid to display a shortcut menu. Click Properties, click the box for TopValues, and enter the desired value as either a number or a percent; for example, 5 to list the top five records, or 5% to display the records that make up the top five percent. The dynaset must be in sequence according to the desired field in order for the TopValues property to work properly.

Run button

Save button

Enter your name

Enter prompt for customer's name in square brackets

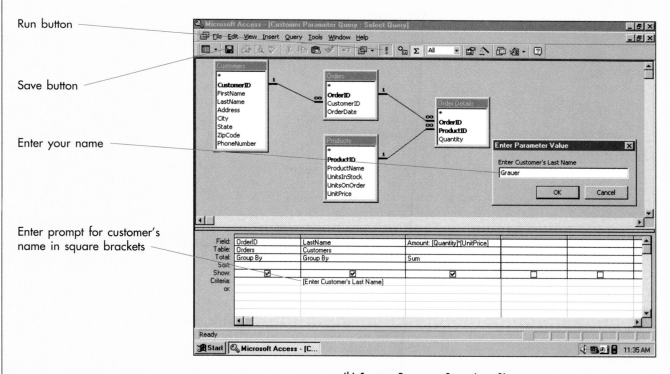

(h) Create a Parameter Query (step 8)

FIGURE 5.10   Hands-on Exercise 3 (continued)

STEP 9: Exit Access

➤ Exit Access if you do not want to continue with the next exercise. (Do not be concerned if Access indicates it will empty the clipboard.)

One of the advantages of an Access database is that it can be easily expanded to include additional data without disturbing the existing tables. The database used throughout the chapter consisted of four tables: a Customers table, a Products table, an Orders table, and an Order Details table. Figure 5.11 extends the database to include a Sales Persons table with data about each member of the sales staff.

The salesperson helps the customer as he or she comes into the store, then receives a commission based on the order. There is a one-to-many relationship between the salesperson and orders. One salesperson can generate many orders, but an order can have only one salesperson. The Sales Persons and Orders tables are joined by the SalesPersonID field, which is common to both tables.

Figure 5.11 is similar to Figure 5.1 at the beginning of the chapter except that the Sales Persons table has been added and the Orders table has been expanded to include a SalesPersonID. This enables management to monitor the performance of the sales staff. Consider:

Query: How many orders has Cori Rice taken?
Answer: Cori has taken five orders.

The query is straightforward and easily answered. You would search the Sales Persons table for Cori Rice to determine her SalesPersonID (S03). You would then search the Orders table and count the records containing S03 in the SalesPersonID field.

The Sales Persons table is also used to generate a report listing the commissions due to each salesperson. The store pays a 5% commission on every sale. Consider:

Query: Which salesperson is associated with order O0003? When was this person hired?
Answer: Cori Rice is the salesperson for order O0003. Ms. Rice was hired on March 15, 1993.

The determination of the salesperson is straightforward, as all you have to do is search the Orders table to locate the order and obtain the SalesPersonID (S03). You then search the Sales Persons table for this value (S03) and find the corresponding name (Cori Rice) and hire date (3/15/93).

Query: What is the commission on order O0003?
Answer: The commission on order O0003 is $209.20.

The calculation of the commission requires a fair amount of arithmetic. First, you need to compute the total amount of the order. Thus, you would begin in the Order Details table, find each product in order O0003, and multiply the quantity of that product by its unit price. The total cost of order O0003 is $4,183.95, based on one unit of product P0005 at $2,599, one unit of product P0020 at $189.95, and one unit of product P0022 at $1,395. (You can also refer to the sales report in Figure 5.9 that was developed in the previous exercise to check these calculations.)

Now that you know the total cost of the order, you can compute the commission, which is 5% of the total order, or $209.20 (.05 × $4,183.95). The complete calculation is lengthy, but Access does it automatically, and therein lies the beauty of a relational database.

(a) Customers Table

CustomerID	First Name	Last Name	Address	City	State	Zip Code	Phone Number
C0001	Benjamin	Lee	1000 Call Street	Tallahassee	FL	33340	(904) 327-4124
C0002	Eleanor	Milgrom	7245 NW 8 Street	Margate	FL	33065	(305) 974-1234
C0003	Neil	Goodman	4215 South 81 Street	Margate	FL	33065	(305) 444-5555
C0004	Nicholas	Colon	9020 N.W. 75 Street	Coral Springs	FL	33065	(305) 753-9887
C0005	Michael	Ware	276 Brickell Avenue	Miami	FL	33131	(305) 444-3980
C0006	Jeffrey	Muddell	9522 S.W. 142 Street	Miami	FL	33176	(305) 253-3909
C0007	Ashley	Geoghegan	7500 Center Lane	Coral Springs	FL	33070	(305) 753-7830
C0008	Serena	Sherard	5000 Jefferson Lane	Gainesville	FL	32601	(904) 375-6442
C0009	Luis	Couto	455 Bargello Avenue	Coral Gables	FL	33146	(305) 666-4801
C0010	Derek	Anderson	6000 Tigertail Avenue	Coconut Grove	FL	33120	(305) 446-8900
C0011	Lauren	Center	12380 S.W. 137 Avenue	Miami	FL	33186	(305) 385-4432
C0012	Robert	Slane	4508 N.W. 7 Street	Miami	FL	33131	(305) 635-3454
C0013	Jessica	Grauer	758 Mangowood Road	Coral Springs	FL	33071	(305) 755-5430

(a) Customers Table

(b) Products Table

Product ID	Product Name	Units In Stock	Units On Order	Unit Price
P0001	Pentium desktop/166 with MMX	50	0	$1,899.00
P0002	Pentium desktop/200 with MMX	25	5	$1,999.00
P0003	Pentium Pro desktop/180	125	15	$2,099.00
P0004	Pentium Pro desktop/200	25	50	$2,299.00
P0005	Pentium laptop/133	15	25	$2,599.00
P0006	15" SVGA Monitor	50	0	$499.00
P0007	17" SVGA Monitor	25	10	$899.00
P0008	20" Multisync Monitor	50	20	$1,599.00
P0009	2.5 Gb IDE Hard Drive	15	20	$399.00
P0010	2 Gb SCSI Hard Drive	25	15	$799.00
P0011	4 Gb SCSI Hard Drive	10	0	$1,245.00
P0012	CD-ROM: 8X	40	0	$249.00
P0013	CD-ROM: 12X	50	15	$449.95
P0014	HD Floppy Disks	500	200	$9.99
P0015	HD Data Cartridges	100	50	$14.79
P0016	2 Gb Tape Backup	15	3	$179.95
P0017	Serial Mouse	150	50	$69.95
P0018	Trackball	55	0	$59.95
P0019	Joystick	250	100	$39.95
P0020	Fax/Modem 56 Kbps	35	10	$189.95
P0021	Fax/Modem 33.6 Kbps	20	0	$65.95
P0022	Laser Printer	100	15	$1,395.00
P0023	Ink Jet Printer	50	50	$249.95
P0024	Color Ink Jet Printer	125	25	$569.95
P0025	Windows 95	400	200	$95.95
P0026	Norton Anti-Virus	150	50	$75.95
P0027	Norton Utilities	150	50	$115.95
P0028	Microsoft Scenes Screen Saver	75	25	$29.95
P0029	Microsoft Bookshelf	250	100	$129.95
P0030	Microsoft Cinemania	25	10	$59.95
P0031	Professional Photos on CD-ROM	15	0	$45.95

(b) Products Table

(c) Orders Table

Order ID	Customer ID	Order Date	SalesPerson ID
O0001	C0004	4/15/97	S01
O0002	C0003	4/18/97	S02
O0003	C0006	4/18/97	S03
O0004	C0007	4/18/97	S04
O0006	C0001	4/21/97	S05
O0007	C0002	4/21/97	S01
O0008	C0002	4/22/97	S02
O0009	C0001	4/22/97	S03
O0010	C0002	4/22/97	S04
O0011	C0001	4/24/97	S05
O0012	C0007	4/24/97	S01
O0013	C0004	4/24/97	S02
O0014	C0006	4/25/97	S03
O0015	C0009	4/25/97	S04
O0016	C0006	4/26/97	S05
O0017	C0011	4/26/97	S01
O0018	C0011	4/26/97	S02
O0019	C0012	4/27/97	S03
O0020	C0012	4/28/97	S04
O0021	C0010	4/29/97	S05
O0022	C0010	4/29/97	S01
O0023	C0008	4/30/97	S02
O0024	C0006	5/1/97	S03
O0025	C0006	5/1/97	S04
O0026	C0013	5/31/97	S05

(c) Orders Table

(d) Order Details Table

Order ID	Product ID	Quantity
O0001	P0013	1
O0001	P0014	4
O0001	P0027	1
O0002	P0001	1
O0002	P0006	1
O0002	P0020	1
O0002	P0022	1
O0003	P0005	1
O0003	P0020	1
O0003	P0022	1
O0004	P0003	1
O0004	P0010	1
O0004	P0022	2
O0006	P0007	1
O0006	P0014	10
O0007	P0028	1
O0007	P0030	3
O0008	P0001	1
O0008	P0004	3
O0008	P0008	4
O0008	P0011	2
O0008	P0012	1
O0009	P0006	1
O0010	P0002	2
O0010	P0022	1
O0010	P0023	1
O0011	P0016	2
O0011	P0020	2
O0012	P0021	10
O0012	P0029	10
O0012	P0030	10
O0013	P0009	4
O0013	P0016	10
O0013	P0024	2
O0014	P0019	2
O0014	P0028	1
O0015	P0018	1
O0015	P0020	1
O0016	P0029	2
O0017	P0019	2
O0018	P0009	1
O0018	P0025	2
O0018	P0026	2
O0019	P0014	25
O0020	P0024	1
O0021	P0004	1
O0022	P0027	1
O0023	P0021	1
O0023	P0028	1
O0023	P0029	1
O0024	P0007	1
O0024	P0013	5
O0024	P0014	3
O0024	P0016	1
O0025	P0012	2
O0025	P0029	2
O0026	P0001	1
O0026	P0014	2
O0026	P0020	1

(d) Order Details Table

(e) Sales Persons Table

SalesPersonID	FirstName	LastName	WorkPhone	HireDate
S01	Linda	Black	(305) 284-6105	2/3/93
S02	Michael	Vaughn	(305) 284-3993	2/10/93
S03	Cori	Rice	(305) 284-2557	3/15/93
S04	Karen	Ruenheck	(305) 284-4641	1/31/94
S05	Richard	Linger	(305) 284-4662	1/31/94

(e) Sales Persons Table

FIGURE 5.11   Super Store Database

The Sales Commission Query

We think it important that you understand how the tables in a database are related to one another and that you can answer conceptual questions such as obtaining the commission for a specific order. Practically speaking, however, you would not do the calculations yourself, but would create the necessary queries to let Access do the work for you.

Consider, for example, Figure 5.12a, which displays the design view of a parameter query to calculate the commissions for a specific salesperson. (This query determines the commissions for Cori Rice, which you computed manually in the previous discussion.) Enter the last name of the sales associate, Rice, and the query returns the dynaset in Figure 5.12b, showing all of her commissions. Note, too, that the commission returned for order O0003 is $209.20, which corresponds to the amount we arrived at earlier.

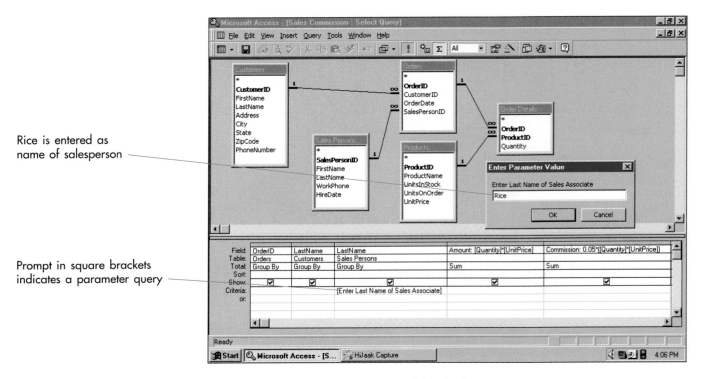

Rice is entered as
name of salesperson

Prompt in square brackets
indicates a parameter query

(a) Design View

Commission earned
on Order O0003

(b) Dynaset

FIGURE 5.12   Sales Commissions

The query in Figure 5.12a includes fields from all five tables in the database. The relationships are shown graphically in the top half of the query window and reflect the earlier discussion—for example, the one-to-many relationship between salespersons and orders. These tables are joined through the SalesPersonID field, which is the primary key in the Sales Persons table but a foreign key in the Orders table. (The Orders table has been modified to include this field.) Each field in the Total row contains either a Group By entry or an aggregate function, as explained in the previous discussion on total queries.

The Get External Data Command

The Computer Store database that you have been using in the hands-on exercises does not include the Sales Persons table. You could, of course, create the table manually, just as you would enter any other table. Alternatively, you could import the table from an external database, if it (the Sales Persons table) had been created independently. This is accomplished through the *Get External Data command,* which imports an object (a table, query, form, or report) from another database.

One benefit of this approach is that you can take advantage of any work that was previously done. The Sales Persons table, for example, may be part of an employee database in a completely different application. The Get External Data command also enables you to divide a large project (perhaps a class project) among many individuals, then subsequently put the objects back into a common database when the individual work is completed.

The following exercise has you import the Sales Persons table from another Access database. It then directs you to modify the existing Orders table to include a SalesPersonID, which references the records in the Sales Persons table, and to modify the Super Store Order Form to include the salesperson data.

HANDS-ON EXERCISE 4

Expanding the Database

Objective: To import a table from another database; to modify the design of an existing table. Use Figure 5.13 as a guide in the exercise.

STEP 1: Import the Sales Persons Table

➤ Open the **Computer Store database.** Click the **Tables tab.**

➤ Pull down the **File menu.** Click **Get External Data** to display a cascaded menu, then click **Import** to display the Import dialog box.

➤ Click (select) the **Sales Persons database** from the **Exploring Access folder,** then click **Import** to display the Import Objects dialog box in Figure 5.13a.

➤ If necessary, click the **Tables tab,** click **Sales Persons** (the only table in this database), then click **OK.** A dialog box will appear briefly on your screen as the Sales Persons table is imported into the Computer Store database.

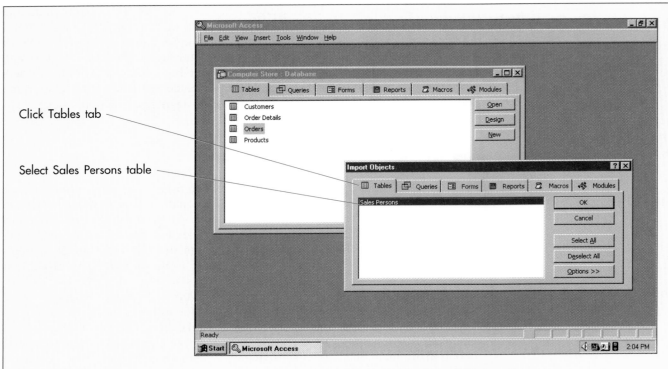

Click Tables tab

Select Sales Persons table

(a) Import the Sales Persons Table (step 1)

FIGURE 5.13   Hands-on Exercise 4

THE DOCUMENTS SUBMENU

One of the fastest ways to get to a recently used file, regardless of the application, is through the Windows 95 Start menu, which includes a Documents submenu containing the last 15 files that were opened. Click the Start button, click (or point to) the Documents submenu, then click the document you wish to open (e.g., Computer Store), assuming that it appears on the submenu. Windows will start the application, then open the indicated document.

STEP 2: Modify the Orders Table Design

➤ Select the **Orders table** from the Database window as shown in Figure 5.13b. Click the **Design button.**

➤ Click in the first available row in the **Field Name** column. Enter **SalesPersonID** as shown in Figure 5.13b. Choose **Number** as the data type. The Field Size property changes to Long Integer by default.

 • Click the **Format** property. Enter **\S00.**

 • Click the **Default Value** property and delete the **0.**

➤ Click the **Save button** to save the modified design of the Orders table.

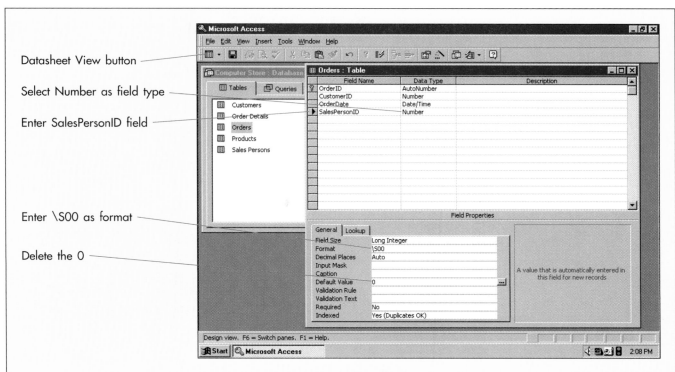

Datasheet View button

Select Number as field type

Enter SalesPersonID field

Enter \S00 as format

Delete the 0

(b) Modify the Orders Table (step 2)

FIGURE 5.13   Hands-on Exercise 4 (continued)

RELATIONSHIPS AND THE AUTONUMBER FIELD TYPE

The join fields on both sides of a relationship must be the same data type—for example, both number fields or both text fields. The Auto-Number field type, however, cannot be specified on both sides of a relationship. Thus, if the join field (SalesPersonID) in the primary table (Sales Persons) is an AutoNumber field, the join field in the related table (Orders) must be specified as a Number field, with the Field Size property set to Long Integer.

STEP 3: Add the Sales Person to Existing Orders

➤ Click the **Datasheet View button** to change to the Datasheet view as shown in Figure 5.13c. Maximize the window.

➤ Enter the **SalesPersonID** for each existing order as shown in Figure 5.13c. Enter only the number (e.g., 1, rather than S01) as the S and leading 0 are displayed automatically through the Format property. (Orders O0001 and O0002 have salespersons 1 and 2 respectively, and are not visible in the figure.)

➤ Close the Orders table.

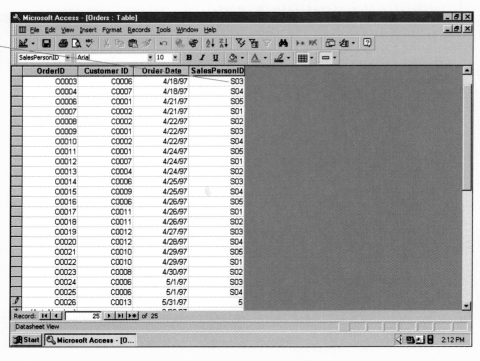

Enter SalesPersonID for each order (enter number only)

OrderID	Customer ID	Order Date	SalesPersonID
O0003	C0006	4/18/97	S03
O0004	C0007	4/18/97	S04
O0006	C0001	4/21/97	S05
O0007	C0002	4/21/97	S01
O0008	C0002	4/22/97	S02
O0009	C0001	4/22/97	S03
O0010	C0002	4/22/97	S04
O0011	C0001	4/24/97	S05
O0012	C0007	4/24/97	S01
O0013	C0004	4/24/97	S02
O0014	C0006	4/25/97	S03
O0015	C0009	4/25/97	S04
O0016	C0006	4/26/97	S05
O0017	C0011	4/26/97	S01
O0018	C0011	4/26/97	S02
O0019	C0012	4/27/97	S03
O0020	C0012	4/28/97	S04
O0021	C0010	4/29/97	S05
O0022	C0010	4/29/97	S01
O0023	C0008	4/30/97	S02
O0024	C0006	5/1/97	S03
O0025	C0006	5/1/97	S04
O0026	C0013	5/31/97	5

Record: 25 of 25

(c) Add the Sales Person (step 3)

FIGURE 5.13   Hands-on Exercise 4 (continued)

HIDE THE WINDOWS 95 TASKBAR

The Windows 95 taskbar is great for novices because it makes task switching as easy as changing channels on a TV. It also takes up valuable real estate on the desktop, and hence you may want to hide the taskbar when you don't need it. Point to an empty area on the taskbar, click the right mouse button to display a shortcut menu, and click Properties to display the Taskbar Properties dialog box. Click the Taskbar Options tab (if necessary), check the box to Auto hide the taskbar, and click OK. The taskbar should disappear. Now point to the bottom of the screen (or the edge where the taskbar was last displayed), and it will reappear.

STEP 4: Add a Relationship

➤ Pull down the **Tools menu.** Click **Relationships** to open the Relationships window as shown in Figure 5.13d. (The Sales Persons table is not yet visible.) Click the **Maximize button.**

➤ If necessary, drag the bottom border of the **Orders table** until you see the SalesPersonID (the field you added in step 2).

➤ Pull down the **Relationships menu.** Click **Show Table.** Click the **Tables tab** if necessary, select the **Sales Persons table,** then click the **Add button** to add the Sales Persons table to the Relationships window. Close the Show Table dialog box.

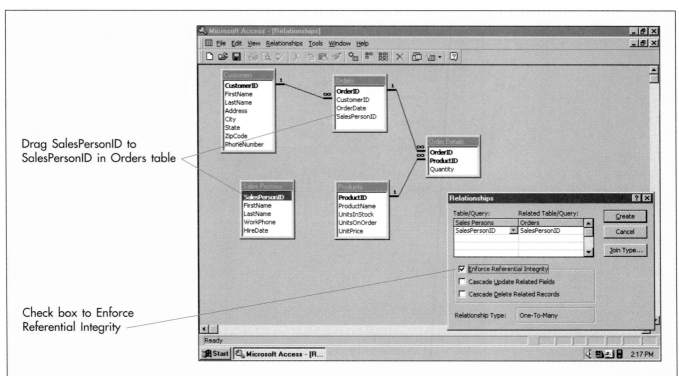

Drag SalesPersonID to SalesPersonID in Orders table

Check box to Enforce Referential Integrity

(d) Create the Relationship (step 4)

FIGURE 5.13   Hands-on Exercise 4 (continued)

➤ Drag the title bar of the **Sales Persons table** to position the table as shown in Figure 5.13d. Drag the **SalesPersonID field** from the Sales Persons table to the SalesPersonID in the Orders table. You will see the Relationships dialog box.

➤ Check the box to **Enforce Referential Integrity.** Click the **Create Command button** to create the relationship.

➤ Click the **Save button** to save the Relationships window. Close the Relationships window.

STEP 5: Modify the Order with Customer Information Query

➤ You should be back in the Database window. Click the **Queries tab,** select the **Order with Customer Information query,** then click the **Design button** to open the query in the Design view as shown in Figure 5.13e.

➤ If necessary, click and drag the border of the **Orders table** so that the newly added SalesPersonID field is displayed. Click the **horizontal scroll arrow** until a blank column in the design grid is visible.

➤ Click and drag the **SalesPersonID** from the Orders table to the last column in the design grid.

➤ Save the query. Close the query.

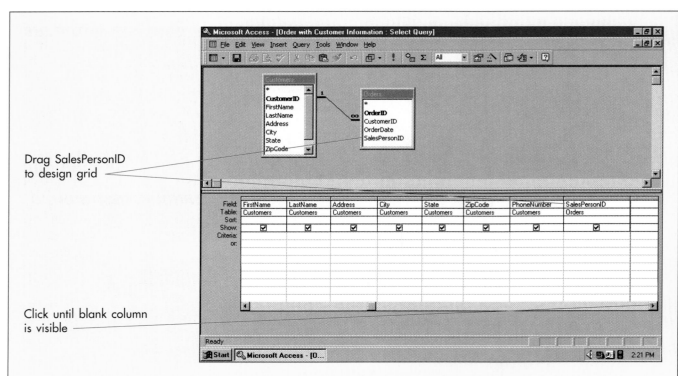

Drag SalesPersonID to design grid

Click until blank column is visible

(e) Modify the Order with Customer Information Query (step 5)

FIGURE 5.13   Hands-on Exercise 4 (continued)

STEP 6: Modify the Order Form

➤ You should be back in the Database window. Click the **Forms tab,** select the **Super Store Order Form,** then click the **Design** button to open the form in the Design view.

➤ Right click the **form selector box** and click **Properties** to display the Form Properties box. Click the **Data tab,** click the **Record Source property,** click the **drop-down arrow,** then select **Order with Customer Information.** This updates the form so that it looks for information from the modified (rather than the original) query. Close the Properties box.

➤ Move and size the controls so that there is room to add a control for the salesperson as shown in Figure 5.13f.

➤ Click the **Combo Box tool** on the Toolbox toolbar. Click and drag in the form where you want the combo box to go. Release the mouse. You will see the first step in the Combo Box Wizard.

• Check the option button that indicates you want the combo box to look up values in a table or query. Click **Next.**

• Choose the **Sales Persons table** in the next screen. Click **Next.**

• Select the **SalesPersonID** and **LastName** from the Available Fields list box for inclusion in the Combo box columns list. Click **Next.**

• Adjust the column widths if necessary. Be sure the box to hide the key column is checked. Click **Next.**

• Click the option button to store the value in the field. Click the **drop-down arrow** to display the fields in the query and select the **SalesPersonID** field. Click **Next.**

• Enter **Salesperson** as the label for the combo box. Click **Finish.**

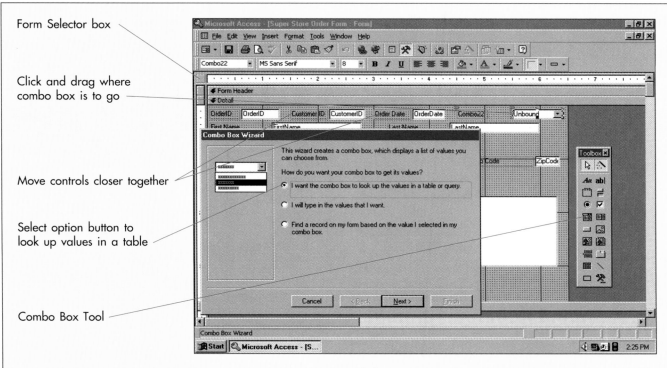

Form Selector box

Click and drag where
combo box is to go

Move controls closer together

Select option button to
look up values in a table

Combo Box Tool

(f) Modify the Super Store Order Form (step 6)

FIGURE 5.13   Hands-on Exercise 4 (continued)

➤ Move and/or size the combo box and its label so that it is spaced attractively
on the form.

➤ Point to the combo box, click the **right mouse button** to display a shortcut
menu, and click **Properties.**

➤ Click the **Other tab.** Change the name of the box to **Sales Person.** Close the
dialog box.

➤ Pull down the **View menu** and click **Tab Order.** Click the **AutoOrder button**
to change the tab order so that the combo box is accessed in sequence. Click
OK.

➤ Save the form. Change to the Form view.

STRUCTURED QUERY LANGUAGE

Structured Query Language (SQL) was developed by IBM during the
1970s and has since become the standard language for accessing a relational database. Access shields you from the subtleties of the SQL syn-
tax through the design grid, which creates the equivalent SQL statement
for you. An SQL statement may appear, however, as the record source
property within the form and can be confusing if you are not familiar with
SQL. Click the Record Source property, click the drop-down arrow to
display the list of queries within the database, then click the desired query
to replace the SQL statement.

STEP 7: The Completed Order Form

➤ You should see the completed form as shown in Figure 5.13g. Click the **New Record button** to display a blank form so that you can place an order.

➤ Click in the **Customer ID text box.** Enter **13** (your customer number from the first exercise), then press the **Tab key** to move to the next field.

- The OrderID is entered automatically as it is an AutoNumber field and assigned the next sequential number.

- All of your customer information (your name, address, and phone number) is entered automatically because of the AutoLookup feature that is built into the underlying query.

- Today's date is entered automatically because of the default value (=Date()) that is built into the Orders table.

➤ Click the **drop-down arrow** on the Sales Person combo box. Select **Black** (or click in the box and type **B**), and the complete name is entered automatically.

➤ Click the **ProductID text box** in the subform. Enter **2** (not P0002) and press the **enter key** to move to the next field. The OrderID (O0027) is entered automatically, as is the Product Name and Unit Price.

➤ Press the **Tab key** three times to move to the Quantity field, enter **1,** and press the **Tab key** twice more to move to the ProductID field for the next item.

➤ Close the Order form.

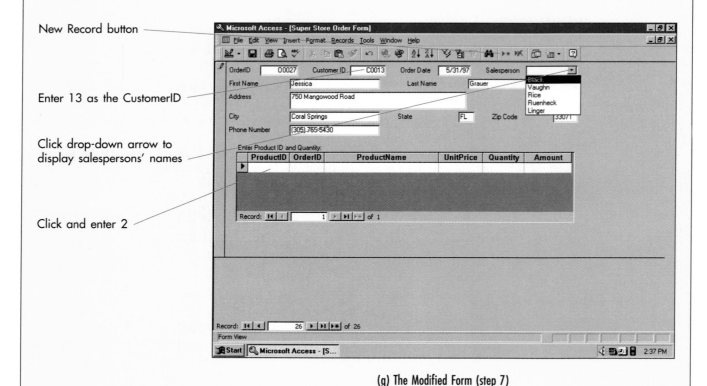

New Record button

Enter 13 as the CustomerID

Click drop-down arrow to display salespersons' names

Click and enter 2

(g) The Modified Form (step 7)

FIGURE 5.13   Hands-on Exercise 4 (continued)

THE STARTUP PROPERTY

The Startup property determines how a database will appear when it is opened. One very common option is to open a form automatically so that the user is presented with the form without having to navigate through the Database window. Pull down the Tools menu, click Startup to display the Startup dialog box, then click the drop-down arrow in the Display Form list box. Select the desired form (e.g., the Super Store Order form developed in this exercise), then click OK. The next time you open the database the designated form will be opened automatically.

STEP 8: Database Properties

➤ You should be back in the Database window. Pull down the **File menu** and click **Database Properties** to display the dialog box in Figure 5.13h.

➤ Click the **Contents tab** to display the contents of the Computer Store database on which you have been working:

- There are five tables (Customers, Order Details, Orders, Products, and Sales Persons).
- There are five queries, which include the Total and Parameter queries you created in exercise 3.
- There are two forms—the main form, which you have completed in this exercise, and the associated subform.

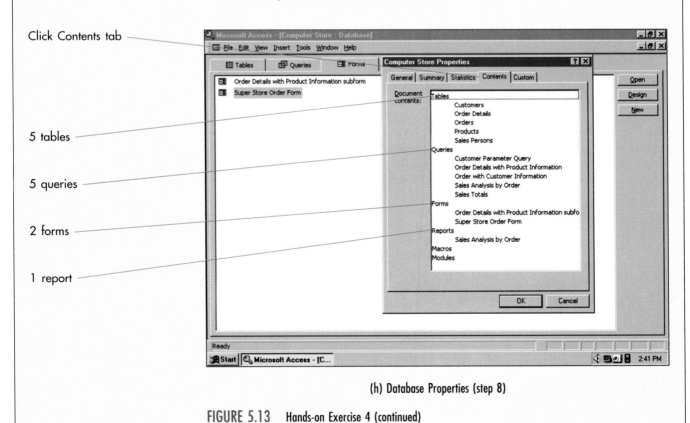

Click Contents tab

5 tables

5 queries

2 forms

1 report

(h) Database Properties (step 8)

FIGURE 5.13 Hands-on Exercise 4 (continued)

- There is one report, the report you created in exercise 3.
- There are no macros or modules. (Macros are covered in the next chapter.)

➤ Close the Properties window.

COMPACTING A DATABASE

The size of an Access database with multiple objects is quite large even if the database contains only a limited number of records. It is important, therefore, to compact the database periodically so that it is stored as efficiently as possible. Close the open database, but remain in Access. Pull down the Tools menu, click Database utilities, then click Compact Database to display a dialog box similar to the Open box. Select (click) the database you wish to compact, then enter a *different file name* for the compacted base. (This ensures that you still have the original database if there is a problem.) Click the Save button to compact the database and close the dialog box. Check that the compacted database is OK, delete the original database, then rename the compacted database to the original name. See online Help for additional information.

STEP 9: Exit Access

➤ Click OK to close the dialog box. Close the Computer Store database. Exit Access. Congratulations on a job well done.

SUMMARY

The implementation of a many-to-many relationship requires an additional table whose primary key consists of (at least) the primary keys of the individual tables. The many-to-many table may also contain additional fields whose values are dependent on the combined key. All relationships are created in the Relationships window by dragging the join field from the primary table to the related table. A many-to-many relationship is implemented by a pair of one-to-many relationships.

Enforcement of referential integrity prevents you from adding a record to the related table if that record contains an invalid value of the foreign key. It also prevents the deletion and/or updating of records on the "one" side of a one-to-many relationship when there are matching records in the related table. The deletion (updating) can take place, however, if the relationship is modified to allow the cascaded deletion (updating) of related records (fields).

There are several reasons to base a form (or subform) on a query rather than a table. A query can contain a calculated field; a table cannot. A query can contain fields from more than one table and take advantage of AutoLookup. A query can also contain selected records from a table and/or display those records in a different sequence from that of the table on which it is based.

A parameter query prompts you for the criteria each time you execute the query. The prompt is enclosed in square brackets and is entered in the Criteria row within the Query Design view. Multiple parameters may be specified within the same query.

Aggregate functions (Avg, Min, Max, Sum, and Count) perform calculations on groups of records. Execution of the query displays an aggregate record for each group, and individual records do not appear. Updating of individual records is not possible in this type of query.

Tables may be added to an Access database without disturbing the data in existing tables. The Get External Data command enables you to import an object(s) from another database.

KEY WORDS AND CONCEPTS

AutoLookup	Join field	Startup property
AutoNumber field	Join line	Sum function
Cascaded deletion	Main form	Table row
Cascaded updating	Many-to-many	TopValues property
Combined key	relationship	Total query
Description property	One-to-many	Total row
Foreign key	relationship	Unmatched Query
Format property	Parameter query	Wizard
Get External Data	Primary key	Zoom box
command	Prompt	
Group By	Referential integrity	

MULTIPLE CHOICE

1. Which tables are necessary to implement a many-to-many relationship between students and the courses they take?
   (a) A Students table
   (b) A Courses table
   (c) A Students-Courses table
   (d) All of the above

2. Which of the following would be suitable as the primary key in a Students-Courses table, where there is a many-to-many relationship between Students and Courses, and further, when a student is allowed to repeat a course?
   (a) The combination of StudentID and CourseID
   (b) The combination of StudentID, CourseID, and semester
   (c) The combination of StudentID, CourseID, semester, and grade
   (d) All of the above are equally appropriate

3. Which of the following is necessary to add a record to the "one" side in a one-to-many relationship in which referential integrity is enforced?
   (a) A unique primary key for the new record
   (b) One or more matching records in the many table
   (c) Both (a) and (b)
   (d) Neither (a) nor (b)

4. Which of the following is necessary to add a record to the "many" side in a one-to-many relationship in which referential integrity is enforced?
  (a) A unique primary key for the new record
  (b) A matching record in the primary table
  (c) Both (a) and (b)
  (d) Neither (a) nor (b)

5. Under which circumstances can you delete a "many" record in a one-to-many relationship?
  (a) Under all circumstances
  (b) Under no circumstances
  (c) By enforcing referential integrity
  (d) By enforcing referential integrity with the cascaded deletion of related records

6. Under which circumstances can you delete the "one" record in a one-to-many relationship?
  (a) Under all circumstances
  (b) Under no circumstances
  (c) By enforcing referential integrity
  (d) By enforcing referential integrity with the cascaded deletion of related records

7. Which of the following would be suitable as the primary key in a Patients-Doctors table, where there is a many-to-many relationship between patients and doctors, and where the same patient can see the same doctor on different visits?
  (a) The combination of PatientID and DoctorID
  (b) The combination of PatientID, DoctorID, and the date of the visit
  (c) Either (a) or (b)
  (d) Neither (a) nor (b)

8. How do you implement the many-to-many relationship between patients and doctors described in the previous question?
  (a) Through a one-to-many relationship between the Patients table and the Patients-Doctors table
  (b) Through a one-to-many relationship between the Doctors table and the Patients-Doctors table
  (c) Both (a) and (b)
  (d) Neither (a) nor (b)

9. A database has a one-to-many relationship between teams and players, which is implemented through a common TeamID field. Which data type and field size should be assigned to the TeamID field in the Players table, if TeamID is defined as an AutoNumber field in the Teams table?
  (a) AutoNumber and Long Integer
  (b) Number and Long Integer
  (c) Text and Long Integer
  (d) Lookup Wizard and Long Integer

10. Which of the following is true about a main form and an associated subform?
  (a) The main form can be based on a query
  (b) The subform can be based on a query
  (c) Both (a) and (b)
  (d) Neither (a) nor (b)

11. A parameter query:
   (a) Displays a prompt within brackets in the Criteria row of the query
   (b) Is limited to a single parameter
   (c) Both (a) and (b)
   (d) Neither (a) nor (b)

12. Which of the following is available as an aggregate function within a select query?
   (a) Sum and Avg
   (b) Min and Max
   (c) Both (a) and (b)
   (d) Neither (a) nor (b)

13. A query designed to take advantage of AutoLookup requires:
   (a) A unique value for the join field in the "one" side of a one-to-many relationship
   (b) The join field to be taken from the "many" side of a one-to-many relationship
   (c) Both (a) and (b)
   (d) Neither (a) nor (b)

14. Which of the following can be imported from another Access database?
   (a) Tables and forms
   (b) Queries and reports
   (c) Both (a) and (b)
   (d) Neither (a) nor (b)

15. Which of the following is true of the TopValues query property?
   (a) It can be used to display the top 10 records in a dynaset
   (b) It can be used to display the top 10 percent of the records in a dynaset
   (c) Both (a) and (b)
   (d) Neither (a) nor (b)

ANSWERS

1. d	**6.** d	**11.** a
2. b	**7.** b	**12.** c
3. a	**8.** c	**13.** c
4. a	**9.** b	**14.** c
5. a	**10.** c	**15.** c

PRACTICE WITH ACCESS 97

1. The Sales Commission report in Figure 5.14 is based on a query similar to the parameter query used to determine the commissions for a particular salesperson. Create the necessary query, then use the Report Wizard to create the report in Figure 5.14. This exercise illustrates the power of Access as both the report and underlying query are based on five different tables.

Sales Commission Report

	Order ID	Order Date	Last Name	Amount	Commission
Black					
	O0001	4/15/97	Colon	$605.86	$30.29
	O0007	4/21/97	Milgrom	$209.80	$10.49
	O0012	4/24/97	Geoghegan	$2,558.50	$127.93
	O0017	4/26/97	Center	$79.90	$4.00
	O0022	4/29/97	Anderson	$115.95	$5.80
	O0027	5/31/97	Grauer	$1,999.00	$99.95
			Sum:	**$5,569.01**	**$278.45**
Linger					
	O0006	4/21/97	Lee	$998.90	$49.95
	O0011	4/24/97	Lee	$739.80	$36.99
	O0016	4/26/97	Muddell	$259.90	$13.00
	O0021	4/29/97	Anderson	$2,299.00	$114.95
	O0026	5/31/97	Grauer	$2,108.93	$105.45
			Sum:	**$6,406.53**	**$320.33**
Rice					
	O0003	4/18/97	Muddell	$4,183.95	$209.20
	O0009	4/22/97	Lee	$499.00	$24.95
	O0014	4/25/97	Muddell	$109.85	$5.49
	O0019	4/27/97	Slane	$249.75	$12.49
	O0024	5/ 1/97	Muddell	$3,358.67	$167.93
			Sum:	**$8,401.22**	**$420.06**
Ruenheck					
	O0004	4/18/97	Geoghegan	$5,688.00	$284.40
	O0010	4/22/97	Milgrom	$5,642.95	$282.15
	O0015	4/25/97	Couto	$249.90	$12.50
	O0020	4/28/97	Slane	$569.95	$28.50
	O0025	5/ 1/97	Muddell	$757.90	$37.90
			Sum:	**$12,908.70**	**$645.43**

Saturday, May 31, 1997   **Page 1 of 2**

FIGURE 5.14   Report for Practice Exercise 1

2. The query in Figure 5.15 identifies products that have never been ordered. The query was created through the Unmatched Query Wizard according to the instructions below.

a. Click the Queries tab in the Database window. Click New, select the Find Unmatched Query Wizard, then click OK.

b. Choose Products as the table whose records you want to see in the query results. Click Next.

c. Choose Order Details as the table that contains the related records. Click Next.

d. ProductID is automatically selected as the matching field. Click Next.

e. Select every field from the Available Fields list. Click Next.

f. Products without Matching Order Details is entered as the name of the query. Click the Finish Command button to exit the Wizard and see the results of the query.

g. What advice will you give to management regarding unnecessary inventory?

h. What advantage (if any) is there in using the Find Unmatched Query Wizard to create the query, as opposed to creating the query by entering the information directly in the Query Design view?

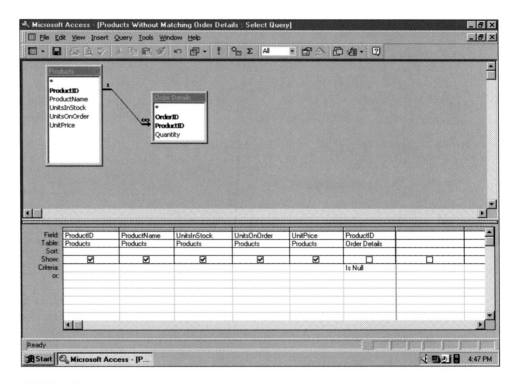

FIGURE 5.15   Screen for Practice Exercise 2

3. Create the form in Figure 5.16, which displays either the information for an existing customer or a blank form to add a new customer. This is accomplished by basing the form on a parameter query rather than the Customers table. Execution of the query displays a blank form when the customer's name is not in the database (as in Figure 5.16), or it will display a completed form when it finds the name. Create the necessary parameter query that

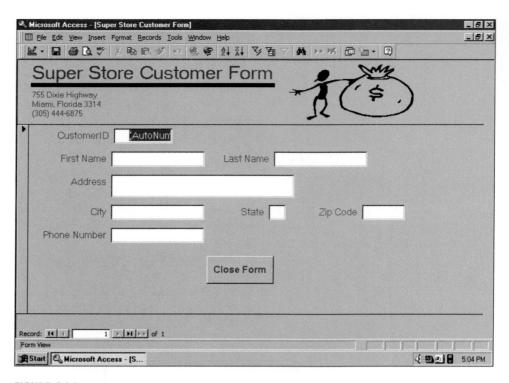

FIGURE 5.16   Screen for Practice Exercise 3

requests the customer's last name followed by the customer's first name, then create the form based on the parameter query. You are free to improve upon our design.

4. The best way to open the Customer form that was created in the previous exercise is by adding a command button to the Super Store Order form as shown in Figure 5.17. The user would click the Find/Add Command button to display the Parameter Value dialog box, then he or she would enter the customer's last name as indicated. The system would return a completed Customer form for an existing customer (from which to obtain the CustomerID) or a blank form to add a new customer. Closing the customer form, in either case, would return you to the Order form where you can enter the CustomerID and the data for the new order.

a. Open the Super Store Order form that was completed in Hands-on Exercise 4, then use the Command Button Wizard to add the buttons in Figure 5.17. The Find/Add a Customer button should open the form from the previous problem. The Add Order button should add a new order, and the Close Form button should close the Order form.

b. You can improve the form further by modifying the subform to display a combo box for the product name. This way, the user clicks on the combo box within an order, and selects the products by name rather than having to enter a ProductID. Open the subform in Design view, delete the existing ProductID and ProductName controls, then follow the procedure that was used to add a combo box for the salesperson (see step 6 on page 236). Remember to change the Tab order.

c. Add the Form Header to improve the appearance of the form.

d. Add a new order for yourself consisting of a Pentium 133, 17-inch monitor, laser printer, and 28.8 bps modem. Print this order (be sure to print only a single order) and submit it to your instructor.

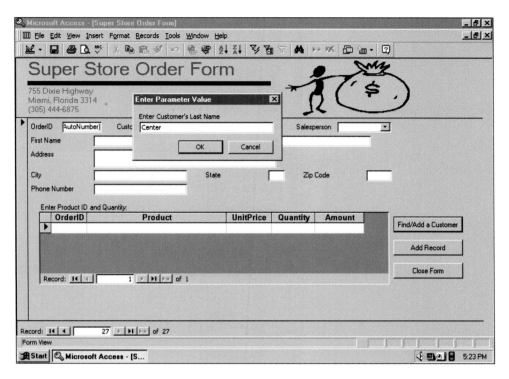

FIGURE 5.17   Screen for Practice Exercise 4

5. Figure 5.18 displays the final version of our Super Store Order form, which contains one additional element—the total amount for the displayed order. Proceed as follows:

a. Open the Super Store Order form in Design view. Click the Subform/Subreport Wizard tool, then click and drag on the design grid under the existing subform control to create a new subform to display the total amount of the order. The subform should be based on the Sales Total query that was created in the third hands-on exercise.

b. Add the OrderID and Amount fields to the new form. Select the option to Show Sales Totals for each record in the Order with Customer Information. Accept the suggested name for the subform.

c. Click off the newly created subform control, then double click the subform to open it. Delete the OrderID controls in the header and detail sections. Delete the Amount label in the Form header. Close the Form header, then size the Amount control to make it smaller.

d. Right click the Form Selector box to display the Properties dialog box. Change the Default View property to Single Form and the Scroll Bars property to Neither. Suppress the record selectors and the navigation buttons. Save the form.

e. Size and move the Sales Total subform within the Order Form. Delete the current label and add a new label for the Order total. Save the form.

f. Change to the Form view, then use the Navigation buttons to move from one order to the next. Each time you view a new order, the total amount is visible at the bottom of the screen.

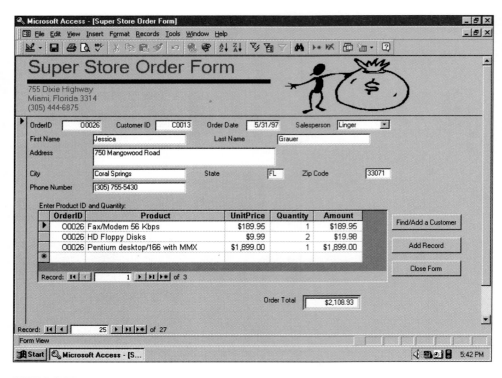

FIGURE 5.18   Screen for Practice Exercise 5

CASE STUDIES

Medical Research

Design a database for a medical research project that will track specific volunteers and/or specific studies. A study will require several subjects, but a specific person may participate in only one study. The system should also be able to track physicians. Many physicians can work on the same study. A given physician may also work on multiple studies.

The system should be able to display all facts about a particular volunteer (subject) such as name, birth date, sex, height, weight, blood pressure, and cholesterol level. It should be able to display all characteristics associated with a particular study—for example, the title, beginning date, ending date, as well as the names of all physicians who work on that study. It should also show whether the physician is a primary or secondary investigator in each study.

Show the required tables in the database, being sure to indicate the primary key and foreign keys in each table. Indicate one or two other fields in each table as appropriate. (You need not list them all.)

The Stock Broker

You have been hired as a consultant to a securities firm that wants to track its clients and the stocks they own. The firm prides itself on its research and maintains a detailed file for the stocks it follows. Among the data for each stock are its symbol (ideal for the primary key), the industry it is in, its earnings, dividend, etc.

The firm requires the usual client data (name, address, phone number, social security number, etc.). One client can hold many different stocks, and the same stock can be held by different clients. The firm needs to know the date the client purchased the stock, the number of shares that were purchased, and the purchase price.

Show the required tables in the database, being sure to indicate the primary key and foreign keys in each table. Indicate one or two other fields in each table (you need not list them all).

The Video Store

You have been hired as a database consultant to the local video store, which rents and/or sells tapes to customers. The store maintains the usual information about every customer (name, address, phone number, and so on). It also has detailed information about every movie, such as its duration, rating, rental price, and purchase price. One customer can rent several tapes, and the same tape will (over time) be rented to many customers.

The owner of the store needs a detailed record of every rental that identifies the movie, the customer, the date the rental was made, and the number of days the customer may keep the movie without penalty.

Class Scheduling

Class scheduling represents a major undertaking at any university. It entails the coordination of course offerings as published in a registration schedule together with faculty assignments. All courses have a formal title but are more commonly known by a six-position course-id. Microcomputer Applications, for example, is better known as CIS120. The first three characters in the course-id denote the department (e.g., CIS stands for Computer Information Systems). The last three indicate the particular course.

The university may offer multiple sections of any given course at different times. CIS120, for example, is offered at four different times: at 9:00, 10:00, 11:00, and 12:00, with all sections meeting three days a week (Mondays, Wednesdays, and Fridays). The information about when a class meets is summarized in the one-letter section designation; for example, section A meets from 9:00 to 9:50 on Mondays, Wednesdays, and Fridays.

The published schedule should list every section of every course together with the days, times, and room assignments. It should also display the complete course title, number of credits, and the name of the faculty member assigned to that section. It should be able to list all classes taught by a particular faculty member or all sections of a particular course. Design a relational database to satisfy these requirements.

BUILDING APPLICATIONS: INTRODUCTION TO MACROS AND PROTOTYPING

6

OBJECTIVES

After reading this chapter you will be able to:

1. Explain how forms are used to develop an automated user interface; create a form with multiple command buttons to serve as a menu.

2. Use the Link Tables command to associate tables in one database with objects in a different database.

3. Describe how macros are used to automate an application; explain the special role of the AutoExec macro.

4. Describe the components of the Macro window; distinguish between a macro action and an argument.

5. Use the On Click property to change the action associated with a command button.

6. Use the Find Unmatched Query Wizard to identify records in one table that do not have a corresponding record in another table.

7. Explain how prototyping facilitates the development of an application; use the MsgBox action as the basis of a prototype macro.

8. Create a macro group; explain how macro groups simplify the organization of macros within a database.

OVERVIEW

You have completed several chapters in our text and have developed some impressive databases. You have created systems with multiple tables that contained both one-to-many and many-to-many relationships. You have created sophisticated forms and queries that relate data from several tables to one another. In short, you have become proficient in Microsoft Access and have learned how to create the objects (tables, forms, queries, and reports) that comprise a database.

You have not, however, developed a user interface that ties the objects together so that the database is easy to use. In other words, you have created a database, but have not yet created an application. An application contains the same objects as a database. The difference is subtle and has to do with how the objects are presented to the user. An application has an intuitive user interface that does not require a knowledge of Microsoft Access on the part of the user.

This chapter has you develop an application for the Coral Springs Soccer Association. The discussion starts with an existing database that is expanded to include a user interface that enables a nontechnical person to use the application. The application includes macros that automate common command sequences and further simplify the system for the end user. And finally, the application includes the concept of prototyping, which enables you to demonstrate its "look and feel" to potential users, even before the application is complete.

Four hands-on exercises are included that progressively build the application. The end result is a system that is fully functional and one that can be used by any youth-oriented sports league.

THE CORAL SPRINGS SOCCER ASSOCIATION

The Coral Springs Soccer Association (CSSA) has approximately three thousand players organized into teams in various age groups. The Association registers the players and coaches, then holds a draft (among the coaches) to divide the players into teams. The Association has designed a database with three tables (Teams, Players, and Coaches) and has implemented the following relationships:

- A one-to-many relationship between teams and players (one team has many players, but a player is assigned to only one team).
- A one-to-many relationship between teams and coaches (one team has many coaches, but a coach is assigned to only one team).

The Access database developed by the CSSA contains multiple forms, queries, and reports based on these tables. There is a Players form through which you add a new player, or edit or delete the record of an existing player. A similar form exists for the Coaches table. There is also a sophisticated main and subform combination for the Teams table that displays the players and coaches on each team, and through which data for any table (Team, Player, or Coach) can be added, edited, or deleted.

The CSSA database contains a variety of reports, including a master list of players in alphabetical order, mailing labels for all coaches and players, a list of players according to their ability rating, and printed team rosters. The CSSA database also contains queries to find a specific player or coach, and to locate all players and/or coaches who have not been assigned to a team.

It would not be difficult for a person knowledgeable in Access to open the database and then select the various objects from the Database window as the need arose. The Soccer database, however, is used by nontechnical volunteers during registration, at which time hundreds of players (accompanied by their parents) sign up for the coming season. It is essential, therefore, that the database be easy to use, and that a nontechnical person be able to register the players and produce the queries and reports. This gives rise to the menu-driven system in Figure 6.1.

The *user interface* (the screens the user sees) is the most important part of any system, at least from the viewpoint of the end-user. A system that is intuitive and easy to use will be successful. Conversely, a system that is difficult to use or visually unappealing is sure to fail. You don't have to know anything about soccer or the workings of our system to use the menu in Figure 6.1.

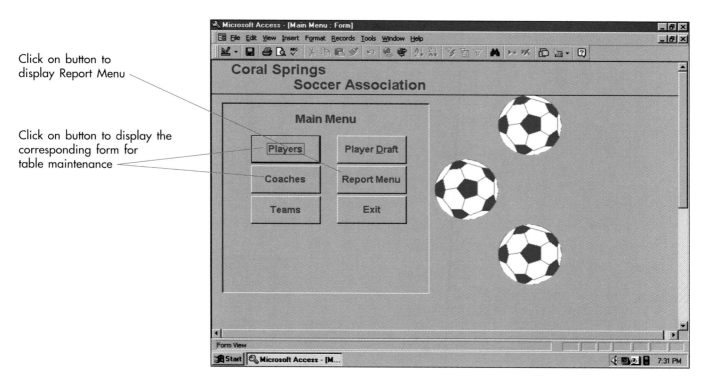

Click on button to display Report Menu

Click on button to display the corresponding form for table maintenance

FIGURE 6.1   A User Interface

You would, for example, click the Players, Coaches, or Teams command buttons and expect a screen that would enable you to maintain records in the corresponding table. In similar fashion, you would click the Report Menu button to display a menu listing the various reports, each of which could be produced by clicking the corresponding button. You would click the Player Draft button to assign players to teams after registration has taken place.

The menu in Figure 6.1 is a form similar to those that you have developed in other chapters. Each of the command buttons was created through the Command Button Wizard. The form is created in such a way that when a user clicks a button, Access interprets the click as an *event* and responds with an action that has been assigned to that event. Clicking the Teams button, for example, causes Access to open the Teams form. Clicking the Players button is a different event and causes Access to open the Players form.

To develop a menu, you create a form, then add command buttons through the Command Button Wizard. The Wizard prompts you for the action you want to take in response to the event (e.g., clicking the button), then creates an *event procedure* for you. The event procedure is a Visual Basic program that executes automatically each time the event occurs. Eventually, you may want to learn Access Basic so that you can develop more advanced applications and create your own procedures. Access Basic is, however, beyond the scope of this text.

THE LINK TABLES COMMAND

All applications consist of tables *and* objects (forms, queries, reports, macros, and modules) based on those tables. The tables and objects may be stored in the same database (as was done throughout the book), or they may be stored in separate databases, as shown in Figure 6.2. In this example the tables are stored in one database (the Soccer Tables database), while the objects are stored in a different database (the Soccer Objects database).

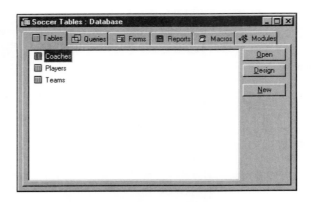

(a) Soccer Tables Database (contains only the tables)

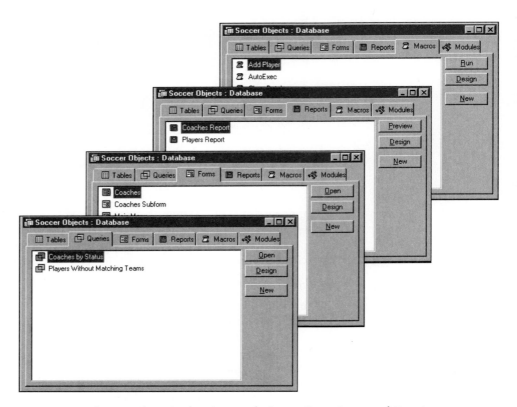

(b) Soccer Objects Database (contains the Queries, Forms, Reports, and Macros)

FIGURE 6.2   Separating the Tables and Objects

One advantage of separating the data from the other objects is that you can create new versions of an application *without* disturbing the data. In other words, you can develop an upgraded release of the application (Soccer Objects Two) and distribute it to the users without affecting the various tables. The new version contains additional and/or improved features (e.g., new reports and queries) but attaches to the original data, and thus retains all of the transactions that have been processed.

The approach also provides flexibility with respect to where the tables and the associated objects are stored. It is common, for example, to store the tables on a network drive, which can be accessed by multiple users. The other objects, however, would be stored on the users' local drives. Thus, you could create different sets of objects for different users. The Director, for example, may be given access to all tables within the database where he or she can perform any type of operation. Other users, however, may be given only restricted access, such as being able to add players or coaches, but prevented from making team assignments.

The tables and objects are tied to one another through the ***Link Tables command,*** which is executed from within the Soccer Objects database. The command associates the tables in one database (Soccer Tables) with the objects in another database (Soccer Objects). Once the Link Tables command has been executed, it is as though the tables were in the Soccer Objects database with respect to maintaining the data. You can add, edit, and delete a record in any (linked) table; you cannot, however, change the design of a linked table from within the Soccer Objects database.

The following exercise has you link the tables from one database to the objects in a different database, then develop the Main Menu (shown earlier in Figure 6.1) for the Coral Springs Soccer Association.

HANDS-ON EXERCISE 1

Creating a User Interface

Objective: To use the Link Tables command to associate tables in one database with the objects in a different database. To create a form with multiple command buttons to provide the user with a menu. Use Figure 6.3 as a guide in the exercise.

STEP 1: Open the Soccer Objects Database

➤ Start Access. Change to the **Exploring Access folder** as you have been doing throughout the text.

➤ Open the **Soccer Objects database** as shown in Figure 6.3a, then click the various tabs in the Database window to view the contents of this database. This database contains the various objects (forms, queries, and reports) in the soccer application, but not the tables.

  • Click the **Tables tab.** There are currently no tables in the database.

  • Click the **Forms tab.** There are six forms in the database.

  • Click the **Queries tab.** There is one query in the database.

  • Click the **Reports tab.** There are currently no reports in the database.

➤ Pull down the **File menu,** click **Database Properties,** then click the **Contents tab** to see the contents of the database as shown in Figure 6.3a. Click **OK** to close the dialog box.

DATABASE PROPERTIES

The tabs within the Database window display the objects within a database, but show only one type of object at a time. You can, for example, see all of the reports or all of the queries, but you cannot see the reports and queries at the same time. There is another way. Pull down the File menu, click Database Properties, then click the Contents tab to display the contents (objects) in the database. You cannot, however, use the Database Properties dialog box to open those objects.

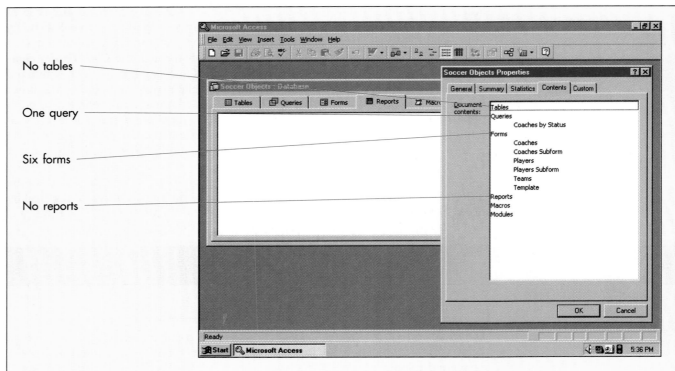

No tables

One query

Six forms

No reports

(a) The Soccer Objects Database (step 1)

FIGURE 6.3 Hands-on Exercise 1

STEP 2: The Link Tables Command

➤ Pull down the **File menu.** Click **Get External Data,** then click **Link Tables** from the submenu. You should see the Link dialog box.

➤ Select the **Exploring Access folder.** Scroll (if necessary) until you can select the **Soccer Tables database,** then click the **Link Command button.**

➤ You should see the Link Tables dialog box in Figure 6.3b. Click the **Select All Command button** to select all three tables, then click **OK.**

➤ The system (briefly) displays a message indicating that it is linking the tables, after which the tables should appear in the Database window. (If necessary, click the **Tables tab** in the Database window.) The arrow next to each table indicates that the table physically resides in another database.

IMPORTING VERSUS LINKING

The Get External Data command displays a cascaded menu to import or link an object from another database. (Any type of object can be imported. A table is the only type of object that can be linked.) Importing an object brings a copy of the object into the current database and does not maintain a tie to the original object. Thus, any changes to the object in the current database are not reflected in the original object. Linking, on the other hand, does not bring the table into the database but only a pointer to the table. Any changes to the data in the linked table are reflected in the original table as well as any other databases that are linked to that table.

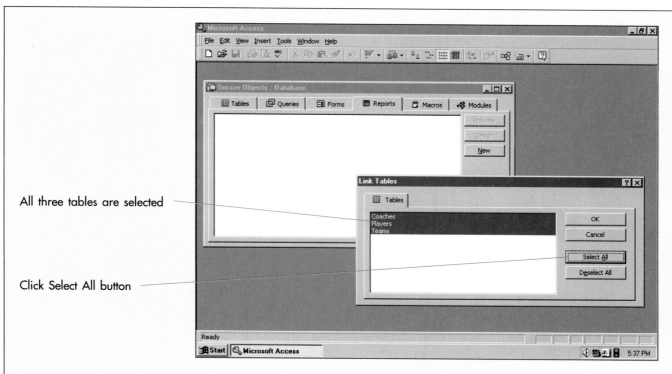

All three tables are selected

Click Select All button

(b) Link Tables Command (step 2)

FIGURE 6.3 Hands-on Exercise 1 (continued)

STEP 3: Add a New Player

➤ Click the **Forms tab** to display the available forms, then double click the **Players form** to open the form. Click the **Maximize button** so that the form takes the entire window as shown in Figure 6.3c.

➤ Click the **Add Player Command button** on the bottom of the form. Click the **text box** to enter your first name. (The PlayerID is an AutoNumber field that is updated automatically.) Enter your name, then press the **Tab key** to move to the next field.

➤ Continue to enter the appropriate data for yourself, but please assign yourself to the **Comets team.** Note, too, that various defaults and data validation have been built into the system:

• As soon as you begin to enter data, a unique PlayerID is assigned automatically since PlayerID is an AutoNumber field.

• The phone number must be numeric and must contain both the area code and phone number.

• Coral Springs and FL are entered as default values for city and state, respectively, but can be changed by entering new values.

• The team is entered via a drop-down list. Type **C** (the first letter in Comets) and Comets is entered automatically from the drop-down list for teams.

• The player rating is a required field (all players are evaluated for ability in order to balance the teams) and must be A, B, C, or D.

➤ Click the **Close Form Command button** to complete the data entry and return to the Database window.

PlayerID is entered
automatically

Click in text box and
enter your first name

Select Comets

Click Add Player button

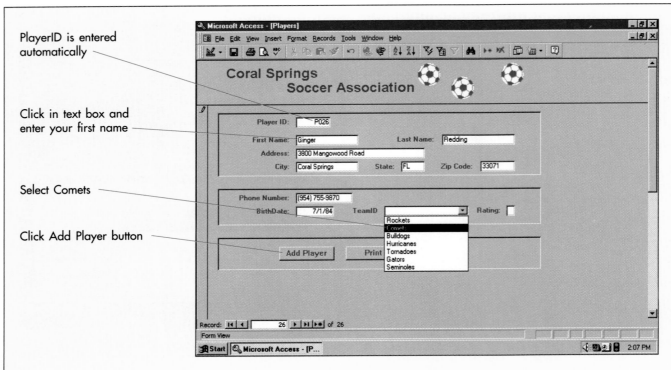

(c) Add a Player (step 3)

FIGURE 6.3   Hands-on Exercise 1 (continued)

A LOOK AHEAD

The Add Record button in the Players form was created through the
Command Button Wizard. The Wizard creates an *event procedure* that
creates a blank record at the end of the underlying table and enables you
to add a new player. The procedure does not, however, position you at a
specific control within the Players form; that is, you still have to click in
the First Name text box to start entering the data. You can, however, create a macro that displays a blank record *and* automatically moves to the
First Name control. See steps 7 and 8 in the next hands-on exercise.

STEP 4: View the Team Form

➤ Double click the **Teams form** to open this form. You will see the players and
coaches for Team T01 (Rockets).

➤ Click the ▶ on the Team status bar (or press the **PgDn key**) to move to the
next team, which is team T02 (Comets) as shown in Figure 6.3d.

➤ Your name has been added as the last player on this team because of the
team assignment you made in the previous step. Don't be concerned that
your team doesn't have a coach, as we will take care of that in step 9.

➤ Click the **Close Form Command button** to return to the Database window.

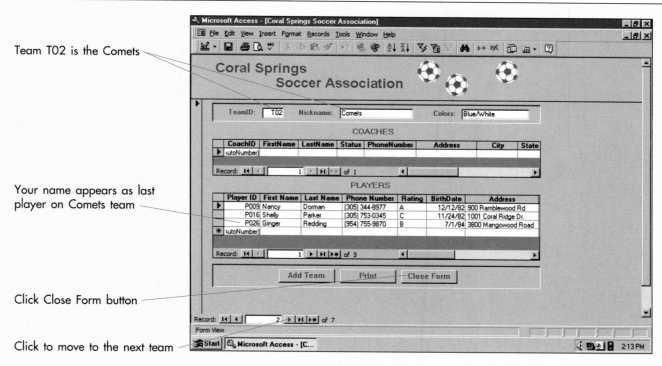

Team T02 is the Comets

Your name appears as last player on Comets team

Click Close Form button

Click to move to the next team

(d) View a Team Roster (step 4)

FIGURE 6.3   Hands-on Exercise 1 (continued)

STEP 5: Create the Main Menu Form

➤ Select (click) the **Template form,** but do *not* open the form. Pull down the **Edit menu** and click **Copy** (or click the **Copy button** on the Database toolbar). The form has been copied to the clipboard, although there is no visible indication that this has been accomplished.

➤ Pull down the **Edit menu** and click **Paste** (or click the **Paste button** on the Database toolbar). You will see the Paste As dialog box in Figure 6.3e.

➤ Type **Main Menu** as the name of the form. Press **enter** or click **OK.** The Database window should now contain the Main Menu form you just created.

USE A TEMPLATE

Avoid the routine and repetitive work of creating a new form by basing all forms for a given application on the same template. A template is a partially completed form that contains graphic elements and other formatting specifications. A template does not, however, have an underlying table or query. We suggest that you create a template for your application and store it within the database, then use that template whenever you need to create a new form. (All you do is copy the template.) It saves you time and trouble. It also promotes a consistent look that is critical to the application's overall success.

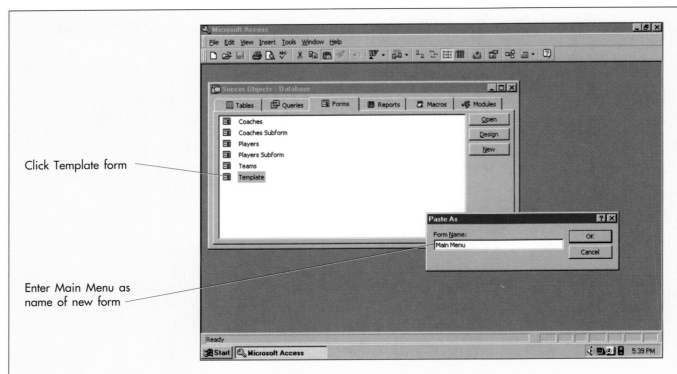

Click Template form

Enter Main Menu as
name of new form

(e) Copy the Template Form (step 5)

FIGURE 6.3   Hands-on Exercise 1 (continued)

STEP 6: Add the Player Command Button

➤ Click the newly created **Main Menu form.** Click the **Design button** to open the form in Design view, then maximize the window.

➤ Click the text box containing the label, **Enter menu name here,** then click and drag to select the text. Enter **Main Menu** to replace the selected text as shown in Figure 6.3f.

➤ Check that the Form Design, Formatting (Form/Report), and Toolbox toolbars are all visible. (See boxed tip to display a missing toolbar.)

➤ Click the **Command button tool.** (The mouse pointer changes to a tiny crosshair attached to a command button when you point anywhere in the form.)

➤ Click and drag in the form where you want the button to go, then release the mouse. This draws a button and simultaneously opens the Command Button Wizard as shown in Figure 6.3f. (The number on your button may be different from ours.)

• Click **Form Operations** in the Categories list box. Select **Open Form** from the list of actions. Click **Next.**

• Select **Players** from the list of available forms. Click **Next.**

• Click the option button to **Open the form and show all the records.** Click **Next.**

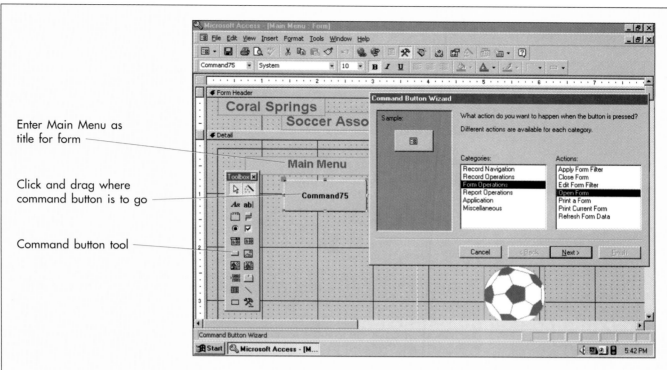

Enter Main Menu as title for form

Click and drag where command button is to go

Command button tool

(f) Add the Command Button (step 6)

FIGURE 6.3   Hands-on Exercise 1 (continued)

- Click the **Text option button,** then click and drag to select the default text (Open Form). Type **Players** in the text box next to the option button. Click **Next.**
- Enter **Players** (in place of the button number) as the name of the button, then click the **Finish Command button.**

➤ The completed command button should appear on your form. This button will open the Players form when clicked.

FIXED VERSUS FLOATING TOOLBARS

A toolbar can be docked (fixed) along the edge of a window, or it can be displayed as a floating toolbar within the window. To move a docked toolbar, drag the move handle in the toolbar background. To move a floating toolbar, drag its title bar. If a desired toolbar is not visible, point to any visible toolbar and click the right mouse button to display a shortcut menu from which you can display other toolbars.

STEP 7: Add the Remaining Command Buttons

➤ Add a command button to open the **Coaches form** following the procedure in the previous step. Click the **Command button tool,** click and drag in the form where you want the button to go, then release the mouse. Choose **Form Operations** in the Categories list box, select **Open Form,** and click **Next.**

➤ Choose **Coaches** from the list of available forms and click **Next.** Click the option button to **Open the form and show all the records.** Click **Next.**

➤ Click the **Text Option button,** enter **Coaches** in the text box, and click **Next.** Enter **Coaches** as the name of the button and click the **Finish Command button.**

➤ Add a **Teams button** in similar fashion.

➤ Add a fourth (and final) command button to close the Main Menu form. Choose **Form Operations,** then select **Close Form** as the action when the button is pressed.

➤ Enter **Exit** as the text to display on the button, and use **Exit** as the name of the button. Save the completed form.

THE FORMAT PAINTER

The Format Painter (common to all Office applications) copies the formatting of the selected object, such as a command button, to another object. Select (click) the object whose formatting you want to copy, then click or double click the Format Painter button. (Clicking the Format Painter will paint only one object. Double clicking will paint continuously until the feature is disabled by clicking the Format Painter button a second time.) Either way, the mouse pointer changes to a paintbrush to indicate that you can paint other objects with the current formatting. Just click the target object, which will assume the identical formatting characteristics as the original object.

STEP 8: Size and Align the Buttons

➤ Your form should contain four command buttons as shown in Figure 6.3g. Size one of the buttons to the height and width you want, then select all four command buttons by pressing and holding the **Shift key** as you click each button.

➤ Pull down the **Format menu.** Click **Size** to display the cascade menu shown in Figure 6.3g. Click **To Widest** to set a uniform width for the selected buttons.

➤ Pull down the **Format menu** a second time, click **Size** to display the cascade menu, and click **To Tallest** to set a uniform height for the selected buttons.

➤ Pull down the **Format menu** once again, click **Vertical Spacing,** then click **Make Equal.**

➤ Pull down the **Format menu** a final time, click **Align,** then click **Left** to complete the alignment.

➤ Click the **drop-down arrow** on the **Font/Fore Color button** on the Formatting toolbar to display the available colors, then click **Blue** to change the text color of all four buttons.

➤ If necessary, move the buttons so they are centered under the Main Menu title. Change the font on the buttons to Arial 12 pt. Make other changes in the formatting and/or spacing of the buttons as necessary.

➤ Save the form.

Form View button

Size one of the buttons to desired height and width

Press Shift key as you click each additional button to select multiple buttons

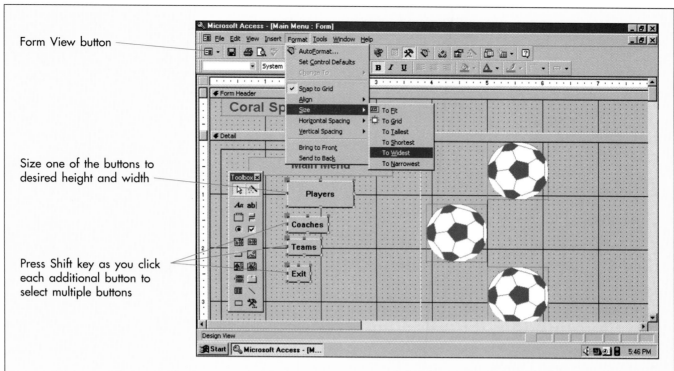

(g) Size and Align the Buttons (step 8)

FIGURE 6.3   Hands-on Exercise 1 (continued)

AVOID CLUTTER

Don't clutter a screen by displaying too much information or too many command buttons. (Seven or eight is the maximum that most people can handle comfortably.) Develop subservient (lower-level) menus if you find yourself with too many buttons on one screen. Don't crowd the command buttons. Make the buttons large enough (and of a uniform size) so that the text within a button is easy to read. Use sufficient blank space around the buttons so that they stand out from the rest of the screen.

STEP 9: Test the Menu

➤ Click the **Form View button** on the Form Design toolbar to switch to the Form view and view the completed menu in Figure 6.3h.

➤ Click the **Coaches Command button** to open this form. You should see a Coaches form similar to the Players and Teams forms.

➤ Click the **Add Coach Command button** at the bottom of the form. Click the text box to enter the coach's first name. (The CoachID is entered automatically as an AutoNumber field.)

➤ Enter data for your instructor as the coach. Click the appropriate **Option button** to make your instructor a **Head Coach.** Assign your instructor to the Comets (Team T02), which is the same team you joined in step 3.

➤ Click the **Close Form Command button** to complete data entry.

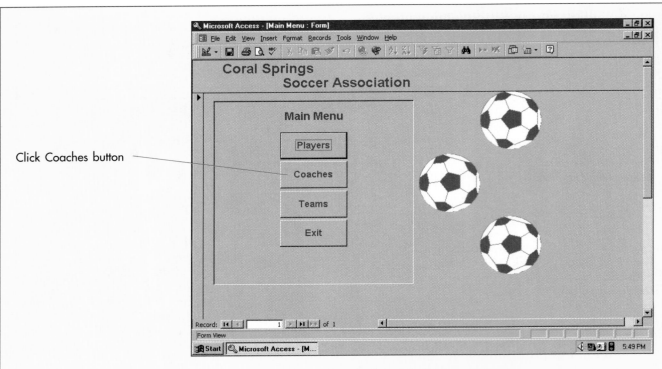

Click Coaches button

(h) The Completed Form (step 9)

FIGURE 6.3   Hands-on Exercise 1 (continued)

➤ Click the **Teams Command button** to open the Teams form, then click the ▶ (next record) or ◀ (previous record) button on the Teams status bar to move to Team T02 (the Comets). You should see your instructor as the head coach and yourself as a player.

➤ Pull down the **Edit menu,** click **Select Record** to select the record for your team, then click the **Print button** on the form to print the roster and prove to your instructor that you have completed the exercise. Click the **Close Form button** to close the Teams form and return to the Main Menu.

SUPPRESS THE RECORD SELECTOR AND NAVIGATION BUTTONS

The Main Menu form is not based on an underlying table and thus the record selector and navigation buttons have no meaning. Change to the Design view for the Main Menu, right click the Form selector box to the left of the ruler, then click the Properties command to display the Properties dialog box. Click the Record Selector text box and click No to disable the Record Selector. Click the Navigation Buttons Text box and click No to disable the buttons. Close the Properties dialog box. Return to the Form view to see the effect of these changes, which are subtle but worthwhile.

STEP 10: Exit Access

➤ Click the **Exit button** to close the Main Menu form. Click **Yes** if asked to save changes to the design of the Main Menu form.

➤ Exit Access if you do not want to continue with the next exercise at this time.

The exercise just completed created a user interface that enables a nontechnical user to maintain the tables in the Soccer application. It did not, however, automate the system completely in that the user still has to open the form containing the Main Menu to get started, and further, has to close the same form at the end of a session to exit Access. You can make the application even easier to use by including macros that perform these tasks automatically.

A *macro* automates a command sequence. Thus, instead of using the mouse or keyboard to execute a series of commands, you store the commands (actions) in a macro and execute the macro. You can create a macro to open a table, query, form, or report. You can create a macro to display an informational message, then beep to call attention to that message. You can create a macro to move or size a window, or to minimize, maximize, or restore a window. In short, you can create a macro to execute any command in any Access menu and thus make an application easy to use.

The Macro Window

A macro is created in the *Macro window* as shown in Figure 6.4. The Macro window has two sections. You enter the *actions* (commands) that make up the macro and any optional comments in the upper section. You supply the additional information (*arguments*) for those actions in the lower section.

The macro in Figure 6.4 consists of a single action (MsgBox), which has four arguments (Message, Beep, Type, and Title). The *MsgBox action* displays a dialog box with the message you define. It's an ideal way to display an informational message to a user and is illustrated later in the chapter. The help area at the bottom right of the Macro window displays help information; the specific help information depends on where you are in the Macro window.

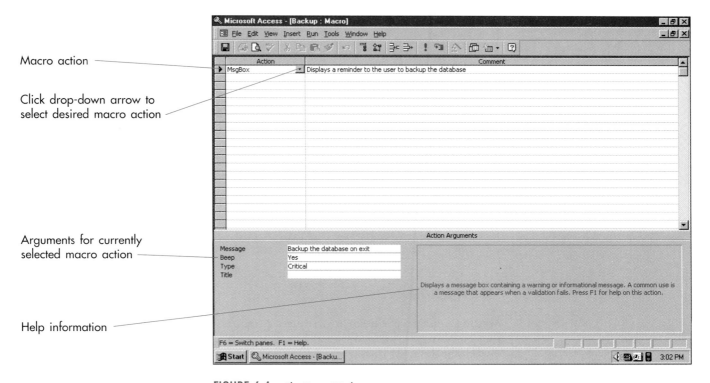

FIGURE 6.4 The Macro Window

A macro is created from the Database window by selecting the Macros tab and clicking the New button. It is stored as an object in the database in the same fashion as a form or report. Actions are added to a macro by choosing the action from a drop-down list or by typing the name of the action. The arguments for an action are entered in similar fashion; that is, by choosing from a drop-down list (when available) or by typing the argument directly. After a macro has been saved, it can be run from the Macro window or the Database window or it can be assigned to run as a response to an event (e.g., clicking a command button) in a form or report.

The *macro toolbar* is displayed at the top of the Macro window and contains buttons that help create and test a macro. Many of the buttons (e.g., the Database Window, Save, and Office Assistant buttons) are common to other toolbars you have used in conjunction with other objects. Other buttons are specific to the Macro window and are referenced in the hands-on exercises as necessary. As with other toolbars, you can point to a button to display its ScreenTip and determine its purpose.

ACCESS MACROS ARE DIFFERENT

Access lacks the macro recorder that is common to Word and Excel. This means that you have to explicitly enter the actions in the Macro window rather than have the recorder do it for you. Nevertheless, you can still create an Access macro to do virtually anything you would do via the keyboard or mouse.

The AutoExec Macro

After a macro is created, it is saved so that it can be run (executed) at a later time. A macro name can contain up to 64 characters (letters and numbers) and may include spaces. The name of the macro appears in the title bar of the Macro window (e.g., Backup in Figure 6.4). You can use any name at all for a macro, as long as you adhere to these simple rules.

One macro name, however, *AutoExec,* is reserved, and this macro has a unique function. The *AutoExec macro* (if it exists) is executed automatically whenever the database in which it is stored is opened. In other words, whenever you open a database, Access looks to see if the database contains an AutoExec macro, and if so, Access runs the macro for you.

The AutoExec macro is essential to automating a system for the end-user. It typically contains an OpenForm action to load the form containing the main (start-up) menu. The AutoExec macro may also perform other housekeeping chores to get the database ready to use, such as maximizing the current window.

Every database can have its own AutoExec macro, but there is no requirement for the AutoExec macro to be present. We recommend, however, that you include an AutoExec macro in every application to help the user get started quickly.

Debugging

Writing a macro is similar to writing a program in that mistakes are virtually certain to be made, and you need a way to correct those mistakes. Should Access encounter an error during the execution of a macro, it displays as much information as it can to help you determine the reason for the error—to assist you in *debugging* your program.

Figure 6.5a contains an erroneous version of the AutoExec macro that will be developed in the exercise that follows shortly. The macro contains two actions, Maximize and OpenForm. The Maximize action maximizes the Database window and affects all subsequent screens that will be displayed in the application. The OpenForm macro opens the form containing the menu developed in the previous exercise. The name of the form is deliberately misspelled to produce the error in Figure 6.5b.

When the AutoExec macro is executed, Access attempts to open the Main Menus form but is unable to do so. It displays the informational message in Figure 6.5b, followed by the Action Failed dialog box in Figure 6.5c. The latter is displayed whenever a macro is unable to execute successfully. Your only course of action is to click the Halt Command button, then attempt to correct the error using the displayed information.

Two macro actions are included

Name of form to be opened is misspelled

Arguments for currently selected macro action (OpenForm)

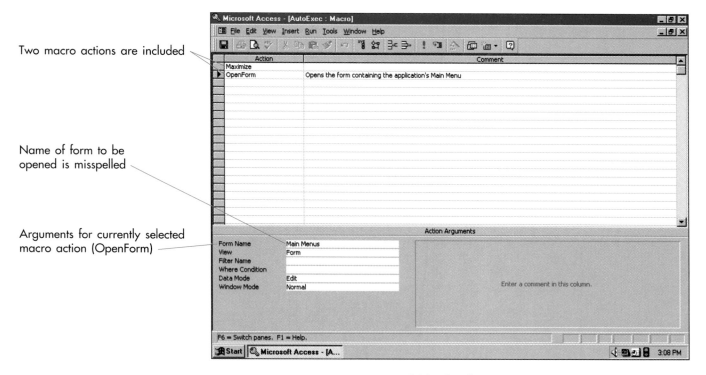

(a) AutoExec Macro

(b) Informational Message

FIGURE 6.5   Debugging

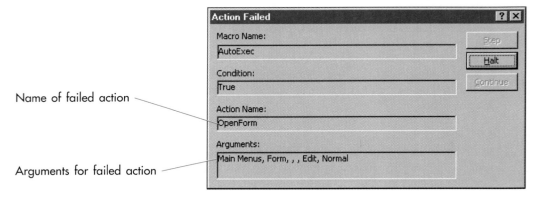

Name of failed action

Arguments for failed action

(c) Action Failed Dialog Box

FIGURE 6.5   Debugging (continued)

The Action Failed dialog box indicates the name of the failed macro (AutoExec). The Action Name indicates the failed action (OpenForm) within the macro, and the Arguments box shows the corresponding values. In this example the error is easy to find. The name of the form should have been Main Menu rather than Main Menus.

THE FIRST BUG

A bug is a mistake in a computer program; hence debugging refers to the process of correcting program errors. According to legend, the first bug was an unlucky moth crushed to death on one of the relays of the electro-mechanical Mark II computer, bringing the machine's operation to a halt. The cause of the failure was discovered by Grace Hopper, who promptly taped the moth to her logbook, noting, *"First actual case of bug being found."*

HANDS-ON EXERCISE 2

Introduction to Macros

Objective: To create an AutoExec macro to open a form automatically; to create a Close Database macro to close the database and exit from the system. To use the On Click property to change the action associated with a command button. Use Figure 6.6 as a guide in the exercise.

STEP 1: Create the AutoExec Macro

➤ Start Access. Open the **Soccer Objects database** from the previous exercise.

➤ Click the **Macros tab** in the Database window (there are currently no macros in the database). Click the **New button** to create a new macro. If necessary, click the **Maximize button** so that the Macro window takes the entire screen as in Figure 6.6a.

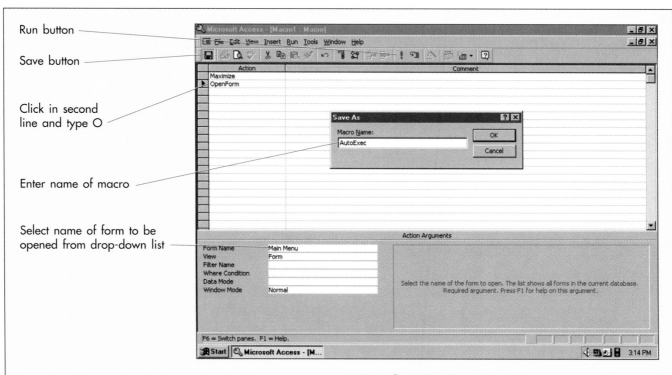

Run button

Save button

Click in second
line and type O

Enter name of macro

Select name of form to be
opened from drop-down list

(a) Create the AutoExec Macro (step 1)

FIGURE 6.6   Hands-on Exercise 2

➤ Click the **drop-down arrow** to display the available macro actions. Scroll through the list until you can select **Maximize.**

➤ Click the **Action box** on the second line. Type the letter **O,** and the Open-Form action appears automatically. Press **enter** to accept this action, then click the text box for the **Form Name** argument in the lower section of the Macro window.

➤ Click the **drop-down arrow** to display the list of existing forms and select **Main Menu** (the form you created in the previous exercise).

➤ Click the **Save button** to display the Save As dialog box in Figure 6.6a. Type **AutoExec** as the macro name and click **OK.**

➤ Click the **Run button** to run the macro, which displays the Main Menu from the previous exercise. (The window is maximized on the screen.) Click the **Exit button** on the Main Menu to close the menu and return to the macro.

➤ Pull down the **File menu.** Click **Close** to close the AutoExec macro.

TYPE ONLY THE FIRST LETTER(S)

Click the Action box, then type the first letter of a macro action to move immediately to the first macro action beginning with that letter. Type an M, for example, and Access automatically enters the Maximize action. If necessary, type the second letter of the desired action; for example, type the letter I (after typing an M), and Access selects the Minimize action, which begins with the letters M and I.

STEP 2: The MsgBox Action

➤ You should be back in the Database window, which should display the name of the AutoExec macro. Click the **New button** to create a second macro, which automatically positions you at the first action.

➤ Type **MS** (the first two letters in the MsgBox action), then press **enter** to accept this action.

➤ Click the text box for the **Type** argument in the lower section of the Macro window. Click the **drop-down arrow** to display the list of message types. Select **Critical.**

➤ Click the text box for the **Message** argument. Press **Shift+F2** to display the zoom box so that you can see the contents of your entire message, then enter the message in Figure 6.6b. Click **OK.**

Run button

Click and type MS

Zoom box

Click and enter
message to be displayed

Click and press Shift+F2
to display zoom box

Click and select Critical
from drop-down list

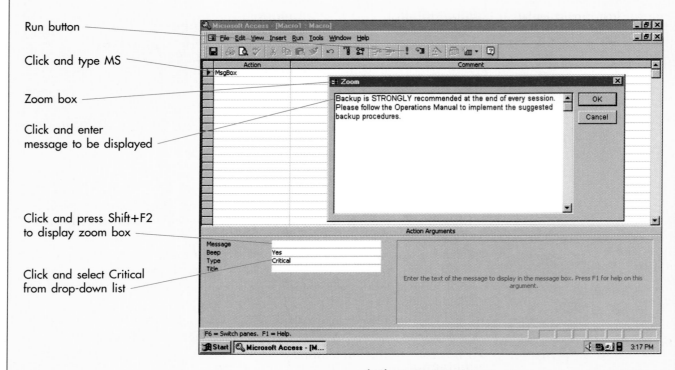

(b) The MsgBox Action (step 2)

FIGURE 6.6   Hands-on Exercise 2 (continued)

BACK UP YOUR DATABASE

It's not a question of if it will happen, but when. Hard disks die, files are lost, and viruses infect a system. Take our word for it, there are few things more unpleasant than searching for a file that isn't there or discovering that the file you do retrieve is missing most of its data. Adequate backup is the only insurance you can obtain against data loss. Backing up a system is easy, but you must remember to do it, and you must do it faithfully, without fail.

➤ Click the **Run button** to test the macro. You will see a message indicating that you have to save the macro. Click **Yes** to save the macro, type **Close Database** as the name of the macro, and click **OK.**

➤ You will see a dialog box containing the text of the message you just created. Click **OK** after you have read the message so that you can continue working on the macro.

STEP 3: Complete the Close Database Macro

➤ Click the **Action box** on the second line. Type **Cl** (the first two letters in *Close*) and press **enter.**

➤ Click the text box for the **Object Type** argument. Click the **drop-down arrow.** Choose **Form** as the Object type. Click the **Object Name** argument, click the **drop-down arrow,** and choose **Main Menu** as the Object (form) name.

➤ Click the **comment line** for this action. Type **Close the Main Menu form** as shown in Figure 6.6c.

➤ Click the **Action box** on the third line. Type **Cl** (the first two letters in *Close*) and press **enter.**

➤ This time no arguments are necessary. The Close command will affect the current window (i.e., the Database window), which closes the database.

➤ Click the **comments line** for this macro action and enter the comment shown in the figure.

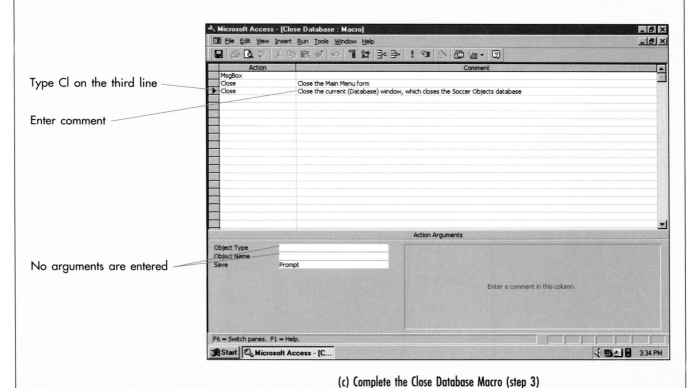

Type Cl on the third line

Enter comment

No arguments are entered

(c) Complete the Close Database Macro (step 3)

FIGURE 6.6   Hands-on Exercise 2 (continued)

➤ Pull down the **File menu** and click **Close** to close the macro. Click **Yes** when prompted whether to save the changes to the Close Database macro.

➤ If necessary, press the **F11 key** to switch to the Database window. You should see the names of both macros (AutoExec and Close Database).

THE F6 KEY

Press the F6 key to move back and forth between the top and bottom halves of the Macro window. You can also use the F6 key to move between the top and bottom portions of the Table and Query windows when they are open in Design view.

STEP 4: The On Click Property

➤ Click the **Forms tab,** select the **Main Menu form,** then click the **Design button** to open the form in Design view. If necessary, maximize the window.

➤ Point to the **Exit command button** (that was created in the first exercise) and click the **right mouse button** to display a shortcut menu. Click **Properties** to display the Properties dialog box in Figure 6.6d. Click the **Event tab.**

➤ Click the **On Click box,** which is currently set to [Event Procedure]. This was set automatically when you used the Command Button Wizard to create the button in step 7 of the previous exercise.

Form View button

Click in box, then click drop-down arrow to display macro names

Point to Exit button, click right mouse button to display shortcut menu

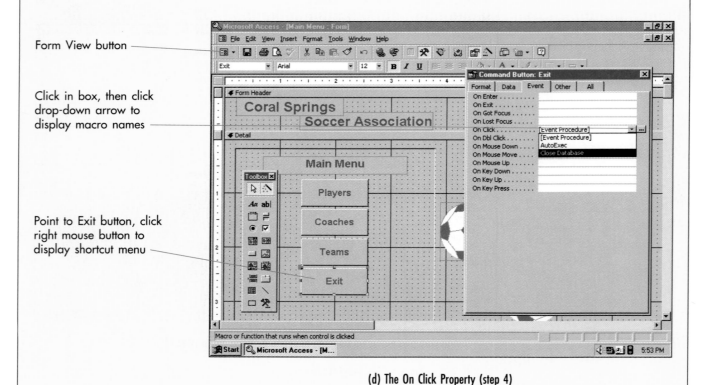

(d) The On Click Property (step 4)

FIGURE 6.6   Hands-on Exercise 2 (continued)

➤ Click the **drop-down arrow** to display the existing macros. Click **Close Data-base** (the macro you just created). Close the Properties dialog box.

➤ Save the form. Click the **Form View button** to switch to Form view so that you can test the macros you just created.

CREATE A HELP BUTTON

One of the nicest features you can provide your users is a means of obtaining technical support either by telephone or via e-mail. Use the MsgBox action to create a simple macro that displays your phone number and e-mail address, then assign that macro to a Help button on your Main Menu. See practice exercise 1 at the end of the chapter.

STEP 5: Test the AutoExec and Close Database Macros

➤ You should see the Main Menu form displayed in Figure 6.6e. Click the **Exit Command button,** which executes the Close Database macro you assigned to the button.

• You should see the informational message shown in the figure. (The message is displayed by the MsgBox action in the Close Database macro.)

• Click **OK** to accept the message. The Close Database macro then closes the database.

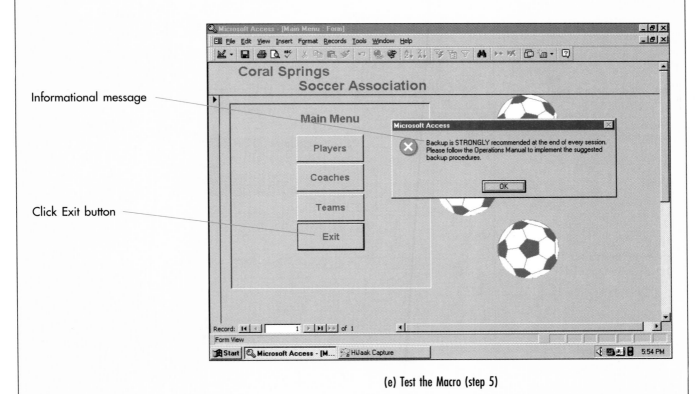

(e) Test the Macro (step 5)

FIGURE 6.6   Hands-on Exercise 2 (continued)

STEP 6: Reopen the Database

➤ Pull down the **File menu,** then click **Soccer Objects** from the list of recently opened databases. The AutoExec macro executes automatically, maximizes the current window, and displays the Main Menu.

➤ Pull down the **File menu** and click **Close** to close the form and continue working on this database. (You cannot click the Exit command button as that would close the database.) You should be back in the Database window.

STEP 7: Create the Add Player Macro

➤ Click the **Forms tab** in the Database window. Double click the **Players form** to open this form.

➤ Click the **Add Player button** on the Players form and note that in order to add a player, you must first click the First Name text box. We will correct this by creating an Add Player macro that will automatically move to the First Name text box. Click the **Close Form button** to exit the Players form.

➤ Click the **Macros tab** in the Database window. Click **New** to create a new macro, then create the Add Player macro as shown in Figure 6.6f:

• Use the **F6 key** to switch between the top and bottom halves of the Macro window.

• The first action, **Go To Record,** has three arguments we must enter: Object Type, Object Name, and Record. Click in the Object Type box, click the drop-down arrow, and select **Form.** Click in the Object Name box, click the drop-down arrow, and select **Players.** Click in the Record box, click the drop-down arrow, and select **New.** The macro action and corresponding arguments are equivalent to moving to the end of the Player table in order to add a new record.

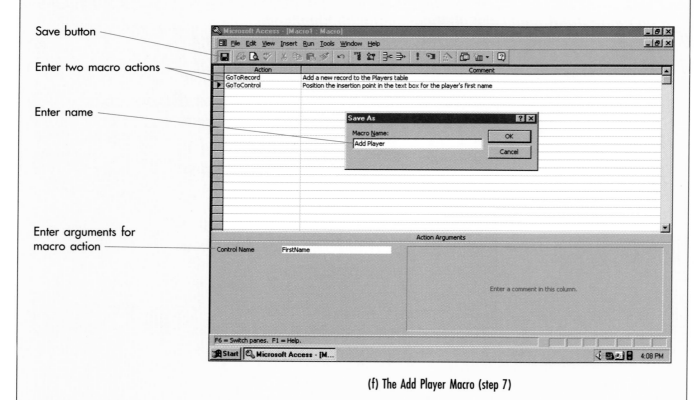

(f) The Add Player Macro (step 7)

FIGURE 6.6   Hands-on Exercise 2 (continued)

- The **GoToControl** action has a single argument, which is the name of the control on the Players form. Type **FirstName** (there is no space in the control name).
- Add the comments as shown.

➤ Save the macro as **Add Player.** Do *not* attempt to run the macro at this time.

➤ Pull down the **File menu** and click **Close** to exit the macro and return to the Database window.

THE DISPLAY WHEN PROPERTY

The Add, Print, and Close Form Command buttons appear on the various forms (Team, Player, or Coach) when the forms are displayed on the screen, but not when the forms are printed. This was accomplished by setting the Display When property of the individual command buttons when the forms were created. Open a form in Design view, point to an existing command button, then click the right mouse button to display a shortcut menu. Click on the line for the Display When property and set the property accordingly.

STEP 8: The On Click Property

➤ Click the **Forms tab** in the Database window and select the **Players form.** Click the **Design button** to open the form in Design view as shown in Figure 6.6g.

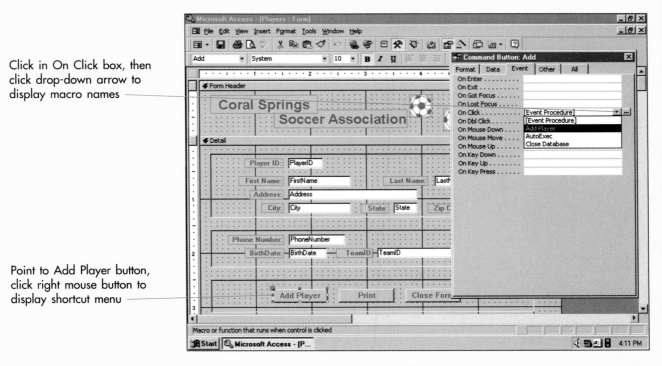

Click in On Click box, then click drop-down arrow to display macro names

Point to Add Player button, click right mouse button to display shortcut menu

(g) The On Click Property (step 8)

FIGURE 6.6   Hands-on Exercise 2 (continued)

➤ Point to the **Add Player command button,** then click the **right mouse button** to display a shortcut menu. Click **Properties** to display the Properties dialog box.

➤ Click the **Event tab.** You will see the On Click property, which is currently set to [Event Procedure]. Click the **On Click property box,** then click the **drop-down arrow** to display the existing macros.

➤ Click **Add Player** (the macro you just created). Close the Properties dialog box.

➤ Click the **Form View button** to switch to Form view and test the Add Player macro.

  • Click the **Add Player command button.** You are automatically positioned in the First Name box (because of the Add Player macro) and can start typing immediately.

  • Enter data for a friend of yours. Assign your friend to the **Comets** (your team).

➤ Click the **Close Form command button** when you have completed the record. Click **Yes** if prompted to save the changes to the Players form.

THE CONTROLTIP TEXT PROPERTY

Point to any button on any Office toolbar and you see a ScreenTip that describes the purpose of that button. Access enables you to create your own ScreenTips through the ControlTip Text property. Open a form in Design view, right click the control for which you want to create a tip, then click the Properties command to open the Properties dialog box. Click the Other (or All) tab, click the ControlTip text box to enter the desired text, then close the dialog box. Change to Form view and point to the control. You will see the ToolTip you just created.

STEP 9: Close the Database

➤ You can close the database in one of two ways:

  • You should be back in the Database window. Pull down the **File menu** and click **Close** to close the Soccer Objects database, *or*

  • Click the **Forms tab,** double click the **Main Menu form** to open this form, click the **Exit button** on the form, then click **OK** in response to the message reminding you to back up the system.

➤ Pull down the **File menu.** Click **Exit** if you do not want to continue with the next exercise at this time.

THE PLAYER DRAFT

The implementation of a player draft is essential to the Soccer Association. Players sign up for the coming season at registration, after which the coaches meet to select players for their teams. All players are rated as to ability, and the CSSA strives to maintain a competitive balance between teams.

The coaches take turns selecting players from the pool of unassigned players as displayed in the form shown in Figure 6.7. The form is based on a query that identifies the players who have not yet been drafted. To aid in the selection process, the unassigned players are listed by ability and alphabetically within ability. Note, too, the use of a ***combo box*** to simplify data entry in conjunction with the team assignment. The user is able to click the drop-down arrow to display a list of team nicknames (or enter the nickname directly) rather than having to remember the associated team number.

In addition to displaying the list of unassigned players, the form in Figure 6.7 also contains three command buttons that are used during the player draft. The Find Player button moves directly to a specific player, and enables a coach to see whether a specific player has been assigned to a team, and if so, to which team. The Update List button refreshes the underlying query on which the list of unassigned players is based. It is used periodically during the draft as players are assigned to teams, to remove those players from the list of unassigned players. The End Draft button closes the form and returns to the Main Menu.

Unassigned players are listed by ability and alphabetically within ability

Drop-down list box simplifies data entry

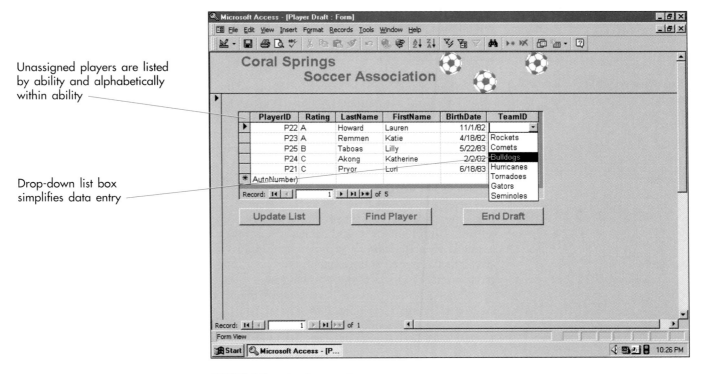

FIGURE 6.7   The Player Draft

SIMPLIFY DATA ENTRY

A drop-down list box simplifies data entry as it lets you select a value from a list, such as a team nickname, rather than having to remember the corresponding team number. A combo box combines the properties of a text box and a list box; that is, you can enter a new value directly in the box, or you can click the drop-down arrow to display a list of values from which to choose.

The Find Unmatched Query Wizard

Think, for a moment, how Access is able to display the list of unassigned players. You need to remember the one-to-many relationship between teams and players (one team has many players, but a player has only one team). Remember, too, that this relationship is implemented through the common TeamID field, which appears in both tables. The TeamID is the primary key in the Teams table and it is a foreign key in the Players table. A player is assigned to a team by entering the team number into the TeamID field in the Players table. Conversely, any player without a value in his or her TeamID field is an unassigned player.

To display a list of unassigned players, you need to create a query, based on the Players table, which selects records without an entry for TeamID. This can be done by creating the query explicitly (and specifying the Null criterion for TeamID) or more easily through the Find Unmatched Query Wizard, which creates the query for you. The Wizard asks the questions in Figure 6.8, then generates the query.

The *Find Unmatched Query Wizard* identifies the records in one table (e.g., the Players table) that do not have matching records in another table (e.g., the Teams table). The wizard begins by asking for the table that contains the unmatched records (Figure 6.8a) and for the related table (Figure 6.8b). It identifies the join field (TeamID in Figure 6.8c), then gives you the opportunity to select the fields you want to see in the query results (Figure 6.8d). The Wizard even suggests a name for the query (Players Without Matching Teams in Figure 6.8e), then displays the dynaset in Figure 6.8f.

The Find Unmatched Query Wizard has multiple applications within the CSSA database. It can identify players without teams (as in Figure 6.8), or conversely, teams without players. It can also identify coaches who have not been assigned to a team, and, conversely, teams without coaches.

Macro Groups

Implementation of the player draft requires three macros, one for each command button. Although you could create a separate macro for each button, it is convenient to create a *macro group* that contains the individual macros. The macro group has a name, as does each macro in the group. Only the name of the macro group appears in the Database window.

Figure 6.9 displays a Player Draft macro group containing three individual macros (Update List, Find Player, and End Draft), which run independently of one another. The name of each macro appears in the Macro Name column (which is displayed by clicking the Macro Names button on the Macro toolbar). The actions and comments for each macro are shown in the corresponding columns to the right of the macro name.

The advantage of storing related macros in a macro group, as opposed to storing them individually, is purely organizational. Large systems often contain many macros, which can overwhelm the developer as he or she tries to locate a specific macro. Storing related macros in macro groups limits the entries in the Database window, since only the (name of the) macro group is displayed. Thus, the Database window would contain a single entry (Player Draft, which is the name of the macro group), as opposed to three individual entries (Update List, Find Player, and End Draft, which correspond to the macros in the group).

Access must still be able to identify the individual macros so that each macro can be executed at the appropriate time. If, for example, a macro is to be executed when the user clicks a command button, the *On Click property* of that command button must specify both the individual macro and the macro group to which it belongs. The two names are separated by a period—for example, Player Draft.Update List—to indicate the Update List macro in the Player Draft group.

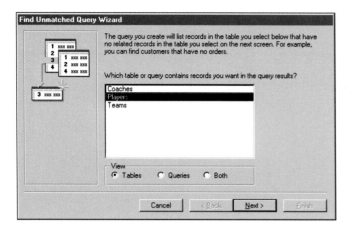

(a) Table Containing the Unmatched Records

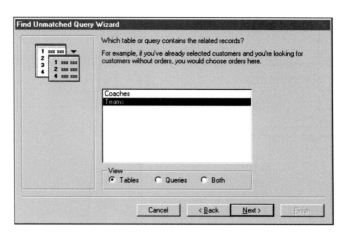

(b) The Related Table

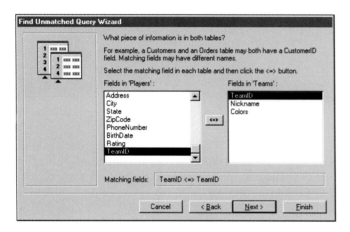

(c) Join Field

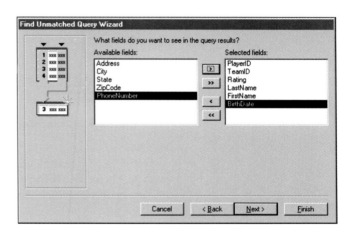

(d) Fields for Dynaset

(e) Suggested Name

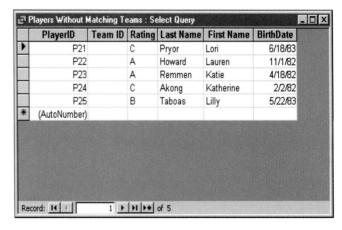

(f) Dynaset

FIGURE 6.8   The Find Unmatched Query Wizard

Macro Name column

Three macros are contained
in the macro group

Macro Names button

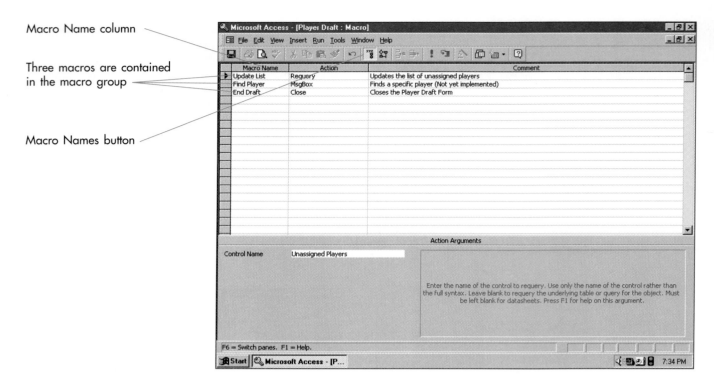

FIGURE 6.9 Macro Groups

As indicated, each macro in Figure 6.9 is assigned to a command button in the Player Draft form of Figure 6.7. The macros are created in the following hands-on exercise, which implements the player draft.

THE MACRO TOOLBAR

The Macro Name and Conditions buttons on the Macro toolbar toggle the corresponding columns on and off. Click either button to display (hide) the indicated column. See practice exercise 3 at the end of the chapter for additional information on the Conditions column.

HANDS-ON EXERCISE 3

The Player Draft

Objective: To create a macro group containing three macros to implement a player draft. Use Figure 6.10 as a guide in the exercise.

STEP 1: The Unmatched Query Wizard

➤ Start Access and open the **Soccer Objects database.** Pull down the **File menu** and click **Close** (or click the **Close button**) to close the Main Menu form but leave the database open. (You *cannot* click the Exit command button as that would close the database.)

➤ Click the **Queries tab** in the Database window. Click **New,** select the **Find Unmatched Query Wizard,** then click **OK** to start the Wizard:

- Select **Players** as the table whose records you want to see in the query results. Click **Next.**
- Select **Teams** as the table that contains the related records. Click **Next.**
- **TeamID** is automatically selected as the matching field. Click **Next.**
- Select the following fields from the Available Fields list: **PlayerID, Rating, LastName, FirstName, BirthDate,** and **TeamID.** Click **Next.**
- **Players Without Matching Teams** is entered as the name of the query. Check that the option button to **View the results** is selected, then click **Finish** to exit the Wizard and see the results of the query.

➤ You should see a dynaset containing five players (Pryor, Howard, Remmen, Akong, and Taboas) as shown in Figure 6.10a. The TeamID field for each of these players is blank, indicating these players are not on a team.

Click to switch to
Design view

TeamID field is blank

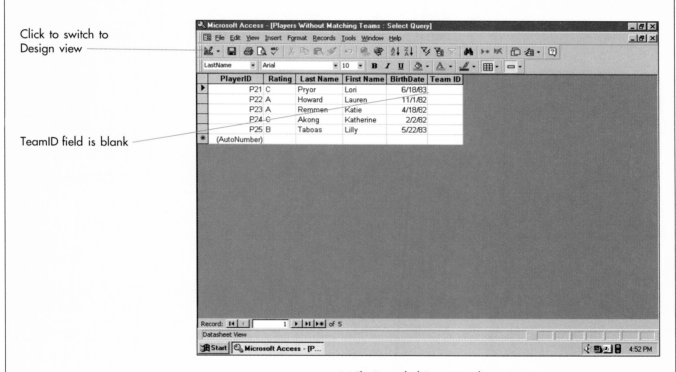

(a) The Unmatched Query Wizard (step 1)

FIGURE 6.10   Hands-on Exercise 3

THE MOST RECENTLY OPENED FILE LIST

An easy way to open a recently used database is to select it from the Microsoft Access dialog box that appears when Access is first started. Check to see if your database appears on the list of the most recently opened databases, and if so, simply double click the database to open it.

STEP 2: Modify the Unmatched Query

➤ Change to Design view to see the underlying query as displayed in Figure 6.10b.

➤ Click and drag the line separating the upper and lower portions of the window. If necessary, click and drag the field lists to match the figure.

➤ Click in the **Sort row** for **Rating,** then click **Ascending** from the drop-down list. Click in the **Sort row** for **LastName,** then click **Ascending** from the drop-down list.

➤ Click the **Run button** to view the revised query, which lists players according to their player rating and alphabetically within rating.

➤ Close the query. Click **Yes** if asked whether to save the changes to the Players Without Matching Teams query.

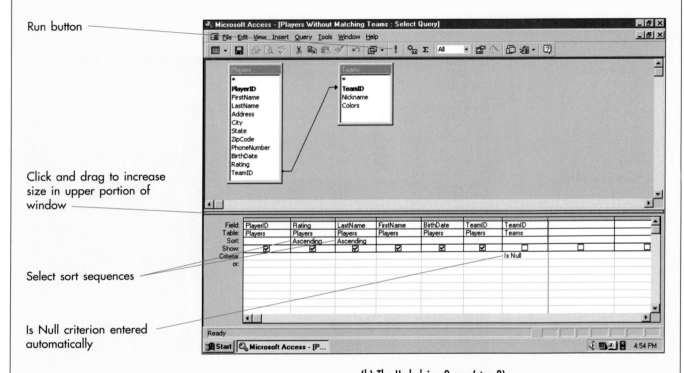

(b) The Underlying Query (step 2)

FIGURE 6.10   Hands-on Exercise 3 (continued)

THE IS NULL CRITERION

The Is Null criterion selects those records that do not have a value in the designated field. It is the essence of the Unmatched Query Wizard, which uses the criterion to identify the records in one table that do not have a matching record in another table. The NOT operator can be combined with the Is Null criterion to produce the opposite effect; that is, the criterion Is Not Null will select records with any type of entry (including spaces) in the specified field.

STEP 3: Create the Unmatched Players Form

➤ Click the **Forms tab** in the Database window, click **New** to display the New Form dialog box, and select **AutoForm:Datasheet.**

➤ Click the **drop-down arrow** to choose a table or query. Select the **Players Without Matching Teams** (the query created in step 2). Click **OK.**

➤ Wait a few seconds as Access creates a form that lists the players who are not currently assigned to a team. The form is displayed in the Datasheet view and resembles the dynaset shown earlier.

➤ Maximize the form if necessary, then change to the Design view as shown in Figure 6.10c. Select the **TeamID control** in the Detail section, then press the **Del key** to delete the TeamID (which will be replaced with a combo box).

➤ Click the **Combo Box tool** on the Toolbox toolbar. Click and drag in the form where you want the combo box to go. Release the mouse. You will see the first step in the Combo Box Wizard:

  • Check the **Option button** that indicates you want the combo box to **look up values in a table or query.** Click **Next.**

  • Choose the **Teams table** in the next screen. Click **Next.**

  • Select the **TeamID** and **Nickname** from the Available Fields list box for inclusion in the combo box columns list. Click **Next.**

  • Adjust the column widths if necessary. Be sure the box to **Hide the key column** is checked. Click **Next.**

  • Click the **Option button** to store the value in the field. Click the **drop-down arrow** to display the fields in the query and select the **TeamID field.** Click **Next.**

  • Enter **TeamID** as the label for the combo box. Click **Finish.**

➤ Click (select) the label next to the control you just created. Press the **Del key** to delete the label.

➤ Point to the combo box, click the **right mouse button** to display a shortcut menu, and click **Properties.** Change the name of the control to **TeamID.** Close the Properties box.

➤ Click the **Save button** to display the Save As dialog box in Figure 6.10c. (Players Without Matching Teams is already entered as the default name.)

➤ Click **OK** to save the form, then close the form.

LIST BOXES VERSUS COMBO BOXES

The choice between a list box and a combo box depends on how you want the control to appear in the form. The advantage of a list box is that it is always visible, and further, that the user is restricted to selecting a value from the list. The advantage of a combo box is that it takes less space because its values are not displayed until you open it. A combo box also enables you to control whether the user can select just the values in the list or whether additional values are permitted. (The Limit to List property is set to Yes and No, respectively.) And finally, a combo box permits you to enter the first few characters in a value to move directly to that value. A list box, however, accepts only the first letter.

Save button

Click and drag where
you want combo box
control to go

Combo Box tool

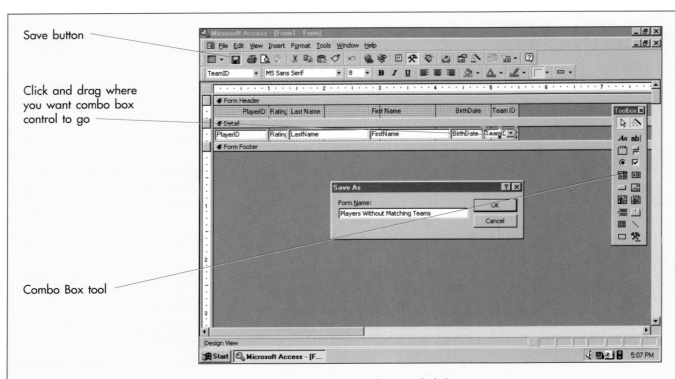

(c) Create the Unmatched Players Form (step 3)

FIGURE 6.10   Hands-on Exercise 3 (continued)

STEP 4: Create the Player Draft Macro Group

➤ Click the **Macros tab** in the Database window. Click **New** to create a new macro, and if necessary, click the **Maximize button** to maximize the Macro window.

➤ If you do not see the Macro Names column, pull down the **View menu** and click **Macro Names** to display the column. (Alternatively, you can click the **Macro Names button** on the Macro toolbar.)

➤ Enter the macro names, actions, and comments as shown in Figure 6.10d. Supply the arguments for each action as indicated below:

• The Requery action (in the Update List macro) has a single argument in which you specify the control name (the name of the query). Type **Players Without Matching Teams,** which is the query you created earlier in step 1.

• The Find Player macro will be implemented as an assignment (see practice exercise 4), but in the interim, it will display a message and contain only the MsgBox action. Enter **Not Yet Implemented** as the text of the message. Select **Information** as the type of message.

• The arguments for the End Draft macro are visible in Figure 6.10d. The Player Draft form will be created in the next step. Thus, you need to enter the form name explicitly since it will not appear in the drop-down list.

➤ Save the Macro group as **Player Draft** as shown in Figure 6.10d. Close the Macro window.

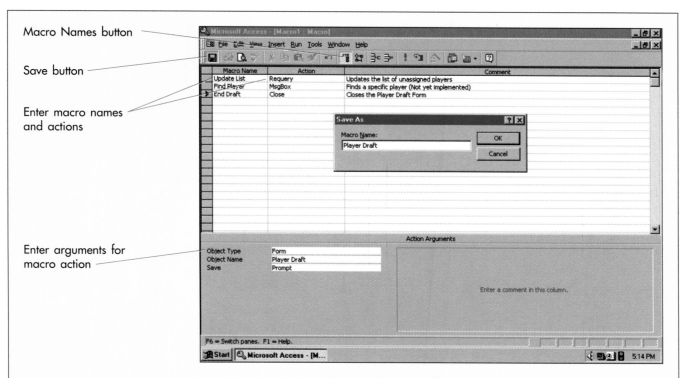

Macro Names button

Save button

Enter macro names
and actions

Enter arguments for
macro action

(d) Create the Player Draft Macro Group (step 4)

FIGURE 6.10   Hands-on Exercise 3 (continued)

REQUERY COMMAND NOT AVAILABLE

Most macros are designed to run at specified times and will fail if tested in isolation. The macros in the Player Draft group, for example, are designed to run only when the Player Draft form is open. Do not be concerned, therefore, if you attempt to test the macros at this time and the Action Failed dialog box appears. The macros will work correctly at the end of the exercise, when the entire player draft is in place. See problem 2 at the end of the chapter.

STEP 5: Create the Player Draft Form

➤ Click the **Forms tab** in the Database window. Select the **Template form,** click the **Copy button** to copy the form to the clipboard, then click the **Paste button** to complete the copy operation. Type **Player Draft** as the name of the copied form. Click **OK.**

➤ Open the **Player Draft form** in Design view. Delete the label and the rectangle from the Details section. Size the soccer balls, then move them to the Form Header section as shown in Figure 6.10e.

➤ Click the **Restore button,** then move and size the windows as shown in Figure 6.10e.

➤ Click the **Database window.** Click and drag the **Players Without Matching Teams form** onto the Player Draft form as shown in Figure 6.10e. Maximize the window.

Form View button

Resize soccer balls and move to Form Header section

Click and drag Players Without Matching Teams form to Player Draft form

Sizing handles

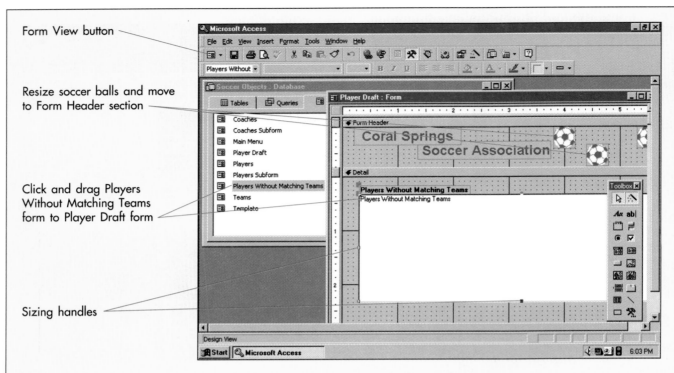

(e) Create the Player Draft Form (step 5)

FIGURE 6.10   Hands-on Exercise 3 (continued)

➤ Click and drag the **sizing handles** in the Players Without Matching Team form so that its size approximates the form in Figure 6.10e.

➤ Click the **Form View button** to view your progress. You should see the Datasheet view of the subform, which displays the players who have not yet been assigned to a team.

➤ Click the **Form Design button** to continue working on the form. If necessary, click off the subform control, then double click the subform control to open the subform in Design view. Switch to the Datasheet view to change the width of the columns within the form.

➤ Continue to switch back and forth between the Form view and the Design view until you are satisfied with the appearance of the subform. Close the form. Click **Yes** when asked whether to save the changes.

➤ Select (click) the **label** of the subform (Players Without Matching Teams), then press the **Del key** to delete the label. Be sure you delete the label and not the subform. (Click the **Undo button** if you make a mistake.) Save the form.

MODIFYING A SUBFORM

To modify the subform, click outside the subform to deselect it, then double click the subform to open it. Once the subform is open, you can change to the Design, Datasheet, or Form view by clicking the drop-down arrow on the Form View button on the Form Design toolbar.

STEP 6: Create the Command Buttons

➤ Click and drag the **Command Button tool** to create a command button, as shown in Figure 6.10f.

➤ Click **Miscellaneous** in the Categories list box. Select **Run Macro** from the list of actions. Click the **Next Command button.**

➤ Select **Player Draft.Update List** from the list of existing macros. Click the **Next Command button.**

➤ Click the **Text Option button.** Click and drag to select the default text (Run Macro), then type **Update List** as the text to display on the button. Click the **Next Command button.**

➤ Enter **Update List** (in place of the button number) and click the **Finish Command button.**

➤ Repeat these steps to create the additional command buttons shown in Figure 6.10f. Assign the Find Player and End Draft macros from the Player Draft group to the additional command buttons.

➤ Size, align, space, and color the command buttons as in the previous exercise. Save the completed form.

➤ Close the form.

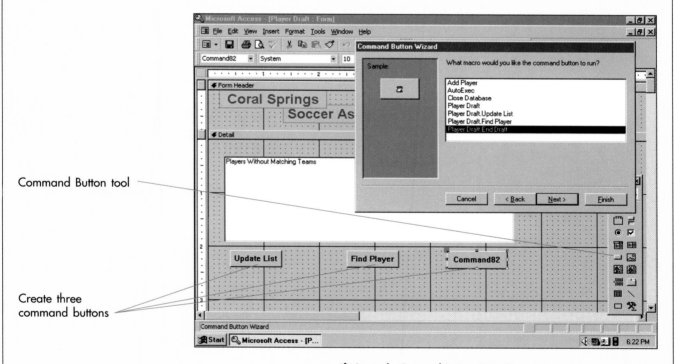

Command Button tool

Create three command buttons

(f) Create the Command Buttons (step 6)

FIGURE 6.10   Hands-on Exercise 3 (continued)

UNIFORM COMMAND BUTTONS

Press and hold the Shift key to select multiple command buttons so that they can be formatted, sized, and aligned in a single command. After the buttons are selected, click the appropriate button on the Formatting toolbar to change the color, font, or point size, or to specify boldface or italics. Check that buttons are still selected, then pull down the Format menu to execute the Size and Alignment commands to arrange the buttons attractively on the form.

STEP 7: Modify the Main Menu

➤ You're almost finished. Open the **Main Menu form** in Design view. Move the four existing buttons to the left.

➤ Click and drag the **Command Button tool** to create the fifth command button as shown in Figure 6.10g. (Your button will display a different number.)

➤ Supply the necessary information to the Command Button Wizard so that the new button opens the Player Draft form just created. The text on the button should read **Player Draft.**

➤ Size, align, space, and color the command buttons as in the previous exercise. (Press and hold the **Shift key** to select multiple command buttons.)

➤ Save the completed form. Close the form, which returns you to the Database window.

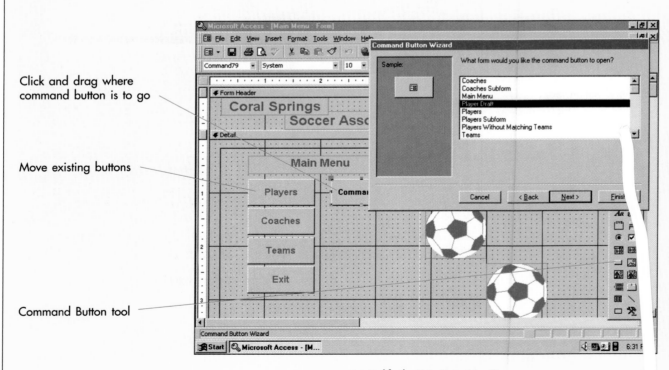

(g) Modify the Main Menu (step 7)

FIGURE 6.10   Hands-on Exercise 3 (continued)

THE F11 KEY

It's easy to lose the Database window, especially when you are maximizing objects within a database. Press the F11 key at any time to make the Database window the active window and place it in front of all the other open objects.

STEP 8: Test the Completed System

➤ Click the **Macros tab** in the Database window. Double click the **AutoExec macro** to execute this macro, as though you just opened the Soccer Objects database.

➤ Click the **Player Draft button** in the Main Menu to display the form you just created, as shown in Figure 6.10h. The Players are listed according to their ratings.

➤ Click the **TeamID field** for Katie Remmen. Type **R** (the first letter in Rockets) and Katie is assigned automatically to this team.

➤ Click the **Update List Command button.** Katie disappears from the list of unassigned players as she has just been drafted by the Rockets.

➤ Click the **End Draft button** to (temporarily) end the draft and return to the Main Menu.

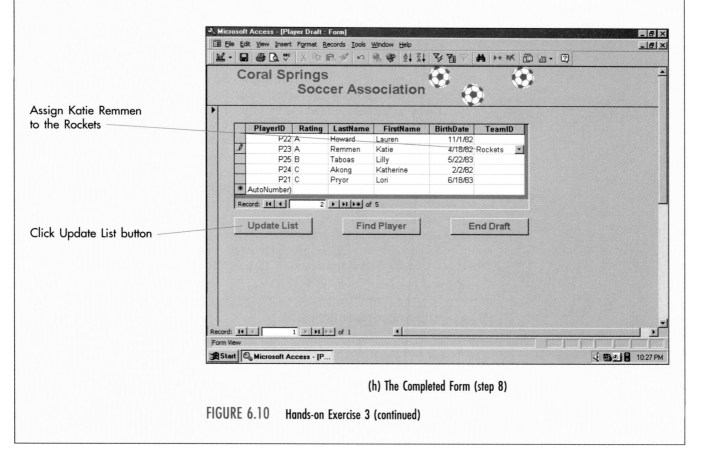

(h) The Completed Form (step 8)

FIGURE 6.10   Hands-on Exercise 3 (continued)

- ➤ Click the **Teams Command button** to view the team rosters. Team T01 (Rockets) is the first team you see, and Katie Remmen is on the roster. Click the **Close Form button** to return to the Main Menu.
- ➤ Click the **Exit Command button** to leave the system. Click **OK** in response to the message reminding you to back up the system.

A SIMPLE STRATEGY FOR BACKUP

We cannot overemphasize the importance of adequate backup. Backup procedures are personal and vary from individual to individual as well as installation to installation. Our suggested strategy is very simple, namely, that you back up whatever you cannot afford to lose and that you do so at the end of every session. Be sure to store the backup at a different location from the original file.

PROTOTYPING

Today's competitive environment demands that you develop applications quickly. This is especially true if you are creating an application for a client, where it is important for that person to see a working system as soon as possible. Prototyping enables you to do precisely that. Not only will the client appreciate your sense of urgency, but the sooner the client sees the initial version, the easier it is for you to make the necessary corrections.

A *prototype* is a partially completed version of an application that demonstrates the "look and feel" of the finished system. Consider, for example, Figure 6.11, which applies prototyping to the soccer application. The Main Menu in Figure 6.11a now includes a command button to display the Report Menu in Figure 6.11b. The Report Menu then enables a user to select any of the available reports.

The reports, however, have not yet been created; that is, clicking any of the command buttons in Figure 6.11b displays a message indicating that the report is not available. Nevertheless, the user has a better appreciation for how the eventual system will work and can provide immediate feedback on the portion of the system that has been completed. He or she may request changes in the user interface, the addition or deletion of reports, and so on. And, as indicated, the sooner the user communicates the requested changes to you, the easier it is for you to make those corrections. Once the prototype has been approved, the individual reports can be implemented one at a time, until the system is complete.

TOP-DOWN IMPLEMENTATION

An application should be developed in stages, beginning at the top (the form containing the Main Menu) and working toward the bottom (subsidiary forms, reports, and queries). Testing should go on continually, even before all of the objects are completed. This is accomplished through prototyping, which always presents a working application to the user, in which lower-level objects need not be completed. Development continues in top-down fashion, with each new version of the application containing additional objects until the system is finished.

New button displays a
Report Menu

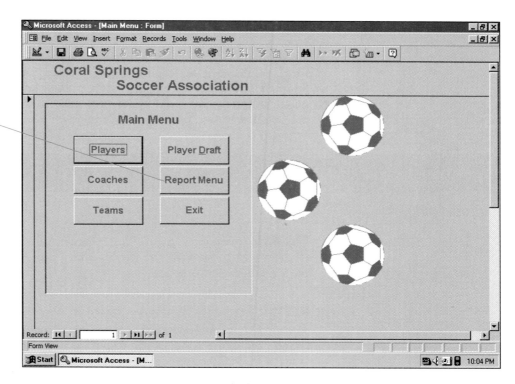

(a) Main Menu

Message displayed when a
report command button is clicked

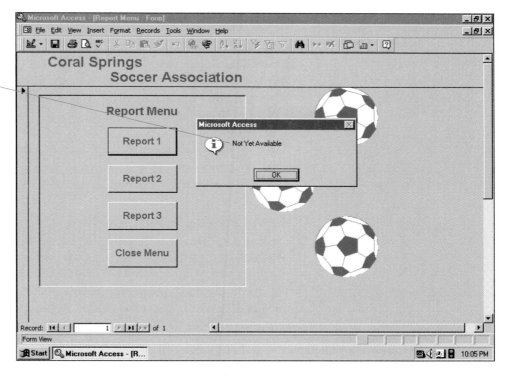

(b) Report Menu

FIGURE 6.11   Prototyping

Realize, too, how easy it is to produce the prototype shown in Figure 6.11. You need to create a macro (containing the MsgBox action) that will display the appropriate message when a report is not available. You also need to create a form that displays the Report Menu, and that form is easily created using the same template you used to create the Main Menu. And finally, you need to add a command button to the Main Menu to display the Report Menu. All of these steps are detailed in the following hands-on exercise.

HANDS-ON EXERCISE 4

Prototyping

Objective: To create a subsidiary Report Menu that is not fully implemented; to use the MsgBox action as the basis of a prototyping macro. Use Figure 6.12 as a guide in the exercise.

STEP 1: Create the Prototype Macro

➤ Start Access and open the **Soccer Objects database.** Pull down the **File menu** and click **Close** (or click the **Close button**) to close the Main Menu form but leave the database open. (You *cannot* click the Exit command button as that would close the database.)

➤ Click the **Macros tab** in the Database window, which contains the four macros from the previous exercise. Click the **New button,** which opens the Macro window and automatically positions you at the first action. If necessary, click the **Maximize button** so that the Macro window takes the entire screen.

➤ Type **MS** (the first two letters in the MsgBox action), then press **enter** to accept this action. Press the **F6 key** or click the **box for the Message argument.** Type **Not Yet Available** as shown in Figure 6.12a.

➤ Press the **down arrow key** twice to move to the box for the **Type argument.** Click the **drop-down arrow** to display the list of message types and select **Information.**

➤ Click the **Save button.** Save the macro as **Prototype.**

➤ Click the **Run button** to test the macro, which displays the informational message in Figure 6.12a. Click **OK** to accept the message. Close the Macro window.

STEP 2: Create the Report Menu Form

➤ Click the **Forms tab** in the Database window. Click the **Template form** (on which all other forms are based), pull down the **Edit menu,** and click **Copy** (or press **Ctrl+C,** a universal Windows shortcut).

➤ Pull down the **Edit menu** a second time and click **Paste** (or click **Ctrl+V,** a universal Windows shortcut). Enter **Report Menu** as the name of the new form. Click **OK.**

➤ Select the newly created **Report Menu form.** Click the **Design button** to open the form in Design view as shown in Figure 6.12b.

➤ Click the **Restore button,** then size and/or move the Database and Form windows so that your desktop matches the arrangement in Figure 6.12b.

➤ Click the **label** in the Detail section, then click and drag to select the text **Enter Menu Name Here.** Enter **Report Menu** to replace the selected text. Save the form.

Run button

Click and type MS

Enter text of message

Select Information
as the message type

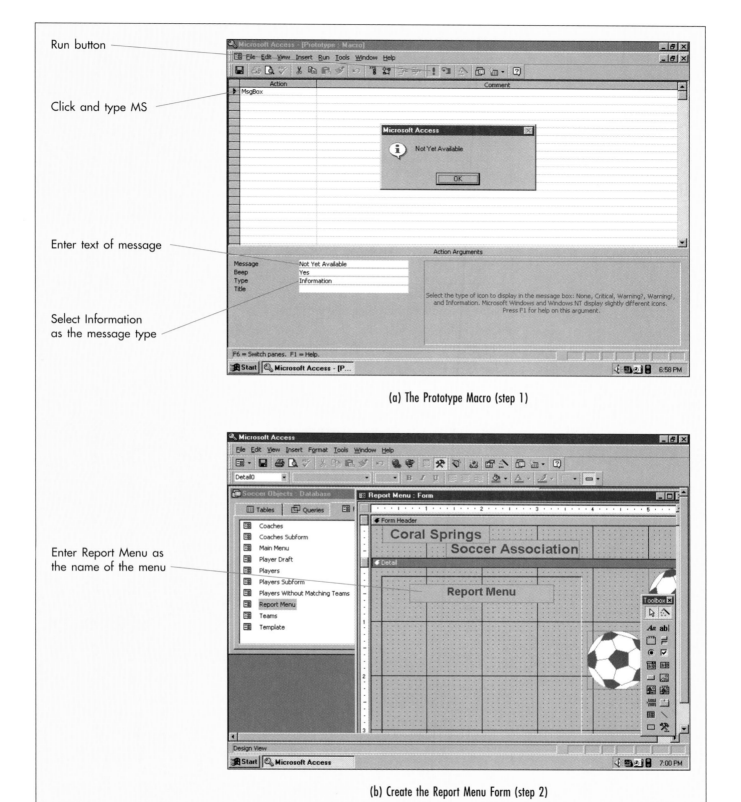

(a) The Prototype Macro (step 1)

Enter Report Menu as
the name of the menu

(b) Create the Report Menu Form (step 2)

FIGURE 6.12   Hands-on Exercise 4

ARRANGE THE DESKTOP

To size a window, point to any border (the mouse pointer changes to a double arrow), then drag the border in the direction you want to go: inward to shrink the window or outward to enlarge it. Alternatively, you can drag a corner to change both dimensions at the same time. To move a window while retaining its size, point to its title bar, then drag the window to its new position. Remember, too, that you cannot size a maximized window; that is, you must restore a maximized window if you want to change its size.

STEP 3: Add the Command Buttons

➤ Click the **Macros tab** in the Database window. Click and drag the **Prototype macro** to the Report Menu form as shown in Figure 6.12c. Release the mouse, and a command button is created that will execute the Prototype macro.

➤ Click and drag to select the name of the button (Prototype), which corresponds to the name of the macro. Type **Report 1** as the new name. (Clicking this button in Form view will still execute the Prototype macro as you have changed only the text of the button, not the underlying macro.)

➤ Repeat these steps to create two additional buttons, **Report 2** and **Report 3,** as shown in Figure 6.12c. Do not worry about the size or position of the buttons at this time.

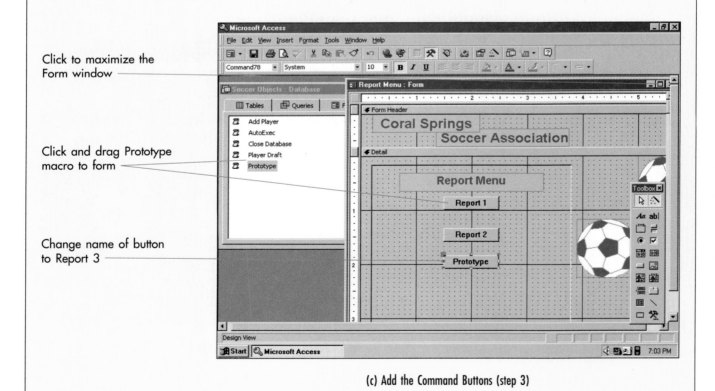

Click to maximize the Form window

Click and drag Prototype macro to form

Change name of button to Report 3

(c) Add the Command Buttons (step 3)

FIGURE 6.12   Hands-on Exercise 4 (continued)

STEP 4: Complete the Report Menu

➤ Maximize the Form window.

➤ Click the **Command Button tool** on the Toolbox toolbar, then click and drag in the form to create the command button shown in Figure 6.12d. (The number of your button will be different from ours.)

➤ The Command Button Wizard prompts you for the next several responses. Choose **Form operations** from the Categories list. Select **Close Form** as shown in Figure 6.12d. Click **Next.**

➤ Click the **Text option,** type **Close Menu** in the text box, and click **Next.** Type **Close Menu** as the name of the button. Click **Finish.**

➤ Size, align, color, and/or move the command buttons as you have done throughout the chapter.

➤ Click the **Form View button** to test the menu. Click the **Report 1 button,** which displays a message indicating that the report is not yet available. Click **OK** in response to the message.

➤ Click the buttons for **Report 2** and **Report 3,** then click **OK** as you see each informational message.

➤ Click the **Close Menu Command button** to close the Report Menu. Click **Yes** when asked whether to save the form.

(d) Complete the Report Menu (step 4)

FIGURE 6.12   Hands-on Exercise 4 (continued)

GIVE YOUR USERS WHAT THEY WANT

Talk to the people who will eventually use your application to determine what they expect from the system. Ask for copies of the (paper) forms they currently have and aim for a similar look in your application. Try to obtain copies of the reports they currently prepare to be sure that your system produces the information expected from it.

STEP 5: Modify the Main Menu

➤ If necessary, click the **Forms tab** in the Database window. Select the **Main Menu form,** then click the **Design button** to open the form in Design view as shown in Figure 6.12e.

➤ Click the **Command Button tool** on the Forms Design toolbar, then click and drag in the form to create the command button shown in Figure 6.12e. (The number of your button will be different from ours.)

➤ The Command Button Wizard prompts you for several responses. Choose **Form operations** from the Categories list. Select **Open Form.** Click **Next.**

➤ Choose **Report Menu** as the name of the form. Click **Next.**

➤ Click the **Text option,** type **Report Menu** in the text box, and click **Next.** Type **Report Menu** as the name of the button. Click **Finish.**

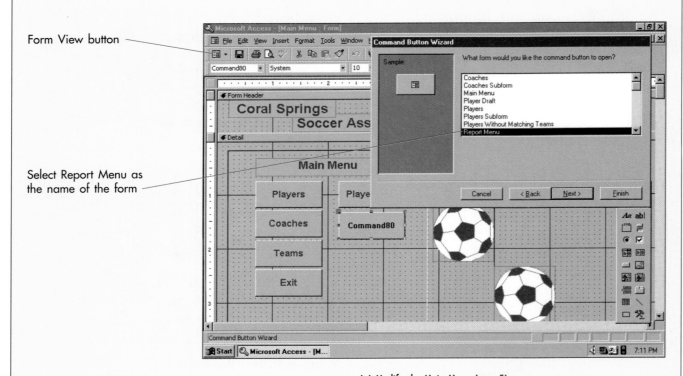

(e) Modify the Main Menu (step 5)

FIGURE 6.12   Hands-on Exercise 4 (continued)

BE CONSISTENT

Consistency within an application is essential to its success. Similar functions should be done in similar ways to facilitate learning and to build confidence in the application. The soccer application, for example, has similar screens for the Players, Coaches, and Teams forms, each of which contains the identical command buttons to add or print a record and close the form. The interface and means of navigation are consistent from one screen to the next.

STEP 6: Test the Completed System

➤ Click the **Form View button** to switch to the Form view and test the system. Click the **Report Menu button** on the Main Menu to display the Report Menu in Figure 6.12f.

➤ Click the command buttons for any of the reports, then click **OK** in response to the informational message.

➤ Click the **Close Menu Command button** to exit the Report Menu and return to the Main Menu.

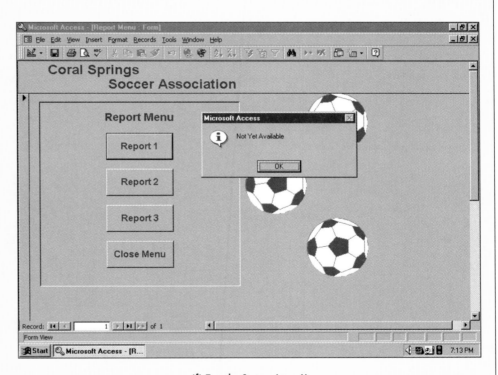

(f) Test the System (step 6)

FIGURE 6.12   Hands-on Exercise 4 (continued)

STEP 7: Additional Properties

➤ Return to the Design view for the Main Menu. Point to the **Form Selector box** to the left of the ruler, click the **right mouse button**, then click the **Properties command** to display the Properties dialog box for the form as shown in Figure 6.12g.

➤ Click the **Format tab** (if necessary), then click in the **Record Selectors text box** to display the drop-down list shown in Figure 6.12g. Click **No** to disable the Record Selector.

➤ Click in the **Navigation Buttons text box** to display its drop-down list, then click **No** to suppress the display of the navigation buttons.

➤ Click the **Player Draft button.** The Properties box displays the properties of the selected object.

➤ Click the **All tab,** then change the caption property to **Player &Draft** by placing an ampersand in front of the "D" in "Draft."

➤ Scroll down to the **ControlTip Text** property and enter **Click this button or press Alt+D** to assign players to teams. Close the Properties box.

➤ If necessary, size and align the command button within the Main Menu. (Press and hold the **Shift key** to select multiple buttons, then use the Size and Align commands on the Format menu.)

➤ Save the completed form.

Form selector box

Change both properties to No

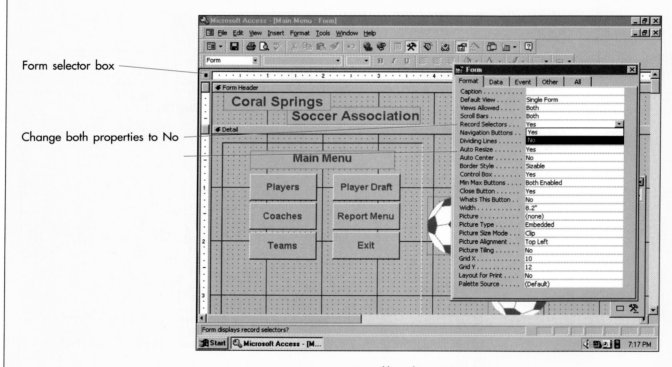

(g) Additional Properties (step 7)

FIGURE 6.12   Hands-on Exercise 4 (continued)

KEYBOARD SHORTCUTS—THE CAPTION PROPERTY

The Caption Property enables you to create a keyboard shortcut for a command button. Right click the button in the Form Design view to display the Properties dialog box for the command button. Click the All tab, then modify the Caption Property to include an ampersand immediately in front of the letter that will become part of the shortcut (e.g., &Help if you have a Help button). Close the dialog box, then go to the Form view. The command button will contain an underlined letter (e.g., Help), which can be activated in conjunction with the Alt key (e.g. Alt+H).

STEP 8: The Finished Form

➤ Return to the Form view to view the finished menu. Neither the Selection Area nor the Navigation buttons are visible in accordance with the property settings in the previous step.

➤ Point to the Player Draft button, which displays the ScreenTip shown in Figure 6.12h. Press **Alt+D** (the keyboard shortcut created in step 7) to return to the player draft that was created earlier in the exercise. Click the **End Draft button** to return to the main form.

➤ Click the **Exit command button** to close the database. Click **Yes** if prompted to save any of the objects created in this exercise.

➤ Exit Access. Congratulations on a job well done.

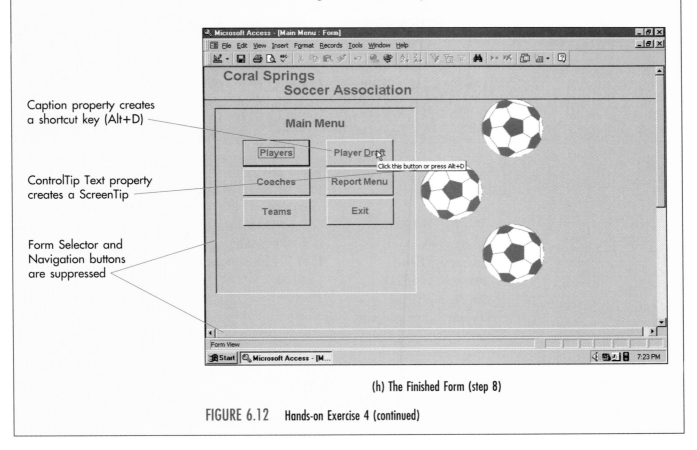

(h) The Finished Form (step 8)

FIGURE 6.12   Hands-on Exercise 4 (continued)

An application contains the same objects as a database. The difference is in how the objects are presented to the user. An application has an intuitive user interface that does not require a knowledge of Microsoft Access on the part of the user.

The tables in a database can be separated from the other objects to enable the distribution of updated versions of the application without disturbing the data. The tables are stored in one database and the objects in another. The Link Tables command associates the tables with the objects.

A form is the basis of a user interface. The form contains text or list boxes in which to enter or edit data, and command buttons to move from one screen to the next. Clicking a command button causes Access to execute the underlying macro or event procedure.

A macro automates a command sequence and consists of one or more actions. An action is a command that performs a specific operation, such as opening a form or running a select query. A macro action has one or more arguments that supply information about how the command is to be executed.

The Macro window has two sections. The upper section contains the name (if any) of the macro, the condition (if any) under which it is executed, and most important, the actions (commands) that make up the macro. The lower section specifies the arguments for the various actions. A macro group consists of multiple macros and is used for organizational purposes.

The AutoExec macro is executed automatically whenever the database in which it is stored is opened. Each database can have its own AutoExec macro, but there is no requirement for an AutoExec macro to be present.

The Unmatched Query Wizard identifies the records in one table (e.g., the Players table) that do not have matching records in another table (e.g., the Teams table).

A prototype is a model (mockup) of a completed application that demonstrates the "look and feel" of the application. Prototypes can be developed quickly and easily through the use of simple macros containing the MsgBox action.

KEY WORDS AND CONCEPTS

Action	Event procedure	Macro window
Application	Find Unmatched Query Wizard	MsgBox action
Argument	Get External Data	On Click property
AutoExec macro	Is Null criterion	Prototype
Combo box	Link Tables command	Requery command
Command button	List box	Template
Database properties	Macro	Top-down implementation
Debugging	Macro group	User interface
Display When property	Macro toolbar	Zoom box
Event		

MULTIPLE CHOICE

1. The user interface of an application is based on a:
   (a) Table
   (b) Form
   (c) Query
   (d) Report

2. Which of the following describes the storage of the tables and objects for the application developed in the chapter?
   (a) Each table is stored in its own database
   (b) Each object is stored in its own database
   (c) The tables are stored in one database and the objects in a different database
   (d) The tables and objects are stored in the same database

3. Which of the following is true regarding the Link Tables command as it was used in the chapter?
   (a) It was executed from the Soccer Objects database
   (b) It was executed from the Soccer Tables database
   (c) Both (a) and (b)
   (d) Neither (a) nor (b)

4. What happens when an Access database is initially opened?
   (a) Access executes the AutoExec macro if the macro exists
   (b) Access opens the AutoExec form if the form exists
   (c) Both (a) and (b)
   (d) Neither (a) nor (b)

5. Which statement is true regarding the AutoExec macro?
   (a) Every database must have an AutoExec macro
   (b) A database may have more than one AutoExec macro
   (c) Both (a) and (b)
   (d) Neither (a) nor (b)

6. Which of the following are examples of arguments?
   (a) MsgBox and OpenForm
   (b) Message type (e.g., critical) and Form name
   (c) Both (a) and (b)
   (d) Neither (a) nor (b)

7. What happens if you drag a macro from the Database window onto a form?
   (a) A command button is created that opens the form
   (b) A command button is created that runs the macro
   (c) Both (a) and (b)
   (d) Neither (a) nor (b)

8. How do you change the properties of a command button on an existing form?
   (a) Open the form in Form view, then click the left mouse button to display a shortcut menu
   (b) Open the form in Form view, then click the right mouse button to display a shortcut menu
   (c) Open the form in Form Design view, then click the left mouse button to display a shortcut menu
   (d) Open the form in Form Design view, then click the right mouse button to display a shortcut menu

9. Which of the following is true regarding the Unmatched Query Wizard with respect to the CSSA database?
   (a) It can be used to identify teams without players
   (b) It can be used to identify players without teams
   (c) Both (a) and (b)
   (d) Neither (a) nor (b)

10. Which of the following can be associated with the On Click property of a command button?
    (a) An event procedure created by the Command Button Wizard
    (b) A macro created by the user
    (c) Either (a) or (b)
    (d) Neither (a) nor (b)

11. Which of the following was suggested as essential to a backup strategy?
    (a) Backing up files at the end of every session
    (b) Storing the backup file(s) at another location
    (c) Both (a) and (b)
    (d) Neither (a) nor (b)

12. The On Click property of a command button contains the entry, *Player Draft.Update List*. Which of the following is true?
    (a) Update List is an event procedure
    (b) Player Draft is an event procedure
    (c) Player Draft is a macro in the Update List macro group
    (d) Update List is a macro in the Player Draft macro group

13. Which columns are always visible in the Macro window?
    (a) Action and Comments
    (b) Macro Name and Conditions
    (c) Both (a) and (b)
    (d) Neither (a) nor (b)

14. The F6 and F11 function keys were introduced as shortcuts. Which of the following is true about these keys?
    (a) The F6 key switches between the top and bottom sections of the Macro window
    (b) The F11 key makes the Database window the active window
    (c) Both (a) and (b)
    (d) Neither (a) nor (b)

15. Which of the following was suggested as a way to organize macros and thus limit the number of macros that are displayed in the Database window?

(a) Avoid macro actions that have only a single argument

(b) Avoid macros that contain only a single action

(c) Create a macro group

(d) All of the above

ANSWERS

1. b	**6.** b	**11.** c
2. c	**7.** b	**12.** d
3. a	**8.** d	**13.** a
4. a	**9.** c	**14.** c
5. d	**10.** c	**15.** c

PRACTICE WITH ACCESS 97

1. Prototyping was demonstrated in the fourth hands-on exercise to create the "look and feel" of the soccer application. It remains, however, to create the three reports in the Report Menu, to create a macro to open each of these reports, and finally to assign each macro to the appropriate command button. Create the following reports:

a. Report 1 is a master list of all players in alphabetical order. Include the player's first and last names, date of birth, rating, phone, and address in that order. Create the report in landscape rather than portrait orientation.

b. Report 2 is a master list of all coaches in alphabetical order. Include the coach's first and last names, phone, and address in that order. Create the report in landscape rather than portrait orientation.

c. Report 3 is to print the team rosters in sequence by TeamID. Each roster is to begin on a new page. The header line should contain the TeamID, nickname, and team colors as well as the name and phone number of the head coach. A detail line—containing the player's first and last names, telephone number, and date of birth—is to appear for each player. Players are to be listed alphabetically.

d. Submit a disk with the CSSA database to your instructor.

2. Figure 6.13 displays a modified version of the Main Menu for the CSSA database, which has been enhanced through the addition of a Help button. The user clicks the Help button to execute a macro, which in turn displays the dialog box shown in the figure.

a. Complete all of the hands-on exercises in the chapter, then add a Help macro containing your telephone and e-mail address. (The macro consists of a single MsgBox action.)

b. Modify the existing Main Menu to include the Help button shown in Figure 6.13, which runs the macro you just created.

c. Submit a disk with the CSSA database to your instructor.

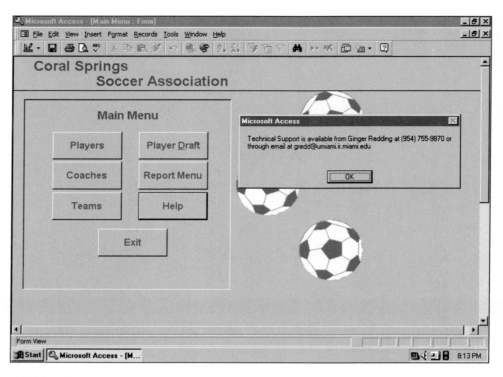

FIGURE 6.13   Screen for Practice Exercise 2

3. Figure 6.14 illustrates the use of the Condition column in the Macro window. The intent of the macro in Figure 6.14 is to display a message to "A"-rated players inviting them to try out for an All-City competitive team that plays against teams from other cities.

   a. Create the macro shown in Figure 6.14. (Click the Conditions button on the Macro toolbar to display the Conditions column in the Macro window.)

   b. Open the Players form in Design view. Right click the Rating control to display its Property sheet, then assign the macro you just created to the On Exit property.

   c. Prove to yourself that the macro works. Change to Form view, then move to the record containing the information you entered for yourself in step 3 of the first hands-on exercise. Click the text box containing the player rating, enter "A", then press the Tab key to move to the next control. You should see a message inviting you to try for the competitive team. Change your rating to a "B" and press the Tab key a second time. This time there is no message.

   d. Submit a disk with the CSSA database to your instructor.

4. The player draft was only partially completed in the fourth hands-on exercise and still requires the completion of the Find Player function. After this has been accomplished, you will be able to click the Find Player button in Figure 6.15 to display the Find Parameter Value dialog box to enter a player's name, and then view the information for that player. Accordingly:

   a. Create a parameter query that requests the last name of a player, then returns *all* fields for that player.

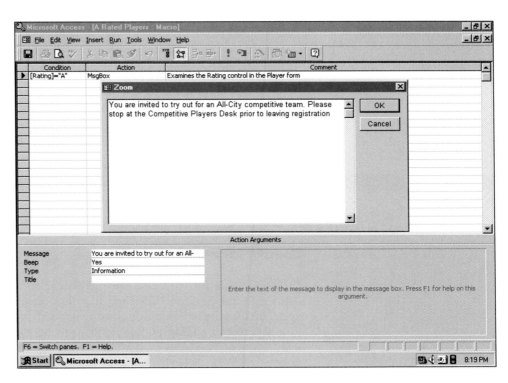

FIGURE 6.14   Screen for Practice Exercise 3

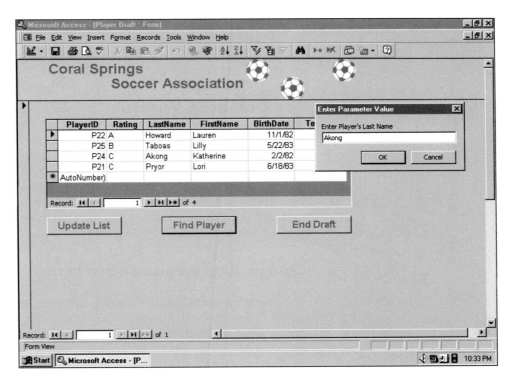

FIGURE 6.15   Screen for Practice Exercise 4

b. Copy the existing Players Form to a new form called Find Player. Change the Record Source property of the Find Player form to the parameter query you created in part a.

c. Change the Find Player macro in the Player Draft group so that it opens the Find Player form you just created.

d. Add the Help button to the Player Draft menu as described in practice exercise 2. Submit the completed disk to your instructor.

Case Studies

Client/Server Applications

The application for the Coral Springs Soccer Association was developed to run on a single PC; in practice, however, it would most likely be implemented on a network. Investigate the additional steps needed to load the Soccer Tables database on a server and enable multiple users (clients) to access the database simultaneously. How does Access prevent two users from modifying the same record simultaneously? What security features are available? How would backup be implemented? Where would the Soccer Objects database be stored?

A Project for the Semester

Choose any of the eight cases at the end of the two previous chapters (with the exception of the Recreational Sports League) and develop a complete system. Design the tables and relationships and provide a representative series of forms to enter and edit the data. Create a representative set of queries and reports. And finally, tie the system together via a system of menus similar to those that were developed in this chapter.

The Database Wizard

The Database Wizard provides an easy way to create a database as it creates the database for you. The advantage of the Wizard is that it creates the tables, forms, and reports, together with a Main Menu (called a switchboard) in one operation. The disadvantage is that the Wizard is inflexible compared to creating the database yourself. Use the online Help facility to learn about the Database Wizard, then use the Wizard to create a simple database for your music collection. Is the Wizard a useful shortcut, or is it easier to create the database yourself?

Compacting versus Compressing

The importance of adequate backup has been stressed throughout the text. As a student, however, your backup may be limited to what you can fit on a single floppy disk, which in turn creates a problem if the size of your database grows beyond 1.4Mb. Two potential solutions involve compacting and/or compressing the database. Compacting is done from within Access, whereas compressing requires additional software. Investigate both of these techniques with respect to the CSSA database created in the chapter. Be sure to indicate to your instructor the reduction in file size that you were able to achieve.

APPENDIX A: TOOLBARS

OVERVIEW

Microsoft Access has 20 predefined toolbars that provide access to commonly used commands. Twelve of the toolbars are tied to a specific view and are displayed automatically when you work in that view. These twelve toolbars are shown in Figure A.1 and are listed here for convenience: the Database, Relationships, Table Design, Table Datasheet, Query Design, Query Datasheet, Form Design, Form View, Report Design, Print Preview, Macro Design, and Visual Basic toolbars.

The remaining toolbars are shown in Figure A.2. The Toolbox and Formatting (Form/Report Design) toolbars are displayed by default in both the Form Design and Report Design views. The Formatting (Datasheet) toolbar is displayed by default in both the Table Datasheet and Query Datasheet views. The Web toolbar can be displayed (hidden) in any view at the discretion of the user. The Filter/Sort toolbar is displayed at the discretion of the user.

Database Toolbar

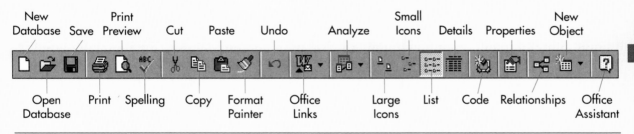

Relationships Toolbar

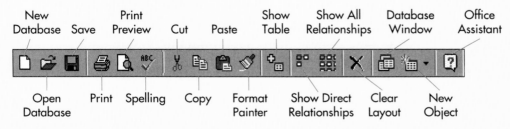

FIGURE A.1   Access Toolbars Tied to Specific Views

Table Design Toolbar

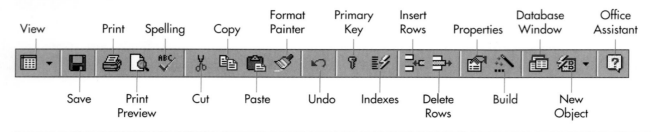

View — Print — Spelling — Copy — Format Painter — Primary Key — Insert Rows — Properties — Database Window — Office Assistant

Save — Print Preview — Cut — Paste — Undo — Indexes — Delete Rows — Build — New Object

Table Datasheet Toolbar

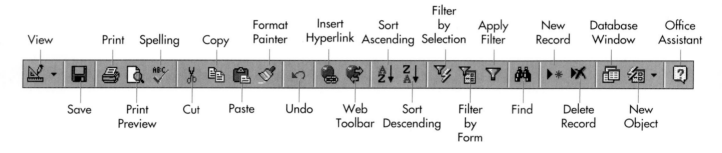

View — Print — Spelling — Copy — Format Painter — Insert Hyperlink — Sort Ascending — Filter by Selection — Apply Filter — New Record — Database Window — Office Assistant

Save — Print Preview — Cut — Paste — Undo — Web Toolbar — Sort Descending — Filter by Form — Find — Delete Record — New Object

Query Design Toolbar

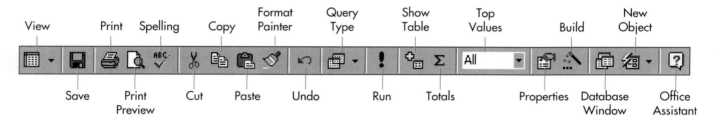

View — Print — Spelling — Copy — Format Painter — Query Type — Show Table — Top Values — Build — New Object

Save — Print Preview — Cut — Paste — Undo — Run — Totals — Properties — Database Window — Office Assistant

Query Datasheet Toolbar

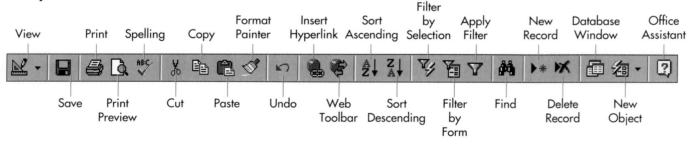

View — Print — Spelling — Copy — Format Painter — Insert Hyperlink — Sort Ascending — Filter by Selection — Apply Filter — New Record — Database Window — Office Assistant

Save — Print Preview — Cut — Paste — Undo — Web Toolbar — Sort Descending — Filter by Form — Find — Delete Record — New Object

Form Design Toolbar

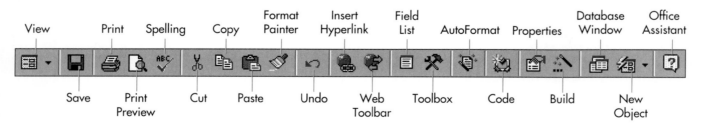

View — Print — Spelling — Copy — Format Painter — Insert Hyperlink — Field List — AutoFormat — Properties — Database Window — Office Assistant

Save — Print Preview — Cut — Paste — Undo — Web Toolbar — Toolbox — Code — Build — New Object

FIGURE A.1 Access Toolbars Tied to Specific Views (continued)

Form View Toolbar

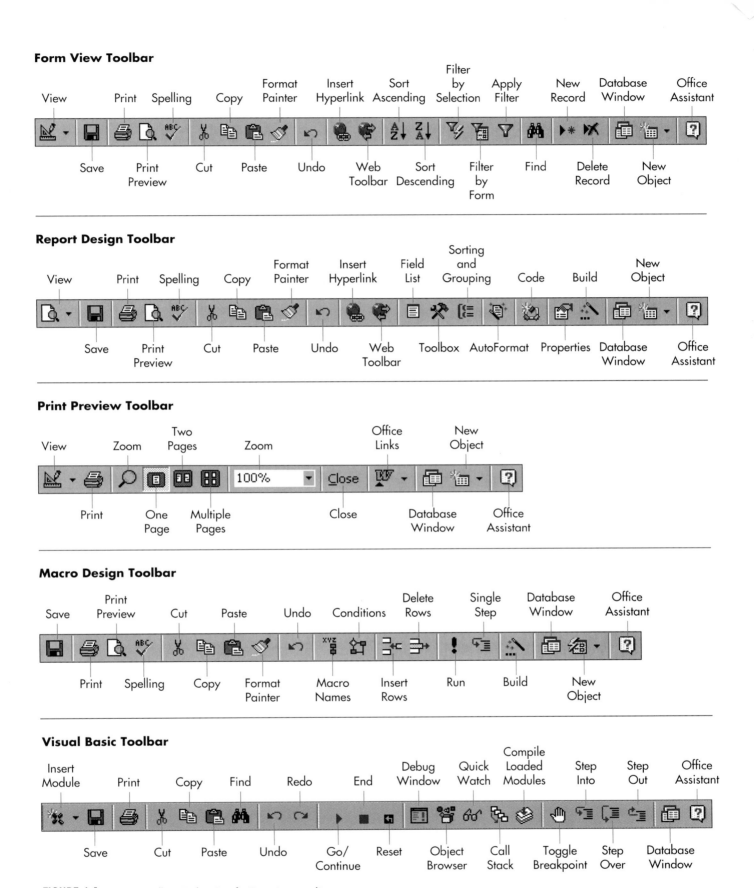

View · Print · Spelling · Copy · Format Painter · Insert Hyperlink · Sort Ascending · Filter by Selection · Apply Filter · New Record · Database Window · Office Assistant

Save · Print Preview · Cut · Paste · Undo · Web Toolbar · Sort Descending · Filter by Form · Find · Delete Record · New Object

Report Design Toolbar

View · Print · Spelling · Copy · Format Painter · Insert Hyperlink · Field List · Sorting and Grouping · Code · Build · New Object

Save · Print Preview · Cut · Paste · Undo · Web Toolbar · Toolbox · AutoFormat · Properties · Database Window · Office Assistant

Print Preview Toolbar

View · Zoom · Two Pages · Zoom · Office Links · New Object

Print · One Page · Multiple Pages · Close · Database Window · Office Assistant

100%

Close

Macro Design Toolbar

Save · Print Preview · Cut · Paste · Undo · Conditions · Delete Rows · Single Step · Database Window · Office Assistant

Print · Spelling · Copy · Format Painter · Macro Names · Insert Rows · Run · Build · New Object

Visual Basic Toolbar

Insert Module · Print · Copy · Find · Redo · End · Debug Window · Quick Watch · Compile Loaded Modules · Step Into · Step Out · Office Assistant

Save · Cut · Paste · Undo · Go/Continue · Reset · Object Browser · Call Stack · Toggle Breakpoint · Step Over · Database Window

FIGURE A.1   Access Toolbars Tied to Specific Views (continued)

Toolbox Toolbar

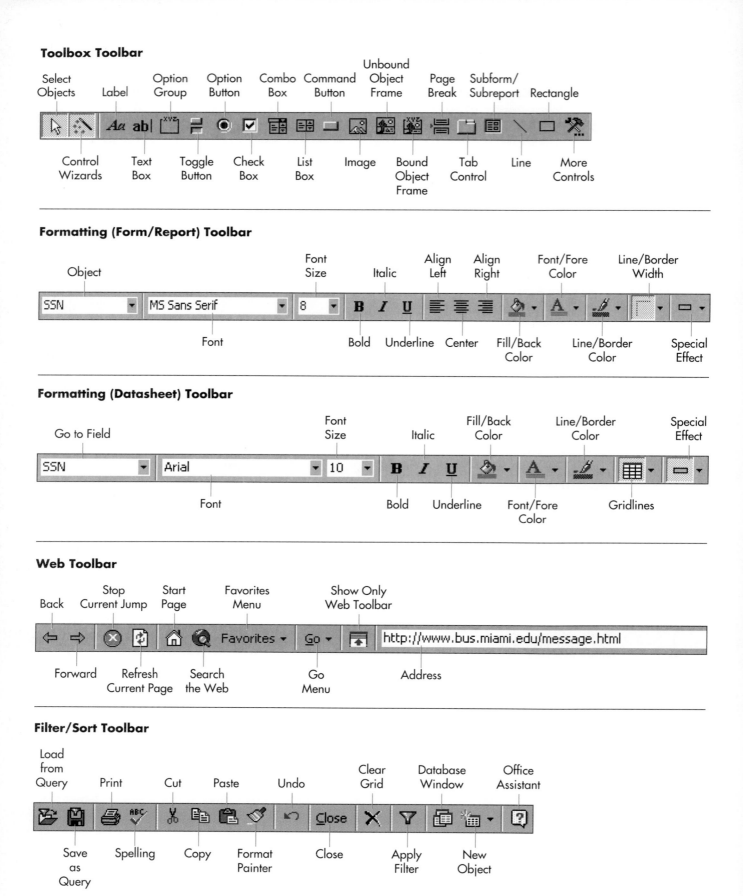

FIGURE A.2   Other Access Toolbars

APPENDIX B: DESIGNING A RELATIONAL DATABASE

OVERVIEW

An Access database consists of multiple tables, each of which stores data about a specific subject. To use Access effectively, you must relate the tables to one another. This in turn requires a knowledge of database design and an understanding of the principles of a relational database under which Access operates.

Our approach to teaching database design is to present two case studies, each of which covers a common application. The first case centers on franchises for fast food restaurants and incorporates the concept of a one-to-many relationship. One person can own many restaurants, but a given restaurant is owned by only one person. The second case is based on a system for student transcripts and incorporates a many-to-many relationship. One student takes many courses, and one course is taken by many students. The intent in both cases is to design a database capable of producing the desired information.

CASE STUDY: FAST FOOD FRANCHISES

The case you are about to read is set within the context of a national corporation offering franchises for fast food restaurants. The concept of a franchise operation is a familiar one and exists within many industries. The parent organization develops a model operation, then franchises that concept to qualified individuals (franchisees) seeking to operate their own businesses. The national company teaches the franchisee to run the business, aids the person in site selection and staffing, coordinates national advertising, and so on. The franchisee pays an initial fee to open the business followed by subsequent royalties and marketing fees to the parent corporation.

The essence of the case is how to relate the data for the various entities (the restaurants, franchisees, and contracts) to one another. One approach is to develop a single restaurant table, with each restaurant record containing data about the owner and contract arrangement. As we shall see, that design leads to problems of redundancy whenever the same person owns more than one restaurant or when several restaurants are governed by the same contract type. A better approach is to develop separate tables, one for each of the objects (restaurants, franchisees, and contracts).

The entities in the case have a definite relationship to one another, which must be reflected in the database design. The corporation encourages individuals to own multiple restaurants, creating a *one-to-many relationship* between franchisees and restaurants. One person can own many restaurants, but a given restaurant is owned by only one person. There is also a one-to-many relationship between contracts and restaurants because the corporation offers a choice of contracts to each restaurant.

The company wants a database that can retrieve all data for a given restaurant, such as the annual sales, type of contract in effect (contract types are described below), and/or detailed information about the restaurant owner. The company also needs reports that reflect the location of each restaurant, all restaurants in a given state, and all restaurants managed by a particular contract type. The various contract arrangements are described below:

Contract 1: 99-year term, requiring a one-time fee of $250,000 payable at the time the franchise is awarded. In addition, the franchisee must pay a royalty of 2 percent of the restaurant's gross sales to the parent corporation, and contribute an additional 2 percent of sales to the parent corporation for advertising.

Contract 2: 5-year term (renewable at franchisee's option), requiring an initial payment of $50,000. In addition, the franchisee must pay a royalty of 4 percent of the restaurant's gross sales to the parent corporation, and contribute an additional 3 percent of sales to the parent corporation for advertising.

Contract 3: 10-year term (renewable at franchisee's option), requiring an initial payment of $75,000. In addition, the franchisee must pay a royalty of 3 percent of the restaurant's gross sales to the parent corporation, and contribute an additional 3 percent of sales to the parent corporation for advertising.

Other contract types may be offered in the future. The company currently has 500 restaurants, of which 200 are company owned. Expansion plans call for opening an additional 200 restaurants each year for the next three years, all of which are to be franchised. There is no limit on the number of restaurants an individual may own, and franchisees are encouraged to apply for multiple restaurants.

Single Table Solution

The initial concern in this, or any other, system is how best to structure the data so that the solution satisfies the information requirements of the client. We present two solutions. The first is based on a single restaurant table and will be shown to have several limitations. The second introduces the concept of a relational database and consists of three tables (for the restaurants, franchisee, and contracts).

The single table solution is shown in Figure B.1a. Each record within the table contains data about a particular restaurant, its franchisees (owner), and contract type. There are five restaurants in our example, each with a *unique* restaurant number. At first glance, Figure B.1a appears satisfactory; yet there are three specific types of problems associated with this solution. These are:

1. Difficulties in the modification of data for an existing franchisee or contract type, in that the same change may be made in multiple places.

Restaurant Number	Restaurant Data (Address, annual sales . . .)	Franchisee Data (Name, telephone, address . . .)	Contract Data (Type, term, initial fee . . .)
R1	Restaurant data for Miami . . .	Franchisee data (Grauer . . .)	Contract data (Type 1 . . .)
R2	Restaurant data for Coral Gables . . .	Franchisee data (Moldof . . .)	Contract data (Type 1 . . .)
R3	Restaurant data for Fort Lauderdale. . .	Franchisee data (Grauer . . .)	Contract data (Type 2 . . .)
R4	Restaurant data for New York . . .	Franchisee data (Glassman . . .)	Contract data (Type 1 . . .)
R5	Restaurant data for Coral Springs . . .	Franchisee data (Coulter . . .)	Contract data (Type 3 . . .)

(a) Single Table Solution

Restaurant Number	Restaurant Data	Franchisee Number	Contract Type
R1	Restaurant data for Miami . . .	F1	C1
R2	Restaurant data for Coral Gables . . .	F2	C1
R3	Restaurant data for Fort Lauderdale. . .	F1	C2
R4	Restaurant data for New York . . .	F3	C1
R5	Restaurant data for Coral Springs . . .	F4	C3

Contract Type	Contract Data
C1	Contract data. . .
C2	Contract data. . .
C3	Contract data. . .

Franchisee Number	Franchisee Data (Name, telephone, address, . . .)
F1	Grauer. . .
F2	Moldof. . .
F3	Glassman. . .
F4	Coulter. . .

(b) Multiple Table Solution

FIGURE B.1   Single versus Multiple Table Solution

2. Difficulties in the addition of a new franchisee or contract type, in that these entities must first be associated with a particular restaurant.

3. Difficulties in the deletion of a restaurant, in that data for a particular franchisee or contract type may be deleted as well.

The first problem, modification of data about an existing franchisee or contract type, stems from *redundancy,* which in turn requires that any change to duplicated data be made in several places. In other words, any modification to a duplicated entry, such as a change in data for a franchisee with multiple restaurants (e.g., Grauer, who owns restaurants in Miami and Fort Lauderdale), requires a search through the entire table to find all instances of that data so that the identical modification can be made to each of the records. A similar procedure would have to be followed should data change about a duplicated contract (e.g., a change in the royalty percentage for contract Type 1, which applies to restaurants R1, R2, and R4). This is, to say the least, a time-consuming and error-prone procedure.

The addition of a new franchisee or contract type poses a different type of problem. It is quite logical, for example, that potential franchisees must apply to the corporation and qualify for ownership before having a restaurant assigned to them. It is also likely that the corporation would develop a new contract type prior to offering that contract to an existing restaurant. Neither of these events is easily accommodated in the table structure of Figure B.1a, which would require the creation of a dummy restaurant record to accommodate the new franchisee or contract type.

The deletion of a restaurant creates yet another type of difficulty. What happens, for example, if the company decides to close restaurant R5 because of insufficient sales? The record for this restaurant would disappear as expected, but so too would the data for the franchisee (Coulter) and the contract type (C3), which is not intended. The corporation might want to award Coulter another restaurant in the future and/or offer this contract type to other restaurants. Neither situation would be possible as the relevant data has been lost with the deletion of the restaurant record.

Multiple Table Solution

A much better solution appears in Figure B.1b, which uses a different table for each of the entities (restaurants, franchisees, and contracts) that exist in the system. Every record in the restaurant table is assigned a unique restaurant number (e.g., R1 or R2), just as every record in the franchisee table is given a unique franchisee number (e.g., F1 or F2), and every contract record a unique contract number (e.g., C1 or C2).

The tables are linked to one another through the franchisee and/or contract numbers, which also appear in the restaurant table. Every record in the restaurant table is associated with its appropriate record in the franchisee table through the franchisee number common to both tables. In similar fashion, every restaurant is tied to its appropriate contract through the contract number, which appears in the restaurant record. This solution may seem complicated, but it is really quite simple and elegant.

Assume, for example, that we want the name of the franchisee for restaurant R5, and further, that we need the details of the contract type for this restaurant. We retrieve the appropriate restaurant record, which contains franchisee and contract numbers of F4 and C3, respectively. We then search through the franchisee table for franchisee F4 (obtaining all necessary information about Coulter) and search again through the contract table for contract C3 (obtaining the data for this contract type). The process is depicted graphically in Figure B.1b.

The multiple table solution may require slightly more effort to retrieve information, but this is more than offset by the advantages of table maintenance. Consider, for example, a change in data for contract C1, which currently governs restaurants R1, R2, and R4. All that is necessary is to go into the contract table, find record C1, and make the changes. The records in the restaurant table are *not* affected because the restaurant records do not contain contract data per se, only the number of the corresponding contract record. In other words, the change in data for contract C1 is made in one place (the contract table), yet that change would be reflected for all affected restaurants. This is in contrast to the single table solution of Figure B.1a, which would require the identical modification in three places.

The addition of new records for franchisees or contracts is done immediately in the appropriate tables of Figure B.1b. The corporation simply adds a franchisee or contract record as these events occur, without the necessity of a corresponding restaurant record. This is much easier than the approach of Figure B.1a, which required an existing restaurant in order to add one of the other entities.

The deletion of a restaurant is also easier than with the single table organization. You could, for example, delete restaurant R5 without losing the associated franchisee and contract data as these records exist in different tables.

Queries to the Database

By now you should be convinced of the need for multiple tables within a database and that this type of design facilitates all types of table maintenance. However, the ultimate objective of any system is to produce information, and it is in this area that the design excels. Consider now Figure B.2, which expands upon the multiple table solution to include additional data for the respective tables.

To be absolutely sure you understand the multiple table solution of Figure B.2, use it to answer the questions at the top of the next page. Check your answers with those provided.

Restaurant Number	Street Address	City	State	Zip Code	Annual Sales	Franchisee Number	Contract Type
R1	1001 Ponce de Leon Blvd	Miami	FL	33361	$600,000	F1	C1
R2	31 West Rivo Alto Road	Coral Gables	FL	33139	$450,000	F2	C1
R3	333 Las Olas Blvd	Fort Lauderdale	FL	33033	$250,000	F1	C2
R4	1700 Broadway	New York	NY	10293	$1,750,000	F3	C1
R5	1300 Sample Road	Coral Springs	FL	33071	$50,000	F4	C3

(a) Restaurant Table

Franchisee Number	Franchisee Name	Telephone	Street Address	City	State	Zip Code
F1	Grauer	(305) 755-1000	2133 NW 102 Terrace	Coral Springs	FL	33071
F2	Moldof	(305) 753-4614	1400 Lejeune Blvd	Miami	FL	33365
F3	Glassman	(212) 458-5054	555 Fifth Avenue	New York	NY	10024
F4	Coulter	(305) 755-0910	1000 Federal Highway	Fort Lauderdale	FL	33033

(b) Franchisee Table

Contract Type	Term (years)	Initial Fee	Royalty Pct	Advertising Pct
C1	99	$250,000	2%	2%
C2	5	$50,000	4%	3%
C3	10	$75,000	3%	3%

(c) Contract Table

FIGURE B.2   Fast Food Franchises

Questions

1. Who owns restaurant R2? What contract type is in effect for this restaurant?
2. What is the address of restaurant R4?
3. Which restaurant(s) are owned by Mr. Grauer?
4. List all restaurants with a contract type of C1.
5. Which restaurants in Florida have gross sales over $300,000?
6. List all contract types.
7. Which contract type has the lowest initial fee? How much is the initial fee? Which restaurant(s) are governed by this contract?
8. How many franchisees are there? What are their names?
9. What are the royalty and advertising percentages for restaurant R3?

Answers

1. Restaurant R2 is owned by Moldof and governed by contract C1.
2. Restaurant R4 is located at 1700 Broadway, New York, NY 10293.
3. Mr. Grauer owns restaurants R1 and R3.
4. R1, R2, and R4 are governed by contract C1.
5. The restaurants in Florida with gross sales over $300,000 are R1 ($600,000) and R2 ($450,000).
6. The existing contract types are C1, C2, and C3.
7. Contract C2 has the lowest initial fee ($50,000); restaurant R3 is governed by this contract type.
8. There are four franchisees: Grauer, Moldof, Glassman, and Coulter.
9. Restaurant R3 is governed by contract C2 with royalty and advertising percentages of four and three percent, respectively.

THE RELATIONAL MODEL

The restaurant case study illustrates a *relational database*, which requires a separate table for every entity in the physical system (restaurants, franchisees, and contracts). Each occurrence of an entity (a specific restaurant, franchisee, or contract type) appears as a *row* within a table. The properties of an entity (a restaurant's address, owner, or sales) appear as *columns* within a table.

Every row in every table of a relational database must be distinct. This is accomplished by including a column (or combination of columns) to uniquely identify the row. The unique identifier is known as the *primary key.* The restaurant number, for example, is different for every restaurant in the restaurant table. The franchisee number is unique in the franchisee table. The contract type is unique in the contract table.

The same column can, however, appear in multiple tables. The franchisee number, for example, appears in both the franchisee table, where its values are unique, and in the restaurant table, where they are not. The franchisee number is the primary key in the franchisee table, but it is a *foreign key* in the restaurant table. (A foreign key is simply the primary key of a related table.)

The inclusion of a foreign key in the restaurant table enables us to implement the one-to-many relationship between franchisees and restaurants. We enter the franchisee number (the primary key in the franchisee table) as a column in the restaurant table, where it (the franchisee number) is a foreign key. In similar fashion, contract type (the primary key in the contract table) appears as a foreign key in the restaurant table to implement the one-to-many relationship between contracts and restaurants.

It is helpful perhaps to restate these observations about a relational database in general terms:

1. Every entity in a physical system requires its own table in a database.
2. Each row in a table is different from every other row because of a unique column (or combination of columns) known as a primary key.
3. The primary key of one table can appear as a foreign key in another table.
4. The order of rows in a table is immaterial.
5. The order of columns in a table is immaterial, although the primary key is generally listed first.
6. The number of columns is the same in every row of the table.

THE KEY, THE WHOLE KEY, AND NOTHING BUT THE KEY

The theory of a relational database was developed by Dr. Edgar Codd, giving rise to the phrase, *"The key, the whole key, and nothing but the key . . . so help me Codd."* The sentence effectively summarizes the concepts behind a relational database and helps to ensure the validity of a design. Simply stated, the value of every column other than the primary key depends on the key in that row, on the entire key, and on nothing but that key.

Referential Integrity

The concept of *referential integrity* requires that the tables in a database be consistent with one another. Consider once again the first row in the restaurant table of Figure B.2a, which indicates that the restaurant is owned by franchisee F1 and governed by contract Type C1. Recall also how these values are used to obtain additional information about the franchisee or contract type from the appropriate tables in Figures B.2b and B.2c, respectively.

What if, however, the restaurant table referred to franchisee number F1000 or contract C9, neither of which exists in the database of Figure B.2? There would be a problem because the tables would be inconsistent with one another; that is, the restaurant table would refer to rows in the franchisee and contract tables that do not exist. It is important, therefore, that referential integrity be strictly enforced and that such inconsistencies be prevented from occurring. Suffice it to say that data validation is critical when establishing or maintaining a database, and that no system, relational or otherwise, can compensate for inaccurate or incomplete data.

CASE STUDY: STUDENT TRANSCRIPTS

Our second case is set within the context of student transcripts and expands the concept of a relational database to implement a *many-to-many relationship.* The system is intended to track students and the courses they take. The many-to-many relationship occurs because one student takes many courses, while at the same time, one course is taken by many students. The objective of this case is to relate the student and course tables to one another to produce the desired information.

The system should be able to display information about a particular student as well as information about a particular course. It should also display information about a student-course combination, such as when a student took the course and the grade he or she received.

Solution

The (intuitive and incorrect) solution of Figure B.3 consists of two tables, one for courses and one for students, corresponding to the two entities in the physical system. The student table contains the student's name, address, major, date of entry into the school, cumulative credits, and cumulative quality points. The course table contains the unique six-character course identifier, the course title, and the number of credits.

There are no problems of redundancy. The data for a particular course (its description and number of credits) appears only once in the course table, just as the data for a particular student appears only once in the student table. New courses will be added directly to the course table, just as new students will be added to the student table.

The design of the student table makes it easy to list all courses for one student. It is more difficult, however, to list all students in one course. Even if this were not the case, the solution is complicated by the irregular shape of the student table. The rows in the table are of variable length, according to the number of courses taken by each student. Not only is this design awkward, but how do we know in advance how much space to allocate for each student?

Course Number	Course Description	Credits
ACC101	Introduction to Accounting	3
CHM100	Survey of Chemistry	3
CHM101	Chemistry Lab	1
CIS120	Microcomputer Applications	3
ENG100	Freshman English	3
MTH100	Calculus with Analytic Geometry	4
MUS110	Music Appreciation	2
SPN100	Spanish I	3

(a) Course Table

Student Number	Student Data	Courses Taken with Grade and Semester												
S1	Student data (Adams...)	ACC101	SP95	A	CIS120	FA94	A	MU100	SP94	B				
S2	Student data (Fox...)	ENG100	SP95	B	MTH100	SP95	B	SPN100	SP95	B	CIS120	FA94	A
S3	Student data (Baker...)	ACC101	SP95	C	ENG100	SP95	B	MTH100	FA94	C	CIS120	FA94	B
S4	Student data (Jones...)	ENG100	SP95	A	MTH100	SP95	A						
S5	Student data (Smith...)	CIS120	SP95	C	ENG100	SP95	B	CIS120	FA94	F			

(b) Student Table

FIGURE B.3   Student Transcripts (repeating groups)

The problems inherent in Figure B.3 stem from the many-to-many relationship that exists between students and courses. The solution is to eliminate the ***repeating groups*** (course number, semester, and grade), which occur in each row of the student table in Figure B.3, in favor of the additional table shown in Figure B.4. Each row in the new table is unique because the *combination* of student number, course number, and semester is unique. Semester must be included since students are allowed to repeat a course. Smith (student number S5), for example, took CIS120 a second time after failing it initially.

The implementation of a many-to-many relationship requires an additional table, with a ***combined key*** consisting of (at least) the keys of the individual entities. The many-to-many table may also contain additional columns, which exist as a result of the combination (intersection) of the individual keys. The combination of student S5, course CIS120, and semester SP95 is unique and results in a grade of C.

Note, too, how the design in Figure B.4 facilitates table maintenance as discussed in the previous case. A change in student data is made in only one place (the student table) regardless of how many courses the student has taken. A new student may be added to the student table prior to taking any courses. In similar fashion, a new course can be added to the course table before any students have taken the course.

Review once more the properties of a relational database, then verify that the solution in Figure B.4 adheres to these requirements. To be absolutely sure

Course Number	Course Description	Credits
ACC101	Introduction to Accounting	3
CHM100	Survey of Chemistry	3
CHM101	Chemistry Lab	1
CIS120	Microcomputer Applications	3
ENG100	Freshman English	3
MTH100	Calculus with Analytic Geometry	4
MUS110	Music Appreciation	2
SPN100	Spanish I	3

(a) Course Table

Student Number	Student Data
S1	Student data (Adams. . .)
S2	Student data (Fox. . .)
S3	Student data (Baker. . .)
S4	Student data (Jones. . .)
S5	Student data (Smith. . .)

(b) Student Table

Student Number	Course Number	Semester	Grade
S1	ACC101	SP95	A
S1	CIS120	FA94	A
S1	MU100	SP94	B
S2	ENG100	SP95	B
S2	MTH100	SP95	B
S2	SPN100	SP95	B
S2	CIS120	FA94	A
S3	ACC101	SP95	C
S3	ENG100	SP95	B
S3	MTH100	FA94	C
S3	CIS120	FA94	B
S4	ENG100	SP95	A
S4	MTH100	SP95	A
S5	CIS120	SP95	C
S5	ENG100	SP95	B
S5	CIS120	FA94	F

(c) Student-Course Table

FIGURE B.4   Student Transcripts (improved design)

that you understand the solution, and to illustrate once again the power of the relational model, use Figure B.4 to answer the following questions about the student database.

Questions

1. How many courses are currently offered?
2. List all three-credit courses.
3. Which courses has Smith taken during his stay at the university?
4. Which students have taken MTH100?
5. Which courses did Adams take during the Fall 1994 semester?
6. Which students took Microcomputer Applications in the Fall 1994 semester?
7. Which students received an A in Freshman English during the Spring 1995 semester?

Answers

1. Eight courses are offered.
2. The three-credit courses are ACC101, CHM100, CIS120, ENG100, and SPN100.
3. Smith has taken CIS120 (twice) and ENG100.
4. Fox, Baker, and Jones have taken MTH100.
5. Adams took CIS120 during the Fall 1994 semester.
6. Adams, Fox, Baker, and Smith took Microcomputer Applications in the Fall 1994 semester.
7. Jones was the only student to receive an A in Freshman English during the Spring 1995 semester.

SUMMARY

A relational database consists of multiple two-dimensional tables. Each entity in a physical system requires its own table in the database. Every row in a table is unique due to the existence of a primary key. The order of the rows and columns in a table is immaterial. Every row in a table contains the same columns in the same order as every other row.

A one-to-many relationship is implemented by including the primary key of one table as a foreign key in the other table. Implementation of a many-to-many relationship requires an additional table whose primary key combines (at a minimum) the primary keys of the individual tables. Referential integrity ensures that the information in a database is internally consistent.

KEY WORDS AND CONCEPTS

Column
Combined key
Entity
Foreign key
Many-to-many relationship

One-to-many relationship
Primary key
Query
Redundancy
Referential integrity

Relational database
Repeating group
Row
Table

APPENDIX C: COMBINING AN ACCESS DATABASE WITH A WORD FORM LETTER

C

OVERVIEW

One of the greatest benefits of using the Microsoft Office suite is the ability to combine data from one application with another. An excellent example is a *mail merge,* in which data from an Access *table* or *query* are input into a Word document to produce a set of individualized form letters. You create the *form letter* using Microsoft Word, then you merge the letter with the *records* in the Access table or query. The merge process creates the individual letters, changing the name, address, and other information as appropriate from letter to letter. The concept is illustrated in Figure C.1, in which John Smith uses a mail merge to seek a job upon graduation. John writes the letter describing his qualifications, then merges that letter with a set of names and addresses to produce the individual letters.

The mail merge process uses two input files (a main document and a data source) and produces a third file as output (the set of form letters). The *main document* (e.g., the cover letter in Figure C.1a) contains standardized text together with one or more *merge fields* that indicate where the variable information is to be inserted in the individual letters. The *data source* (the set of names and addresses in Figure C.1b) contains the data that varies from letter to letter and is a table (or query) within an Access database. (The data source may also be taken from an Excel list, or alternatively it can be created as a table in Microsoft Word.)

The main document and the data source work in conjunction with one another, with the merge fields in the main document referencing the corresponding fields in the data source. The first line in the address of Figure C.1a, for example, contains three merge fields, each of which is enclosed in angle brackets, *<<Title>> <<FirstName>> <<Last-Name>>*. (These entries are not typed explicitly but are entered through special commands as described in the hands-on exercise that follows shortly.) The merge process examines each record in the data

John H. Smith

426 Jenny Lake Drive • Coral Gables, FL 33146 • (305) 666-4801

April 13, 1997

<<Title>> <<FirstName>> <<LastName>>
<<JobTitle>>
<<Company>>
<<Address1>>
<<City>>, <<State>> <<PostalCode>>

Dear <<Title>> <<LastName>>:

I am writing to inquire about a position with <<Company>> as an entry-level computer programmer. I have just graduated from the University of Miami with a bachelor's degree in Computer Information Systems (May 1997), and I am very interested in working for you. I have a background in both microcomputer applications (Windows 95, Word, Excel, PowerPoint, and Access) as well as extensive experience with programming languages (Visual Basic, C++, and COBOL). I feel that I am well qualified to join your staff as over the past two years I have had a great deal of experience designing and implementing computer programs, both as a part of my educational program and during my internship with Personalized Computer Designs, Inc.

I am eager to put my skills to work and would like to talk with you at your earliest convenience. I have enclosed a copy of my résumé and will be happy to furnish the names and addresses of my references, if you so desire. You may reach me at the above address and phone number. I look forward to hearing from you.

Sincerely,

John H. Smith

(a) The Form Letter (a Word document)

FIGURE C.1   The Mail Merge

source and substitutes the appropriate field values for the corresponding merge fields as it creates the individual form letters. For example, the first three fields in the first record will produce *Mr. Jason Frasher;* the same fields in the second record will produce, *Ms. Lauren Howard,* and so on.

In similar fashion, the second line in the address contains the <<*JobTitle*>> field. The third line contains the <<*Company*>> field. The fourth line references the <<*Address1*>> field, and the last line contains the <<*City*>>, <<*State*>, and <<*Postalcode*>> fields. The salutation repeats the <<*Title*>> and <<*LastName*>> fields. The first sentence in the letter uses the <<*Company*>> field a second time. The mail merge prepares the letters one at a time, with one letter created for every record in the data source until the file of names and addresses is exhausted. The individual form letters are shown in Figure C.1c. Each letter begins automatically on a new page.

Contacts : Table

Title	First Name	Last Name	JobTitle	Company	Address1	City	State	Postal Code
Mr	Jason	Frasher	President	Frasher Systems	100 S. Miami Avenue	Miami	FL	33103-
Ms.	Lauren	Howard	Director of Human Resources	Unique Systems	475 LeJeune Road	Coral Gables	FL	33146-
Ms.	Elizabeth	Scherry	Director of Personnel	Custom Computing	8180 Kendall Drive	Miami	FL	33156-

Record: 1 of 3

(b) The Data Source (an Access Table or Query)

John H. Smith
426 Jenny Lake Drive • Coral Gables, FL 33146 • (305) 666-4801

April 13, 1997

Ms. Elizabeth Scherry
Director of Personnel
Custom Computing
8180 Kendall Drive
Miami, FL 33156

Dear Ms. Scherry:

I am writing to inquire about a position with Custom Computing as an entry-level computer programmer. I have just graduated from the ... Computer Information Systems (May 1997), a... background in both microcomputer applicatio... Access) as well as extensive experience with ... COBOL). I feel that I am well qualified to jo... great deal of experience designing and implem... educational program and during my internshi...

I am eager to put my skills to work and woul... have enclosed a copy of my résumé and will ... references, if you so desire. You may reach m... forward to hearing from you.

Sincerely,

John H. Smith

John H. Smith
426 Jenny Lake Drive • Coral Gables, FL 33146 • (305) 666-4801

April 13, 1997

Ms. Lauren Howard
Director of Human Resources
Unique Systems
475 LeJeune Road
Coral Gables, FL 33146

Dear Ms. Howard:

I am writing to inquire about a position with Unique Systems as an entry-level computer programmer. I have just graduated from t... Computer Information Systems (May 1997... background in both microcomputer applica... Access) as well as extensive experience wi... COBOL). I feel that I am well qualified t... great deal of experience designing and imp... educational program and during my intern...

I am eager to put my skills to work and w... have enclosed a copy of my résumé and w... references, if you so desire. You may reac... forward to hearing from you.

Sincerely,

John H Smith

John H. Smith
426 Jenny Lake Drive • Coral Gables, FL 33146 • (305) 666-4801

April 13, 1997

Mr. Jason Frasher
President
Frasher Systems
100 S. Miami Avenue
Miami, FL 33103

Dear Mr. Frasher:

I am writing to inquire about a position with Frasher Systems as an entry-level computer programmer. I have just graduated from the University of Miami with a bachelor's degree in Computer Information Systems (May 1997), and I am very interested in working for you. I have a background in both microcomputer applications (Windows 95, Word, Excel, PowerPoint, and Access) as well as extensive experience with programming languages (Visual Basic, C++, and COBOL). I feel that I am well qualified to join your staff as over the past two years I have had a great deal of experience designing and implementing computer programs, both as a part of my educational program and during my internship with Personalized Computer Designs, Inc.

I am eager to put my skills to work and would like to talk with you at your earliest convenience. I have enclosed a copy of my résumé and will be happy to furnish the names and addresses of my references, if you so desire. You may reach me at the above address and phone number. I look forward to hearing from you.

Sincerely,

John H. Smith

(c) The Printed Letters

FIGURE C.1 The Mail Merge (continued)

Mail Merge Helper

A mail merge can be started from either *Microsoft Word* or *Microsoft Access.* Either way two input files are required—the form letter (main document) and the data source. The order in which these files are created depends on how the merge is initiated. When starting in Microsoft Word, you begin with the form letter, then create the data source. The process is reversed in Access—you start with a table or query, then exit to Word to create the form letter. The merge itself, however, is always performed from within Microsoft Word through the *Mail Merge Helper* as indicated in the next hands-on exercise.

The Mail Merge Helper guides you through the process. It enables you to create (or edit) the main document, to create or edit the data source, and finally, it enables you to merge the two.

PAPER MAKES A DIFFERENCE

Most of us take paper for granted, but the right paper can make a significant difference in the effectiveness of the document. Reports and formal correspondence are usually printed on white paper, but you would be surprised how many different shades of white there are. Other types of documents lend themselves to colored paper for additional impact. In short, the paper you use is far from an automatic decision. Our favorite source for paper is a company called Paper Direct (1-800-APAPERS). Ask for a catalog, then consider the use of a specialty paper the next time you have an important project, such as the cover letter for your résumé.

HANDS-ON EXERCISE 1

Mail Merge

Objective: To combine an Access table and a Word form letter to implement a mail merge and produce a set of form letters. Use Figure C.2 as a guide in the exercise.

STEP 1: Open the Names and Addresses Database

➤ Start Access. Open the **Names and Addresses** database in the **Exploring Access folder.** The **Tables tab** is selected. The **Contacts table** is the only table within the database.

➤ Pull down the **Tools menu,** click **Office Links** to display a cascaded menu in Figure C.2a, then click **Merge It with MS Word** to begin the mail merge.

➤ The dialog box for the Microsoft Word Mail Merge Wizard appears after a few seconds.

➤ The option button to link your data to an existing Microsoft Word document is already selected. (We have created the form letter for you on the data disk.) Click **OK.**

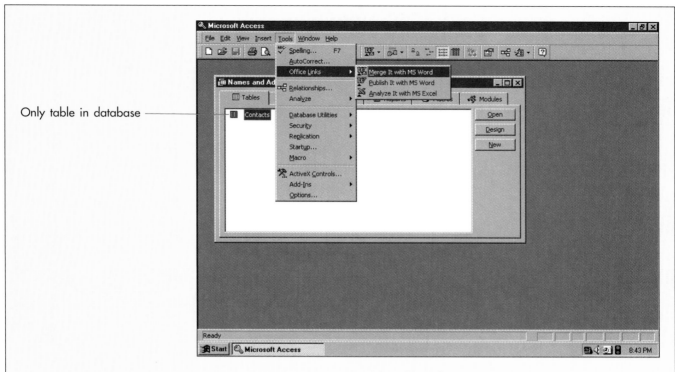

Only table in database

(a) Open the Database (step 1)

FIGURE C.2   Hands-on Exercise 1

STEP 2: Open the Form Letter

➤ You should see the dialog box to select the form letter as shown in Figure C.2b. If necessary, change to the **Exploring Access folder,** then select the **Form Letter document.** Click **Open.**

➤ Maximize the window containing the Word document (form letter). Pull down the **File menu,** click the **Save As** command to display the Save As dialog box, enter **Completed Form Letter** as the name of the document, then click the **Save command button.**

➤ There are now two identical copies of the file on disk: "Form Letter," which we supplied, and "Completed Form Letter," which you just created. The title bar references the latter, which is the document in memory. (You can always return to the original document if you modify this one beyond repair.)

THE MAIL MERGE TOOLBAR

The Microsoft Word Mail Merge toolbar is displayed automatically as soon as a merge is initiated. The toolbar contains various buttons that are used in conjunction with a mail merge and is referenced explicitly in step 5 of this exercise. Remember, too, that you can right click any toolbar in any Office application to display a shortcut menu, which enables you to explicitly display or hide the toolbars in that application.

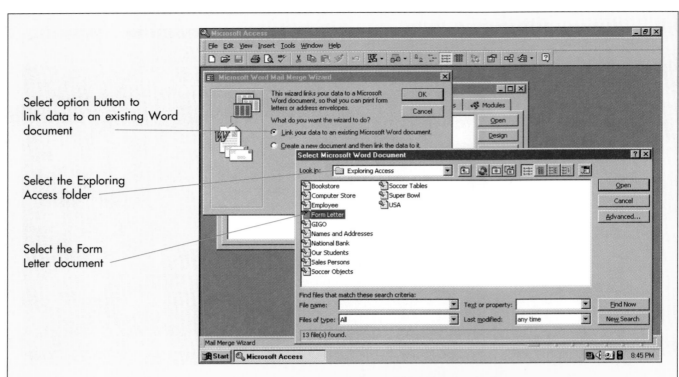

Select option button to link data to an existing Word document

Select the Exploring Access folder

Select the Form Letter document

(b) Open the Form Letter (step 2)

FIGURE C.2   Hands-on Exercise 1 (continued)

STEP 3: Insert Today's Date

➤ The form letter should be visible on your monitor as shown in Figure C.2c.

- If necessary, pull down the **View menu** and click **Page Layout** (or click the Page Layout button above the status bar).

- If necessary, click the **Zoom control arrow** on the Standard toolbar to change to **Page Width.**

➤ Click to the left of the "D" in Dear Sir, then press **enter** twice to insert two lines. Press the **up arrow** two times to return to the first line you inserted.

➤ Pull down the **Insert menu** and click the **Date and Time** command to display the dialog box in Figure C.2c.

➤ Select (click) the date format you prefer and, if necessary, check the box to insert the date as a field. Click **OK** to close the dialog box

---

FIELD CODES VERSUS FIELD RESULTS

All fields in Microsoft Word are displayed in a document in one of two formats, as a *field code* or as a *field result.* A field code appears in braces and indicates instructions to insert variable data when the document is printed; a field result displays the information as it will appear in the printed document. You can toggle the display between the field code and field result by selecting the field and pressing Shift+F9 during editing.

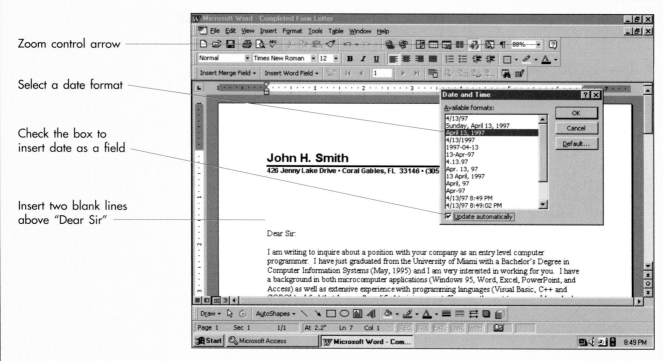

Zoom control arrow

Select a date format

Check the box to insert date as a field

Insert two blank lines above "Dear Sir"

(c) Insert the Date (step 3)

FIGURE C.2   Hands-on Exercise 1 (continued)

STEP 4: Insert the Merge Fields

➤ Click in the document immediately below the date. Press **enter** to leave a blank line between the date and the first line of the address.

➤ Click the **Insert Merge Field** button on the Mail Merge toolbar to display the fields within the data source, then select (click) **Title** from the list of fields. The title field is inserted into the main document and enclosed in angle brackets as shown in Figure C.2d.

➤ Press the **space bar** to add a space between the words. Click the **Insert Merge Field** button a second time. Click **FirstName.** Press the **space bar.**

➤ Click the **Insert Merge Field** button again. Click **LastName.**

➤ Press **enter** to move to the next line. Enter the remaining fields in the address as shown in Figure C.2d. Be sure to add a comma as well as a space after the **City field.**

➤ Delete the word "Sir" in the salutation and replace it with the **Title** and **Last Name fields** separated by spaces. Delete the words "your company" in the first sentence and replace them with the **Company field.**

➤ Save the document.

STEP 5: The Mail Merge Toolbar

➤ The Mail Merge toolbar enables you to preview the form letters before they are created. Click the **<<abc>> button** on the Mail Merge toolbar to display field values rather than field codes.

➤ You will see, for example, Mr. Jason Frasher (instead of <<Title>> <<First-Name>> <<LastName>>) as shown in Figure C.2e

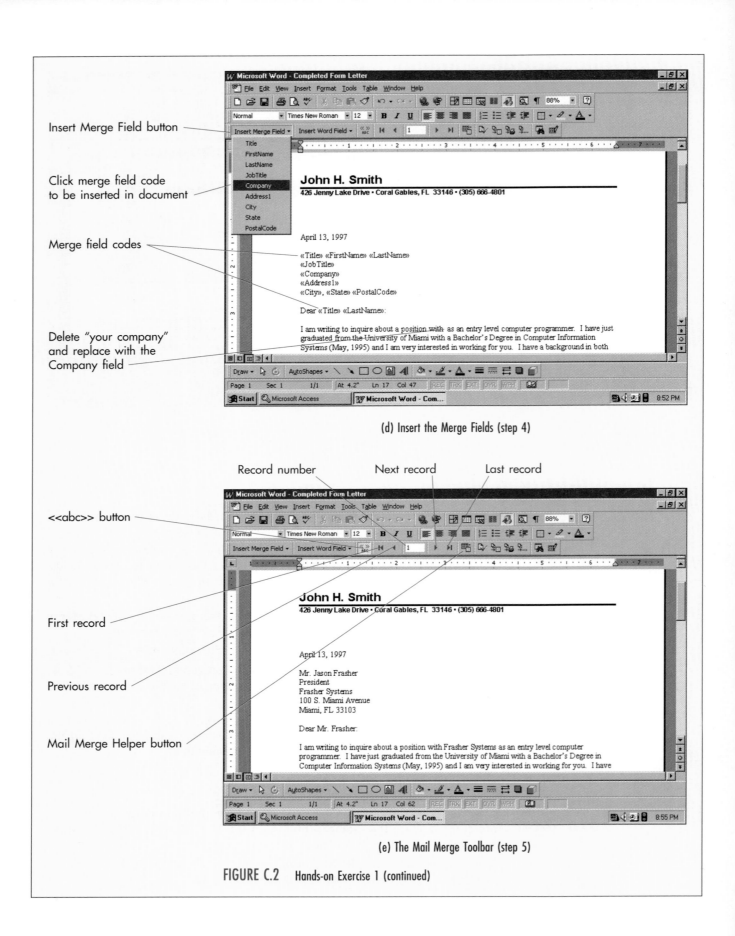

Insert Merge Field button

Click merge field code
to be inserted in document

Merge field codes

Delete "your company"
and replace with the
Company field

(d) Insert the Merge Fields (step 4)

Record number   Next record   Last record

<<abc>> button

First record

Previous record

Mail Merge Helper button

(e) The Mail Merge Toolbar (step 5)

FIGURE C.2   Hands-on Exercise 1 (continued)

➤ The **<<abc>> button** functions as a toggle switch. Click it once and you switch from field codes to field values; click it a second time and you go from field values back to field codes. End with the field values displayed.

➤ Look at the text box on the Mail Merge toolbar, which displays the number 1 to indicate that the first record is displayed. Click the ▶ **button** to display the form letter for the next record (Ms. Lauren Howard, in our example).

➤ Click the ▶ **button** again to display the form letter for the next record (Ms. Elizabeth Scherry). The toolbar indicates you are on the third record. Click the ◀ **button** to return to the previous (second) record.

➤ Click the |◀ **button** to move directly to the first record (Jason Frasher). Click the ▶| **button** to display the form letter for the last record (Elizabeth Scherry).

➤ Toggle the **<<abc>> button** to display the field codes.

STEP 6: The Mail Merge Helper

➤ Click the **Mail Merge Helper button** on the Merge toolbar to display the dialog box in Figure C.2f.

➤ The Mail Merge Helper shows your progress thus far:

• The main document has been created and saved as Completed Form Letter on drive C.

• The data source is the Contacts table within the Names and Addresses database.

➤ Click the **Merge command button** to display the Merge dialog box in Figure C.2f. The selected options should already be set, but if necessary, change your options to match those in the figure.

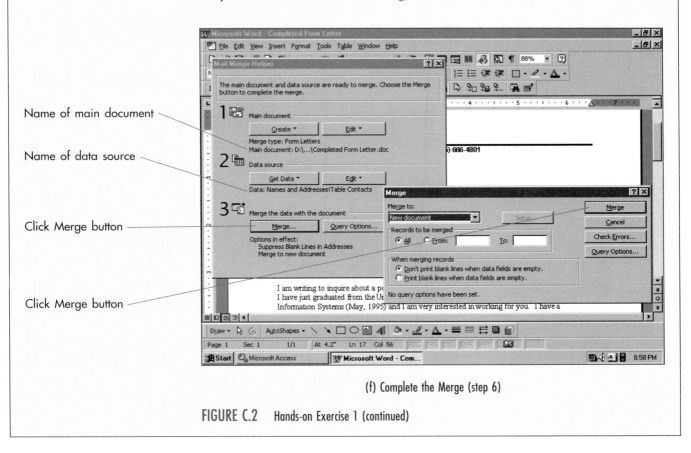

(f) Complete the Merge (step 6)

FIGURE C.2   Hands-on Exercise 1 (continued)

➤ Click the **Merge command button.** Word pauses momentarily, then generates the three form letters in a new document, which becomes the active document and is displayed on the monitor. The title bar of the active window changes to Form Letters1.

STEP 7: The Form Letters

➤ Scroll through the individual letters in the FormLetters1 document to review the letters one at a time.

➤ Pull down the **View menu.** Click **Zoom.** Click **Many Pages.** Click the **monitor icon,** then click and drag the icon within the resulting dialog box to display three pages side by side. Click **OK.** You should see the three form letters as shown in Figure C.2g.

➤ Print the letters to prove to your instructor that you did this exercise.

➤ Pull down the **File menu** and click **Exit** to exit Word. Pay close attention to the informational messages that ask whether to save the modified file(s):

• There is no need to save the merged document (Form Letters1) because you can always re-create the merged letters, provided you have saved the main document and data source.

• Save the Completed Form Letter if you are asked to do so.

➤ Exit Access. Congratulations on a job well done. We wish you good luck in your job hunting!

Title bar shows a new document

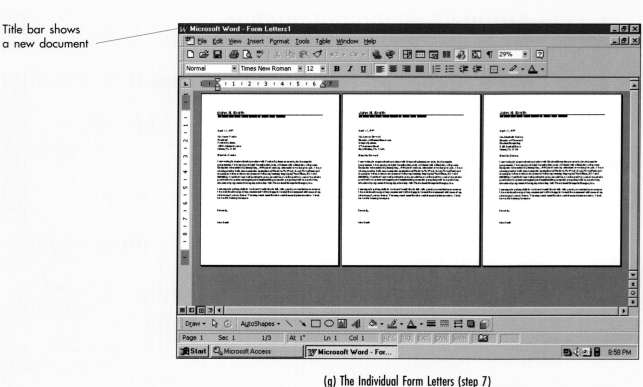

(g) The Individual Form Letters (step 7)

FIGURE C.2   Hands-on Exercise 1 (continued)

APPENDIX D:
A SEMESTER PROJECT

OVERVIEW

This appendix describes the student project we require in our introductory course in Microsoft Access at the University of Miami. It is intended for both students and instructors as it describes the various milestones in the administration of a class project. Our experience has been uniformly positive. Students work hard, but they are proud of the end result, and we are continually impressed at the diversity and quality of student projects. The project is what students remember most about our course and it truly enhances the learning experience.

We begin our course with detailed coverage of Access as it pertains to a single table (Chapters 1 through 3) so that students can develop proficiency with basic skills. Once this is accomplished, we move into a discussion of database design (Appendix A) and relational databases (Chapters 4 and 5). It is at this point that we introduce the class project, which becomes the focal point of our course for the rest of the semester. The class is divided into groups of three or four students each, and students work together to submit a collective project.

It is important that the groups be balanced with respect to student abilities. Our groups are always formed after the first exam, when we have additional information with which to create the groups. We distribute a questionnaire in which we ask students who they want to work with (and conversely, if there is anyone they would be uncomfortable working with). We always honor the latter request and do our best to honor the former as well. We also make continual use of peer evaluations so that the groups work as smoothly as possible.

Once the groups have been formed, we establish a series of milestones that are described in the remainder of the appendix. There is absolutely no requirement for you or your class to follow our milestones exactly. We have found, however, that providing detailed feedback through a series of continual assignments is very effective in moving the groups toward their final goal. We hope this appendix is useful to you and we look forward to receiving your comments.

Phase I—Preliminary Design

Describe, in a one- or two-page narrative, the relational database that your group will design and implement. You can select any of the case studies at the end of the chapters on one-to-many or many-to-many relationships, or alternatively, you can choose an entirely different system. Regardless of which system you choose, however, the preliminary design is one of the most important aspects of the entire project as it is the basis for the eventual Access database. A good design will enable you to implement the project successfully, and hence you should give considerable thought to the document you prepare. Your project need not be unduly complex, but it must include at least three tables. The relationships between the tables can be one-to-many or many-to-many. Your document should describe the physical system for which you will create the database. It should also contain a "wish list" describing in general terms the information the system is to produce.

Phase II—Detailed Design

Implement the refinements (if any) to the preliminary design from Phase I, then expand that design to include all of the necessary fields in each table. You also need to develop the properties for each field at this time. Be sure to include adequate data validation and to use input masks as appropriate. One additional requirement is that the primary key of at least one table be an AutoNumber field.

After you have completed the design, create an Access database containing the necessary tables, with all the fields in each table, but no other objects. You do not have to enter any data at this time, but you are required to document your work. To do so, pull down the Tools menu, click the Relationships command, define the various relationships, then press the PrintScreen key to capture the screen to the clipboard. Start Word, then paste the contents of the clipboard (containing the relationships diagram) into your Word document. This creates a one-page document that gives you a visual overview of your database. Submit this document to your instructor.

You are also asked to provide detailed documentation for each table. Pull down the Tools menu, click Analyze, then click Documentor. Select Tables in the Object Type drop-down list box, then select all of the tables. Click the Options button, then include for each table the Properties and Relationships but not the Permissions by User and Group. Include for each field Names, Data types, Sizes, and Properties. Do not include any information on indexes. Print the information for each table in the database and submit it to your instructor for review.

Phase III—The User Interface

Phase III focuses on the development of a template, which will be replicated throughout the system. The template, or user interface, is critical to the success of any system as a user spends his or her day in front of the screen. The interface must be functional and it helps if it is visually compelling. We have found that the best way for the group to arrive at a template is for each member to submit a design independently, after which the group can select the best design.

Your template should contain a logo for the project and establish a color scheme. You do *not* have to put actual command buttons on the template, but you are to use the rectangle tool to indicate the placement of the buttons. Use clip art as appropriate, but clip art for the sake of clip art is often juvenile. You may want to use different fonts and/or simple graphics (e.g., horizontal or vertical lines are often quite effective). A simple design is generally the best design.

After the individual templates have been created, they are to be merged into a database, which consists solely of the four individual templates; there will be no tables or other objects in the database. (This is accomplished through the File Import command.) Bring this database to class and be prepared to show off the competing designs for your project. Choose the winning template for your system, then use that design as the basis for the remainder of the project.

Phase IV—Create the Forms and Enter Test Data

Phase IV has you create the forms in which to enter test data based on the template of Phase III. You need a form (or subform) for every table to add, edit, and delete records in that table. You are required, however, to have at least one subform, and you must structure your forms to facilitate data entry in a logical way. All forms should have a consistent look (via a common template).

The forms should be user friendly and display command buttons so that there is no requirement on the part of the end user to know Access. Each form is to include buttons to add, delete, find and print a record, and to close the form. A Help button is a nice touch. Include drop-down list boxes to facilitate data entry in at least two places. The forms should be designed so that they fit on one screen and do not require the user to scroll to access all of the fields and/or the command buttons. Design for the lowest common denominator (e.g., 640 × 480).

Once they have been created, use the forms to enter test data for each table. (Each table should contain 10 to 15 records.) Be sure that the data will adequately test all of the queries and reports that will be in your final system. Submit a print-out of the data in each table to your instructor. (You can print the Datasheet view of each table.) In addition, submit a printed copy of each form to your instructor.

Phase V—Prototyping

Phase V has you develop a "complete" system using the prototyping described in the text. The main menu should be displayed automatically (via an AutoExec macro) when the database is opened, and the user should be able to step through the entire system. The final reports and queries need not be implemented at this time (a "not yet implemented" message is fine at this stage). The user should, however, be able to go from one form to the next, without encountering an error message. Realize, too, that the main menu is not based on a table or query, and thus it should not display the Record Selector and Navigation buttons.

Phase VI—The Completed System

Submit the completed Access database on disk. You will be judged on whether your system actually works; that is, the instructor will enter and/or modify data at random. The effects of the new data should be manifest in the various reports and queries. To obtain a grade of A, you will need to satisfy the following requirements (many of which have been completed) in the earlier phases:

1. Use of the Data Validation and Input Mask properties to validate and facilitate data entry. In addition, at least one table is to contain an AutoNumber field as its primary key.
2. Existing data in all tables, with 10 to 15 records in each table.
3. An AutoExec macro to load the main menu and maximize the window.
4. A help button on one or more screens that displays the name of the group and an appropriate help message (e.g., a phone number).
5. A working form (or subform) for each table in the database so that you can maintain each table. You must have at least one subform in your system. The forms should have a consistent look (via a common template). The system

and especially the forms should make sense; just because you have all of the forms does not mean you satisfy the requirements of the project. Your forms should be designed to facilitate data entry in a logical way.

6. The forms should be user friendly so that there is no requirement on the part of the end user to know Access. Each form is to include buttons to add, delete, find and print a record, and to close the form. Include drop-down list boxes to facilitate data entry in at least two places.

7. All forms should be designed for the lowest common denominator (640 × 480). The screens should be sufficiently compact so that no scrolling is required.

8. Five working reports, at least one of which is a group/total report.

9. Inclusion of a parameter query to drive a form or report.

10. At least one unmatched query and one top-value query.

11. The completed system should be as visually compelling as possible. Clip art for the sake of clip art tends to dilute the desired effect. In general, a consistent logo (one image) is much better from slide to slide than multiple images. No clip art is better than poor clip art or too much clip art.

The Written Document

In addition to demonstrating a working system, you are to submit a written document. The submission of the written project will be an impressive (lengthy) document, but easily generated as much of the material is created directly from Access. The objective is for you to have a project of which you will be proud and something that you can demonstrate in the future. Include the following:

1. Title page plus table (list) of the contents; pages need not be numbered, but please include "loose-leaf" dividers for each section.

2. A one- or two-page description of the system.

3. Technical documentation. Pull down the Tools menu, click Analyze, then click the Documentor command to print the definition of each table. Include the Properties and Relationships, but do *not* include Permissions by User and Group. Choose the option to print the Names, Data types, Sizes, and Properties for each field. Do not print anything for the indexes.

4. Hard copy of each form (one per page).

5. Hard copy of each report (one per page).

6. A working disk.

A Final Word

Throughout the project, you will be working with different versions of your database on different machines. You will also need to share your work with other members of your group. And, of course, you need to back up your work. The floppy disk is the medium of choice but its capacity is only 1.4MB and an Access database can quickly exceed that.

It is important, therefore, that you master certain skills as early as possible. In particular, you should learn how to *compact* an Access database, after which you can take advantage of a *file compression program* to reduce the size even further. You might also explore the use of *FTP* as an alternate means of transferring a file. You should also learn how to separate the data from the other objects in a database to further reduce storage requirements.

PREREQUISITES: ESSENTIALS OF WINDOWS 95

OBJECTIVES

After reading this appendix you will be able to:

1. Describe the objects on the Windows desktop; describe the programs available through the Start button.
2. Explain the function of the minimize, maximize, restore, and close buttons; move and size a window.
3. Discuss the function of a dialog box; describe the elements in a dialog box and the various ways in which information is supplied.
4. Use the Help menu to learn about features in Windows 95; format a floppy disk and implement a screen saver by following instructions from the Help menu.
5. Use the Internet Explorer to access the Internet and download the practice files for the *Exploring Windows* series.
6. Use Windows Explorer to locate a specific file or folder; describe the views available for Windows Explorer.
7. Describe how folders are used to organize a disk; create a new folder; copy and/or move a file from one folder to another.
8. Delete a file, then recover the deleted file from the Recycle Bin.

OVERVIEW

Windows 95 is a computer program (actually many programs) that controls the operation of your computer and its peripherals. *Windows 97* improves on Windows 95 to bring elements of the Internet to the desktop. Windows 97 was not available when we went to press, but we expect it to follow the same conventions as Windows 95. Thus, our introduction applies to both, as it emphasizes the common features of file management in support of Microsoft Office 97. (Microsoft Office runs equally well under Windows 95, Windows 97, or Windows NT.)

One of the most significant benefits of the Windows environment is the common user interface and consistent command structure that is imposed on every Windows application. Once you learn the basic concepts and techniques, you can apply that knowledge to every Windows application. This appendix teaches you those concepts so that you will be able to work productively in the Windows environment. It is written for you, the computer novice, and assumes no previous knowledge about a computer or about Windows. Our goal is to get you "up and running" as quickly as possible so that you can do the work you want to do.

We begin with an introduction to the Windows desktop, the graphical user interface that lets you work in intuitive fashion by pointing at icons and clicking the mouse. We identify the basic components of a window and describe how to execute commands and supply information through various elements in a dialog box. We introduce you to My Computer, an icon that is present on every Windows desktop, then show you how to use My Computer to access the various components of your system.

The appendix also shows you how to manage the hundreds (indeed, thousands) of files that are stored on the typical system. We show you how to create a new folder (the electronic equivalent of a manila folder in a filing cabinet) and how to move or copy a file from one folder to another. We show you how to rename a file, how to delete a file, and how to recover a deleted file from the Recycle Bin.

The appendix also contains four hands-on exercises, which enable you to apply the conceptual discussion in the text at the computer. The exercises are essential to the learn-by-doing philosophy we follow throughout the *Exploring Windows* series.

THE DESKTOP

Windows creates a working environment for your computer that parallels the working environment at home or in an office. You work at a desk. Windows operations take place on the ***desktop.***

There are physical objects on a desk such as folders, a dictionary, a calculator, or a phone. The computer equivalents of those objects appear as ***icons*** (pictorial symbols) on the desktop. Each object on a real desk has attributes (properties) such as size, weight, and color. In similar fashion, Windows assigns properties to every object on its desktop. And just as you can move the objects on a real desk, you can rearrange the objects on the Windows desktop.

Figure 1a displays the desktop when Windows is first installed on a new computer. This desktop has only a few objects and is similar to the desk in a new office, just after you move in. Figure 1b displays a different desktop, one with several open windows, and is similar to a desk during the middle of a working day. Do not be concerned if your Windows desktop is different from ours. Your real desk is arranged differently from those of your friends, and so your Windows desktop will also be different.

The simplicity of the desktop in Figure 1a helps you to focus on what is important. The ***Start button,*** as its name suggests, is where you begin. Click the Start button (mouse operations are described on page 9) and you see a menu that lets you start any program (e.g., Microsoft Word or Microsoft Excel) on your computer. The Start button also contains a ***Help command*** through which you can obtain information about every aspect of Windows.

Each icon on the desktop in Figure 1a provides access to an important function within Windows. ***My Computer*** enables you to browse the disk drives and optional CD-ROM drive that are attached to your computer. ***Network Neighborhood*** extends your view of the computer to include the accessible drives on the network to which your machine is attached, if indeed it is part of a network. (You

Double click to browse disk drives

Double click to access network drives

Double click to recover deleted files

Double click to start the Internet Web browser

Click the Start button to display a menu

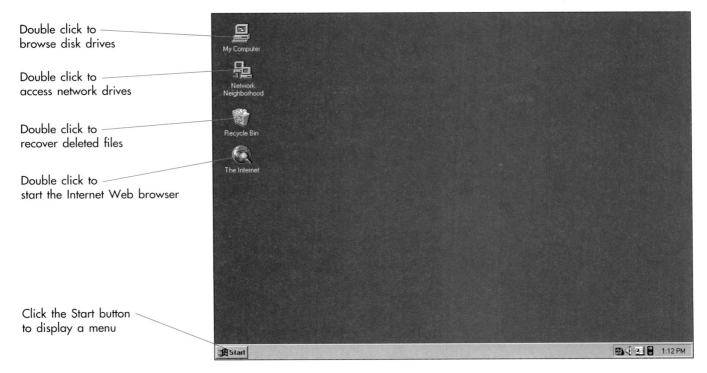

(a) New Desktop

Microsoft Word is in memory

Microsoft Excel is in memory

Internet Web browser is in memory

My Computer is in memory and shows disk drives and folders

Taskbar shows all programs currently in memory

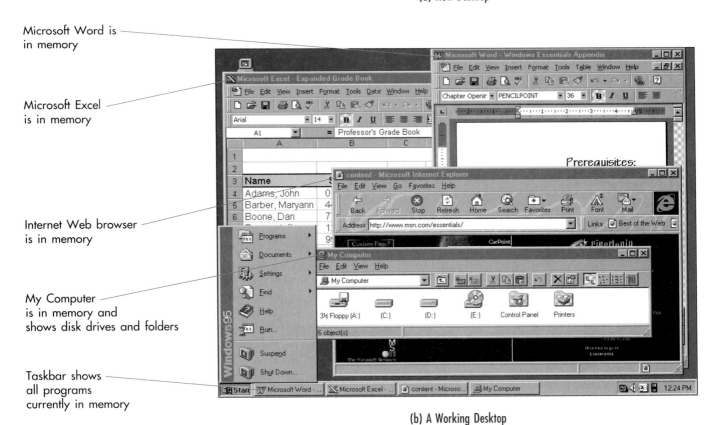

(b) A Working Desktop

FIGURE 1   The Windows Desktop

will not see this icon if you are not connected to a network.) The **Recycle Bin,** described later in the appendix, allows you to recover a file that was previously deleted. Double clicking the **Internet icon** starts the Web browser and initiates a connection to the Internet (assuming you have the necessary hardware).

Each icon on the desktop in Figure 1a opens into a window containing additional objects when you open (double click) the icon. Double click My Computer in Figure 1a, for example, and you see the objects contained in the My Computer window of Figure 2. The contents of the My Computer window depend on the hardware of the specific computer system. Our system, for example, has one floppy drive, two hard (fixed) disks, and a CD-ROM. The My Computer window also contains the Control Panel and Printer folders, which allow access to functions that control other elements in the environment on your computer. (A **folder,** called a directory under MS-DOS, may in turn contain other folders and/or individual files.)

The desktop in Figure 1b contains additional windows that display programs that are currently in use. Each window has a title bar that displays the name of the program and the associated document. You can work in any window as long as you want, then switch to a different window. **Multitasking,** the ability to run several programs at the same time, is one of the major benefits of the Windows environment. It lets you run a word processor in one window, a spreadsheet in a second window, surf the Internet in a third window, play a game in a fourth window, and so on.

The **taskbar** at the bottom of the desktop shows all of the programs that are currently active (open in memory). It contains a button for each open program and lets you switch back and forth between those programs by clicking the appropriate button. The taskbar in Figure 1a does not contain any buttons (other than the Start button) since there are no open applications. The taskbar in Figure 1b, however, contains four additional buttons, one for each open window.

ANATOMY OF A WINDOW

Figure 2 displays two views of the My Computer window and labels its essential elements. Every window has the same components as every other window, which include a title bar, a minimize button, a maximize or restore button, and a close button. Other elements that may be visible include a horizontal and/or vertical scroll bar, a menu bar, a status bar, and a toolbar. Every window also contains additional objects (icons) that pertain specifically to the programs or data associated with that window.

The **title bar** appears at the top of the window and displays the name of the window—for example, My Computer in both Figures 2a and 2b. The icon at the extreme left of the title bar provides access to a control menu that lets you select operations relevant to the window. The **minimize button** shrinks the window to a button on the taskbar. The **maximize button** enlarges the window so that it takes up the entire desktop. The **restore button** (not shown in Figure 2) appears instead of the maximize button after a window has been maximized, and restores the window to its previous size. The **close button** closes the window and removes it from the desktop.

The **menu bar** appears immediately below the title bar and provides access to pull-down menus (as discussed later in the appendix). A **toolbar** appears below the menu bar and lets you execute a command by clicking a button as opposed to pulling down a menu. The **status bar** at the bottom of the window displays information about the window as a whole or about a selected object within a window.

A **vertical** (or **horizontal**) **scroll bar** appears at the right (or bottom) border of a window when its contents are not completely visible and provides access

Close button ─────

Minimize button ─────

Maximize button ─────

Hard drive ─────

CD-ROM drive ─────

Large Icons button ─────

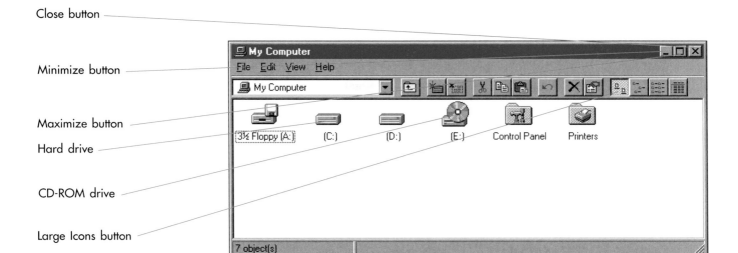

(a) Large Icons View

Close button ─────

Minimize button ─────

Maximize button ─────

Details button ─────

CD-ROM drive ─────

Total size of drive ─────

Remaining space on drive ─────

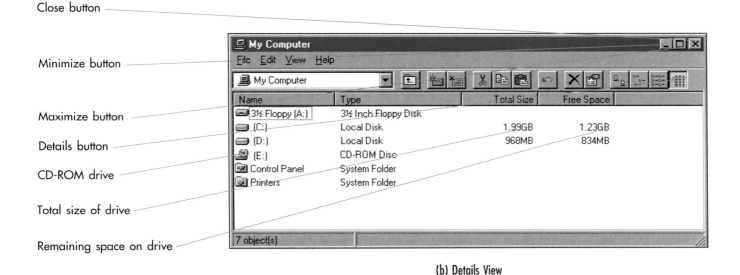

(b) Details View

FIGURE 2   Anatomy of a Window

to the unseen areas. Scroll bars do not appear in Figure 2 since all six objects in the window are visible.

The objects in any window can be displayed in four different views according to your preference or need. The choice between the views depends on your personal preference. You might, for example, choose the **Large Icons view** in Figure 2a if there are only a few objects in the window. The **Details view** in Figure 2b displays additional information about each object including the type of object, the total size of the disk, and the remaining space on the disk. You switch from one view to the next by choosing the appropriate command from the View menu or by clicking the corresponding button on the toolbar.

Moving and Sizing a Window

A window can be sized or moved on the desktop through appropriate actions with the mouse. To *size a window,* point to any border (the mouse pointer changes to a double arrow), then drag the border in the direction you want to go—inward to shrink the window or outward to enlarge it. You can also drag a corner (instead of a border) to change both dimensions at the same time. To **move a window** while retaining its current size, click and drag the title bar to a new position on the desktop.

Pull-down Menus

The menu bar provides access to **pull-down menus** that enable you to execute commands within an application (program). A pull-down menu is accessed by clicking the menu name or by pressing the Alt key plus the underlined letter in the menu name; for example, press Alt+V to pull down the View menu. Three pull-down menus associated with My Computer are shown in Figure 3.

The commands within a menu are executed by clicking the command or by typing the underlined letter (for example, C to execute the Close command in the File menu) once the menu has been pulled down. Alternatively, you can bypass the menu entirely if you know the equivalent keystrokes shown to the right of the command in the menu (e.g., Ctrl+X, Ctrl+C, or Ctrl+V to cut, copy, or paste as shown within the Edit menu).

A **dimmed command** (e.g., the Paste command in the Edit menu) means the command is not currently executable, and that some additional action has to be taken for the command to become available.

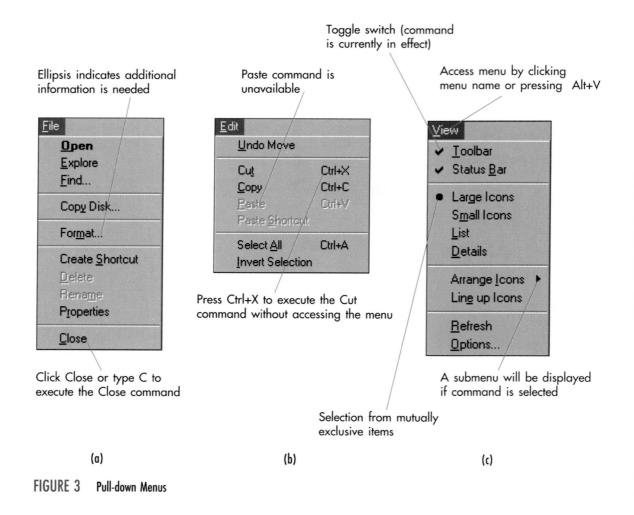

(a)   (b)   (c)

FIGURE 3   Pull-down Menus

An *ellipsis* (...) following a command indicates that additional information is required to execute the command; for example, selection of the Format command in the File menu requires the user to specify additional information about the formatting process. This information is entered into a dialog box (discussed in the next section), which appears immediately after the command has been selected.

A *check* next to a command indicates a toggle switch, whereby the command is either on or off. There is a check next to the Toolbar command in the View menu of Figure 3, which means the command is in effect (and thus the toolbar will be displayed). Click the Toolbar command and the check disappears, which suppresses the display of the toolbar. Click the command a second time and the check reappears, as does the toolbar in the associated window.

A *bullet* next to an item (e.g., Large Icons in Figure 3c) indicates a selection from a set of mutually exclusive choices. Click another option within the group (e.g., Small Icons) and the bullet will disappear from the previous selection (Large Icons) and appear next to the new selection (Small Icons).

An *arrowhead* after a command (e.g., the Arrange icons command in the View menu) indicates that a *submenu* (also known as a cascaded menu) will be displayed with additional menu options.

Dialog Boxes

A *dialog box* appears when additional information is needed to execute a command. The Format command, for example, requires information about which drive to format and the type of formatting desired.

Option (radio) buttons indicate mutually exclusive choices, one of which must be chosen—for example, one of three Format Type options in Figure 4a. Click a button to select an option, which automatically deselects the previously selected option.

Check boxes are used instead of option buttons if the choices are not mutually exclusive or if an option is not required. Multiple boxes can be checked as in Figure 4a, or no boxes may be checked as in Figure 4b. Individual options are selected (cleared) by clicking the appropriate check box.

A *text box* is used to enter descriptive information—for example, Bob's Disk in Figure 4a. A flashing vertical bar (an I-beam) appears within the text box when the text box is active, to mark the *insertion point* for the text you will enter.

A *list box* displays some or all of the available choices, any one of which is selected by clicking the desired item. A *drop-down list box,* such as the Capacity list box in Figure 4a, conserves space by showing only the current selection. Click the arrow of a drop-down list box to display the list of available options. An *open list box,* such as those in Figure 4b, displays multiple choices at one time. (A scroll bar appears within an open list box if some of the choices are not visible and provides access to the hidden choices.)

A *tabbed dialog box* provides multiple sets of options. The dialog box in Figure 4c, for example, has two tabs, each with its own set of options. Click either tab (the General tab is currently selected) to display the associated options.

The *What's This button* (a question mark at the right end of the title bar) provides help for any item in the dialog box. Click the button, then click the item in the dialog box for which you want additional information. The *Close button* (the X at the extreme right of the title bar) closes the dialog box.

All dialog boxes also contain one or more *command buttons,* the functions of which are generally apparent from the specific button's name. The Start button, in Figure 4a, for example, initiates the formatting process. The OK command button in Figure 4b accepts the settings and closes the dialog box. The Cancel button does just the opposite—it ignores (cancels) any changes made to the settings, then closes the dialog box without further action.

Click here to see other options

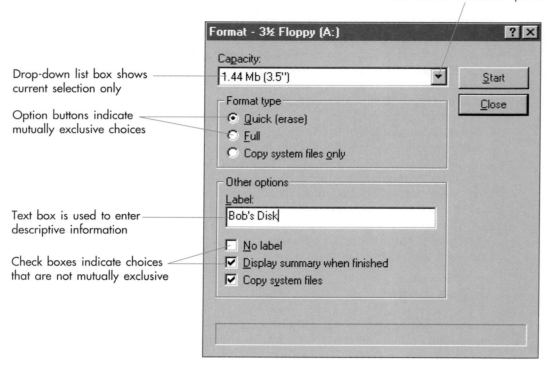

Drop-down list box shows current selection only

Option buttons indicate mutually exclusive choices

Text box is used to enter descriptive information

Check boxes indicate choices that are not mutually exclusive

(a) Option Boxes and Check Boxes

Command buttons

Open list box displays multiple options

Scroll bar indicates that not all options are visible

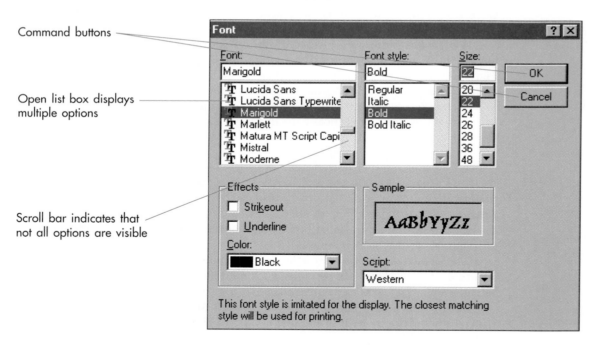

(b) List Boxes

FIGURE 4   Dialog Boxes

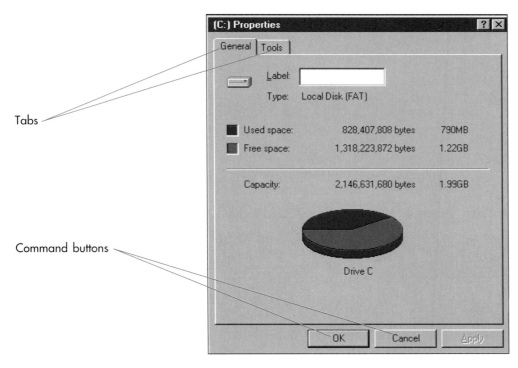

Tabs

Command buttons

(c) Tabbed Dialog Box

FIGURE 4   Dialog Boxes (continued)

THE MOUSE

The mouse is indispensable to Windows and is referenced continually in the hands-on exercises throughout the text. There are four basic operations with which you must become familiar:

- To *point* to an object, move the mouse pointer over the object.
- To *click* an object, point to it, then press and release the left mouse button; to *right click* an object, point to the object, then press and release the right mouse button.
- To *double click* an object, point to it, then quickly click the left button twice in succession.
- To *drag* an object, move the pointer to the object, then press and hold the left button while you move the mouse to a new position.

The mouse is a pointing device—move the mouse on your desk and the *mouse pointer,* typically a small arrowhead, moves on the monitor. The mouse pointer assumes different shapes according to the location of the pointer or the nature of the current action. You will see a double arrow when you change the size of a window, an I-beam as you insert text, a hand to jump from one help topic to the next, or a circle with a line through it to indicate that an attempted action is invalid.

The mouse pointer will also change to an hourglass to indicate that Windows is processing your command, and that no further commands may be issued until the action is completed. The more powerful your computer, the less frequently the hourglass will appear, and conversely, the less powerful your system, the more you see the hourglass.

THE MICROSOFT INTELLIMOUSE

Microsoft has created a new mouse for Office 97. The mouse contains a wheel between the left and right buttons, allowing you to scroll through a document by rotating the wheel forward or back. You can also increase (or decrease) the magnification by holding the Ctrl key as you rotate the wheel on the mouse. Additional information is available from the IntelliPoint Online User's Guide. (Click the Start button, point to Programs, point to Microsoft Input Devices, and then point to Mouse.)

The *Mouse* Versus the Keyboard

Almost every command in Windows can be executed by using either the mouse or the keyboard. Most people start with the mouse but add keyboard shortcuts as they become more proficient. There is no right or wrong technique, just different techniques, and the one you choose depends entirely on personal preference in a specific situation. If, for example, your hands are already on the keyboard, it is faster to use the keyboard equivalent. Other times, your hand will be on the mouse and that will be the fastest way.

In the beginning, you may wonder why there are so many different ways to do the same thing, but you will eventually recognize the many options as part of Windows' charm. It is not necessary to memorize anything, nor should you even try; just be flexible and willing to experiment. The more you practice, the sooner all of this will become second nature to you.

THE HELP MENU

Windows has an extensive *Help menu* that contains information about virtually every topic in Windows. We believe that the best time to learn about Help is when you begin your study of Windows. Help is available at any time, and is accessed most easily by clicking the *Help command* on the Start menu, which displays the Help Topics dialog box in Figure 5.

The *Contents tab* in Figure 5a is similar to the table of contents in an ordinary book. The major topics are represented by books, each of which can be opened to display additional topics. These topics may be viewed and/or printed to access the indicated information.

The *Index tab* in Figure 5b is analogous to the index of an ordinary book. Type the first several letters of the topic you want to look up, click the topic when it appears in the window, then click the Display button to view the information. The Help screens are task-specific and provide easy-to-follow instructions.

The *Find tab* (not shown in Figure 5) contains a more extensive listing of entries than does the Index tab. It lets you enter a specific word (or Windows term), then it returns every Help screen that contains that word.

MICROSOFT ON THE WEB

The Microsoft Web site provides information beyond that found in the Help menu. Go to the Microsoft home page (www.microsoft.com), then click the Support tab where you choose the application. You will find articles about new features in the application, answers to frequently asked questions, as well as the knowledge base used by Microsoft support engineers.

Contents tab is selected —————

Books represent —
major topics

Open book displays —————
more specific topics

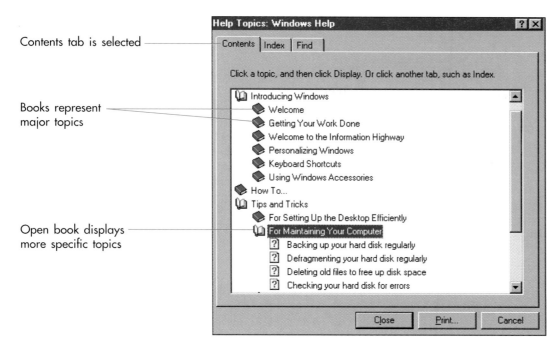

(a) Contents Tab

Index tab is selected —————

Type first letters of topic —————

Click desired topic —————

Click Display button —————

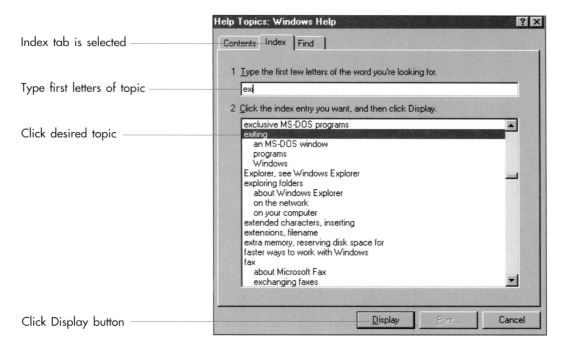

(b) Index Tab

FIGURE 5   The Help Command

FORMATTING A FLOPPY DISK

You will soon begin to work on the computer, which means that you will be using various applications to create different types of documents. Each document is saved in its own file and stored on disk, either on a hard disk (e.g., drive C) if you have your own computer, or on a floppy disk (drive A) if you are working in a computer lab at school.

Even if you have your own machine, however, you will want to copy files from the hard disk to a floppy disk for backup. Thus, you need to purchase a floppy disk(s), and further, you need to format the floppy disk so that it will be able to store the files you create. (You can purchase preformatted floppy disks, but it is very easy to format your own, and we provide instructions in the hands-on exercise that follows.) Be aware, however, that formatting erases any data that was previously on a disk, so be careful not to format a disk with important data (e.g., one containing today's homework assignment).

Formatting is accomplished through the *Format command.* The process is straightforward and has you enter all of the necessary information into a dialog box. One of the box's options is to copy system files onto the disk while formatting it. These files are necessary to start (boot) your computer, and if your hard disk were to fail, you would need a floppy disk with the system (and other) files in order to start the machine. (See Help for information on creating a *boot disk* containing the system files.) For ordinary purposes, however, you do not put the system files on a floppy disk because they take up space you could use to store data.

FORMAT AT THE PROPER CAPACITY

A floppy disk should be formatted at its rated capacity or else you may be unable to read the disk. There are two types of 3½-inch disks, double-density (720KB) and high-density (1.44MB). The easiest way to determine the type of disk you have is to look at the disk itself for the label DD or HD, for double- and high-density, respectively. You can also check the number of square holes in the disk; a double-density disk has one, whereas a high-density disk has two.

LEARNING BY DOING

Learning is best accomplished by doing, and so we come to the first of four hands-on exercises in this appendix. The exercises enable you to apply the concepts you have learned, then extend those concepts to further exploration on your own. The exercise welcomes you to Windows 95, shows you how to open, move, and size a window on the desktop, how to format a floppy disk, and how to use Help to install a screen saver.

A *screen saver* is a special program that protects your monitor by producing a constantly changing pattern after a designated period of inactivity. It is a delightful way to personalize your computer and an excellent illustration of how the Help menu can aid you in accomplishing a specific task. The answer to almost everything you need to know is found in one type of help or another. Start with the Help menu, then go to the Microsoft web site (www.microsoft.com) if you need additional information.

Welcome to Windows

Objective: To turn on the computer and start Windows; to use the Help facility; to open, move, and size a window; and to format a floppy disk. Use Figure 6 as a guide in the exercise.

STEP 1: Start the Computer

➤ The floppy drive should be empty prior to starting your machine. This ensures that the system starts by reading files from the hard disk (which contains the Windows files) as opposed to a floppy disk (which does not).

➤ The number and location of the on/off switches depend on the nature and manufacturer of the devices connected to the computer. The easiest possible setup is when all components of the system are plugged into a surge protector, in which case only a single switch has to be turned on. In any event, turn on the monitor, printer, and system unit.

➤ Your system will take a minute or so to get started after which you should see the desktop in Figure 6a. Do not be concerned if the appearance of your desktop is different from ours.

➤ You may see additional objects on the desktop in Windows 95 and/or the active desktop content in Windows 97.

Click the Start button
to see a menu

(a) Start the Computer (step 1)

FIGURE 6   Hands-on Exercise 1

STEP 2: Open My Computer

➤ Point to the **My Computer icon,** click the **right mouse button,** then click the **Open command** from the shortcut menu. (Alternatively, you can double click the icon to open it directly.)

➤ My Computer will open into a window as shown in Figure 6b. Do not be concerned if the contents of your window or its size and position on the desktop are different from ours.

➤ Pull down the **View menu** (point to the menu and click). Make or verify the following selections (you have to pull down the menu each time you choose a different command):

  • The **Toolbar command** should be checked. The Toolbar command functions as a toggle switch. Click the command and the toolbar is displayed; click the command a second time and the toolbar disappears.

  • The **Status bar command** should be checked. The status bar command also functions as a toggle switch.

  • **Large Icons** should be selected as the current view.

➤ Click the **Details button** on the toolbar to change to this view. Click the **Large Icons button** to return to this view.

➤ Pull down the **View menu** a final time. Click the **Arrange Icons command** and (if necessary) click the **AutoArrange command** so that a check appears.

➤ Click outside the menu (or press the **Esc key**) if the command is already checked.

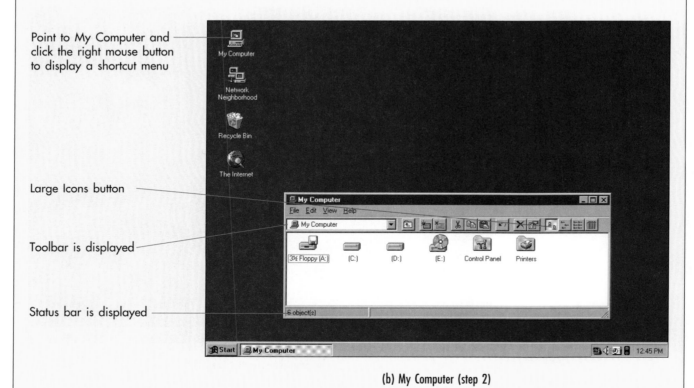

Point to My Computer and click the right mouse button to display a shortcut menu

Large Icons button

Toolbar is displayed

Status bar is displayed

(b) My Computer (step 2)

FIGURE 6   Hands-on Exercise 1 (continued)

DESIGNATING THE DEVICES ON A SYSTEM

The first (usually only) floppy drive is always designated as drive A. (A second floppy drive, if it were present, would be drive B.) The first (often only) hard disk on a system is always drive C, whether or not there are one or two floppy drives. A system with one floppy drive and one hard disk (today's most common configuration) will contain icons for drive A and drive C. Additional hard drives (if any) and/or the CD-ROM are labeled from D on.

STEP 3: Move and Size a Window

➤ Click the **maximize button** so that the My Computer window expands to fill the entire screen.

➤ Click the **restore button** (which replaces the maximize button and is not shown in Figure 6c) to return the window to its previous size.

➤ Click the **minimize button** to shrink the My Computer window to a button on the taskbar. Click the My Computer button to reopen the window.

➤ Move and size the My Computer window on your desk to match the display in Figure 6c:

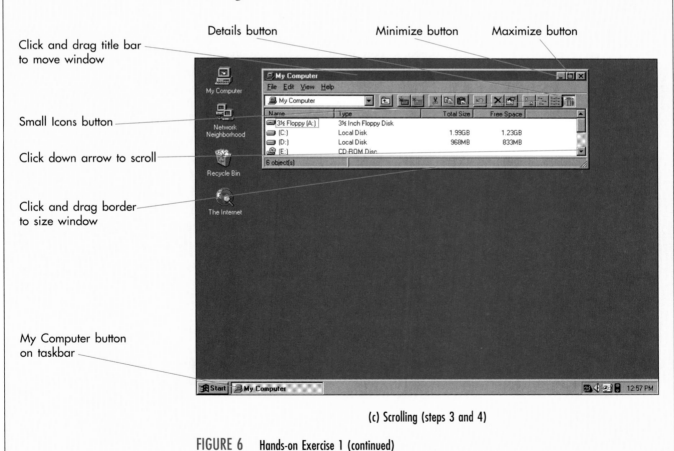

(c) Scrolling (steps 3 and 4)

FIGURE 6   Hands-on Exercise 1 (continued)

- To change the width or height of the window, click and drag a border (the mouse pointer changes to a double arrow) in the direction you want to go; drag the border inward to shrink the window or outward to enlarge it.
- To change the width and height at the same time, click and drag a corner rather than a border.
- To change the position of the window, click and drag the title bar.

➤ Click the **minimize button** to shrink the My Computer window to a button on the taskbar. My Computer is still open and remains active in memory.
➤ Click the **My Computer button** on the taskbar to reopen the window.

THE CONTROL PANEL

The Control Panel contains the utility programs (tools) used to change the hardware and/or software settings for the devices on your system (e.g., modem, monitor, mouse, and so on). Double click the Control Panel icon within My Computer to open the Control Panel window, then double click the icon of the device whose settings you want to modify. Additional information can be obtained through the Help facility.

STEP 4: Scrolling

➤ Pull down the **View menu** and click **Details** (or click the Details button on the toolbar). You are now in the Details view as shown in Figure 6c.
➤ If necessary, click and drag the bottom border of the window inward so that you see the vertical scroll bar in Figure 6c. The scroll bar indicates that the contents of the window are not completely visible.
➤ Click the **down arrow** on the scroll bar. The top line (for drive A) disappears from view and a new line containing the Control Panel comes into view.
➤ Click the **down arrow** a second time, which brings the Printers folder into view at the bottom of the window as the icon for drive C scrolls off the screen.
➤ Click the **Small icons** button on the toolbar. The scroll bar disappears because the contents of the window become completely visible.
➤ Click the **Details button** on the toolbar. The scroll bar returns because you can no longer see the complete contents. Move and/or size the window to your personal preference.

SCREENTIPS

Point to any button on the toolbar and Windows displays a ScreenTip containing the name of the button, which is indicative of its function. You can also point to other objects on the desktop to see similar ScreenTips. Point to the clock at the right end of the taskbar, for example, and you will see a ScreenTip with today's date. Point to the Start button and you will see a ScreenTip telling you to click here to begin.

STEP 5: Online Help

➤ Click the **Start button** on the taskbar, then click the **Help command** to display the Help Topics dialog box in Figure 6d.

➤ Click the **Index tab** as shown in Figure 6d. Type **For** (the first letters in formatting, the topic you are searching for). The Help system automatically displays the topics beginning with the letters you enter.

➤ Click **Disks** (under formatting) from the list of displayed topics, then click the **Display command button** (or double click the topic to avoid having to click the command button).

➤ The Help Topics dialog box is replaced by a Windows Help window with instructions on how to format a floppy disk.

Index tab

Type For

Click to select disks from list of topics

Start button

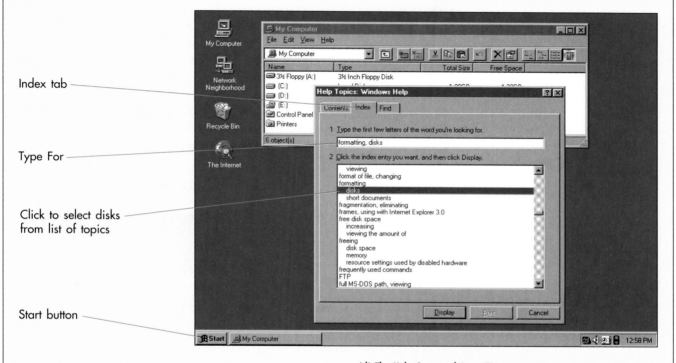

(d) The Help Command (step 5)

FIGURE 6   Hands-on Exercise 1 (continued)

PRINT THE HELP TOPIC

You can print the contents of any Help window by pointing anywhere within the window and clicking the right mouse button to display a shortcut menu. Click Print Topic, then click the OK command button in the resulting dialog box to print the topic.

STEP 6: Format a Floppy Disk

➤ Place a floppy disk in drive A. Remember, formatting erases everything on the disk, so be sure that you do not need anything on the disk you are about to format. Read the instructions in the Help window in Figure 6.3e, then follow our instructions, which provide more detail.

➤ Click the icon for **drive A.** Pull down the **File menu** and click **Format.** You will see the dialog box in Figure 6e.

• Set the **Capacity** to match the floppy disk you purchased (1.44MB for a high-density disk and 720KB for a double-density disk).

• Click the **Full option button** to choose a full format. This option is well worth the extra time as it ensures the integrity of your disk.

• Click the **Label text box** if it's empty or click and drag over the existing label if there is an entry. Enter a new label (containing up to 11 characters) such as **Bob's Disk** as shown in Figure 6e.

• Click the **Start command button** to begin the formatting operation. This will take about a minute and you can see the progress of the formatting process at the bottom of the dialog box.

➤ After the formatting process is complete, you will see an informational dialog box with the results of the formatting operation. Read the information, then click the **Close command button** to close the informational dialog box.

➤ Close the Format dialog box. Close the Help window.

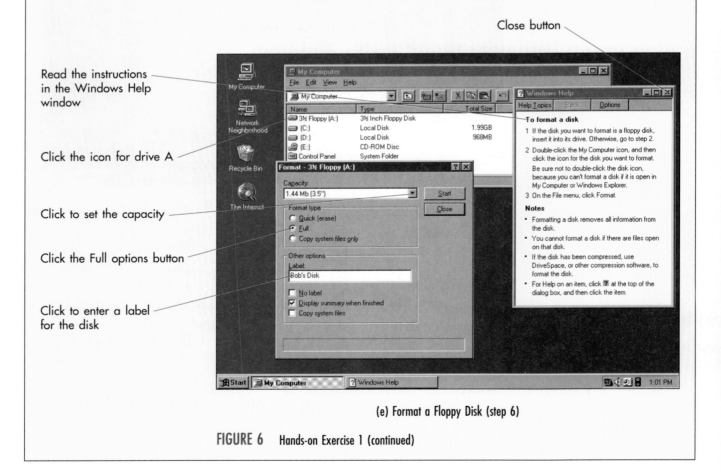

(e) Format a Floppy Disk (step 6)

FIGURE 6 Hands-on Exercise 1 (continued)

STEP 7: Implement a Screen Saver

➤ If you are working in a lab environment, it is possible that your network administrator has disabled the ability to implement a screen saver, and that you will be unable to complete this step. If this is true at your site, skip the instructions below and go to step 8.

➤ Click the **Start button,** click the **Help command** to display the Help Topics dialog box, then click the **Index tab.** Type **Scr** (the first letters in *screen,* the topic you are searching for).

➤ Click **Screen Savers** from the list of displayed topics, then click the **Display button.** (You can also double click the topic to avoid having to click the command button.)

➤ You will see a second dialog box listing the available topics under Screen Savers. **Double click** the topic that begins **Protecting your screen.** You should see the Help window in Figure 6f. Click the **shortcut jump button** to display the Display Properties dialog box.

➤ Click the **drop-down arrow** in the Screen Saver box to display the available screen savers. Click one or more of the available screen savers until you come to one you like.

➤ Click the **OK command button** to accept the screen saver and exit the dialog box. Click the **Close button** to close the Windows Help window.

STEP 8: Exit Windows

➤ Click the **Start button,** then click the **Shut Down command.** You will see a dialog box asking whether you're sure that you want to shut down the computer. (The option button to shut down the computer is already selected.)

➤ Click the **Yes command button,** then wait as Windows gets ready to shut down your system. Wait until you see another screen indicating that it is OK to turn off the computer.

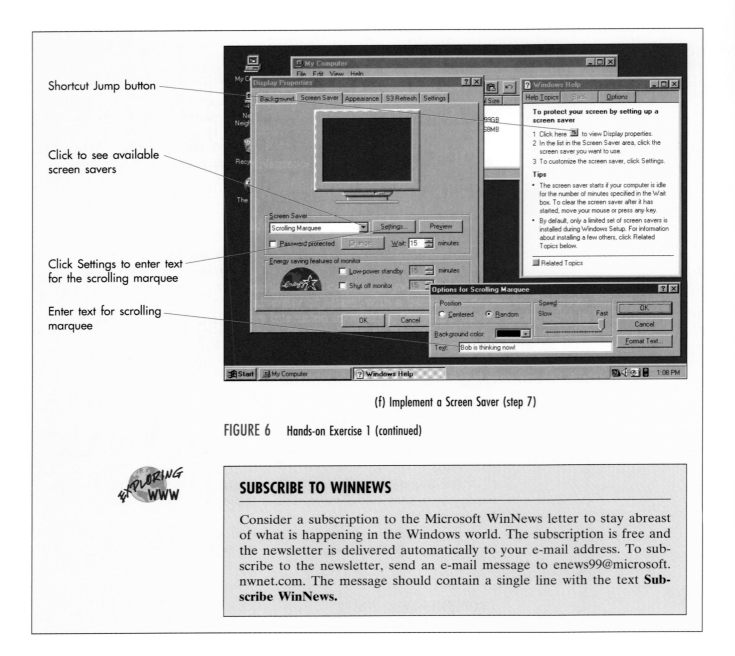

Shortcut Jump button

Click to see available screen savers

Click Settings to enter text for the scrolling marquee

Enter text for scrolling marquee

(f) Implement a Screen Saver (step 7)

FIGURE 6   Hands-on Exercise 1 (continued)

SUBSCRIBE TO WINNEWS

Consider a subscription to the Microsoft WinNews letter to stay abreast of what is happening in the Windows world. The subscription is free and the newsletter is delivered automatically to your e-mail address. To subscribe to the newsletter, send an e-mail message to enews99@microsoft.nwnet.com. The message should contain a single line with the text **Subscribe WinNews.**

FILES AND FOLDERS

The ultimate purpose of any computer system is to do useful work. This, in turn, requires the acquisition of various application software, such as Microsoft Office. Each document, spreadsheet, presentation, or database that you create is stored in a file on a disk, be it a hard disk or a floppy disk. It is important, therefore, that you understand the basics of file management so that you will be able to retrieve these files at a later time.

A *file* is data that has been given a name and stored on disk. There are, in general, two types of files, *program files* and *data files.* Microsoft Word and Microsoft Excel are program files. The documents and spreadsheets created by these programs are data files. A *program file* is executable because it contains instructions that tell the computer what to do. A *data file* is not executable and can be used only in conjunction with a specific program.

A file must have a name so that it can be identified. The file name can contain up to 255 characters and may include spaces and other punctuation. (This is very different from the rules that existed under MS-DOS, which limited file names to eight characters followed by an optional three-character extension.) Long file names permit descriptive entries such as *Term Paper for Western Civilization* (as opposed to a more cryptic *TPWCIV* that would be required under MS-DOS).

Files are stored in **folders** to better organize the hundreds (often thousands) of files on a hard disk. A Windows folder is similar in concept to a manila folder in a filing cabinet and contains one or more documents (files) that are somehow related to each other. An office worker stores his or her documents in manila folders. In Windows, you store your data files (documents) in electronic folders on disk.

Folders are the key to the Windows storage system. You can create any number of folders to hold your work just as you can place any number of manila folders into a filing cabinet. You can create one folder for your word processing documents and a different folder for your spreadsheets. Alternatively, you can create a folder to hold all of your work for a specific class, which may contain a combination of word processing documents and spreadsheets. The choice is entirely up to you and you can use any system that makes sense to you. Anything at all can go into a folder—program files, data files, even other folders.

Figure 7 displays two views of a folder containing six documents. The name of the folder (Homework) appears in the title bar next to the icon of an open folder. The minimize, maximize, and close buttons appear at the right of the title bar. A toolbar appears below the menu bar in each view.

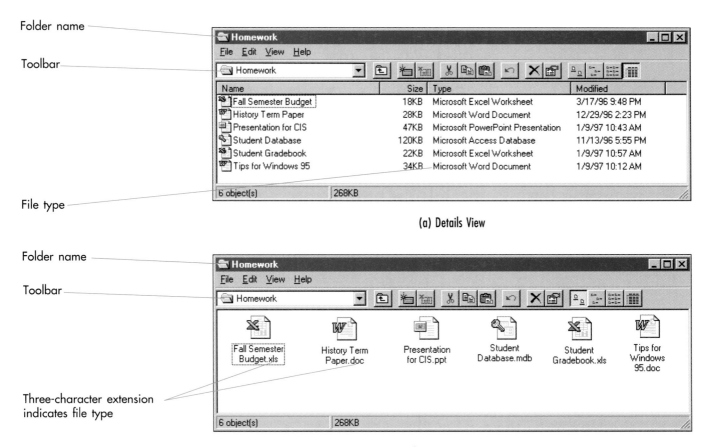

(a) Details View

(b) Large Icons View

FIGURE 7   The Homework Folder

The Details view in Figure 7a displays a small icon representing the application that created the file. It also shows the name of each file in the folder (note the descriptive file name), the file size, the type of file, and the date and time the file was last modified. Figure 7b illustrates the Large Icons view, which displays only the file name and an icon representing the application that created the file. The choice between views depends on your personal preference. (A Small Icons view and List view are also available.)

File Type

Every data file has a specific *file type* that is determined by the application used to create the file. One way to recognize the file type is to examine the Type column in the Details view as shown in Figure 7a. The History Term Paper, for example, is a Microsoft Word document. The Student Gradebook is a Microsoft Excel worksheet.

You can also determine the file type (or associated application) from any view by examining the application icon displayed next to the file name. Look carefully at the icon next to the History Term Paper in Figure 7a, for example, and you will recognize the icon for Microsoft Word. The application icon is recognized more easily in the Large Icons view in Figure 7b.

Still another way to determine the file type is through a three-character extension, which is appended to the file name. (A period separates the filename from the extension.) Each application has a unique extension that is automatically assigned to the file name when the file is created. DOC and XLS, for example, are the extensions for Microsoft Word and Excel, respectively. The extension may be suppressed or displayed according to an option in the View menu of My Computer (or the Windows Explorer), but is best left suppressed in Windows 95/97.

My Computer

It is important to be able to locate a folder and/or its documents so that you can retrieve a document and go to work. Assume, for example, that you are looking for a term paper in American History that you began yesterday and saved in a folder called Homework. You know the folder is somewhere on drive C, but you are not quite sure where. You need to locate the folder in order to open the term paper and continue working. One way to accomplish this is through My Computer as shown in Figure 8.

You begin by double clicking the My Computer icon on the desktop to open the My Computer window and display the devices on your system. Next, you double click the icon for drive C since it contains the folder you are looking for. This opens a second window, which displays all of the folders on drive C. And finally, you double click the icon for the Homework folder to open a third window containing the documents in the Homework folder. Once in the Homework folder, you can double click the icon of an existing document, which starts the associated application and opens the document, enabling you to begin work.

The Exploring Windows Practice Files

There is only one way to master Windows 95 and that is to practice at the computer. One of the most important skills you need to acquire is that of file management; that is, you must be proficient in moving and copying files from one drive (or folder) to another. To do so requires that you have a series of files with which to work. Accordingly, we have created a set of practice files that we reference in the next several hands-on exercises. Your instructor will make these files available to you in a variety of ways:

Double click My Computer ——

Double click icon for drive C ——

Double click the Homework folder ——

Double click document name to start associated application and open the document ——

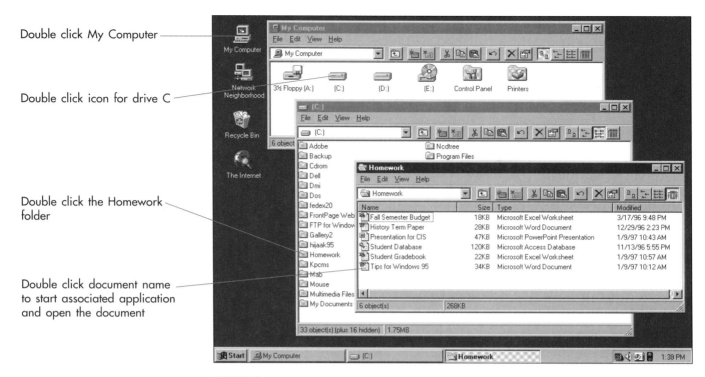

FIGURE 8   Browsing My Computer

- The files can be downloaded from our Web site, as described in the next hands-on exercise. This assumes you have access to the Internet, and further, that you have a basic proficiency with a browser such as the *Internet Explorer.*
- The files might be on a network drive, in which case you can use My Computer (or the Windows Explorer, which is discussed later in the chapter) to copy the files from the network drive to a floppy disk. The procedure to do this is described in hands-on exercise 3 later in the chapter.
- There may be an actual data disk in the computer lab. Go to the lab with a floppy disk, then use the Copy Disk command to duplicate the data disk to create a copy for yourself.

It doesn't matter how you obtain the practice files, only that you are able to do so. Indeed, you may try different techniques in order to gain additional practice with the Windows environment. All three methods will place the practice files on a floppy disk; hence you need the formatted floppy disk that was created in the first hands-on exercise. Note, too, the techniques described in the hands-on exercises apply to the practice files for any book in the *Exploring Windows* series.

THE EXPLORING WINDOWS SERIES

The text you are reading is one of several books in the *Exploring Windows* series, many of which reference a series of practice files for use with the hands-on exercises. One way to access these files is from the Prentice Hall Web site at www.prenhall.com/grauer. You can also go to Bob Grauer's home page (www.bus.miami.edu/~rgrauer) and click the *Exploring Windows* link. Bob's home page also provides links to the classes he is teaching at the University of Miami.

The Practice Files (via the World Wide Web)

Objective: To download the practice files from the *Exploring Windows* Web site. The exercise requires a formatted floppy disk and access to the Internet. Use Figure 9 as a guide in the exercise.

STEP 1: The *Exploring Windows* Series

➤ Start Internet Explorer. If you are working in class, your instructor will provide additional instructions. At home, however, it is incumbent on you to be able to know how to access the Internet.

➤ If necessary, click the **maximize button** so that the Internet Explorer takes the entire desktop. Enter the address of the site you want to visit as shown in Figure 9a.

   • Pull down the **File menu,** click the **Open command** to display the Open dialog box, and enter **www.prenhall.com/grauer** (the http:// is assumed). Click **OK.**

   • *Or,* click in the **Address box** below the toolbar, which automatically selects the current address (so that whatever you type replaces the current address). Enter the address of the site you want to visit, **www.prenhall. com/grauer** (the http:// is assumed). Press the **enter key.**

➤ You should see the *Exploring Windows* home page as shown in Figure 9a. Click the book **Exploring Office 97** to display the page for this series. Click the link to **Office 97.**

Enter the address of the site you want to visit

Click the link to Office 97

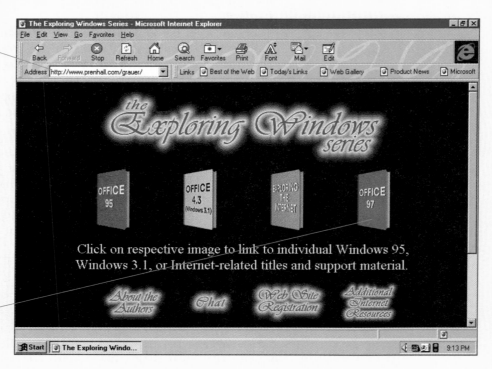

(a) The *Exploring Windows* series (step 1)

FIGURE 9   Hands-on Exercise 2

UNABLE TO LOCATE SERVER OR SERVER NOT RESPONDING

Two things must occur in order for Internet Explorer to display the requested document—it must locate the server on which the document is stored, and it must be able to connect to that computer. The error message "Unable to Locate Server" will appear if you enter the Web address incorrectly. Click the Address bar and re-enter the Web address, being sure to enter it correctly. You may also see the message "Server Down or Not Responding," which implies that Internet Explorer located the server but was unable to connect because the site is busy. This means that too many visitors are already there and you need to try again later in the day.

STEP 2: Download the Practice Files

➤ You should see a screen listing the various books for Office 97. Click the link to **Windows Prerequisites** to display the screen in Figure 9b. (The Save As dialog box is not yet visible.)

➤ Click **prerequisites.exe** (the file you will download to your PC). The File Download window opens, and after a few seconds, an Internet Explorer dialog box opens as well. The option button to **Save it to disk** is selected. Click **OK** to display the Save As dialog box in Figure 9b:

• The **desktop** is selected as the destination in the Save in box. If this is not the case, click the **drop-down arrow** on the Save in box and select the desktop. Click **Save** to download the file.

(b) Download the Practice Files (step 2)

FIGURE 9   Hands-on Exercise 2 (continued)

- If you are unable to save to the desktop because your network administrator has disabled this capability at your site, select drive A in the Save in box instead of the desktop (place a formatted floppy disk in drive A).

➤ The File Download window will reappear on your screen and show you the process of the downloading operation. Be patient, as this may take a few minutes. (The Exploring Prerequisites file is 52KB in size.) The File Download window will close automatically when downloading is complete.

➤ Minimize (do not close) Internet Explorer. The Internet Explorer window shrinks to a button on the taskbar, but the application remains open in memory. (We return to Internet Explorer in step 5.)

ABOUT INTERNET EXPLORER

Pull down the Help menu and click About Internet Explorer to see which version of the Internet Explorer you are using. Our exercises were done with Version 3.00, but you may have a later version if you installed the software after publication of our text. The command structure may vary slightly from one version to the next, but you should be able to complete the exercise without a problem, as long as you are running Version 3.00 or higher.

STEP 3: Install the Practice Files

➤ Double click the **Prerequisites icon** from the desktop or drive A, depending on where you downloaded the file.

- If you downloaded the file to the desktop, the Prerequisites icon should be visible on the desktop and you can simply double click the icon.

- If you downloaded the file to a floppy disk, double click the **My Computer icon** on the desktop to open the My Computer window, double click the icon for **drive A,** then double click the **Prerequisites icon.**

➤ You will see a dialog box thanking you for selecting the *Exploring Windows* series. Click **OK** when you have finished reading the dialog box to begin (or cancel) the installation.

FILE COMPRESSION

Software and other files are typically compressed to reduce the amount of storage space a file requires on disk and/or the time it takes to download the file. In essence, you download a compressed file from a Web site, then you uncompress the file on a local drive. Ideally a compressed file is created as a self-extracting (executable) file as opposed to a zip file, which requires a utility program outside Windows 95. Our files are executable. Thus, all you have to do is double click the executable file after it has been downloaded, and it will automatically install (uncompress) the practice files for you.

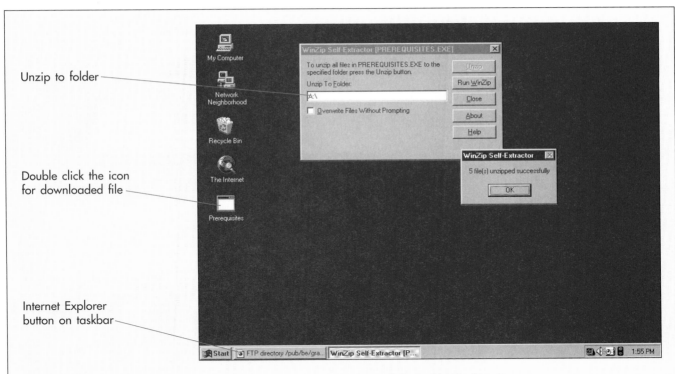

Unzip to folder

Double click the icon
for downloaded file

Internet Explorer
button on taskbar

(c) Install the Practice Files (step 3)

FIGURE 9   Hands-on Exercise 2 (continued)

➤ If necessary, place a floppy disk in drive A, then verify that the Unzip to Folder text box is specified as A:\ (the floppy disk). If it is not, enter **A:** in the text box as shown in Figure 9c.

➤ Click the **Unzip button** to extract the practice files and copy them into the designated folder.

➤ Click **OK** after you see the message indicating that the files have been unzipped successfully. Close the WinZip dialog box.

➤ The practice files have been extracted and copied to drive A.

STEP 4: Open My Computer

➤ Double click **My Computer** to open the My Computer window in Figure 9d. If necessary, pull down the **View menu** to display the toolbar. Click the **Large Icons view.**

➤ Double click the icon for **drive A** to open a second window, which displays the contents of drive A. Use the **View menu** to display the toolbar, then change to the **Details view.**

➤ You should see five files, which are the practice files on the data disk. (There are three Word files, one Excel file, and one PowerPoint file.) These are the files that will be used in a hands-on exercise later in the chapter.

➤ Select (click) the **Prerequisites icon** on the desktop. Press the **Del key** to erase this file as it is no longer needed. Click **Yes** when asked whether to remove this file.

➤ Close the windows for drive A and My Computer as they are no longer needed in this exercise.

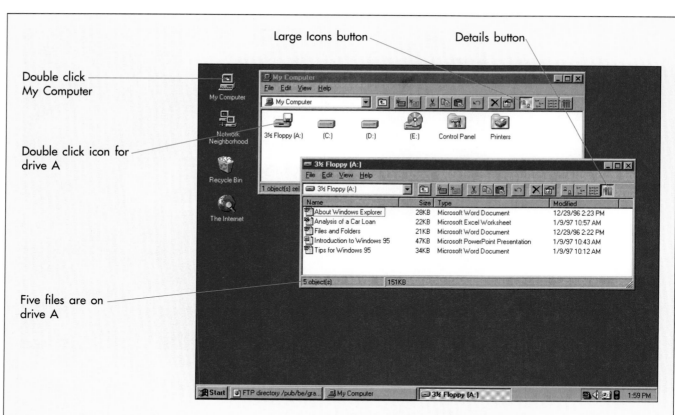

Large Icons button

Details button

Double click My Computer

Double click icon for drive A

Five files are on drive A

(d) Open My Computer (step 4)

FIGURE 9   Hands-on Exercise 2 (continued)

ONE WINDOW OR MANY

By default, My Computer opens a new window every time you open a new drive or folder. The multiple windows can clutter a desktop rather quickly, and hence you may prefer to change the display in the current window to the new drive or folder rather than open a new window. Pull down the View menu, click Options, click the Folder tab, then click the option button to browse folders using a single window.

STEP 5: Microsoft on the Web

➤ Click the **Internet Explorer button** on the taskbar to return to Internet Explorer. Click in the **Address box** below the toolbar. Enter **www.microsoft. com** Press the **enter key.**

➤ You should see Microsoft's home page. Click the link to **Products,** then scroll until you can click the link to **Windows 95** to display the page in Figure 9e.

➤ Your screen will be different from ours, as Microsoft is continually updating its information. Click any links that appeal to you to view additional information that is available from Microsoft via the Web.

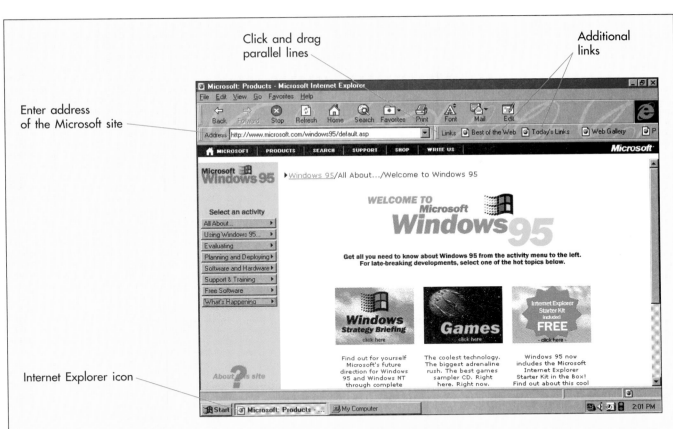

Click and drag parallel lines

Additional links

Enter address of the Microsoft site

Internet Explorer icon

(e) Windows 95 Home Page (step 5)

FIGURE 9   Hands-on Exercise 2 (continued)

➤ You may also want to view additional sites suggested by Internet Explorer. If necessary, click and drag the parallel lines that appear to the right of the address box (the mouse pointer changes to a two-headed arrow) to display additional links.

➤ Click the **Best of the Web** or the **Today's Links button** to explore the current cool sites suggested by Internet Explorer.

➤ We don't know what you will find, but you can expect something interesting every day.

➤ Click the hyperlinks that interest you and off you go. Happy surfing!

SET A TIME LIMIT

We warn you that the Web is addictive, and that once you start surfing, it is difficult to stop. We suggest, therefore, that you set a time limit before you begin, and that you stick to it. Tomorrow is another day, with new places to explore.

One of the most important skills you need to acquire is the ability to locate a specific folder or file so that you can go to work. In essence you need to be able to copy, move, rename, and even delete the various files and folders on your system. There are two basic ways to accomplish these tasks. You can use My Computer to open successive windows until you come to the file or folder you are looking for. Alternatively, you can use the **Windows Explorer** to locate the object by navigating the hierarchical structure of your system. The difference between the two is shown in Figure 10.

Assume, for example, that you are taking five classes this semester, and that you are using the computer in each course. You've created a separate folder to hold the work for each class and have stored the contents of all five folders on a single floppy disk. Assume further that you need to retrieve your third English assignment so that you can modify it and submit the revised version.

You can use My Computer to browse the system as shown in Figure 10a. You would start by opening My Computer, double clicking the icon for drive A to open a second window, then double clicking the icon for the English folder to display its documents. The process is intuitive, but it can quickly lead to a desktop cluttered with open windows. And what if you next needed to work on a paper for Art History? That would require you to open the Art History folder, which produces yet another open window on the desktop.

The Windows Explorer in Figure 10b offers a more sophisticated way to browse the system, as it shows both the hierarchy of folders and the contents of the selected folder. The Explorer window is divided into two panes. The left pane contains a **tree diagram** of the entire system showing all drives and, optionally, the folders in each drive. One (and only one) object is always selected in the left pane, and its contents are displayed automatically in the right pane.

Look carefully at the tree diagram in Figure 10b and note that the English folder is currently selected. The icon for the selected folder is an open folder to differentiate it from the other folders, which are closed and are not currently selected. The right pane displays the contents of the selected folder (English in Figure 10b) and is seen to contain three documents, Assignments 1, 2, and 3. The right pane is displayed in the Details view, but could just as easily have been displayed in another view (e.g., Large or Small Icons) by clicking the appropriate button on the toolbar.

As indicated, only one folder can be selected (open) at a time in the left pane, and its contents are displayed in the right pane. To see the contents of a different folder (e.g., Accounting), you would click the Accounting folder, which automatically closes the English folder and opens the Accounting folder.

The tree diagram in the left pane displays the drives and their folders in hierarchical fashion. The desktop is always at the top of the hierarchy and contains My Computer, which in turn contains various drives, each of which contains folders, which in turn contain documents and/or additional folders. Each object may be expanded or collapsed by clicking the plus or minus sign, respectively.

Look again at the icon next to My Computer in Figure 10b and you see a minus sign, indicating that My Computer has been expanded to show the various drives on the system. There is also a minus sign next to the icon for drive A to indicate that it too has been expanded to show the folders on the disk. Note, however, the plus sign next to drives C and D, indicating that these parts of the tree are currently collapsed and thus their subordinates are not visible.

A folder may contain additional folders and thus individual folders may also be expanded or collapsed. The minus sign next to the Finance folder in Figure 10b, for example, shows that the folder has been expanded and contains two

Double click My Computer

Double click icon for drive A

Double click icon for English folder

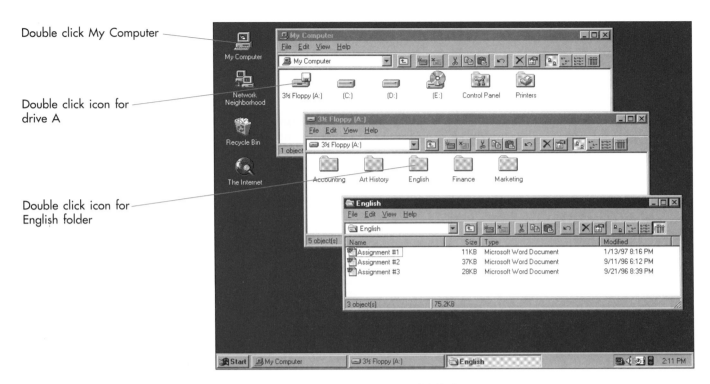

(a) My Computer

Tree diagram

Contents pane displays contents of selected folder

Minus sign indicates drive/folder is expanded (subordinates are visible)

Currently selected folder

No subordinates exist

Plus signs indicate drive/folder is collapsed (subordinates are not visible)

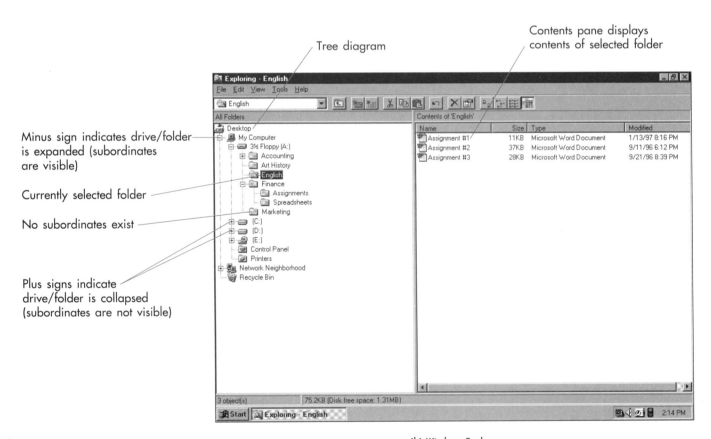

(b) Windows Explorer

FIGURE 10 Working with Files and Folders

additional folders, for Assignments and Spreadsheets, respectively. The plus sign next to the Accounting folder, however, indicates the opposite; that is, the folder is collapsed and its subordinate folders are not currently visible. A folder with neither a plus or minus sign, such as Art History or Marketing, does not contain additional folders and cannot be expanded or collapsed.

The advantage of the Windows Explorer over My Computer is the uncluttered screen and ease with which you switch from one folder to the next. If, for example, you wanted to see the contents of the Art History folder, all you would do would be to click its icon in the left pane, which automatically changes the display in the right pane to show the documents in Art History. The Explorer also makes it easy to move or copy a file from one folder or drive to another, as you will see in the hands-on exercise, which follows shortly.

ORGANIZE YOUR WORK

Organize your folders in ways that make sense to you, such as a separate folder for every class you are taking. You can also create folders within folders; for example, a correspondence folder may contain two folders of its own, one for business correspondence and one for personal letters. Use descriptive names for your folders so that you will remember their contents. (A name may contain up to 255 characters, including spaces.)

The Practice Files

As indicated, there are several ways to obtain the practice files associated with the various books in the *Exploring Windows* series. You can download the files from our Web site as described in the previous hands-on exercise. Alternatively, you can use the Windows Explorer to copy the files from a network drive (at school) to a floppy disk, as will be demonstrated in the following hands-on exercise.

The Windows Explorer is especially useful for moving or copying files from one folder or drive to another. You simply select (open) the folder that contains the file, use the scroll bar in the left pane (if necessary) so that the destination folder is visible, then click and drag the file(s) from the right pane to the destination folder. The Explorer is a powerful tool, but it takes practice to master.

EXPLORE THE PRACTICE FILES

The practice files are intended to teach you the basics of file management, but they are also interesting in and of themselves. The *Tips for Windows 95* document, for example, contains several tips that appeared throughout this appendix. The *Introduction to Windows 95* presentation summarizes much of the material in this appendix. *Analysis of a Car Loan* is an Excel workbook that computes a monthly car payment based on the cost of a car and the parameters of a loan. Double click any of these files from within the Windows Explorer to start the application and load the document.

The Practice Files (via a local area network)

Objective: To use the Windows Explorer to copy the practice files from a network drive to a floppy disk. The exercise requires a formatted floppy disk and access to a local area network. Use Figure 11 as a guide in the exercise.

STEP 1: Start the Windows Explorer

➤ Click the **Start Button,** click (or point to) the **Programs command,** then click **Windows Explorer** to start this program. Click the **maximize button** so that the Explorer takes the entire desktop as shown in Figure 11a. Do not be concerned if your screen is different from ours.

➤ Make or verify the following selections using the **View menu.** (You have to pull down the View menu each time you choose a different command.)

• The **Toolbar command** should be checked.

• The **Status bar command** should be checked.

• The **Large Icons view** should be selected.

➤ Click (select) the **Desktop icon** in the left pane to display the contents of the desktop in the right pane.

➤ Our desktop contains only the icons for My Computer, Network Neighborhood, the Recycle Bin, and the Internet icon. Your desktop may have different icons, but your screen should otherwise match Figure 11a.

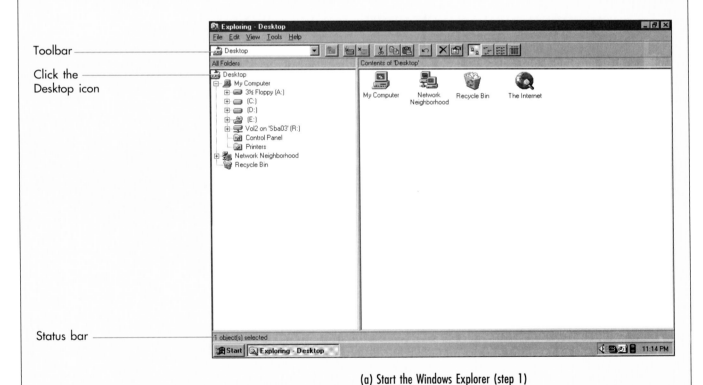

(a) Start the Windows Explorer (step 1)

FIGURE 11   Hands-on Exercise 3

FILE EXTENSIONS

Long-time DOS users remember a three-character extension at the end of a file name to indicate the file type—for example, DOC or XLS to indicate a Word document or Excel workbook, respectively. The extensions are displayed or hidden according to the option you establish through the View menu of the Windows Explorer. Pull down the View menu, click the Options command to display the Options dialog box, click the View tab, then check (or clear) the box to hide (or show) MS-DOS file extensions. Click OK to accept the setting and exit the dialog box. We prefer to hide the extensions.

STEP 2: Additional Practice

➤ The objective of this exercise is to obtain the practice files by copying files from a local area network (such as a computer lab at school) using the Windows Explorer. If you already downloaded the practice files from our Web site in the previous hands-on exercise, you can:

  • Use the practice files you already have and go to step 6 to continue with this exercise, *or*

  • Erase all of the files on your floppy disk (just reformat the disk), then proceed with steps 3 through 5 in this exercise.

➤ We suggest you continue with step 3 in order to practice with the Windows Explorer.

THE QUICK FORMAT COMMAND

The fastest way to erase the entire contents of a floppy disk is to use the Quick Format command. Start the Windows Explorer and select any drive except the floppy drive. (You cannot format a floppy disk in drive A when drive A is selected). Point to the icon for drive A in the left pane, click the right mouse button to display a shortcut menu, then click the Format command to display the Format dialog box. Click the option button for the Quick (erase) Format, then click the Start button to format the disk and erase its contents.

STEP 3: Collapse the Individual Drives

➤ Click the **minus** (or the plus) **sign** next to My Computer to collapse (or expand) My Computer and hide (display) the objects it contains.

➤ Toggle the signs back and forth a few times for practice. End with a minus sign next to the My Computer icon as shown in Figure 11b.

➤ Place a formatted floppy disk in drive A, then click the **plus sign** next to drive A. The plus sign disappears, as drive A does not have any folders.

Click icon to select drive A

Click the plus sign to expand drive

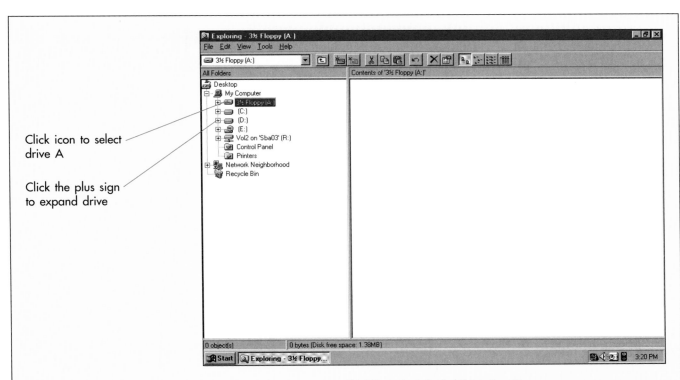

(b) Collapse the Individual Drives (step 3)

FIGURE 11   Hands-on Exercise 3 (continued)

➤ Click the **plus** (minus) **sign** next to the other drives to toggle back and forth between expanding (collapsing) the individual drives on your system.

➤ End this step with every drive collapsed; that is, there should be a **plus sign** next to every drive, as shown in Figure 11b.

➤ Click the drive icon next to drive A to select the drive and display its contents in the right pane. The disk does not contain any files, and hence the right pane is empty.

THE PLUS AND MINUS SIGN

Any drive, be it local or on the network, may be expanded or collapsed to display or hide its contents. A minus sign indicates that the drive has been expanded and that its folders are visible. A plus sign indicates the reverse; that is, the device is collapsed and its folders are not visible. Click either sign to toggle to the other. Clicking a plus sign, for example, expands the drive, then displays a minus sign next to the drive to indicate that the folders are visible. Clicking a minus sign has the reverse effect— it collapses the drive, hiding its folders.

STEP 4: Select the Network Drive

➤ Click the **plus sign** for the network drive, which contains the files you are to copy (e.g., drive R in Figure 11c). Select (click) the **Exploring Prerequisites**

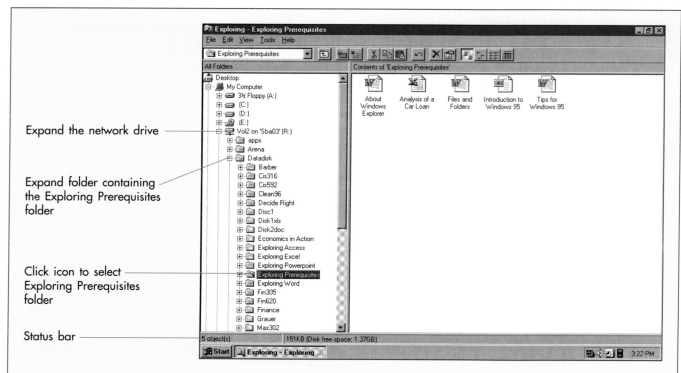

Expand the network drive

Expand folder containing the Exploring Prerequisites folder

Click icon to select Exploring Prerequisites folder

Status bar

(c) Select the Exploring Prerequisites Folder (step 4)

FIGURE 11   Hands-on Exercise 3 (continued)

folder to select this folder. (You may need to expand other folders on the network drive as per instructions from your professor.) Note the following:

- The Exploring Prerequisites folder is highlighted in the left pane, its icon has changed to an open folder, and its contents are displayed in the right pane.

- The status bar indicates that the folder contains five objects and the total file size is 151KB.

➤ Click the icon next to any other folder to select the folder, which in turn deselects the Exploring Prerequisites folder. (Only one folder in the left pane can be selected at a time.) Reselect (click) the **Exploring Prerequisites folder** and its contents are again visible in the right pane.

➤ Pull down the **View menu** and select **Details** (or click the **Details button** on the toolbar) to change to the Details view. This enables you to see the file sizes of the individual files.

THE VIEW MENU

The objects in any window can be displayed in four different views—Large Icons, Small Icons, Details, and List—according to your preference or need. The choice of views depends on your personal preference. You can change from one view to another from the View menu, or by clicking the appropriate button on the toolbar. (Windows 97 provides access to a fifth view, the Web view, which displays the addresses of recently visited Web sites.)

STEP 5: Copy the Individual Files

➤ Select (click) the file **About Windows Explorer,** which highlights the file as shown in Figure 11d. The Exploring Prerequisites folder is no longer highlighted because a different object has been selected. The folder is still open, however, and its contents are displayed in the right pane.

➤ Click and drag the selected file in the right pane to the **drive A icon** in the left pane:

- You will see the ⊘ symbol as you drag the file until you reach a suitable destination (e.g., until you point to the icon for drive A). The ⊘ symbol will change to a plus sign when the icon for drive A is highlighted, indicating that the file can be copied successfully.
- Release the mouse to complete the copy operation. You will see a pop-up window, which indicates the progress of the copy operation. This may take several seconds, depending on the size of the file.

➤ Select (click) the file **Tips for Windows 95,** which automatically deselects the previously selected file (About Windows Explorer). Copy the selected file to drive A by dragging its icon from the right pane to the drive A icon in the left pane.

➤ Copy the three remaining files to drive A as well. (You can select multiple files at the same time by pressing and holding the **Ctrl key** as you click each file in turn. Point to any of the selected files, then click and drag the files as a group.)

➤ Select (click) drive **A** in the left pane, which in turn displays the contents of the floppy disk in the right pane. You should see the five files you have copied to drive A.

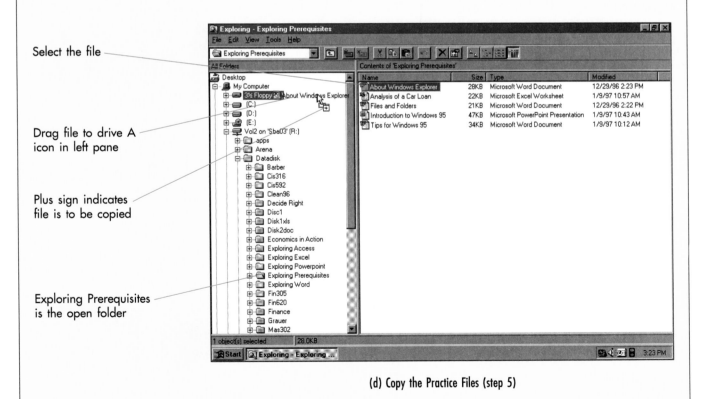

Select the file

Drag file to drive A icon in left pane

Plus sign indicates file is to be copied

Exploring Prerequisites is the open folder

(d) Copy the Practice Files (step 5)

FIGURE 11   Hands-on Exercise 3 (continued)

SELECT MULTIPLE FILES

Selecting (clicking) one file automatically deselects the previously selected file. You can, however, select multiple files by pressing and holding the Ctrl key as you click each file in succession. You can also select multiple files that are adjacent to one another by using the Shift key; that is, click the icon of the first file, then press and hold the Shift key as you click the icon of the last file. You can also select every file in a folder through the Select All command in the Edit menu (or by clicking in the right pane and pressing Ctrl+A).

STEP 6: Check Your Work

➤ Prove to your instructor that you have done the exercise correctly by capturing the Exploring Windows screen, which appears on your monitor. The easiest way to do this is to use the Paint accessory as shown in Figure 11e. Accordingly:

• Press the **Print Screen key** to copy the current screen display to the clipboard (an area of memory that is available to every Windows application). Nothing appears to have happened, but the screen has in fact been copied to the clipboard.

• Click the **Start button,** click **Programs,** click **Accessories,** then click **Paint** to open the Paint accessory. If necessary, click the **maximize button** so that the Paint window takes the entire desktop.

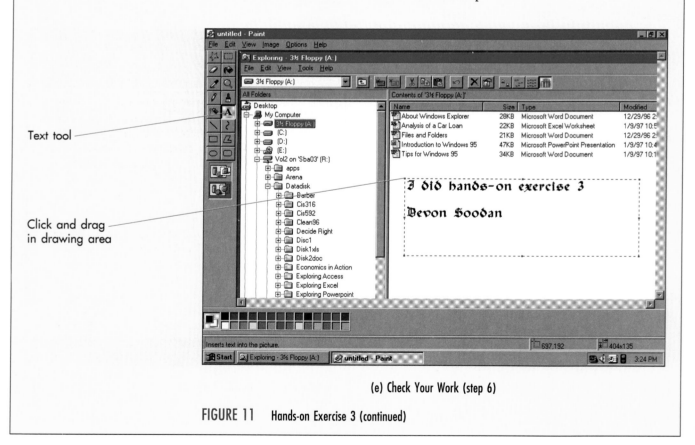

(e) Check Your Work (step 6)

FIGURE 11   Hands-on Exercise 3 (continued)

- Pull down the **Edit menu.** Click **Paste** to copy the screen from the clip-board to the drawing.
- Click the **text tool** (the capital A), then click and drag in the drawing area to create a dotted rectangle that will contain the message to your instructor. Type the text indicating that you did your homework. Click outside the rectangle to deselect it.
- Pull down the **File menu** and click the **Page Setup** command to display the Page Setup dialog box. Click the Landscape option button. Change the margins to one inch all around. Click **OK.**
- Pull down the **File menu** a second time. Click **Print.** Click **OK.** Click the **Close button** to exit Paint. Click **No** if asked to save the file.

➤ Close the Windows Explorer. Exit Windows if you do not want to continue with the next exercise at this time.

THE PAINT ACCESSORY

The Paint Accessory is included in Windows 95 and is an ideal way to create simple (or, depending on your ability, complex) drawings. There is also a sense of familiarity because the Paint accessory shares the common user interface of every Windows application, which includes a title bar, menu bar, minimize, restore, and close buttons, and vertical and horizontal scroll bars. You may also recognize a familiar command structure. The Print and Paste commands, for example, are found in the File and Edit menus, respectively, in Paint, as they are in every Windows application.

THE BASICS OF FILE MANAGEMENT

The exercise just completed had you copy the practice files from a drive on a local area network to your own floppy disk. As you grow to depend on the computer, you will create files of your own in various applications (e.g., Word or Excel). Learning how to manage those files is one of the most important skills you can acquire. This section describes the basic operations you will use.

Moving and Copying a File

Moving and copying a file from one location to another is the essence of file management. It is accomplished most easily by clicking and dragging the file icon from the source drive or folder, to the destination drive or folder, within the Windows Explorer. There is a subtlety, however, in that the result of dragging a file (whether the file is moved or copied) depends on whether the source and destination are on the same or different drives. Dragging a file from one folder to another folder on the same drive moves the file. Dragging a file to a folder on a different drive copies the file. (You can also click and drag a folder, in which case every file in that folder is moved or copied as per the rule for an individual file.)

This process is not as arbitrary as it may seem. Windows assumes that if you drag an object (a file or folder) to a different drive (e.g., from drive C to drive A), you want the object to appear in both places. Hence, the default action when you click and drag an object to a different drive is to copy the object. You can, however, override the default and move the object by pressing and holding the Shift key as you drag.

Windows also assumes that you do not want two copies of an object on the same drive as that would result in wasted disk space. Thus, the default action when you click and drag an object to a different folder on the same drive is to move the object. You can override the default and copy the object by pressing and holding the Ctrl key as you drag. It's not as complicated as it sounds, and you get a chance to practice in the hands-on exercise, which follows shortly.

Deleting Files

The **Delete command** deletes (removes) a file from a disk. The command can be executed in different ways, most easily by selecting a file, then pressing the Del key. Even after a file is deleted, however, you can usually get it back because it is not physically deleted from the hard disk, but moved instead to the Recycle Bin from where it can be recovered.

The **Recycle Bin** is a special folder that contains all files that were previously deleted from any hard disk on your system. Think of the Recycle Bin as similar to the wastebasket in your room. You throw out (delete) a report by tossing it into a wastebasket. The report is gone (deleted) from your desk, but you can still get it back by taking it out of the wastebasket as long as the basket wasn't emptied. The Recycle Bin works the same way. Files are not deleted from the hard disk per se, but are moved instead to the Recycle Bin from where they can be restored to their original location.

The Recycle Bin will eventually run out of space, in which case the files that have been in the Recycle Bin the longest are deleted to make room for additional files. Once a file is deleted from the Recycle Bin, however, it can no longer be recovered, as it has been physically deleted from the hard disk. Note, too, that the protection afforded by the Recycle Bin does not extend to files deleted from a floppy disk. Such files can be recovered, but only through utility programs outside of Windows 95.

Backup

It's not a question of whether it will happen, but when—hard disks die, files are lost, or viruses may infect a system. It has happened to us and it will happen to you, but you can prepare for the inevitable by creating adequate backup *before* the problem occurs. The essence of a backup strategy is to decide which files to back up, how often to do the backup, and where to keep the backup. Once you decide on a strategy, follow it, and follow it faithfully!

Our strategy is very simple—back up what you can't afford to lose, do so on a daily basis, and store the backup away from your computer. You need not copy every file, every day. Instead copy just the files that changed during the current session. Realize, too, that it is much more important to back up your data files than your program files. You can always reinstall the application from the original disks, or if necessary, go to the vendor for another copy of an application. You, however, are the only one who has a copy of the term paper that is due tomorrow. Forewarned is forearmed.

Write Protection

A floppy disk is normally **write-enabled** (the square hole is covered) so that you can change the contents of the disk. Thus, you can create (save) new files to a write-enabled disk and/or edit or delete existing files. Occasionally, however, you may want to **write-protect** a floppy disk (by sliding the tab to expose the square hole) so that its contents cannot be modified. This is typically done with a backup disk when you want to prevent the accidental deletion of a file or the threat of virus infection.

Our Last Exercise

As we have indicated throughout the appendix, the ability to move and copy files is of paramount importance. The only way to master these skills is through practice, and so we offer one last exercise in which you execute a variety of commands to reinforce the material.

The exercise begins with the floppy disk containing the five practice files in drive A. We ask you to create two folders on drive A (step 1) and to move the various files into these folders (step 2). Next, you copy a folder from drive A to drive C (step 3), modify one of the files in the folder on drive C (step 4), then copy the modified file back to drive A (step 5). We ask you to delete a file in step 6, then recover it from the Recycle Bin in step 7. There is a lot to do, so let's get started.

HANDS-ON EXERCISE 4

The Windows Explorer

Objective: To use the Windows Explorer to move, copy, and delete a file, then recover a deleted file from the Recycle Bin. Use Figure 12 as a guide in the exercise.

STEP 1: Create a New Folder

➤ Start the Windows Explorer and maximize its window. Place the floppy disk (from hands-on exercise 2 or 3) in drive A.

➤ Select (click) the icon for **drive A** in the left pane of the Explorer window. Drive A should contain the files shown in Figure 12a. It does not contain any folders.

➤ Point to a blank area anywhere in the **right pane,** then click the **right mouse button** to display a context-sensitive menu.

➤ Click (or point to) the **New command** in the menu, then click **Folder** to create a new Folder on drive A.

➤ The icon for a new folder will appear with the name of the folder (New Folder) highlighted. Type **Computing 101** to change the name of the folder. Press the **enter key.**

➤ Click the icon for **drive A** once again. Pull down the **File menu,** click (or point to) the **New command,** and click **Folder** as the type of object to create.

➤ Type **Other Files** to change the name of the folder. Press **enter.** The right pane should now contain five documents and two folders.

➤ Pull down the **View menu.** Click (or point to) the **Arrange icons command** to display a submenu, then click the **By Name command.** The folders are displayed in alphabetical order followed by the files in alphabetical order.

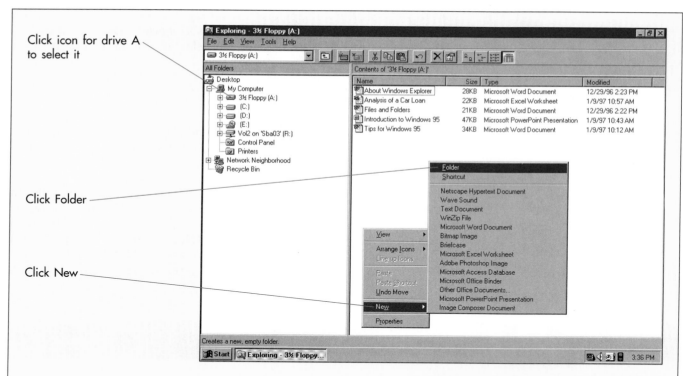

Click icon for drive A to select it

Click Folder

Click New

(a) Create a New Folder (step 1)

FIGURE 12   Hands-on Exercise 4

RENAME COMMAND

Point to a file or a folder, then click the right mouse button to display a menu with commands pertaining to the object. Click the Rename command. The name of the file or folder will be highlighted with the insertion point (a flashing vertical line) positioned at the end of the name. Enter a new name, to replace the selected name, or click anywhere within the name to change the insertion point and edit the name.

STEP 2: Move a File

➤ Click the **plus sign** next to drive A to expand the drive as shown in Figure 12b. Note the following:

• Drive A is selected in the left pane. The right pane displays the contents of drive A (the selected object in the left pane). The folders are shown first and appear in alphabetical order. The file names are displayed after the folders and are also in alphabetical order.

• There is a minus sign next to the icon for drive A in the left pane, indicating that its folders have been expanded. Thus, the folder names also appear under drive A in the left pane.

➤ Click and drag the icon for the file **About Windows Explorer** from the right pane to the **Computing 101 folder** in the left pane. This moves the file into that folder.

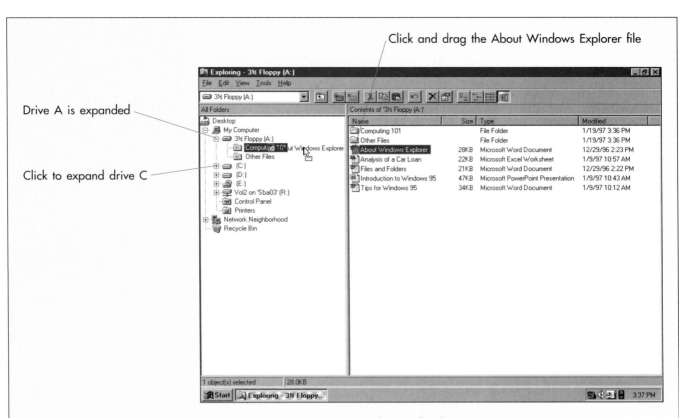

Click and drag the About Windows Explorer file

Drive A is expanded

Click to expand drive C

(b) Move the Files (step 2)

FIGURE 12   Hands-on Exercise 4 (continued)

➤ Click and drag the **Tips for Windows 95 icon** and the **Files and Folders icon** to the **Computing 101 folder** to move these files into the folder.

➤ Click the **Computing 101 icon** in the left pane to select the folder and display its contents in the right pane. You should see the three files that were just moved.

➤ Click the icon for **drive A** in the left pane, then click and drag the remaining files, **Analysis of a Car Loan** and **Introduction to Windows 95** to the **Other Files folder.**

USE THE RIGHT MOUSE BUTTON

The result of dragging a file with the left mouse button depends on whether the source and destination folders are on the same or different drives. Dragging a file to a folder on a different drive copies the file. Dragging the file to a folder on the same drive moves the file. If you find this hard to remember, and most people do, click and drag with the right mouse button to display a shortcut menu asking whether you want to copy or move the file. This simple tip can save you from making a careless (and potentially serious) error. Use it!

STEP 3: Copy a Folder

➤ If necessary, click the **plus sign** next to the icon for drive C to expand the drive and display its folders as shown in Figure 12c.

➤ Do *not* click the folder icon for drive C, as drive A is to remain selected. (You can expand or collapse an object without selecting it.)

➤ Point to the **Computing 101 folder** in either pane, click the **right mouse button** and drag the folder to the icon for **drive C** in the left pane, then release the mouse to display a shortcut menu. Click the **Copy Here** command.

➤ You should see the Copy files dialog box as the individual files within the folder are copied from drive A to drive C.

Point to Computing 101 folder, then click right mouse button and drag to icon for drive C

Click Copy Here

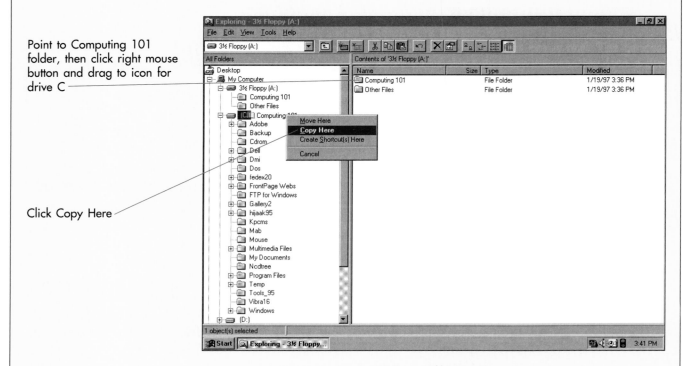

(c) Copy a Folder (step 3)

FIGURE 12   Hands-on Exercise 4 (continued)

CUSTOMIZE THE EXPLORER WINDOW

Increase (or decrease) the size of the left pane within the Explorer Window by dragging the vertical line separating the left and right panes in the appropriate direction. You can also drag the right border of the various column headings (Name, Size, Tip, and Modified) in the right pane to increase (or decrease) the width of the column in order to see more (or less) information in that column. Double click the right border of a column heading to automatically adjust the column width to accommodate the widest entry in that column.

➤ If you see the Confirm Folder Replace dialog box, it means that the previous student forgot to delete the Computing 101 folder when he or she did this exercise. Click the **Yes to All button** so that the files on your floppy disk will replace the previous versions on drive C.

➤ Please remember to **delete** the Computing 101 folder on drive C, as described in step 8 at the end of the exercise.

STEP 4: Modify a Document

➤ Click (select) the **Computing 101 folder** on drive C to open the folder as shown in Figure 12d. The contents of this folder are shown in the right pane.

➤ Double click the **About Windows Explorer** file to open the file and edit the document. Press **Ctrl+End** to move to the end of the document. Add the sentence shown in Figure 12d followed by your name. (See boxed tip on page 46 if you are unable to read the document.)

➤ Pull down the **File menu** and click **Save** to save the modified file (or click the **Save button** on the Standard toolbar). Pull down the **File menu** and click **Exit** to exit from Microsoft Word.

➤ The entire Windows Explorer window is again visible. Pull down the **View menu** and click **Refresh** (or press the **F5 key**) to update the contents of the right pane. The date and time associated with the About Windows Explorer file has been changed to indicate that the file has just been modified.

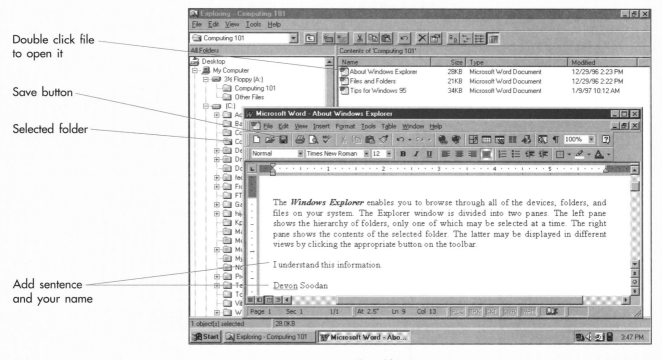

Double click file to open it

Save button

Selected folder

Add sentence and your name

(d) Modify a Document (step 4)

FIGURE 12   Hands-on Exercise 4 (continued)

FILE FORMATS ARE INCOMPATIBLE

If you are unable to open the Word document in our exercise, it is because you are using Microsoft Word 7.0 (also known as Microsoft Word for Windows 95) rather than Word 97. The new release can read documents created in the earlier version, but the converse is not true—that is, Word 7.0 cannot read documents created by Word 97. (Our file was created in Word 97.) The incompatibility between Office 97 and its predecessor Office 95 is a potential problem for millions of users.

STEP 5: Copy (Back Up) a File

➤ Verify that the **Computing 101 folder** on drive C is the active folder as denoted by the open folder icon. Click and drag the icon for the **About Windows Explorer** file from the right pane to the **Computing 101 folder** on **drive A** in the left pane.

➤ You will see the message in Figure 12e, indicating that the folder (drive A) already contains a file called About Windows Explorer and asking whether you want to replace the existing file.

➤ Click **Yes** because you want to replace the previous version of the file on drive A with the updated version on drive C.

➤ You have just backed up the file; in other words, you have created a duplicate copy of a file on drive C on drive A. Thus, you can use the floppy disk to restore the file should anything happen to drive C.

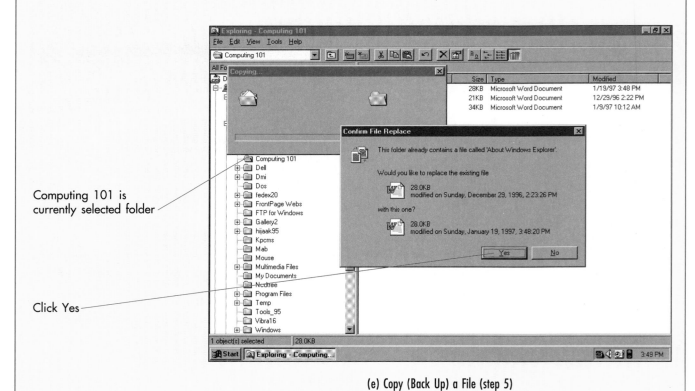

Computing 101 is currently selected folder

Click Yes

(e) Copy (Back Up) a File (step 5)

FIGURE 12 Hands-on Exercise 4 (continued)

COPYING FROM ONE FLOPPY DISK TO ANOTHER

You've learned how to copy a file from drive C to drive A, or from drive A to drive C, but how do you copy a file from one floppy disk to another? It's easy when you know how. Place the first floppy disk in drive A, select drive A in the left pane of the Explorer windows, then copy the file(s) from the right pane to a temporary folder on drive C in the left pane. Remove the first floppy disk, and replace it with the second. Press the F5 key to refresh the display in the right pane. Select the temporary folder on drive C in the left pane, then click and drag the file(s) from the left pane to the floppy disk in the right pane.

STEP 6: Delete a Folder

➤ Select (click) the **Computing 101 folder** on drive C in the left pane. Pull down the **File menu** and click **Delete** (or press the **Del key**).

➤ You will see the dialog box in Figure 12f asking whether you are sure you want to delete the folder (that is, send the folder and its contents to the Recycle Bin). Note the green recycle logo within the box, which implies that you will be able to restore the file.

➤ Click **Yes** to delete the folder. The folder disappears from drive C. Pull down the **Edit menu.** Click **Undo Delete.** The deletion is cancelled and the folder reappears in the left pane.

Select the Computing 101 folder

Click Yes

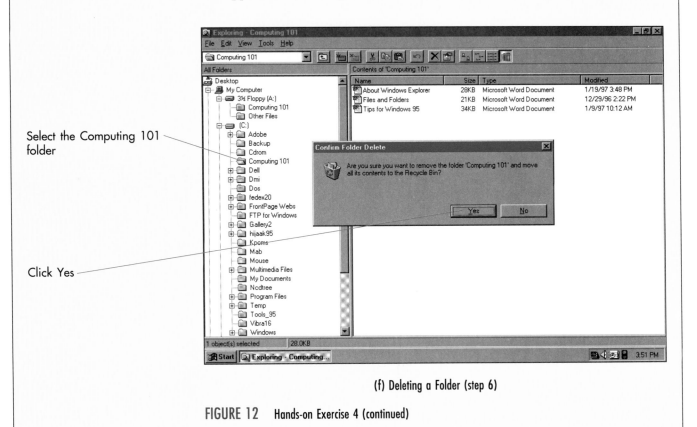

(f) Deleting a Folder (step 6)

FIGURE 12   Hands-on Exercise 4 (continued)

STEP 7: The Recycle Bin

➤ If necessary, select the **Computing 101 folder** on drive C in the left pane. Select (click) the **About Windows Explorer** file in the right pane. Press the **Del key,** then click **Yes** when asked whether to delete the file.

➤ Double click the **Recycle Bin icon** on the desktop if you can see its icon, *or* Double click the **Recycled icon** within the window for drive C. (You may have to scroll in order to see the icon.)

➤ The Recycle Bin contains all files that have been previously deleted from drive C, and hence you may see a different number of files than those displayed in Figure 12g.

➤ Point to the **About Windows Explorer** file, click the **right mouse button** to display the shortcut menu in Figure 12g, then click **Restore.** The file disappears from the Recycle Bin because it has been returned to the Computing 101 folder. Select the folder and verify the file is back.

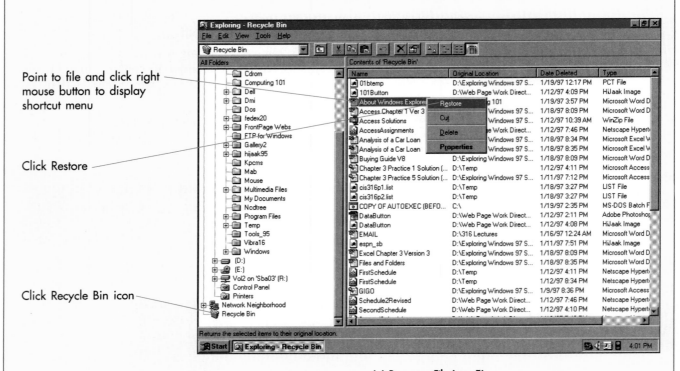

Point to file and click right mouse button to display shortcut menu

Click Restore

Click Recycle Bin icon

(g) Recover a File (step 7)

FIGURE 12   Hands-on Exercise 4 (continued)

STEP 8: Complete the Exercise

➤ Delete the **Computing 101 folder** on **drive C** as a courtesy to the next student.

➤ Click the **Computing 101 folder** on drive A in the left pane. Repeat the steps described on page 38 to capture the screen and prove to your instructor that you did the exercise.

➤ Exit Windows. Congratulations on a job well done. You have mastered the basics and are ready to begin working in Microsoft Office.

INDEX